TRAINING EMPLOYEES WITH DISABILITIES

Strategies to Enhance Learning & Development For an Expanding Part of Your Workforce

WILLIAM R. TRACEY

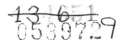

amacom
American Management Association

New York • Atlanta • Boston • Chicago • Kansas City • San Francisco • Washington, D.C.
Brussels • Mexico City • Tokyo • Toronto

This book is available at a special
discount when ordered in bulk quantities.
For information, contact Special Sales Department,
AMACOM, a division of American Management Association,
135 West 50th Street, New York, NY 10020.

Library of Congress Cataloging-in-Publication Data

Tracey, William R.
    Training employees with disabilities : strategies to enhance
learning & development for an expanding part of your workforce /
William R. Tracey.
        p.   cm.
    Includes bibliographical references and index.
    ISBN 0-8144-0220-8
    1. Employees—Training of—United States.   2. Handicapped—
Employment—United States.   I. Title.
HF5549.5.T7T66225   1995
658.3'1245—dc20   94-26610
                                                             CIP

Printing number

10   9   8   7   6   5   4   3   2   1

For my parents, foster parents, godparents, sisters and brothers, aunts and uncles, friends, students, and co-workers, who have had a variety of disabilities, including alcoholism, amyotrophic lateral sclerosis, amputation, arthritis, attention deficit disorder, bipolar disorder, blindness, cancer, clinical depression, diabetes mellitus, Down syndrome, epilepsy, facial disfigurement, heart disease, mental retardation, panic disorder, and schizophrenia—and lived full and productive lives. They taught me a great deal about disability and served as the inspiration for this book.

Contents

Preface

It has been estimated that 43 million Americans have some form of physical disability, and only about one-third of them are employed. Those figures do not include persons who are mentally and emotionally disabled, the great majority of whom are unemployed. Yet by the turn of the century, at least eight of every ten new workers will be women, minorities, and people with disabilities. Because the American labor pool is changing and shrinking, all organizations will have to learn how to take advantage of new sources of qualified employees. One of the best sources is people with disabilities.

A Louis Harris poll conducted for the National Organization on Disability and released in September 1991, *Public Attitudes toward People with Disabilities*, showed that one-third of all Americans have a relative who is disabled. Forty-seven percent of the respondents said they personally knew someone who was disabled; of those, 24 percent had a person with a disability in their household, and 45 percent had a relative with a disability living elsewhere.

The education and training of people with disabilities has changed greatly since the first residential schools (for blind children) were opened in the 1830s. Early in the twentieth century, local school districts established special classes for people with sensory impairments, enabling some children to live at home. And in the mid-twentieth century, local school districts instituted special classes for people with mental retardation. However, beyond special schools and colleges, rehabilitation clinics, and hospitals, little was done to educate, train, and develop adults with disabilities. Only in isolated cases did business and industry provide training and development programs for people with impairments.

Recently socially responsible companies, without fanfare, have provided training for persons with disabilities, particularly veterans. Most of these organizations maintain that people with disabilities are their best employees. Now such training is mandated by law for many Americans.

Few organizations will be able to avoid their responsibility to employ and train people with disabilities.

The Americans with Disabilities Act of 1990 (ADA), unquestionably one of the most far-reaching pieces of legislation passed by the Congress in the last thirty years, extends the same protections to people with disabilities as earlier civil rights acts accorded to all Americans regardless of race, color, religion, national origin, age, and sex. Since its passage, the ADA has resulted in changes in the policies and practices of public entities and private corporations and in a dramatic increase in the number of charges of discrimination filed. The Equal Employment Opportunity Commission reported that 27,944 ADA charges were filed between July 27, 1992, the day after the law's employment provisions went into effect, and May 31, 1994. Some of those are certain to be based on discrimination in training and development programs, as well as on discrimination in hiring and promotion.

The obligations and responsibilities of organizations go far beyond the letter of the law. They must take affirmative action to support the spirit of the law as well. Organizations and their training departments must be ready to accommodate larger numbers of employees with disabilities. To do that, trainers and other employees will need to rid themselves of inaccurate perceptions about trainees with disabilities and replace them with correct understandings. Here are some of the most important:

- Bridges of understanding must be built between nondisabled workers and persons with disabilities. Too many people are misinformed about what people with impairments can do and offer in the workplace, and they can offer it only if they are accepted.
- Too many people are troubled by or uneasy about persons with disabilities because they cannot "fix" their disabilities. They must abandon that attitude.
- The way trainees with disabilities think, learn, and behave is not different from that of other trainees. The difference is mainly one of degree.
- It is impossible to prejudge what most persons with disabilities can learn.
- Those with disabilities must be treated first of all as people who need to express their individuality, and accommodations for their differences must be made within that framework.
- Accommodations for people with disabilities are not made out of a spirit of altruism; they are a means of ensuring the success of a worker and his or her contribution to corporate productivity.

- People with disabilities become stronger and more independent when their issues and challenges are shared with others.
- Low self-esteem is one of the biggest problems persons with disabilities face.
- Some disabilities do limit the performance of those who have them, but that fact should not close the door to employment, training and development, and opportunities for advancement in the workplace.

Although the key to the successful employment of people with disabilities is sensitive, knowledgeable, and well-trained supervisors, most, and perhaps all, workers need training of some type (orientation, entry-level technical, remedial, and upgrading training) as well as training that will enhance their personal and professional development and promotability. For that reason, trainers need to be able to make needed accommodations for people with disabilities of all types. They also need to be able to employ methods, techniques, and devices that will enable learners with disabilities to undergo training and development in regular classes (mainstreaming) whenever possible.

Trainers and supervisors need to understand the nature of the types of disabilities they are likely to encounter in the workplace and in a training environment. Specifically, they need to have some idea of the limitations imposed by sensory; mobility and motion; health and medical; mental, developmental, and emotional; learning; and speech and language disabilities. They also need to know what is available and what works when dealing with various types of disabilities.

This book, directed to trainers and supervisors in public and private organizations, focuses on two aspects of working with and training people with disabilities: (1) knowledge of the effects of various types of disabilities on capabilities and need for accommodation and (2) the development and implementation of instructional methods and materials that will assist trainees with disabilities to make the transition from unemployed to contributing and self-confident members of the workforce.

The objective of this book is *not* to provide information and direction to specialists in rehabilitating and training people with various types of disabilities. Nor is it my intention to provide medical advice. I am neither a physician nor a trained specialist on the disabilities discussed. Rather, the purpose of this book is to provide ideas, practical suggestions, and assistance to corporate trainers, supervisors, and others who work with people with all types of disabilities in the workplace.

I must also emphasize that my purpose is not to make trainers rehabilitation specialists. Rather, it is to give them some broad guidelines and some specific suggestions that will help them to improve learning conditions and learning outcomes for trainees with disabilities. I hope that organization trainers and other readers will find my suggestions to be relevant, useful, and doable, but not overwhelming. And it is important that they use the strategies and methods that seem to best fit their own situation.

This book describes various disabilities, training methods, techniques, and assistive devices. Some chapters are more detailed than others and some provide clearer generalizations and rules than others, because more is known about some topics than others.

Many organizations and individuals have not only contributed to the ideas in this book but have also given me assistance, suggestions, and feedback during its development. I thank them for their expert counsel and willingness to help.

I would be remiss if I neglected to thank the fine editorial staff at AMACOM. Without their cooperation, support, and assistance, this book would not be what it is. Special thanks go to Adrienne Hickey, senior acquisitions and planning editor, and Barbara Horowitz, associate editor.

                                                                                          W.R.T.

Acknowledgments

I thank the following professionals who provided advice and assistance during the preparation of this book.

Nile L. Albright, M.D., president, Advanced Medical Research Foundation, and Partner, Albright Associates, Boston, Massachusetts.

Robert J. Beall, Ph.D., president and chief executive officer, Cystic Fibrosis Foundation, Bethesda, Maryland.

Joseph Binowski, area director, Executive Office of Human Services, Massachusetts Rehabilitation Commission, Hyannis, Massachusetts.

Peter Birrell, disability consultant, Workforce Diversity, Aetna Human Resources, Hartford, Connecticut.

Patricia L. Bowen, administrative assistant, Better Hearing Institute, Annandale, Virginia.

M. Louis Camardo, equal employment planning manager, Ford Motor Company, Dearborn, Michigan.

J. T. Childs, director, Workforce Diversity Programs, Workforce Solutions, an IBM Company, Armonk, New York.

Peter Damiri, public relations director, Multiple Sclerosis Association of America, Oaklyn, New Jersey.

Charles C. Diggs, Ph.D., director, Consumer Affairs Division, American Speech-Language-Hearing Association, Rockville, Maryland.

Loraine DiPietro, director, National Information Center on Deafness, Gallaudet University, Washington, D.C.

James Dobson, president, Society for Muscular Dystrophy Information International, Bridgewater, Nova Scotia, Canada.

John F. Fiorita, EOP director, National Spinal Cord Injury Association, 600 West Cummings Park, Woburn, Massachusetts.

Susan Fliegel, LICSW, director of chapter services, Massachusetts Chapter, National Multiple Sclerosis Society, Waltham, Massachusetts.

Laurie M. Flynn, executive director, National Alliance for the Mentally Ill, Arlington, Virginia.

Mildred Frank, Council of Citizens with Low Vision, International, Daytona Beach, Florida.

Jane Fraser, president, Stuttering Foundation of America, Washington, D.C.

Mary Jane Garcia, resource specialist, National Down Syndrome Congress, Atlanta, Georgia.

Mary Gawlick, senior coordinator, Center for Career Programs, Gallaudet University, Washington, D.C.

Harry Geller, compliance specialist/consultant, Sears Roebuck & Company, Hoffman Estates, Illinois.

Becky Gilliam, director, Equal Employment Opportunity/Affirmative Action, GenCorp, Akron, Ohio.

Renee Heartlove, Hearing HelpLine coordinator, Better Hearing Institute, Washington, D.C.

Jack A. Honeck, senior project leader, Workforce Diversity Programs, Workforce Solutions, an IBM Company, Armonk, New York.

Linda Iacelli, coordinator, Employer Outreach and Training, Center on Employment, National Technical Institute for the Deaf, Rochester Institute of Technology, Rochester, New York.

Robert Ingram, program manager, Corporate Diversity, Hewlett-Packard Company, Palo Alto, California.

Sol Kaminski, secretary, National Amputation Association, Malverne, New York.

George McCauley, training coordinator, Executive Office of Health and Human Services, Department of Mental Retardation, Commonwealth of Massachusetts, Fall River, Massachusetts.

Gerald McGaughran, coordinator, Co-op Internship, Center for Career Programs, Gallaudet University, Washington, D.C.

William M. McLin, executive vice president, Epilepsy Foundation, Landover, Maryland.

Edward J. Madara, director, American Self-Help Clearinghouse, St. Charles–Riverside Medical Center, Denville, New Jersey.

Phillip J. Manhardt, Ph.D., director, Personnel Research, Human Resources Department, The Prudential Insurance Company of America, Newark, New Jersey.

Anne Nissen, director, Center for Career Programs, Gallaudet University, Washington, D.C.

Charles W. Pearson, president, Adult Attention Deficit Foundation, Birmingham, Michigan.

Patricia A. Peck, vice president, Human Resources, Woolworth Corporation, New York, New York.

Louise K. Perna, coordinator, Disability Program, DuPont Human Resources, E. I. duPont de Nemours and Company, Wilmington, Delaware.

Dianne B. Piastro, syndicated columnist on disability issues, Cryptography Incorporated, Long Beach, California.

Pat (Patricia) Price, president & editor, Council of Citizens with Low Vision International, Indianapolis, Indiana.

Frank Reid, vice president of human resources, Jostens Learning Corporation, Phoenix, Arizona.

Judith Rosenthal, senior career coordinator, Center for Career Programs, Gallaudet University, Washington, D.C.

Diana L. Sauter, Ph.D., psychologist, Cincinnati, Ohio.

Marc Schenck, D.C., assistant director, Research and Education, Eastern Paralyzed Veterans Association, Jackson Heights, New York.

Patricia A. Smoot, manager human resources, Masonite, Chicago, Illinois.

Robert Steele, coordinator, Outreach Satellite Office for Cape Cod and the Islands, Perkins School for the Blind, Hyannis, Massachusetts.

Elizabeth Traubert, rehabilitation specialist, Outreach Satellite Office for Cape Cod and the Islands, Perkins School for the Blind, Hyannis, Massachusetts.

Cathleen Urbain, Ph.D., coordinator, Minnesota Supported Employment Parent Training Project, The PACER Center, Minneapolis, Minnesota.

Betsy Wilson, director, Let's Face It, Concord, Massachusetts.

Ellen Winogrond, public information manager, American Academy of Ophthalmology, San Francisco, California.

Part I

DISABILITY AND THE CHANGING WORKPLACE

1

The Nature of Disability

Two-thirds of all Americans with disabilities between the ages of 16 and 64 are unemployed, yet most want to work.[1] Studies have demonstrated that workers with disabilities perform just as well as employees without disabilities, that the cost of employer-provided insurance is unaffected by hiring workers with disabilities, and that the cost of job accommodations is minimal. Nevertheless, thousands of people with disabilities, including those who have been properly trained for work, still are confronted with misunderstanding, unfair employment practices, accessibility barriers, and technology shortfalls.

Many myths surround people with disabilities. One of the most prevalent is that those who have achieved in professions and occupations once closed to them are especially talented. Another is that those with sensory disabilities have acquired extraordinary and compensating abilities in one or more of the unaffected senses. But people with disabilities are like everyone else. They have equal amounts of intellect, sensitivity, good humor, wit, and perceptiveness—as well as their fair share of anxiety, tension, temper, eccentricity, arrogance, and prejudice—as their nondisabled peers. It is also important to remember that no two people with the same disability are any more alike than two nondisabled people. Blind people, deaf people, and people who use wheelchairs are not homogeneous groups.

Definitions

Among the many definitions of disability is this one: *"any condition which results in functional limitations that interfere with an individual's ability to perform his or her customary work."*[2] It focuses on people who have been in the workforce and through accident, injury, or disease become disabled—unable to continue their employment—for a long or short period of time (temporary disability) or indefinitely (permanent disability).

The definition of disability most commonly found in insurance contracts is very narrow. Typically, insurance policies define disability as an inability to perform the "material duties" of an occupation. In this case, "material" connotes job duties and tasks that are important, significant, critical, or crucial. Although conditions that insurers consider disabilities are almost certain to be regarded as disabilities under most definitions, current legal definitions are much broader.

Other definitions are germane to the issue; the most important are those used by the Americans with Disabilities Act of 1990, the Rehabilitation Act of 1973, the Social Security Administration, the President's Committee on Employment of People with Disabilities, and the Department of Defense and Department of Veterans Affairs.

Americans with Disabilities Act of 1990 (ADA)

The ADA defines disability as a physical or mental impairment that substantially limits one or more of the major life activities of an individual, a record of such an impairment, or being regarded as having such an impairment. Under ADA, the determination as to whether an individual has a disability is made without regard to mitigating measures, such as medications, auxiliary aids, and reasonable accommodations. Therefore, if a person has an impairment that substantially limits a major life activity, he or she is protected under the ADA, regardless of the fact that the disease or condition or its effects may be corrected or controlled. For example, if an employee has diabetes and takes insulin daily to control the disease, he or she is protected by ADA. On the other hand, if an employee has a broken arm that will heal but is temporarily unable to perform the essential functions of a keyboard operator, he or she is not protected by ADA. Although the employee does have an impairment, it does not substantially limit a major life activity, is of limited duration, and will have no long-term effect.

Rehabilitation Act of 1973

This legislation included three definitions, each for a specific subchapter of the law. For subchapters I and III, which relate to rehabilitation services, an individual with handicaps is defined as one who "(i) has a physical or mental disability which for such individual constitutes or results in a substantial handicap to employment and (ii) can reasonably be expected to benefit in terms of employability from vocational rehabilitation services."

For subchapters IV and V, which relate to employment in the executive branch of the government and employment under federal contracts, grants, and programs, an individual with handicaps means "any person who (i) has a physical or mental impairment which substantially limits one or more of such person's major life activities, (ii) has a record of such an impairment, or (iii) is regarded as having such an impairment." The term does not include individuals who are current alcoholic or drug abusers whose use of alcohol or drugs prevents them from performing the duties of the job in question or whose employment would constitute a direct threat to the property or safety of others. Nor does the term include individuals who have a contagious disease or infection that would constitute a direct threat to the health or safety of others or are unable to perform the duties of the job.

The law also provides a definition of an individual with severe handicaps as one

> (i) who has a severe physical or mental disability which seriously limits one or more functional capacities (such as mobility, communication, self-care, self-direction, interpersonal skills, work tolerance, or work skills) in terms of employability; (ii) whose vocational rehabilitation can be expected to require multiple vocational rehabilitation services over an extended period of time; and (iii) who has one or more physical or mental disabilities resulting from amputation, arthritis, autism, blindness, burn injury, cancer, cerebral palsy, cystic fibrosis, deafness, head injury, heart disease, hemiplegia, hemophilia, respiratory or pulmonary dysfunction, mental retardation, mental illness, multiple sclerosis, muscular dystrophy, musculo-skeletal disorders, neurological disorders (including stroke or epilepsy), paraplegia, quadriplegia, and other spinal cord conditions, sickle cell anemia, specific learning disabilities, end-stage renal disease, or another disability or combination of disabilities, determined on the basis of evaluation of rehabilitation potential to cause comparable substantial functional limitation.

Social Security

Disability under social security is based on an individual's inability to work. The law states that a person (worker, widow, or widower) is disabled if he or she has a physical or mental condition(s) that prevents him or her from engaging in any substantial gainful work for which he or she is suited, and the disability is expected to last (or has lasted) for 12 months, or is expected to result in death.

Disabling conditions that make individuals eligible for social security include (1) damage to the brain, or brain abnormality, that resulted in severe loss of judgment, intellect, orientation, or memory; (2) cancer that is progressive and has not been controlled or cured; (3) diseases of the digestive system that result in severe malnutrition, weakness, and anemia; (4) progressive degenerative disease that has resulted in the loss of most bodily functions (e.g., multiple sclerosis, Buerger's disease, rheumatoid arthritis); (5) loss of major function of both arms, both legs, or a leg and an arm, due to trauma or disease; (6) mental illness resulting in marked impaired ability to get along with other people; and (7) blindness.

Department of Defense and Department of Veterans Affairs

For veterans and retired military personnel, a disabled person is defined as one who has been granted a disability rating of any percentage (typically ranging from 10 to 100 percent) by either the Department of Defense or the Department of Veterans Affairs. That definition applies to federal laws and regulations that pertain to disabled veterans, for example, the Vietnam Era Veterans Readjustment and Assistance Act of 1974 and the Persian Gulf Conflict Supplemental Authorization and Personnel Benefits Act of 1991.

Workers' Opinions

Many workers do not consider all of the conditions identified by the ADA as qualified disabilities. A survey of 687 workers commissioned in 1992 by the Bureau of National Affairs found that a majority of respondents did not consider alcoholism, drug addiction, cancer, AIDS, and diabetes as disabilities.[3] Figure 1-1 shows the percentage of respondents who considered various conditions to be disabilities.

The Definition Used in This Book

In this book, disability is considered to be any physical, mental, or emotional condition, whether congenital or due to disease, accident, or injury, work related or not, that has been an obstacle to or disqualifer for initial employment or continuation of employment. That definition intentionally excludes such classifications of disability as permanent or temporary, or stable or progressive, although such distinctions may have application under specific circumstances.

Here are some statistics and facts about people with disabilities:

- By the year 2000, at least eight out of every ten new workers will be women, minorities, and people with disabilities. One of the greatest challenges facing human resources managers and practi-

Figure 1-1. Workers' opinions of conditions that should be considered disabilities.

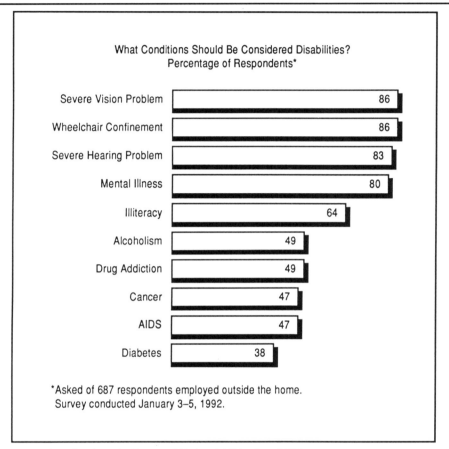

What Conditions Should Be Considered Disabilities?
Percentage of Respondents*

Severe Vision Problem	86
Wheelchair Confinement	86
Severe Hearing Problem	83
Mental Illness	80
Illiteracy	64
Alcoholism	49
Drug Addiction	49
Cancer	47
AIDS	47
Diabetes	38

*Asked of 687 respondents employed outside the home.
Survey conducted January 3–5, 1992.

Source: Based on data from the Bureau of National Affairs, Inc., 1992.

tioners will be hiring, training, and retaining these people in large numbers.

■ Americans with disabilities represent the largest unemployed group: 72.9 percent are unemployed, 18.2 percent are employed full time, and 8.9 percent are employed part time. At the start of 1990, 8.2 million working-age adults with disabilities who wanted to work were unemployed.

■ There are about 43 million people with disabilities in the United States.

■ More than one-quarter of all employed men and women with disabilities are in managerial, professional, or sales occupations.

- Twenty-two percent of African Americans are disabled, as are 20 percent of U.S. Hispanics.
- More than 6 million American children and adults have mental retardation. It affects more people than blindness, muscular dystrophy, polio, cerebral palsy, and rheumatic heart disease combined.
- There are an estimated 2 million wheelchair users in the United States.
- About 8.5 million Americans have a visual impairment.
- About 22 million Americans have a hearing impairment.
- Approximately 2 million people with disabilities reside in institutions (including more than 1.3 million in nursing homes), mental hospitals, residential facilities, and mental retardation facilities.
- Having a disability is not worse or better than not having one; it is just different.
- Candidates for jobs who happen to have disabilities are intelligent and motivated people who are capable of making important contributions to any organization.
- According to an October 1993 report of the Centers for Disease Control and Prevention, the number of work-disabled people totaled more than 12.8 million in 1990 (81.5 Americans per 1,000 ages 16–64), which costs the nation about $111.6 billion each year in medical costs and lost wages.
- People with disabilities are ready, willing, and able to take on the demands of the U.S. workplace; all they need is the opportunity.

Disability Culture

There is a disability culture, although most people are not conscious of it. It is not new; it has always existed. Syndicated columnist Dianne B. Piastro says:

> If you can get beyond seeing disabilities only as medical problems that need to be cured, overcome, or hidden, and think in terms of how this group of people interacts with society and deals with their environment, disability culture becomes apparent. The disability cultural movement is becoming increasingly important. It is about individuals' stories celebrating who we are, learning who we have been. And through them all weaves a common thread of survival, restricted choices, enforced poverty, and benign oppression that will no longer be suppressed. There is strength in our stories. There is power in our differ-

ences. . . . And, as more and more disabled people discard the roles of isolated victims, and reflect pride in their shared experience, disability culture will simply become accepted as an integral part of the cultural diversity of this country.

But she also notes what she calls a "pervasive problem." She explains:

Many people, whether or not their disability is visible, mild, or severe, refuse to identify with the disability movement because of the social stigma, as well as the usual lower economic opportunity that goes with being identified as disabled. But distinct cultural experiences bind people in each of society's minorities. Many who don't recognize this bond say they don't think of themselves as disabled, that they're just like everybody else. Unfortunately, what these people really are doing is buying into society's devaluation of disabled people.

It is sad when people try so hard not to be something that is a fact of life for them. In doing so they isolate themselves from the majority culture as well as the disability culture. The majority culture won't really allow disabled people to forget their difference, even though many think they'll be accepted if they just work hard enough and don't make waves. But we won't reach a state of dignified coexistence in a predominately nondisabled society if many of us continue to deny that an integral part of ourselves is important and valid.[4]

Types of Disabilities

Physical Disabilities

People with physical disabilities are individuals whose limitations are attributable primarily to lowered or impaired physical or sensory capacity caused by congenital or inherited physical defects; disease or injury suffered before, during, or immediately after birth; accidents or illnesses in childhood or adulthood; inadequate diet; or impaired maturation due to inadequate nourishment or insufficient physical activity and stimulation over a prolonged period of time.

Blindness and Vision Impairments

The term *blind* is used most frequently to describe a severe loss of vision. The terms *persons with visual impairments* or *persons with low vision* are used when referring to people who are not totally or legally blind. People with severe vision loss today work in all occupations, but it is estimated that 70 percent of those who are able to work do not have jobs or work only part time in sheltered workshops.

Two and one-half million Americans are severely visually impaired, unable to read a newspaper. Of those, 120,000 are totally blind and 600,000 are legally blind. More than 50,000 Americans become blind every year.

Deafness and Hearing Impairments

Deafness is the term used most frequently to describe profound hearing loss. *Hearing impairment* describes any degree of hearing loss from slight to profound. About 22 million Americans are hearing impaired; 2 million are deaf. Hearing impairments may be congenital or the result of accidents, injuries, diseases, or infections.

Mobility and Motion Impairments

Mobility and motion impairments involve the loss or the loss of use of limbs, bones, or muscles due to disease, injury, or deformity (such as amputation, head injuries, spinal cord injuries, cerebral palsy, amyotrophic lateral sclerosis [Lou Gehrig's disease], multiple sclerosis, tuberculosis of the bones and joints, and congenital deformities). Many people with these types of impairments use wheelchairs; many others use crutches or canes; still others use prostheses (artificial hands or grasping devices, arms, legs, or feet) of one type or another. It is estimated that upward of 25 million people have limited mobility. Of that number, 2 million use wheelchairs.

Down Syndrome

Down syndrome is a chromosome disorder that usually causes delay in physical, intellectual, and language development. The exact causes of the chromosomal rearrangement and primary means of preventing Down syndrome are unknown. It is one of the leading clinical causes of mental retardation in the world; approximately 250,000 families in the United States are affected by Down syndrome. It is not related to race, nationality, or socioeconomic status.

Disfigurement

These are people whose physical appearance is very different from the norm, such as burn survivors and those with physical deformities. The source of the disability may be hereditary (birth defects), disease, or accident. The disfigurement may be facial or associated with the body, back, head, or limbs.

Health and Medical Problems

These are people with such illnesses as AIDS, human immunodeficiency virus (HIV) (whether symptomatic or asymptomatic), asthma, cancer, diabetes, epilepsy, heart conditions, or tuberculosis, or those who are profoundly obese.

Mental, Developmental, and Emotional Disabilities[5]

Mental illness describes any severe mental disorder such as schizophrenia, depression, and emotional disorders. It has been estimated that between 30 and 45 million Americans have been diagnosed as mentally ill. One American family in four has a member with a serious mental disorder. *Developmental disability* describes any severe mental disorder that began before age 22 and continues indefinitely. Individuals with mental retardation, cerebral palsy, and other similar long-term disabilities are considered to have developmental disabilities. *Emotional disability* describes disorders characterized by behavioral irregularities that are severe enough to interfere with daily living or job performance. These disabilities may be due to heredity, rearing, a traumatic experience, or, most commonly, excessive stress. Because of their inability to cope with tension, people with emotional disabilities may engage in defensive actions, such as aggressive behavior, passivity, withdrawal, or the use of drugs or alcohol.

Mental illness takes many forms. The term encompasses a group of disorders that cause severe disturbances in thinking, feeling, and relating to others. Those conditions result in significantly diminished ability to deal with the ordinary requirement of living and working with others. Mental illnesses can affect persons of any age, and they can occur in any family. Mental illness is not the same as mental retardation, which is congenital or inborn. People with mental illnesses usually have normal intelligence, but they may have difficulty performing at an ordinary level because of their illness.

The causes of biologically based brain diseases are not well understood, although it is believed that the functioning of the brain's neurotransmitters is involved. Many factors may contribute to this unsettled functioning. Heredity may play a role. Stress may contribute to its onset. Drugs may also be responsible but are unlikely to be the single cause.

Because the root causes of mental illnesses are not known, there is no effective prevention; however, treatment can improve the functioning of persons with these illnesses. Medications can markedly reduce the symptoms for many people. Psychotherapy, supportive counseling, self-help support groups, and community rehabilitation programs can promote recovery, build self-confidence, and develop independent living and work skills. With appropriate treatment, many mentally ill people can function in society, hold responsible jobs, and enjoy life. However, negative attitudes, stereotypes, and misunderstandings about mental illness create immense barriers for people with mental illness and their families.

Mental, developmental, and emotional disabilities often provide no obvious signs of their presence during, and even following, the hiring process. When that is the case and the individual does not report his or her condition, the employer has no obligations under ADA. However, if the individual or medical or employment records identify the individual as previously diagnosed or classified as impaired, the person is considered to have a record of disability (even if the individual has overcome the condition), and ADA regulations apply.

Mental health professionals include psychiatrists (medical doctors), psychiatric social workers, psychologists, psychiatric nurses, and mental health counselors. In addition, self-help organizations, clergy, and laypersons can also provide assistance to persons with mental illnesses.

Learning Disabilities

People who have problems acquiring knowledge and skills are said to have learning disabilities. These disabilities range from dyslexia to less severe disorders that obstruct, encumber, or hamper learning success. People with learning disabilities have difficulty receiving and processing information and, as a consequence, have reading, writing, speaking, or computational deficiencies that get in the way of job performance and reduce their trainability. Examples include simple memory deficiencies (inability to recall facts or steps in a process) and perceptual disorders (such as inability to judge time or distances, make comparisons, or anticipate obstacles or outcomes).

Speech and Language Disorders[6]

People with speech and language disorders have speech difficulties or impediments to oral communication that are congenital or caused by stroke, accidents, or injuries. These disorders include stuttering, voice and articulation problems, aphasia, cleft palate, lisping, and lallation. Others have had serious diseases, such as cancer, or accidents that resulted in loss of the speech apparatus—the larynx.

One in ten Americans has a communication disorder. Many Americans have speech and language disorders because of stroke, stuttering problems, an undetected hearing loss, a head injury, a movement or muscle problem, a language disorder, or some other problem that interferes with speech, language, or hearing.

Speech and language pathologists can help people develop their communication abilities as well as treat speech, language, and voice disorders. Their services include prevention, identification, evaluation and treatment of communication disorders.

Disability Management

Three elements are crucial to success in hiring, training, developing, and promoting people with disabilities: attitudes, knowledge, and skills. The underpinnings of these elements are basic beliefs and values, which result in the formulation of a philosophy of management.

J. T. Childs, Jr., has identified the key components of a management philosophy that led to successful integration of people with disabilities at IBM:

- *Top management commitment:* Providing personal support to ADA training for all managers
- *Respect for the individual:* Creating a work environment in which an individual with a disability can develop to his or her full potential
- *A focus on abilities:* Building on people's abilities, not their disabilities, and maximizing their abilities through accommodation
- *Mainstreaming:* Providing full access to all aspects of employment, including training, growth and development, and career opportunities, to people with disabilities
- *Making accessibility a way of life:* Considering the needs of people with disabilities in the design of buildings, products, programs, and services[7]

The Language of Disability

The English language is replete with expressions and terms that are insensitive, tactless, demeaning, or outrightly offensive to people with disabilities. These terms, moreover, are overlaid with stereotypes, patronizing attitudes, and sentimentality. Only recently have people become more empathetic and more considerate of the feelings of those with disabilities.

There are four rules to follow when speaking or writing about people with disabilities:

1. Avoid clichés and platitudes.
2. Don't use words or constructs that are patronizing, diminishing, demeaning, or condescending.
3. Always use value-neutral terms and constructions.
4. Always put people, not the disability, first.

General Guidelines

- Avoid referring to people with disabilities as *"the* disabled" or *"the* handicapped."
- Never use the term *handicapped.*
- Avoid calling persons with disabilities "patients."
- Never refer to people with disabilities as "victims," "burdened," "stricken," "suffering," "unfortunate," "crippled," "handicappers," or "invalids." Such terms are dehumanizing because they define people in terms of condition only, and conjure up images that are demeaning. Instead, say "a person with a physical disability."
- Avoid euphemisms like "physically challenged," "inconvenienced," "handi-capable," and "differently abled."
- Never use patronizing terms like "brave," "courageous," "superhuman," "valiant," "inspiring," "game," "gutsy," "special," or "heroic."
- Don't use "defective"; use "congenital disability."
- Avoid terms like "afflicted by" or "afflicted with." Instead say, "a person who has a disability resulting from . . ."
- Avoid referring to persons without disabilities as "able-bodied," "fit," "healthy," "sound," or "normal." The appropriate term is "nondisabled."
- Don't use "confined to," "suffers from," "afflicted with," "victim of," "condemned to," "burdened with," "plagued by," or any other emotionally loaded language.
- Keep it simple, like "has muscular dystrophy," "uses a wheelchair," or "has Down syndrome."
- Never use the terms "wretched," "unfortunate," "pitiful," "poor," "pathetic," or any other words that are judgmental or stereotyping.
- Avoid awkward constructs like "accessible seating" or "handicapped parking." Illogical, ridiculous constructs result from improper use of the word "disabled" as an adjective—for example,

"disabled housing." Correct constructs include "buses equipped to serve persons with disabilities," "parking for disabled people," "housing for people with disabilities," "assistive devices," "disability advocates," and "disability community."

Sensory Disabilities

- Avoid such terms as *"the* blind," *"the* deaf." Use "blind people," "visually impaired," "deaf citizens," and "hard of hearing" or "hearing impaired."
- Don't use the terms "deaf and dumb," "deaf-mute," or "dummy." They are objectionable and inappropriate. Use "deaf," "hearing impaired," or "speech impaired."
- Don't use "sightless," "unsighted," or "four-eyed." Use "blind," "partially sighted," or "vision impaired."

Mental, Developmental, and Emotional Disabilities

- Never refer to *"the* retarded"; instead say, "persons with mental retardation," "persons with schizophrenia," or "someone with mental retardation."
- Such terms as "borderline," "borderline retarded," "low normal," "dull," and "backward," often used to describe persons with mild retardation, contribute to the stereotypes and unclear thinking about the aptitudes, talents, achievements, abilities, and intelligence of many people.
- Terms like "abnormal," "psychotic," "neurotic," and "schizo" are inappropriate.
- Words like "slow," "dotty," "balmy," "simple," "feeble-minded," "crazy," "psycho," "lunatic," "demented," "looney," "daffy," "dim-witted," and "touched" are offensive.
- Never use terms such as "abnormal," "deviant," "unsound," "peculiar," "tard," "retard," "spaz," and "spastic." They stigmatize people who are mentally ill. Use "has a mental disability" or "emotional disability."
- Never use "lunatic asylum," "laughing academy," or "loony bin." Use "hospital," "clinic," or "institution for people with mental illness."

Mobility and Motion Impairments

- Never refer to someone as "lame," "crippled," "paralytic," "gimpy" "misshapened," "grotesque," "malformed," "wheelchair bound," or "confined to a wheelchair." Instead, use "walks with a cane," "uses crutches," "has a disabled hand," "uses a wheelchair."

- Avoid using labels for conditions, such as "arthritic." Use "a person who has arthritis" or "a person with cerebral palsy."

Other Impairments

- Avoid referring to an individual as "brain damaged." Instead use "brain injured" or "has a head injury."
- Don't refer to a short-statured person as a "midget." Use "dwarf" or "little person."
- Never use such terms as "monster," "monstrosity," "vegetable," "freak," or "creature" to describe people with disfiguring disabilities. Instead use words like "the individual has severe disabilities" or "has facial disfigurement."

The Etiquette of Disability

Disability has its own rules of etiquette, which supplement the codes of conduct that guide and direct human communication and interaction. Trainers and other staff members must learn and scrupulously follow these if they are to avoid offending people with disabilities. The most important do's and don'ts follow.

General

- Always use language that is diversity neutral: age neutral, gender neutral, racial neutral, ethnic neutral, and disability neutral.
- Never raise your voice; instead, slow your speaking pace and enunciate clearly.
- Do not expect people with disabilities to reward or commend you for your consideration or your help. You should do no less.
- Never assume that people with disabilities need help, but always greet them and tell them that you're available for assistance. If you are rebuffed, just remember that there are all kinds of people with disabilities as well nondisabled people.
- Always speak directly to a person who has a disability; never assume that a companion will communicate for him or her.
- Offer your help to a person with a disability, but wait for an affirmative reply before touching the individual or taking his or her arm.
- Treat adults as adults. Use first names only if everyone in the

group is addressed by first name. Otherwise use the customary honorifics (Mr., Mrs., Ms., Dr., Professor, and so on).

- Never ask personal questions that you wouldn't ask someone without a disability.
- Never commend a person with a disability for accomplishments learned out of necessity.

Persons Who Have Vision Impairments

- Don't mix or compound disabilities. Just because a person is visually impaired does not mean that he or she is deaf. There is no need to speak louder than usual to a person who is visually impaired.
- Always make your presence known, and do it before you get too close to a person who is blind.
- When you enter a room occupied by a person who is blind, speak first and identify yourself by name. Don't assume that your voice will be recognized.
- When meeting a person with severe loss of vision, identify yourself and anyone who may be with you. Speak normally and indicate when you move from one place to another or need to end the conversation.
- Speak directly to the individual. If your gaze wanders, your voice follows.
- Use words, not gestures or facial expressions. Remember that the individual cannot see the nod, motion, or smile that is intended to change the meaning of your words and may take your words literally.
- Speak naturally, but be alert to signs or signals that your meaning has been misunderstood.
- Never address a blind person through his or her companion or guide. The impression you convey is that the individual is unable to speak for himself or herself.
- When talking with a group that includes a person who is blind, address the individual by name so that he or she will know that the question or remark is directed to him or her.
- Don't be afraid to use expressions such as, "Would you like to see . . ." or "I'm glad to see you again."
- Volunteer assistance, such as, "I'm on my way downtown. Is there something I could get for you?" Most people are reluctant to ask for help. Your offer to help will be appreciated.
- Always leave doors and drawers as you found them—closed or open. Persons who are blind remember them that way. And don't

move chairs or other objects around a room occupied by a blind person.

- Don't push or pull the individual by the arm or clothing. Offer guidance and assistance, but don't assume that the person always needs it.
- Avoid all unnecessary touching of people with visual disabilities. When possible, use oral directions.
- When walking with a person who is visually impaired, identify obstacles, such as curbs, potholes, radical changes in surface, and low-hanging branches.
- When directing a person with visual impairments, use expressions such as "right," "left," "in front of," or "in back of" in relation to where the person is standing, not where you are standing. Even if the person has some vision, do not say "over there" while pointing to the destination.
- Familiarize a blind person with the surroundings by giving pertinent facts, such as the location of doors and objects that could become obstacles.
- When serving food to a blind person who is eating without a sighted companion, offer to read the menu, including the price of each item. As you place each item on the table, call his or her attention to it. If the person wants you to cut up the food or serve it from a casserole or platter, he or she will ask for that help. As you place each item on the plate, use the clock face to help in locating it. It's never bad form to offer, even if the person doesn't request the help.
- When leaving a person with visual impairments, it is best to let him or her stand against a wall or other sturdy object that can serve as a reference point. Being left standing in open space can be disorienting.

Persons Who Have Speech and Hearing Impairments

- When speaking to a person with a hearing disability, get his or her attention by tapping lightly on his or her shoulder or waving your hand. Never speak until you have the person's visual attention.
- Don't be offended if a deaf person taps your shoulder to get your attention.
- Always look at the deaf person when you are speaking, even when an interpreter is present.
- Take time to communicate and allow extra time. Be sure to speak slowly and clearly. Don't exaggerate or shout. Face the person directly, and keep your hands or objects away from your mouth.

- Maintain eye contact and use natural gestures and facial expressions; don't exaggerate your mouth movements.
- Don't beat around the bush. Communicate in a direct manner. Verify understanding before the person leaves.
- Use open-ended questions, ones that require more than "yes" or "no" answers.
- When speaking to someone with speech difficulties, be encouraging and patient. Ask short questions that require brief answers.
- Never pretend to understand if you don't. Repeat or rephrase what you hear so that the person's reaction can confirm or deny your understanding.
- Never say, "Oh, never mind. It doesn't matter," when a deaf person asks you to repeat something.

People with Mobility or Motion Impairments

- Before assisting anyone in a wheelchair or on crutches, ask permission. Never touch the individual before he or she has told you where and how you can help. If your offer is declined, don't stay near; stay clear. If your offer is accepted, ask the person exactly what he or she wants you to do.
- Give people in wheelchairs a lot of space—and time. Open doors and wait patiently for them to go through.
- Wheelchairs and crutches usually require the use of hands and arms, so be prepared to open doors, carry packages, and hold chairs. But don't do anything without first asking, "May I help?" or at the very least informing the person of what you are about to do.
- Don't hang or lean on a person's wheelchair when conversing. If the conversation is more than a passing comment, a request, or an answer to a question, seat yourself at the level of the person in the wheelchair.
- Speak directly to the person in the wheelchair, not to someone else nearby.
- Never move a wheelchair out of the reach of its user.
- Never start to push a person's wheelchair without first getting permission. Ask if he or she needs assistance.

Persons with Disfigurement

Every year thousands of people are confronted with the pain and anguish of disfigurement caused by accidents, cancer, and birth defects— and the feelings of rejection and isolation that often accompany facial or bodily differences. Their families, too, have to deal with the distress and heartache by seeing a loved one with disfigurement.

When most people first meet someone with a severe disfigurement, they are startled. They look; too often they stare. Some laugh nervously. Many then turn their eyes away. These actions are accompanied by feelings of discomfort, uneasiness, anxiety, pity, revulsion, or even fear. Such reactions are the result of the collective experiences of a whole culture and the impact of ingrained values on what beauty is and what people should look like—mental programming, if you like. People have been conditioned from childhood by parents, siblings, friends, educators, the media, business, and the general public that certain physical characteristics are desirable. Any significant departure from these standards is likely to produce negative reactions among many people.

The first two reactions—being startled and looking—are perfectly natural. Staring, laughing nervously, and avoiding eye contact are not. They are demeaning and therefore unacceptable. They should be replaced by understanding, empathy, and appreciation. The key to cultivating proper responses is experiential learning—contact with people with a variety of disfigurements, first by means of photographs and video and then by direct face-to-face interaction, both accompanied by feedback on the appropriateness of responses. After meeting the person, immerse yourself in the business or conversation and socialization, and you'll quickly forget the disfigurement.

Let's Face It provides the following suggestions for supporting people with disfigurement:

- Look them in the eyes.
- Accept their feelings.
- Acknowledge their anger, fear, and bewilderment . . . and perhaps your own.
- Remember that laughter is often the best medicine.
- If you love them, tell them so.[8]

Work Adjustment

Because this book focuses on hiring and training adults with disabilities, it is important that the term "work adjustment" be understood. It has two meanings, which sometimes results in misunderstanding, misuse, and ambiguity. The first meaning is concerned with the rehabilitation process whereby the individual with a disability learns the basic workplace skills needed for employment. In this context, work adjustment is a therapeutic process designed to enhance the employment potential of a person with a disability by developing physical and mental capacities, tolerances, and stamina, providing information and experiences, and cultivating appropriate behaviors. The second meaning focuses on the relationships, skills, and conditions required for *success* on the job. In this context, the goal of work adjustment is to help the individual learn the skills needed to function in an occupation and adjust to work as a lifetime pursuit. In this book we shall deal only with the second concept.

Summary

There are many definitions of disability. Some reflect legal and legislative concerns while others express corporate forms or social protocols. In this book, disability is considered to be any physical, mental, developmental, emotional, or learning condition, whether inherited or due to disease, accident, or injury, work related or not, that has been an obstacle to or disqualifier for initial employment or continuation of employment.

The many myths about disability have resulted in the erection of barriers to the employment and advancement of people who, in fact, are more like the rest of us than they are different. People with disabilities display the range of intellect, sensitivity, good humor, and talents as nondisabled people as well as their share of ordinary human frailties.

All too often people with disabilities have been subjected to terms and labels that are insensitive, degrading, and offensive. Although not usually intentionally demeaning, those terms have demonstrated the tendency of people to adopt stereotypes or to be patronizing, overly sentimental, or tactless. Nondisabled people must learn to avoid words or constructs that are diminishing, use terms that are value neutral, and always put people first. Then they must learn and scrupulously follow the rules of etiquette and codes of conduct that should guide and direct human interaction and communication with people who have disabilities.

For Further Reading, Viewing, and Listening*

Bailey, Ian L., and Amanda Hall. *Visual Impairment: An Overview.* New York: American Foundation for the Blind, 1990.

Building Bridges—Access to American's Hot New Market. Available from National Easter Seal Society.

duPont de Nemours & Company. *Serious Mental Illness: Myths and Realities.* Available from National Alliance for the Mentally Ill.

*Full addresses for the organizations in this listing are found in Appendixes B and C.

Epilepsy Foundation of America. *Questions and Answers about Epilepsy*. Landover, MD: EFA, n.d.

Face Facts Video Tapes. 1991. Five videos: *Cleft Lip and Palate*, 25:55 minutes; *Craniosynostosis*, 26:16 minutes; *Hemifacial Microsomia*, 25:12 minutes; *Treacher Collins Syndrome*, 26:09 minutes; *Orbital Hypertelorism*, 25:36 minutes. Available from Forward Face.

Given the Opportunity: A Guide to Interaction in the Workforce. Video package (video, implementation guide, presentation slide set with script, leader's guide, employee handbook, and audiocassette). Available from Meridian Education Corporation.

I Work with a Guy Who's Deaf and Blind. 1992. 11-minute video. Available from Salenger Films.

Mirror, Mirror. 1990. Videocassette on facial disfigurement. Available on loan for educational programs from About Face.

Morrissey, Patricia. *Disability Etiquette in the Workplace*. Washington, D.C.: Equal Employment Advisory Council and Employment Policy Foundation, 1991. Available from Society for Human Resource Management.

News from Medicine: Peace of Mind. 1988. 60-minute video. Cable News Network.

No One Is Burning Wheelchairs. 1992. 15-minute video. Available from National Easter Seal Society.

Part of the Team. 1991. 17-minute video. Available from the National Easter Seal Society.

Pueschel, Siegfried (ed.). *Down Syndrome: Growing and Learning*. Kansas City, Mo.: Andrews & McMeel, 1978.

Shapiro, Joseph P. *No Pity: People with Disabilities Forging a New Civil Rights Movement*. New York: Times Books, 1993.

Succeeding Together at Work. 1993. 7-minute video. Available from Salenger Films.

Tingey, Carol. *Down Syndrome: A Resource Handbook*. Waltham, Mass.: College-Hill Press/Little, Brown, 1988.

Unseen Courage. 1991. 23-minute video. Produced by Advantage Media.

Welcome to the Team: Disability Etiquette in the Workplace. 1992. 20-minute video. Produced by Advantage Media.

When the Music Stops: The Reality of Serious Mental Illness. 1987. 20-minute video. Available from National Alliance for the Mentally Ill.

Notes

1. President's Committee on Employment of People with Disabilities, *Ready Willing and Available: A Business Guide for Hiring People with Disabilities* (Washington, D.C.: The Committee, August 1992), p. i.
2. Sheila H. Akabas, Lauren B. Gates, and Donald E. Galvin, *Disability Management: A Complete System to Reduce Costs, Increase Productivity, Meet Employee Needs, and Ensure Legal Compliance* (New York: AMACOM, 1992), p. 3.
3. "Workers Are Willing to Accommodate Coworkers with Disabilities," *HR Fo-*

cus, Special Report on the Americans with Disabilities Act, American Management Association, 1992.

4. Dianne B. Piastro, "Living with a Disability: Cultural Movement Increasingly Important," *Cape Cod Times,* July 16, 1993, p. C-2.

5. Much of this material was provided by the National Alliance for the Mentally Ill. Used by permission.

6. Much of this material was provided by the American Speech-Language Hearing Association. Used by permission.

7. J. T. Childs, Jr., keynote speech presented at the EOP Careers and the dis-ABLED Exposition, Washington, D.C., February 25, 1993. Used by permission.

8. *Let's Face It: A Network for People with Facial Difference* (Concord, Mass.: Let's Face It, n.d.).

2

Disability and the Law

Government concern about Americans with disabilities can be traced to legislation from the late 1960s and early 1970s. However, it was not until the 1980s that helping people with disabilities lead independent and fuller lives as workers became a national policy affecting both the government and private institutions.

Most states have laws protecting persons with disabilities, but many of those laws exclude people with mental disabilities. And even when such laws contain provisions to protect people with mental disabilities, relatively few complaints have been filed because of the stigma associated with mental illnesses and disabilities. Recent federal laws are much more encompassing and make the hiring, training, and advancement of people with all types of disabilities mandatory.

Americans with Disabilities Act of 1990 (ADA)

The ADA, the most significant nondiscrimination legislation in 25 years, has had a great impact on all types of organizations. The act provides civil rights protections parallel to those provided by the Civil Rights Act of 1964 to individuals on the basis of race, color, national origin, sex, and religion. The ADA applies to individuals with disabilities in the areas of employment, public accommodations, state and local government services, telecommunications, and transportation. It prohibits discrimination on the basis of disability by private entities in places of public accommodation and requires that all new places of public accommodation and commercial facilities be designed and constructed so as to be readily accessible to and usable by persons with disabilities.

The act protects people with most physical or mental impairments and those with a record of such disabilities. It also protects people perceived as disabled, such as accident or burn survivors with severe facial scarring. Specifically, the act protects people who have physical or mental impairments that substantially limit a "major life activity," have a record of such an impairment, or are regarded as having such an impairment.

An impairment is defined as "any physiological disorder or condition, cosmetic disfigurement, or anatomical loss affecting one or more of the . . . body systems." The regulations define the term "substantially limit" as impairments that preclude a person from performing a major life activity or significantly restrict the condition, manner, or duration under which a person can perform a particular major life activity as compared with the average person in the general population. "Major life activities" include "functions such as caring for oneself, performing manual tasks, walking, seeing, hearing, speaking, breathing, and learning, and working."

A physical or mental impairment is "(1) any physiological disorder, or condition, cosmetic disfigurement, or anatomical loss affecting one or more of the following body systems: neurological, musculoskeletal, special sense organs, respiratory (including speech organs), cardiovascular, reproductive, digestive, genito-urinary, hemic and lymphatic, skin, and endocrine; or (2) any mental or psychological disorder, such as mental retardation, organic brain syndrome, emotional or mental illness, and specific learning disabilities."

Physical or mental impairments include, but are not limited to, such contagious and noncontagious diseases and conditions as orthopedic, visual, speech, and hearing impairments; cerebral palsy, epilepsy, muscular dystrophy, multiple sclerosis, cancer, heart disease, diabetes, mental retardation, emotional illness, specific learning disabilities, human immunodeficiency virus disease (whether symptomatic or asymptomatic), tuberculosis, drug addiction, and alcoholism. Individuals who currently use illegal drugs are not protected by ADA.

Under ADA, homosexuality and bisexuality are not classified as physical or mental impairments, nor are transvestism, transsexualism, pedophilia, exhibitionism, voyeurism, gender identification disorders, compulsive gambling, kleptomania, or pyromania.

Although a current user of drugs is not protected by ADA, a person who currently uses alcohol is not automatically denied protection. An alcoholic is a person with a disability if he or she is qualified to perform the essential functions of job, and an employer may be required to provide an accommodation to an alcoholic. However, an employer can discipline, discharge, or deny employment to an alcoholic whose use of alcohol affects conduct or performance.

The ADA requires employers of 15 or more workers to make reasonable accommodations to enable a person with a disability to do a job. That includes training and development.

Employment (Title I)

Title I of the ADA regulates employment of people with disabilities and is the responsibility of the Equal Employment Opportunity Commission (EEOC). Employers, employment agencies, labor organizations, and joint labor-management committees can no longer screen out people with disabilities in the recruitment and hiring processes, nor can they discriminate in any area of employment, including training. They can no longer conduct preemployment medical screening (with some exceptions) or make inquiries into the nature of an applicant's disability.

The ADA applies to all qualified individuals with a disability. A qualified individual with a disability is a person who meets legitimate skill, experience, education, or other requirements of an employment position that he or she holds or seeks and who can perform the "essential functions" of the position with or without reasonable accommodation.

Essential Job Functions. The term "essential functions" means "the fundamental job duties of the employment position the individual with a disability holds or desires." Requiring an individual to perform essential functions means that an individual will not be considered unqualified simply because of inability to perform marginal or incidental job functions. If an individual is considered qualified to perform essential job functions except for limitations caused by a disability, the employer must consider making reasonable accommodations to enable the individual to perform the functions, unless undue hardship would result, that is, the accommodation would be unduly costly, substantial, or disruptive or would fundamentally alter the nature or operation of the business. Determination of undue hardship involves consideration of such factors as the nature and cost of the accommodation, size and total resources of the organization (financial and nonfinancial), nature and structure of its operation, and the tax credits, deductions, and outside funding available to the company.

Reasonable Accommodation. Reasonable accommodation includes the provision of an aid, device, assistance, relief, or help of any other kind that permits a person with a disability to perform the essential functions of a job without undue hardship to the employer. It is to be decided on a case-by-case basis. However, the EEOC has stated that it will consider an employer's good-faith compliance on reasonable accommodation if the employer can provide evidence, in the form of written documentation, of its decision-making process in its compliance efforts.

The obligation to provide reasonable accommodation applies only to known physical or mental limitations. An employer who is not aware of a physical or mental impairment is not obliged to make any accommodation. However, that does not mean that an applicant or employee must always inform the employer of a disability. If an impairment is obvious—for example, the individual uses crutches or a wheelchair—the employer knows of the disability even if the person never mentions it.

An employer may ask an applicant to "self-identify" as having a disability on a job application form or by other preemployment inquiry under these conditions:

- Federal contractors and subcontractors when required to do so by the affirmative action requirements of section 503 of the Rehabilitation Act of 1973, provided that the requirements of the law are observed in obtaining the information and that the information is maintained as a separate, confidential record.
- If required by any other federal law or regulation, such as those applicable to disabled veterans and veterans of the Vietnam era, to identify applicants or clients with disabilities in order to provide them with required special services.

The requirement for an accommodation is usually generated by a request from the individual with the disability, who frequently can suggest an appropriate accommodation. Although consideration should be given to the preference of the individual involved, the employer has the discretion to choose among effective accommodations and may select the one that is least expensive or easiest to provide.

If a particular accommodation is deemed to be an undue hardship, the employer must identify a substitute. If cost is the problem, consideration must be given to whether funding for the accommodation is available from an outside source, such as a vocational rehabilitation agency, and if the cost of providing the accommodation can be offset by state or federal tax credits or deductions. The applicant or employee must also be given the opportunity to provide the accommodation or pay for the portion of the accommodation that constitutes an undue hardship.

The test of an accommodation is effectiveness—whether the accommodation will allow the person to perform the essential functions of the job. If an applicant refuses to accept the accommodation offered by an employer, the individual may be considered unqualified. If an employee declines an accommodation, the employer must consider reassigning the employee to an existing position that he or she can perform with or without a reasonable accommodation. However, the employer is not required to create a new position or to bump another employee to generate a vacancy.

The ADA extends the concept of reasonable accommodation beyond job or worksite modification to allow workers with disabilities to function on a more nearly level playing field. For example, it calls for reasonable accommodation in the job application process to allow workers to be considered for positions or a modification or adjustment that would permit them to receive the same benefits and privileges extended to similarly situated but nondisabled workers. These may include access to break areas, lunch rooms and cafeterias, training facilities, gymnasiums, and transportation, as well as training and development programs and services.

A word of caution: The ADA prohibits employers from limiting, segregating, or classifying people on the basis of their disabilities and requires that all applicants for positions be judged on the basis of their individual abilities and not on any preconceived notions of what a person with a disability may be capable of doing.

Job Performance Standards. Employers may hold employees with disabilities to the same standards of performance and production as employees without disabilities for performing essential job functions, with or without reasonable accommodations. They may also hold employees with disabilities to the same standards as other employees for the performance of marginal functions unless the disability affects the person's ability to perform those marginal functions. If the ability to perform marginal functions is affected by the disability, the employer must provide some type of reasonable accommodation, such as job restructuring, but the employer may not exclude the employee if he or she is satisfactorily performing the job's essential functions.

Compensation and Benefits. Organizations must ensure that discrimination toward qualified employees or applicants who have disabilities does not occur in any term, condition, or privilege of employment, including compensation and benefits. Employees with disabilities cannot be denied insurance or be subjected to different terms or requirements based exclusively on disability, provided that the disability does not pose increased insurance risk. They cannot limit available coverage or charge different rates for the same coverage simply because the worker has a physical or mental impairment, except when the decision is based on sound risk assessment, risk classification, or actuarial principles. In addition, employers are prohibited from disqualifying for employment or terminating a person with a disability because additional health care costs may be incurred, nor can employers refuse to hire or fire an employee who has a dependent with a disability who is not currently covered by the plan and who, if added, may increase costs.

Employers may offer health insurance policies that contain clauses pertaining to preexisting conditions, even when they adversely affect workers with disabilities, so long as they are not used as a subterfuge to circumvent ADA. Employers may offer policies that limit coverage for certain medical, rehabilitative, or therapeutic procedures or limit treatment to a specified number of visits, months, or years, so long as the limitations apply to nondisabled workers and persons with disabilities are not denied coverage for other medical, rehabilitative, or therapeutic procedures.

The ADA limits employer redesign of health insurance plans. It prohibits employment discrimination against any employee with a disability; therefore, an employer may not fire or refuse to hire a person with a disability solely on the basis that the employer's health insurance plan does not cover the disability or because covering the disability would increase the employer's health care premiums.

The effect of ADA on the design of new health insurance is less clear, although it is reasonably clear that a preexisting condition clause is permissible, even if it adversely affects persons with disabilities. Similarly, a plan may limit reimbursements for certain drugs or treatment, provided that these restrictions are applied uniformly to all employees.

The applicability of health insurance policy limitations for the treatment of AIDS is also unclear. Although ADA specifically defines AIDS as a covered disability (and a clause excluding or limiting treatment for AIDS would appear to be a violation), ADA makes specific exceptions of exclusions based on accepted principles of risk assessment or risk classification. Court decisions following litigation should clarify this contradiction.

As of June 8, 1993, the EEOC prohibited many forms of discrimination found in employee health plans. It declared that employers may not refuse to hire people with disabilities because of their concern about their effect on insurance costs, that workers with disabilities must generally be given equal access to any health insurance provided to other employees, and that employers may not set a lower level of benefits for AIDS or any other "discrete group of disabilities."

Although the policy permits employers to make some disability-based distinctions (such as providing more generous coverage for physical ailments than for mental and emotional conditions), it stipulates that employers will have to prove that their practices are justified and not merely a means of evading the law. That means that an employer will be liable for any discrimination resulting from a contract or agreement with an insurer, health maintenance organization, or other entity to provide or administer a health insurance plan for its workers. To prove that a provision of a plan is not a subterfuge to evade the law, employers must demonstrate that:

- The distinction being challenged is not disability based.
- Disparate treatment is justified by actuarial data or experience.
- Disparate treatment is necessary to maintain the financial soundness of the plan.
- No nondiscrimination-based distinction or treatment could prevent either a drastic premium increase or reduced coverage.
- Coverage for a disability-specific treatment was denied because it had no medical value.

In summary, employees with disabilities must have access to all types of benefits plans under the same terms and conditions as nondisabled employees, including the following:

- Assignment, transfer, promotion, upgrading, rehiring, and award of tenure.
- Layoff, demotion, reassignment, and termination.
- Job classification, compensation, changes in compensation, and bonuses.
- Sick leave, family and medical leave, vacations, leaves of absence, or any other type of leave.
- Benefits, including retirement annuities, health, life, other insurance coverage available to all employees, and company-sponsored fitness, social, or recreational programs.
- Selection and financial support for training and development, including apprenticeships, technical and other training, supervisory and management development, service on committees and task forces, professional and technical memberships, and attendance at professional and technical meetings and conferences.

Attendance and Leave Policies. Attendance and leave policies may be applied to employees with disabilities as long as they are uniformly applied to all employees. Employers may not refuse leave requested by an employee with a disability if other employees are granted such leave. However, an employer may be required to make adjustments in leave policy as a reasonable accommodation, such as leave flexibility and unpaid leave, so long as it would not impose an undue hardship.

Workers Compensation. Only injured workers who meet the ADA's definition of disability are considered disabled under ADA, regardless of whether they meet the criteria for receiving benefits under workers compensation or other disability laws. A worker must also be qualified (with or without accommodation) to be protected under ADA. Because on-the-job injuries do not always cause physical or mental impairments severe enough to limit a major life activity substantially and because many injuries cause only temporary impairments, many injured workers who qualify for workers compensation or other disability benefits laws may not be protected by ADA.

People with Mental Illnesses. The law protects the rights of workers with mental illnesses. Once hired, employees with a history of mental illness are entitled to extra support and accommodation from their employers so long as they can perform the essential duties and tasks of their jobs. The law covers a broad range of mental problems, including mental retardation, learning disabilities, and workers who have overcome substance abuse (recovering drug and alcohol abusers). Other covered illnesses include schizophrenia, manic-depressive disorders, major depression, anxiety disorders, and personality problems.

Accommodations required by the law for persons with mental disabilities have not been identified but will undoubtedly be clarified as a result of lawsuits. However, special provisions may be as simple and inexpensive as providing more frequent breaks and quieter work areas.

Specific Provisions of Title I. Employers must accommodate the disabilities of qualified applicants for positions unless an undue hardship would result, but they may reject applicants or terminate employees who pose a direct threat to the health or safety of other individuals in the workplace as determined by a qualified health professional based on the most current medical knowledge, clear understanding of the essential functions of the job in question, and objective evidence about the condition of the worker. In addition, the EEOC requires that the employer consider the following factors: (1) the duration of the risk, (2) the nature and severity of the potential harm, (3) the likelihood that the potential harm will occur, and (4) the immediacy of potential harm.

Applicants and employees are not protected from personnel actions based on their current illegal use of drugs (drug testing is not affected by the act).

Employers may not discriminate against a qualified applicant or employee because of the known disability of an individual with whom the applicant or employee is known to have a relationship or association.

Religious organizations may give preference in employment to their own members and may require applicants and employees to conform to their religious tenets.

Public Services (Title II)

Title II deals with public entities—any state or local government and any of its departments, agencies, or other instrumentalities, including the legislative and judicial branches of state and local government. All activities, services, and programs of public entities are covered, including town meetings, police and fire departments, motor vehicle licensing, and employment. Also covered is public bus and rail transportation.

Specifically, under the act, state and local governments:

■ May not refuse to allow qualified individuals with disabilities to participate in a service, program, or activity simply because of a disability. Qualified individuals are persons who meet the essential eligibility requirements for the program or activity offered by a public entity.

■ Must provide programs and services in an integrated setting, unless separate or different measures are necessary to ensure equal opportunity.

■ Must eliminate unnecessary eligibility standards or rules that deny individuals with disabilities an equal opportunity to enjoy their services, programs, or activities unless "necessary" for the provisions of the service or activity. Requirements that are essential for the safe operation of the program, such as requirements for eligibility for drivers' licenses, may be imposed if they are based on actual risks and not on mere speculation, stereotypes, or generalizations about persons with disabilities.

■ Are required to make reasonable modifications in policies, practices, and procedures that deny equal access to individuals with disabilities, unless a fundamental alteration of the program would result. However, State and local governments may not require an individual with a disability to accept a special accommodations or benefit if the individual chooses not to accept it.

■ Must ensure that individuals with disabilities are not excluded from service, programs, and activities because buildings are inaccessible. However, they need not remove physical barriers, such as stairs, in all existing buildings, as long as they make their programs accessible to individuals who are unable to use an existing facility.

■ May provide the services, programs, and activities offered in the facility to individuals with disabilities through alternative methods, if physical barriers are not removed. Alternatives include relocating services to an accessibly facility, providing an aide or personal assistant to help an individual with a disability obtain the service, or provide benefits or services at the individuals's home or at an alternative accessible site. State and local governments may not carry an individual with a disability as a means of providing program access except in "manifestly" exceptional circumstances.

■ Must ensure that newly constructed buildings and facilities are free of architectural and communication barriers that restrict access or use by individuals with disabilities.[1] Alterations to an existing building must be accessible. However, ADA does not require retrofitting of existing buildings to eliminate barriers.

■ Must furnish auxiliary aids and services to individuals with hearing, vision, or speech impairments when necessary to ensure effective communication. Auxiliary aids include such services or devices as nonverbal alarms, computer-generated speech, qualified interpreters, assistive listening devices, television closed and open captioning and decoders, telecommunications devices for deaf persons (TDDs), video text displays, readers, taped texts, Braille materials, and large print materials.

■ Are not required to provide auxiliary aids that would result in a fundamental alteration in the nature of a service, program, or activity or in undue financial and administrative burdens. However, public entities must furnish another auxiliary aid, if available, that does not result in a fundamental alteration or undue burdens. Individuals with disabilities may not be charged for the use of such aids.

■ May provide special benefits, beyond those required by the regulation, to individuals with disabilities.

■ May not place special fees or charges on individuals with disabilities to cover the costs of measures needed to ensure nondiscriminatory treatment, such as making modifications required to provide program accessibility or providing qualified interpreters.

■ Must operate their programs so that, when viewed in their entirety, they are readily accessible to and usable by individuals with disabilities.

Public Accommodations (Title III)

Title III of the ADA refers to public accommodations, defined as facilities operated, owned, or leased by private entities and open to the public and commercial facilities (office buildings, factories, warehouses, and the like whose operations affect commerce). This section requires that individuals with disabilities be given full and equal access to the goods, services, facilities, privileges, advantages, and accommodations of any place of public accommodation. In providing these goods and services, public accommodations may not use eligibility requirements that exclude or segregate individual with disabilities, unless the requirements are necessary for the operation of the public accommodation.

Places of public accommodations include businesses and services owned by private entities, such as inns, restaurants, theaters, stadiums, entertainment establishments, retail establishments, shopping centers, retail service establishments (bakeries, dry cleaners, shoe repair, etc.), health care providers, and places of education. Private entities that offer examinations and courses related to educational and occupational certification are also covered by the legislation. The act does not include entities controlled by religious organizations, private clubs, and state and local governments (which are covered by Title II).

The act requires that public accommodations:

■ Make reasonable changes in policies, practices, and procedures that deny equal access to individuals with disabilities, unless a fundamental alteration would result in the nature of the goods and service provided.

■ Provide goods and services in an integrated setting, unless separate or different measures are needed to ensure equal opportunity.

■ Eliminate eligibility standards or rules that deny individuals with disabilities an equal opportunity to enjoy the goods and services of a place of public accommodation. Safety requirements may be imposed only if they are necessary for the safe operation of a place of public accommodation. Such requirements must be based on actual risks and not on mere speculation, stereotypes, or generalizations about people with disabilities.

■ Provide auxiliary aids and services to individuals with vision or hearing impairments to ensure effective communication unless an undue burden or fundamental alteration would result. However, a public accommodation is not required to provide personal devices, such as wheelchairs; individually prescribed devices, such as prescription eyeglasses or hearing aids; or services of a personal nature, such as assistance in eating, toileting, or dressing.

■ Remove architectural and structural communication barriers in existing facilities where readily available and provide readily achievable alternative measures when removal of barriers is not readily achievable, and they must remove physical barriers (such as furniture and equipment that interfere with access to individuals with wheelchairs) in existing facilities, particularly in assembly areas, such as in lecture halls and conference rooms, if removal is readily achievable (without much difficulty or expense). Otherwise, alternative methods of providing the services must be offered, if those methods are readily achievable. Barrier removal measures include installing ramps; making curb cuts at sidewalks and entrances; rearranging tables, chairs, vending machines, display racks, and furniture; widening doorways; installing grab bars in toilet stalls; and adding raised letters or braille to elevator buttons. Alternatives to barrier removal include providing goods and services at the door, sidewalk, or curb; providing home delivery; retrieving merchandise from inaccessible shelves or racks; and relocating activities to accessible locations.

■ Design new construction and alterations in public accommodations to make them accessible.[2] When alterations to a primary function area are made, an accessible path of travel to the altered area (as well as to the bathrooms, telephones, and drinking fountains serving that area) must be provided to the extent that the added accessibility costs are not disproportionate to the overall cost of the alterations. Costs are deemed to be disproportionate if they exceed 20 percent of the cost of the alteration originally planned.

■ Ensure that all newly constructed or renovated facilities used for public accommodations are barrier-free. Existing private facilities housing public accommodations must be altered to make them accessible to the extent that such alterations can be readily achieved without too much difficulty or expense.

■ Serve individuals with disabilities in an equal and unsegregated manner. That may be accomplished by eliminating architectural and communication barriers, training personnel, providing auxiliary aids, and modifying policies, practices, and procedures.

■ If places of public accommodation offer examinations or courses related to applications, licensing, certification or credentialing for secondary or postsecondary education, professional, or trade purposes, they must offer them in an accessible place and manner or provide alternative accessible arrangements.

Telecommunications Relay Services (Title IV)

The telecommunications section of the ADA requires that individuals with hearing impairments have access to a telephone system that allows them to communicate with individuals who do not have hearing impairments. By law, telephone services must establish nationwide telecommunications relay services facilities equipped with specialized equipment and staffed by qualified communications assistants who relay conversation between people who use text telephones and people who use the general telephone network. The act prohibits telephone companies from imposing monthly, fixed charges to recover the costs of this new service. In addition, telephone companies cannot charge relay users higher rates than voice users based on time of day, length of call, or distance between callers.

The law also establishes mandatory minimum standards for operational, technical, and functional procedures to carry out the requirement. In addition, the law requires that televised public service announcements produced or funded by the federal government must include closed captioning of the verbal content of the message.

Documents issued by the Federal Communications Commission since the passage of ADA have made some important changes in terminology to accommodate current technology; however, the changes have not yet come into widespread use. The major change is the use of the term "telecommunications relay services" (TRS) instead of "telecommunications device for the deaf" (TDD) because it more accurately describes the services and equipment used and promotes national understanding and acceptance of persons with disabilities.[3] TRS are defined as telephone transmission services that enable individuals with hearing or speech disabilities to communicate by wire or radio with hearing persons in a manner that is functionally equivalent to the ability of an individual who does not have a hearing or speech disability to communicate using voice communication services by wire or radio.

Transportation (Titles II and III)

The ADA addresses transportation in two ways: transportation provided by public entities and systems offered by private organizations. Over the long term, ADA requires all public and private transportation systems to be fully accessible for individuals with disabilities. For public entities, that means that all new buses must have lifts, new rail cars must have fold-up seats and storage space for wheelchairs, and transit stations and platforms must be accessible. For private bus and van companies, new buses ordered on or after July 26, 1996 (July 26, 1997, for small companies) must be accessible. Other new vehicles, such as vans, must also be accessible, unless the transportation company provides service to individuals with disabilities that is equivalent to that offered to the general public.

Additionally, transportation services provided to employees must be made equally available to workers with disabilities. The law also requires that, for both public and private organizations, architectural barriers that impede access must be removed.

Miscellaneous Provisions (Title V)

Title V includes provisions on a variety of topics. Of particular interest to employers are the following:

- Prohibition of coercion of retaliation against employees who invoke rights under the ADA.
- Availability of attorneys' fees to the prevailing party in ADA-related proceedings.
- The relationship of ADA to other state and federal laws.
- The fact that underwriting and risk classification procedures in relation to employee benefits plans are permitted only as long as

they are consistent with state law and do not serve as a means of circumventing the objectives of ADA.

The ADA and Current Employees

The ADA replies with equal force to current employees who become disabled as well as to job applicants. All of the items that constitute discrimination apply to job posting, reassignments and transfers, and promotions. For both applicants and employees who become disabled, reasonable accommodations are the same. In addition, however, for current employees who become disabled, reasonable accommodation includes:

- Holding the job open until the employee recovers, unless that action would cause undue hardship for the business or organization
- Reassigning the employee to another position
- Limiting hours or making modifications or adjustments to facilities or equipment to make it possible for the employee to continue working

Although not required by ADA, voluntary accommodation may be provided, for example, medical rehabilitation to help the employee return to his or her job or a program of vocational rehabilitation to qualify the employee for another position.

Related Laws and Regulations

Several other federal laws and regulations, including changes to the Internal Revenue Code, deal with disability.

Service Members Occupational Conversion and Training Act of 1993 (SMOCTA)

This legislation, administered jointly by the Departments of Defense (DOD), Labor (DOL), and Veterans Affairs (DVA), offers employers monetary incentives to hire and train eligible veterans. The DOL is authorized by the act to reimburse employers up to $10,000 of a trainee's wages during the training period and $12,000 if the veteran has a service-connected disability. To be eligible, veterans must have served on active duty for more than 90 days and been discharged after August 1, 1990. The veteran must also meet one of the following criteria: (1) be unemployed for at least 8 of the last 15 weeks before applying, (2) as determined by

DOD, have a military occupational specialty not easily transferable to the civilian workplace, or (3) have at least a 30 percent disability rating from DVA. To be eligible, employers must provide training programs of between 6 and 18 months in duration and be approved by DVA. Training for seasonal or temporary jobs, jobs based on commissions, positions with the federal government, or jobs outside the United States are ineligible.

Protection and Advocacy for Mentally Ill Individuals Amendments Act of 1991

This legislation amends and extends the Protection and Advocacy for Mentally Ill Individuals Act of 1986 to ensure that the rights of individuals with mental illnesses are protected and to assist the states to establish and operate a protection and advocacy service.

Internal Revenue Code Amendments of 1990

Certain amendments to the Internal Revenue Code relate to tax credits and other benefits to employers who hire or accommodate persons with disabilities.

Disabled Access Credit (DAC), Section 4. The Omnibus Budget Reconciliation Act of 1990 (public law 101-508) contains a tax incentive to encourage small business to comply with the ADA. Section 44 allows an eligible small business to take a general business credit of up to $5,000 annually for expenditures incurred to comply with ADA requirements.[4] The code permits a nonrefundable tax credit equal to 50 percent of costs that exceed $250 to remove barriers and/or provide auxiliary aids and equipment, up to a maximum of $10,250. The credit can be carried forward up to 15 years and back for 3 years, although there is no carryback to any year before 1990. Businesses may take this credit every year that they make an expenditure for accessibility, regardless of whether it is for purchase of equipment, provision of communications assistance, or removal of architectural barriers.

Eligible access expenditures include amounts paid or incurred:

- To remove architectural, communication, physical, or transportation barriers
- To provide qualified interpreters or other means of making aurally delivered materials available to individuals with hearing impairments

- To provide qualified readers, taped texts, and other methods of making visually delivered materials available to individuals with visual impairments
- To acquire or modify equipment or devices for individuals with disabilities
- To provide other similar services, modifications, materials, or equipment

Architectural and Transportation Barrier Removal Deduction, Section 190. An amendment to the Tax Reform Act in 1990, Section 190 extended permanently the $35,000 tax deduction for the removal of architectural and transportation barriers. The Omnibus Budget Reconciliation Act of 1990 amended section 190 and reduced the deduction from $35,000 to $15,000, effective for tax years after 1990.

Section 190 now allows any business a deduction of up to $15,000 per taxable year paid or incurred for expenses associated with the removal of qualified architectural and transportation barriers at existing places of business or trade and that are not chargeable to a capital account. Qualified expenses include only those specifically attributable to the removal of existing barriers, such as transportation vehicles, inaccessible parking spaces, curbs, ramps, steps, and elevators, warning signals, entrances, narrow doors, floors, water fountains, public telephones, and inaccessible toilet facilities. Modifications must meet the requirements of standards established under section 190 of the Internal Revenue Code, *(26 CFR sec. 1.190)*, that is, they must conform to design standards prepared by the U.S. Architectural and Transportation Barriers Compliance Board and compliance with the Uniform Accessibility Standard.

Targeted Jobs Tax Credit (TJTC), Section 51. The Targeted Jobs Tax Credit offers employers a tax credit against their tax liability if they hire individuals from nine targeted groups, including persons with disabilities. The credit applies only to workers hired by a business or trade and is not available to employers of maids, chauffeurs, or other household employees. The credit is equal to 40 percent of the first-year wages, up to $6,000 per employee, for a maximum credit of $2,444 per employee for the first year of employment.

Television Decoder Circuitry Act of 1990

An amendment to the Communications Act of 1934 was enacted to achieve compliance with the auxiliary aids and services requirements of the ADA. It requires all television sets with screens of 13 inches or more to have built-in decoder circuitry capable of displaying closed captions, making it unnecessary for deaf citizens and people with impaired hearing to use portable decoders.

Technology-Related Assistance for Individuals With Disabilities Act of 1988

Known as the "Tech Act," it established grants to states to set up programs to encourage the use of assistive technology for people with disabilities and national programs, including studies to investigate the financing of technology, the development of an information and referral network (Title I), and a public education campaign to enable workers with disabilities to live more independently, perform a greater variety of jobs, or return to work more quickly (Title II). The act encourages employers and employees in states that have such technology programs to obtain help from the local organization to develop technological accommodations for employees. The law is the only federal legislation to define persons with disabilities as consumers, and it uses the term "consumer" and "principles of consumerism" to empower people with disabilities.

Rehabilitation Act Amendments of 1986

The 1986 amendments to the Rehabilitation Act of 1973 directly affect the provision of assistive technology services to clients of the Vocational Rehabilitation Program by providing a definition of assistive technology devices and services. The legislation includes three new requirements:

1. To receive funds, states must submit a plan to the federal government, updated annually, that describes how rehabilitation services will be provided.
2. When consumers are evaluated for vocational rehabilitation services, their potential to benefit (from an employment standpoint) from rehabilitation technology services must be assessed by a person skilled in those services.
3. A statement must be included in the Individualized Written Rehabilitation Plan (required by the original law for all receiving vocational rehabilitation services) as to what specific technology services will be provided.

Job Training Partnership Act of 1982 (JTPA)

This is the federal government's largest job-skills training program. It targets educationally disadvantaged and displaced youth and adults, especially women, minorities, people with disabilities, the disadvantaged, veterans with disabilities, veterans of the Vietnam era, and veterans recently separated from military service. JTPA funnels federal training funds to the states for local use. The legislation requires states to establish service delivery areas (SDAs), local areas in which JTPA services are developed, implemented, and provided. SDAs provide such services as client assessment, basic education and remediation services, job training, and placement services free of change for all JTPA participants. SDAs broker services, buying them from community colleges, private proprietary schools, adult basic education programs, and vocational educational training by local or state agencies. The act allows employers a 50 percent wage reimbursement of the first six months of employment for disabled individuals who meet established economic guidelines. The program is administered by local private industry councils.

Earlier Federal Legislation

Vietnam Era Veterans Readjustment and Assistance Act of 1974 (VEVRA)

VEVRA is legislation passed by Congress to promote the hiring of qualified disabled veterans and Veterans of the Vietnam era. The act prohibits discrimination against those veterans and requires affirmative action to hire and promote them. Qualified disabled veterans are defined as those who receive disability compensation for a 30 percent or greater disability or who were discharged or released from active duty for an injury received or aggravated in the line of duty.

Veterans of the Vietnam era are defined as individuals who were on active duty more than 180 days between August 5, 1964, and May 5, 1975, were not dishonorably discharged or were on active duty between those dates, and were released for a service-connected disability. The act requires employers to take affirmative action to employ and advance qualified veterans. It applies only to federal contractors and subcontractors with contracts of $10,000 or more. Larger contractors (with contracts worth $50,000 or more and 50 or more employees) are also required to prepare affirmative action programs. The Office of Federal Contract Compliance enforces this legislation.

Rehabilitation Act of 1973

The act, as amended, prohibits discrimination on the basis of disability in all programs and activities funded or conducted by the federal government and covers all recipients of federal funds, including state and local governments, most colleges and universities, nonprofit organizations receiving federal grants and assistance, most hospitals and long-term care facilities, and all federal contractors and subcontractors.

The act established the federal Interagency Committee on Handicapped Employees to provide a focus for federal and other employment of individuals with disabilities, review in cooperation with the EEOC the adequacy of hiring, placement, and advancement practices with respect to individuals with disabilities, and submit to the EEOC an affirmative action plan for the hiring, placement, and advancement of people with disabilities by departments and agencies of the executive branch of the government.

The act requires the EEOC to develop for referral to state agencies policies and procedures that would facilitate the hiring, placement, and advancement of people who have received rehabilitation services under state vocational rehabilitation programs, veterans' programs, or any other program for individuals with disabilities, including the promotion of job opportunities for such individuals. Title I of the act encourages state agencies to provide counseling, guidance, referral, and placement services; vocational and training services; physical and mental restoration services; an income stipend during the rehabilitation program; interpreter and reader services; transportation to rehabilitation facilities; and assistive aids and devices.

Section 503 of the act requires employers with a contract or subcontract of $50,000 or more and employing 50 or more persons to develop, maintain, and disseminate a written affirmative action plan inside and outside the organization. The plan must clearly state the company's nondiscrimination policy as it pertains to people with disabilities, be published and distributed internally (bulletin board notices, orientation briefings, and handbooks and other company publications) and externally (notification to schools, state employment service agencies, and rehabilitation groups), describe internal review procedures, highlight initiatives to prepare, monitor, and execute the plan, and explain internal complaint procedures. Additionally,

> A recipient [of federal funds] to which this subpart applies shall educate, or shall provide for the education of, each qualified handicapped person in its jurisdiction with persons who are not handicapped to the maximum extent appropriate to the needs of the handicapped person. A recipient shall place a handicapped person in the regular educational environment operated by the recipient unless it is demonstrated by the recipient that the education of the persons in the regular environment with

the use of supplementary aids and services cannot be achieved satisfactorily.

Architectural Barriers Act of 1968 (ABA)

The ABA mandated the design, construction, or modification of public buildings and facilities owned or leased in whole or in part by the federal government (or financed or aided by federal funds) to provide means of access to handicapped individuals. As result, uniform federal accessibility standards have been developed that establish uniform standards for the design, construction, and alteration of buildings. Although these standards apply to federally supported facilities, many states have adopted them, developed their own, or included them in their fair employment practices statutes or building codes. The Architectural Barriers Compliance Board (ABCB), a federal entity that monitors compliance with the act, was created by a 1974 amendment to the Vocational Rehabilitation Act of 1973.

Veterans Readjustment Benefits Act of 1966 (VRBA)

VRBA was designed to meet the special employment and training needs of disabled veterans and Vietnam era veterans and increase their opportunities to obtain employment, job training, counseling, and job placement services. The act established an assistant secretary of labor for veterans' employment and training within DOL to promulgate and administer policies and programs to provide employment and training services and programs.

State and Local Statutes

Most states and local governments have statutes that make it illegal to discriminate against anyone with a disability in public or private employment. Some states specifically prohibit discrimination against people who have physical and mental disabilities; others forbid discrimination against people with disabilities in human rights acts that provide protection for others based on race, color, religion, sex, age, national origin, marital status, and so on.

Some states have revised their statutes to conform with the ADA, although provisions vary by states. For example, state or local statutes may cover employees with fewer employees or provide different remedies. It is important to remember, however, that ADA does not supersede state and local laws that prohibit discrimination against people with disabilities. Where ADA provides greater protection, its provision apply; where state or local laws provide greater protection, their provisions apply.

Disability and Workers Compensation

All states have workers compensation laws, statutes designed to protect workers from the hazards and consequences of accidents, injuries, illnesses, and death to themselves and their families as a result of their employment. Although the laws vary widely, all require that employers contribute some part of the salaries of workers with disabilities to their support if the incapacitating illness or injury is attributable to the work environment or sustained when performing the job.

Benefits are paid to workers who sustain job-related physical, mental, or emotional accidents, injuries, disabilities, or disfigurement or who aggravate preexisting physical or mental conditions at work. In addition to death benefits, they typically include weekly payments based on earnings and size of family, medical and hospital bills, scheduled loss (amputation, loss of use or loss of a bodily function), payments for scarring, rehabilitation, retraining, settlements, travel expenses, and attorney fees paid to the employee or his or her surviving spouse or children.

Controlling the cost of workers compensation has been one of the biggest problems employers have faced over the years. These premiums continue to soar, fueled primarily by increasing health care costs and the expanding list of disabilities. Although many employers fear that the ADA will complicate the management of employees disabled by accidents on the job, the fact that the employee was injured at work does not necessarily mean that the worker will be considered a ''qualified individual with disability'' under the ADA.

Employers are responsible for determining if and when an employee injured on the job will be able to return to work. Two questions must be answered: Is the employee capable of performing the usual and customary duties and tasks of the job without risking reinjury, aggravating the injury, or placing others in jeopardy? Is an accommodation needed? If the answer to the first question is no, the worker is disabled, and the employer is under no obligation to assign duties to the employee nor is the employee obligated to return to work. If the answer to the question is yes, the employer may require the absent worker to return to work with or without accommodation. When the employee is judged to be disabled as defined by the ADA, an accommodation may be necessary— for example, modifying work schedules, adapting equipment, acquiring assistive devices, redesigning the job, or making existing facilities accessible.

If the employee declines or challenges the appropriateness of the accommodation and claims that the employer has unlawfully discriminated or retaliated against him or her, the employer must demonstrate that good-faith efforts were made to reinstate the worker by offering alternative and reasonable accommodations. Under such circumstances the employee will have difficulty proving discrimination or retaliation in a workers compensation proceeding.

Summary

In recent years, federal and state laws have dramatically changed the way thousands of U.S. employers manage the recruitment, selection, assignment, transfer, training and development, promotion, and termination of people with disabilities. The intent of the laws has not only been to eliminate discrimination on the basis of disability but also to promote the employment of one of the nation's most underused resources and enhance employment opportunities, increase the availability of services, and improve the quality of life for all Americans with disabilities.

Managers, staff officers, and supervisors in all types of organizations, public and private, must be familiar with these laws and fully understand and meet their obligations if they are to help achieve the purposes of the legislation and avoid the severe penalties imposed for their violation. Foremost among these laws is the ADA, far-reaching legislation that builds on the Civil Rights Act of 1964 and the Rehabilitation Act of 1973 by extending the rights and protections of those laws to people with disabilities. Employers must also recognize that the ADA sets only minimum standards. State laws that are more exacting take precedence over ADA.

For Further Reading and Viewing*

ABC's of ADA. Computerized database of ADA issues. Available from Wonderlic Personnel Test.

Accommodation and Accessibility: Implementing the ADA on a Local Level. New York: American Foundation for the Blind, 1992.

ADA 101—Final Exam. 1992. 40-minute video. Available from Society for Human Resource Management.

ADA Facts and Fears. 1992. 42-minute video. Available from Society for Human Resource Management.

*Full addresses for the organizations in this listing are found in Appendixes B and C.

The ADA Maze: What You Can Do. 1992. 16-minute video. Available from United Training Media.

The ADA on Video. 1992. Two videos: *Focusing on Ability*, 25 minutes, and *Reasonable Accommodations*, twenty-one minutes. Available from United Training Media.

Bureau of National Affairs. *The Americans with Disabilities Act: A Practical and Legal Guide to Impact, Enforcement, and Compliance.* Washington, D.C.: Bureau of National Affairs, 1990.

Department of Justice. Office of the Attorney General. "Part III, Nondiscrimination on the Basis of Disability by Public Accommodations and in Commercial Facilities; Final Rule, 28 CFR Part 36." *Federal Register*, July 26, 1991.

———. "Part IV, Nondiscrimination on the Basis of Disability in State and Local Government Services; Final Rule, 28 CFR Part 35." *Federal Register*, July 26, 1991.

Dixon, M. B., and M. Mobley. *The Americans with Disabilities Act: Impact on Training.* INFO-LINE 9203. Alexandria, Va.: American Society for Training and Development, 1992.

Equal Employment Opportunity Commission. *The Americans with Disabilities Act: Your Responsibilities as an Employer.* Washington, D.C.: EEOC, 1991.

———. *Americans with Disabilities Act of 1990.* Washington, D.C.: EEOC, Office of Communications and Legislative Affairs, 1990.

———. "Part V, Equal Employment Opportunity for Individuals with Disabilities; Final Rule, 29 CFR Part 1630" and "Recordkeeping and Reporting under Title VII of the Civil Rights Act of 1964 and the Americans with Disabilities Act (ADA); Final Rule, 29 CFR Parts 1602 and 1627." *Federal Register*, July 26, 1991.

Equal Employment Opportunity Commission and Department of Justice. Civil Rights Division. *The Americans with Disabilities Act: Questions and Answers.* Washington, D.C.: EEOC, September 1992.

Federal Communications Commission. *Report and Order and Request for Comments.* FCC 91-213, CC Docket No. 90-571. Washington, D.C.: FCC, July 26, 1991.

———. *Telecommunications Relay Services: An Information Handbook.* Washington, D.C.: FCC, January 1992.

Fersh, Don, and Peter W. Thomas. *Complying with the Americans with Disabilities Act: A Guidebook for Management and People with Disabilities.* Westport, Conn.: Quorum Books, 1993.

How to Comply with the Americans with Disabilities Act: A Detailed Guide. Madison, Conn.: Business and Legal Reports, 1993.

Jones, Timothy L. *The Americans with Disabilities Act: A Review of Best Practices.* AMA Management Briefing. New York: AMA Membership Publications Division, 1993.

Lotito, Michael J., Michael J. Soltis, and Richard Pimentel. *The Americans with Disabilities Act: A Comprehensive Guide to Title I.* Alexandria, Va.: Society for Human Resource Management, 1992.

Lotito, Michael J., Richard Pimentel, and Denise Bissonnette. *What Managers and*

Supervisors Need to Know about the ADA. Alexandria, Va.: Society for Human Resource Management, 1992.

Making the ADA Work for You. 1992. 23-minute video. Available from Barr Films.

Making the ADA Work for You: A Video Training Seminar. 1992. 2-hour videocassette. Available from American Foundation for the Blind.

Morrissey, Patricia. *Survival Guide to the Americans with Disabilities Act.* Horsham, Pa.: LRP Publications, 1992.

National Easter Seal Society. *Americans with Disabilities Act: An Easy Checklist for Business.* Chicago: NESS.

Ogletree, Deakins, Nash, Smoak, and Stewart. *Americans with Disabilities Act: Employee Rights and Employer Obligations.* New York: Matthew Bender, 1992.

Perritt, H. H. *Americans with Disabilities Handbook.* New York: Wiley, 1990.

Pimentel, Richard, Michael J. Lotito, and Francis P. Alvarez. *The Americans with Disabilities Act: Making the ADA Work for You.* 2d ed. Alexandria, Va.: Society for Human Resource Management, 1992.

Pioneer/ADA Interactive Training System. 1993. Interactive video series. Available from Pioneer New Media Technology.

Rothwell, William J. "HRD and the Americans with Disabilities Act." *Training and Development* (August 1991): 45–47.

Schneid, Thomas D. *The Americans with Disabilities Act: A Practical Guide for Managers.* New York: Van Nostrand Reinhold, 1992.

———. *The Americans with Disabilities Act: A Compliance Manual.* New York: Van Nostrand Reinhold, 1993.

Tucker, Bonnie P., and Bruce A. Goldstein. *Legal Rights of Persons with Disabilities: An Analysis of Federal Law.* Horsham, Pa.: LRP Publications, 1991.

Vernon-Oehmke, Arlene. *The Human Resources Manager's Guide to ADA Compliance.* Atlanta, Ga.: Life Office Management Association, 1992.

Notes

1. Public entities may choose between two technical standards for accessible design: *The Uniform Accessibility Standard*, established under the Architectural Barriers Act, or the *Americans with Disabilities Act Accessibility Guidelines*, adopted by the Department of Justice for places of public accommodation and commercial facilities covered by Title III of the ADA.

2. In accordance with the standards contained in the *Americans with Disabilities Act Accessibility Guidelines* issued by the Architectural and Transportation Barriers Compliance Board and incorporated in the final Department of Justice Title III regulation.

3. *Report and Order and Request for Comments, FCC 91-213 38199* (Washington, D.C.: Federal Communications Commission, July 26, 1991); *Telecommunications Relay Services: An Information Handbook* (Washington, D.C.: Federal Communications Commission, January 1992).

4. An eligible small business is one with gross receipts of no more than $1 million and 30 or fewer full-time employees (30 hours per week for 20 or more weeks a year) for the year preceding the taxable year.

3

Federal and State Programs and Services

The federal government provides special programs, benefits, and services for persons who are blind, deaf, and developmentally disabled in such areas as vocational rehabilitation, education, employment, work incentives, financial assistance, medical assistance, housing, tax benefits, and transportation. Much of the federal contribution to services for individuals with disabilities is made to states, which then determine how to spend the funds within certain guidelines. Most states also provide services they finance out of their own resources. Human resources managers and practitioners need to know about these programs and services so that they can assist employees in obtaining them.

Special Benefits and Assistance[1]

Program for Developmental Disabilities

This program uses existing services in health, welfare, education, and rehabilitation to provide for the long-range needs of people with developmental disabilities. The services include diagnosis, evaluation, and treatment of the disabling condition; personal care, day care, and special living arrangements; training for jobs, education, and sheltered employment; recreation programs; social and legal services; information and referral services; and transportation. Each state has an agency designated to administer the program.

Vocational Rehabilitation

Vocational rehabilitation services may be federally supported, state-operated programs designed to help individuals with disabilities become employable, independent, and integrated into the community. If the disability constitutes a mental, physical, or emotional limitation that presents a barrier to employment, individuals who meet the criteria are eligible for the services. Services are provided through state departments of vocational rehabilitation or by the division, commission, or department of rehabilitation services for people with visual impairments funded by federal and state governments.

Individuals disabled as a result of military service are most often provided rehabilitation services through regional offices of the U.S. Department of Veterans Affairs. Hospitals and other agencies such as Goodwill, Jewish Vocational Services, Easter Seal Society, and United Cerebral Palsy provide rehabilitation services supported by both public and private funds.

Private agencies as well provide vocational rehabilitation. These proprietary companies work mainly with workers compensation claimants who have incurred on-the-job injuries. Fees for these services are usually paid by insurance carriers under policies purchased by employers to facilitate quick rehabilitation and return of the worker to the job or one as nearly equal to it as possible.

Services. Services provided by rehabilitation agencies include medical examinations; counseling and guidance; medical, surgical, psychiatric, and hospital services; artificial limbs, braces, hearing devices, and eyeglasses; job training; educational opportunities and payment of tuition, fees, and other expenses; financial assistance during rehabilitation for room and board, transportation, and other necessary assistance; referral and job placement; and on-the-job help.

State departments of rehabilitation, the state divisions of services to the blind, and other public agencies, such as the U.S. Department of Veterans Affairs, offer employers partial reimbursement for initial training and employment opportunities made available to the clients they sponsor. In addition, local special and vocational education and Job Training Partnership Act (JTPA) programs can provide contacts for qualified workers with disabilities.

The Process. The first step in vocational rehabilitation is to assess the individual's aptitudes, abilities, and attitudes by administering medical, psychological, and vocational tests. The results are used to set up a rehabilitation plan, which might include physical, occupational, speech, or hearing therapy. Some disabilities might require physical aids such as hearing aids or artificial limbs. Other people with disabilities may require remedial training in mathematics, reading, or communication skills.

The plan then focuses on the development of the skills required to fill targeted jobs and involves classroom instruction, individual tutoring, and simulated work. When the skills have been acquired, job-seeking skills, such as résumé preparation and job interviewing, are taught. Finally, after a client has been placed, the rehabilitation service provides follow-up to ensure that the job match is successful.

Focus on Return to Work. Because of the dramatically increasing costs of disability and workers compensation claims, employers are now focusing on rehabilitation as a viable return-to-work strategy. According to a study by the Northwestern National Life Insurance Company, every dollar invested in rehabilitation saves $30 in disability costs. A relatively obscure accounting rule, Financial Accounting Standard (FAS) 112, is certain to reemphasize the need for that attention. Employers must now account for accrued postemployment benefit liabilities in the areas of long-term disability, workers compensation, continuation of health care and life insurance coverage under the Consolidated Omnibus Budget Reconciliation Act (COBRA), severance pay, and survivor benefits. This rule will force employers to reduce or limit their liability and improve claims administration and their rehabilitation programs and practices.

Employment

More than 2,000 local employment service offices (commonly called state employment services or state job services) throughout the United States help employers find workers and workers find jobs. They have been given responsibility to help persons with disabilities and are required by law to employ a specialist trained to work with them.

Federal Jobs

All federal jobs for regular appointment are announced to the public and filled competitively. However, there is a small number of special appointment positions for individuals with disabilities that are not competitive for individuals with mental retardation who have been referred by their vocational rehabilitation counselor and people with severe physical disabilities who have been referred by their vocational rehabilitation counselor or are taking a 700-hour trial appointment.

Federal Job Information Centers

The Office of Personnel Management maintains centers to provide federal job information and to help people, including those with disabilities, to apply for federal employment. Special arrangements are available, including braille, large type, and recorded forms of some of the tests used in screening federal job applicants. Where such test accommodations are not available, the Job Information Center is required to provide reader assistance.

Job Accommodation Network (JAN)

JAN is an international information network and consulting resource established to help qualified workers with disabilities to be hired or retained. It enables employers, rehabilitation professionals, and people with disabilities to share information about practical ways, including methods and equipment, of making accommodations for employees and applicants with disabilities.

Job Opportunities for the Blind (JOB)

JOB is a joint program of the U.S. Department of Labor and the National Federation of the Blind that provides workshops, publications, and information about reasonable accommodations for the blind. JOB also provides a free, nationwide service to employers in locating and hiring qualified blind applicants and assists employees who are blind or become legally blind while on the job.

Job Training Partnership Program (JTPP)

JTPP is the federal government's largest job-skills training program targeted at educationally disadvantaged and displaced youth and adults, especially women, minorities, people with disabilities, disadvantaged, disabled veterans, veterans of the Vietnam era, and veterans recently separated from military service. It funnels federal training funds to the states for local use through state-operated service delivery areas (SDAs) that provide client assessment, basic education and remediation services, job training, and placement services free of charge for all participants. SDAs broker services, buying them from community colleges, private proprietary schools, adult basic education programs, and vocational educational training by local or state agencies.

Training and Placement Service (TAPS) Program

TAPS is an employment initiative, funded by the Department of Labor and operated by the Epilepsy Foundation of America (EFA). The Foundation is a national, voluntary health organization dedicated to the prevention and cure of seizure disorders, the alleviation of their effects, the promotion of independence, increased job preparation, and employment opportunities, and an optimal quality of life for people who have these disorders. The TAPS program provides job search assistance, training in job-seeking skills, and employer education.

Financial Assistance

Two federal programs and one state-operated program provide direct and continuing financial assistance to persons with disabilities. Social security disability insurance benefits and supplemental security income are federal programs; workers compensation and short-term disability programs are operated by states.

Social Security Disability Benefits (SSDI)

Social security disability insurance benefits may be paid to workers with disabilities under age 65 or their families when earnings are lost or reduced due to the disability. Individuals are considered disabled if they have physical or mental impairments that prevent them from working and are expected to last for at least 12 months or result in death. A person is considered blind if central visual acuity is 20/200 or less in the better eye with the use of corrective lenses or a visual field reduction of 20 degrees or less.

Disability under social security is designed to provide a continuing source of income to the individual and his or her family when the worker is unable to do so. Benefits continue as long as the individual remains disabled. Periodically a continuing disability review (CDR) is conducted to determine eligibility for these benefits. The time between reviews depends on the beneficiary's age and the nature and severity of the medical condition on which the benefits are based, including the chance of medical improvement. Following the review, beneficiaries are placed in one of three medical reexamination categories: (1) medical improvement expected—review scheduled within 6 to 18 months of the most recent medical decision; (2) medical improvement possible—status scheduled for review every 3 years; or (3) medical improvement not expected—status scheduled for review every 7 years. A full medical review involves an indepth field office interview, evaluation of the medical evidence of record by a state disability determination service (DDS) examiner, and possibly a consultative medical examination to obtain any additional information needed to assess the possibility of medical improvement of the beneficiary's present condition. A team consisting of a physician or psychologist and a disability evaluation specialist conducts this review.

Eligibility. To receive benefits, a worker must have credit for a certain amount of work under social security. The amount of work credit needed depends on the worker's age. In addition, monthly benefits may be paid to the dependents of a worker with disabilities:

- Unmarried children under 18 (or under 19 if full-time high school or elementary school students)
- Unmarried children 18 or older who were severely disabled before age 22 and continue to be disabled
- Spouse 62 or older
- Wife under 62 if she is caring for the worker's child who is under 16 or disabled and receiving a benefit based on the earnings of the worker with the disability

A person can receive social security disability benefits at any age (over the age of 65, the benefits become retirement benefits) but must have worked long enough and recently enough under social security. Workers earn up to a maximum of four credits per year, and the amount of earnings required for a credit increases each year as general wage levels rise. The number of credits needed depends on the age of the worker when he or she becomes disabled. Family members who qualify for benefits on the worker's work record do not need work credits.

The amount of the monthly disability benefit is based on the worker's lifetime earnings covered by social security.

Rules for Blind Persons. The social security disability program has special rules for blind persons. Those who qualify may receive benefits on the basis of blindness or disability. An individual is considered blind under social security rules if his or her vision cannot be corrected to better than 20/200 in the better eye or if the visual field is 20 degrees or less, even with corrective lens. A blind person can earn up to the current monthly amount of the annual earnings limit that applies to nondisabled beneficiaries. That is generally higher than the "substantial gainful activity" level of $500 that applies to nonblind disabled workers.

Disability Payments under Supplemental Security Income (SSI)

SSI payments are made to persons (including children) with limited income and assets who are blind or have other qualifying disabilities. Not all income and resources are counted in determining eligibility. Generally, the first $20 per month of unearned income and the first $65 per month in earnings are not counted, nor is a home or the land adjacent to it. Personal property, such as household goods, a car, and life insurance, may not count, depending on their value.

Eligibility. Medical requirements for disability payments are the same for social security and SSI, and a person's disability is determined by the same procedure for both programs. However, there are some differences:

- No disability waiting period is required under SSI because it is assumed that the individual does not have the financial resources to handle short-term health problems.
- Under SSI, the individual may qualify for immediate disability payments if his or her condition is obviously disabling and the SSI income and resource limits are met.
- Different work incentive rules apply to SSI recipients. The major difference is that cash benefits and Medicaid continue as long as the SSI income does not exceed the "substantial" income level.
- Money may be set aside for up to 48 months for a work goal.

Other special rules apply to blind persons, students with disabilities, and people with disabilities who work in sheltered workshops.

Reporting Requirements. Workers who receive SSI because of a disability or blindness (there are special rules that apply only to blind persons) must inform the social security office if their condition improves. Social security occasionally reviews cases to make certain that individuals are still disabled, and special tests may be administered. If the disability ends, SSI is terminated after a short adjustment period. Workers who receive SSI because of a disability may be contacted by their state's vocational rehabilitation agency. The agency may offer help so that the worker can return to work. If such an offer is made and the worker refuses to accept the services, SSI payments can be stopped.

Workers Compensation and Other Disability Payments

Ordinarily disability payments from other sources do not affect social security benefits; however, if the disability payment is workers compensation or other public disability payment (such as civil service, military, or state temporary disability benefits or state or local government retirement benefits based on disability), the social security benefits of the individual and his or her family may be reduced. When the combined amount of the social security benefit received and workers compensation exceeds 80 percent of the individual's average current earnings, the excess amount is deducted from the social security benefit. The deduction continues until the month the individual reaches age 65 or the month his or her workers compensation and/or other disability payment stops, whichever comes first.

Payments that do not affect social security disability benefits include Department of Veterans Affairs benefits, federal benefits, and state and local government benefits if the work done to earn them was covered by social security, private pensions or insurance benefits, and SSI payments.

Short-Term Disability Programs

Five states and one territory (California, Hawaii, New Jersey, New York, Rhode Island, and Puerto Rico) have mandatory short-term disability programs that provide wage replacement benefits of varying lengths (ranging from 26 to 52 weeks) for employees who have become disabled off the job. In most cases there is a waiting period of seven days before benefits begin, and benefits are offset by other sources of income. Different states have different maximum benefit levels.

Medical Assistance

There are four primary sources of federally supported medical assistance for persons with disabilities: Medicare, Medicaid, Crippled Children's Services, and the Early Periodic Screening, Diagnosis and Treatment Program.

Medicare

If disabled before age 65, workers and certain members of their families may qualify for monthly medicare benefits. Medicare coverage (Parts A and B) is provided for a person after being entitled to social security disability benefits for 24 consecutive months. People who need dialysis treatments or kidney transplants because of permanent kidney failure are also eligible for Medicare coverage. People with disabilities who have worked long enough in federal employment may also be eligible for Medicare.

Disability benefits under social security continue as long as the individual is disabled, although, as noted previously, cases are reviewed periodically. Also, benefits will be discontinued if the person works at a "substantial" level (earnings of $500 or more per month) or the person's medical condition improves to the point where he or she is no longer considered disabled. If a beneficiary's social security disability insurance benefits stop because earnings are at the substantial gainful activity level but the individual is still disabled, Medicare can continue for at least 39 months after the trial work period ends.

If a disabled person is receiving Medicare, he or she continues to receive it during the trial work period and extended period of eligibility and for 3 months, for a total of 51 months. The coverage prevents the individual from losing health care benefits suddenly and thus acts as a shield work incentive to allow the person to return to work without fear of losing medical coverage. If a worker who was previously entitled to Medicare starts receiving social security disability benefits again within 5 years, Medicare protection resumes immediately.

Medicaid

People may be eligible for Medicaid if they are receiving welfare, other public assistance, or SSI or are blind or disabled. Individuals with incomes that exceed the limits established by their state, or their children, may be eligible for Medicaid supplemental medical care assistance if medical expenses exceed a given percentage of their annual income.

Crippled Children's Services (CSS)

CSS is a joint federal-state program established to provide medical and related services to children with disabilities from birth to age 21. All states are required to provide free medical diagnosis and evaluation for all children. Additional treatment or hospital care services vary in range and cost from state to state. However, all programs accept third-party payments, such as Medicaid, Blue Cross and Blue Shield, and other medical insurance.

Early Periodic Screening, Diagnosis and Treatment Program (EPSDT)

EPSDT screens children from poor families to determine whether health care or related services may be necessary and provides preventive and remedial care. Children whose families are receiving state Aid to Families with Dependent Children benefits and children whose parents or guardians are receiving Medicaid and/or local or state public assistance benefits are eligible for EPSDT.

Work Incentives

Work incentives are federal rules designed to provide support for social security and SSI beneficiaries who have disabilities and want employment. Although there are different rules for social security and SSI, both programs provide cash benefits and continue Medicare or Medicaid while the person attempts to work on a regular basis, assist with the work expenses resulting from the disability, and help with vocational rehabilitation and training for a new type of work.

Vocational Rehabilitation Services

Workers who are ineligible for social security disability benefits may be considered for vocational rehabilitation services by state vocational rehabilitation agencies, which provide counseling, training, and many other services that persons with disabilities may need to help them get back to work. If a person with disabilities recovers medically while participating in a program that is likely to lead to the individual's becoming self-supporting, benefits may continue until the program ends.

Vocational Rehabilitation On-the-Job Training Program. Vocational rehabilitation on-the-job training is an incentive to hire workers with disabilities in the form of a wage reimbursement awarded to the employer for a limited period of time. To qualify, the disabled worker employed must be an office of vocational rehabilitation client, and the job must be full time and permanent.

Trial Work Period. A trial work period permits social security beneficiaries who go back to work despite severe disabilities to continue receiving benefits for up to nine months (not necessarily consecutive). If the nine months of trial work do not fall within a five-year period, beneficiaries may have even longer to test their ability to work.

Not until after the trial work period is a decision made as to whether the work done by the beneficiary shows that he or she has regained the ability to perform substantial gainful work. If the individual is found able to engage in substantial work and is no longer disabled within the meaning of the law, he or she will be paid benefits for three additional months. If the worker becomes unable to continue working within a year after benefits stop, benefits are reinstated automatically. Legislation extends this trial work period to widows and widowers with disabilities.

Extended Period of Eligibility

For at least three years after a successful trial work period, if a beneficiary continues to work while disabled, he or she may receive a benefit whenever monthly earnings fall below the substantial gainful activity level currently $500 per month for people with disabilities and considerably higher for people who are blind.

A person with a disability who loses his or her job during the first 36 months after returning to work can reestablish eligibility without having to apply for it. The check starts immediately without the usual waiting period. This extended period of eligibility is an addition to the trial work period "lifeline" designed to help workers with disabilities to make the transition to the workplace without fear of losing their benefits permanently.

The extended period of eligibility begins the month after the trial work period ends. If the individual has to stop work for any reason and does not earn enough in that month to exceed the substantial gainful activity level, he or she can receive SSDI for that month. The extended period of eligibility does not restart at that point; it continues until the 36 months are up.

Earned Income Exclusion

For people with disabilities who receive SSI but also have unearned income (such as benefits from a family trust), the SSA subtracts all but $20 of that amount from the monthly check. Earned income, such as wages and salary, is treated differently. An earned income exclusion allows a person to earn up to $500 per month and still receive some benefits. The first $20 of earned income are excluded under the general income exclusion and the next $65 plus one-half of the remainder are excluded under the earned income exclusion. SSI benefits are then reduced by the amount of the remainder.

A person can earn up to $500 ($850 if blind) and still receive some SSI benefits. When earned income exceeds $500, the individual may be eligible to switch to a similar program, the Section 1619 program.

Medicare for People with Disabilities Who Work

This optional work incentive, probably the most important of the work incentives created by the Congress, allows people to "buy into" Medicare by paying a monthly premium. For those who choose the option, state governments automatically pay the premium for hospitalization coverage (Medicare Part A), and the subscriber pays the premium for supplemental medical insurance (Medicare Part B).

This work incentive is allowed only to people who have already had the continuation of medicare coverage work incentive and must be applied for between January 1 and March 1 of the year in which continuation of medicare coverage will expire.

Students with Disabilities

Most scholarships or grants used to pay for tuition, books, and other expenses directly related to an educational program are not counted as income if a student with disabilities is enrolled in a school or training program. Students with disabilities under age 22 who receive SSI and attend college for at least 8 hours per week or a secondary school or work training program at least 12 hours per week can earn up to $400 per month, up to $1,620 per year, under the student earned income exclusion. They can use the exclusion even if they are receiving homebound instruction because their health does not permit them to attend school.

Impairment-Related Work Expenses

Certain expenses for items needed by persons with disabilities to work may be deducted when counting earnings to determine if they are performing substantial work. Expenses must be necessary for the individual to do work satisfactorily, for goods or services not required or used, other than incidentally, in personal activities and not specifically covered under other income tax laws. For example, a person who is blind may deduct payments made to a reader who provides the service at work during regular working hours (not at home). A person who uses a wheelchair, travels out of town on business, and needs a helper to carry luggage and assist in other ways may deduct the helper's expenses while on such trips.

Work Expenses for Blind Persons Exclusion

Persons who receive SSI because they are blind can exclude from their benefits all of their work-related expenses, such as guide dogs, transportation to and from work, federal, state, and local payroll taxes, FICA, personal assistance, visual and sensory aids, translation of materials into braille or transfer to tape or disk, professional association fees and dues, union dues, adaptive equipment, and computer expenses. Such expenses do not have to be related to blindness, just necessary to work.

The blind work expenses work incentive is in addition to the earned income exclusion. Blind work expenses are deducted first, and then the earned income exclusion is computed. Most persons with vision impairments who work are eligible for both.

Plan for Achieving Self-Support (PASS)

PASS allows an individual to put money aside to help him or her become fully employed. It helps with expenses such as education, vocational training, adaptive devices, personal care, special work-related medical expenses, work-related equipment or tools, vehicle modification, or starting a business. Transportation to and from work is not usually approved. Having a plan usually means that the individual can keep more of his or her SSI because the money set aside will not lower the SSI payment.

A PASS consists of a written blueprint, covering up to three years of activities (extendable for one additional year), that lists the steps a person with disabilities will take to prepare for a job, the amount of money needed, the expenses that will be incurred, the source or sources of the income to be used for the PASS, and a timetable that shows when each phase of the plan will be completed. The plan must be approved by the local Social Security Administration field office and is subject to periodic review.

A PASS helps persons with disabilities keep income that otherwise disqualifies them from receiving SSI. That income can be earned or unearned as long as it is set aside to help find and keep a job. PASS can be used to help keep workers compensation benefits, insurance benefits, settlement from a lawsuit, and money given by the family.

Property Essential to Self-Support

This work incentive allows persons with disabilities to keep property owned (or that they may acquire) that is essential to a job or business in which they earn their living. All tangible goods, such as tools and vehicles, are covered completely, as is a home and land on which a business resides or crops are raised for the consumption of the owner. Up to $6,000 of equity in a nonbusiness property needed for self-support is also included in the exclusion.

Individual Income Tax Credits and Deductions

The federal income tax code provides tax credits and both ordinary and special deductions for persons with disabilities in addition to those given to nondisabled persons.

Special Training Schools

Payments to a special school for persons with mental or physical disabilities are deductible if the principal reason for attendance is the institution's resources for ameliorating the disability. And tax credits are allowed by the IRS for the costs of disabled dependent or disabled spouse care, as well as payments to relatives who provide this care, if the relative is not the dependent of the taxpayer or his or child under age 19.

Workers Compensation Payments

Amounts paid to individuals as workers compensation for an occupational injury or illness are fully exempt from tax if they are paid under a workers compensation act or statute. This exemption also applies for survivors if the payments otherwise qualify as workers compensation. If the individual returns to work after qualifying for workers compensation and the benefits are continued while the worker is assigned to transitional or light-duty employment, payments are taxable. Other nontaxable amounts received as compensation for injury or illness include:

- Compensatory damages (but not punitive damages in cases not involving physical injury or illness)
- Benefits received under an accident or health insurance policy paid for by the worker
- Disability benefits received for loss of income or earning capacity as a result of injuries under a no-fault car insurance policy
- Compensation received for permanent loss or loss of use of a part or function of the body or for permanent disfigurement
- Reimbursement for medical care
- Disability pensions for combat-related injuries or illnesses (military and government employees)
- Veterans' benefits

Tax Credits

Although there is no longer an additional personal exemption for persons who are blind, the Tax Reform Act of 1986 entitles blind persons to a higher standard deduction amount than sighted persons. Tax credits are also allowed by the IRS for qualified persons with disabilities, including individuals who are under age 65 retired on permanent and total disability (or who have stopped working because of their disability). And tax credits are given to persons who are physically or mentally impaired and engaged in certain work (called sheltered employment) offered at qualified locations (such as sheltered workshops, hospitals, homebound programs, and Department of Veterans Affairs homes).

Business Tax Incentives

Three types of tax incentives are available to businesses that help persons with disabilities: deductions for the costs of removing architectural or transportation barriers, credit for the costs of providing access for disabled individuals, and tax credits for hiring members of certain targeted groups, including those with disabilities.

Deduction for the Removal of Barriers

A business may deduct expenses incurred in making a facility (road, parking lot, walk, building, or structure) or public transportation vehicle owned or leased for use in a trade or business more accessible to and usable by people with disabilities. Specific standards have been established for these expenses to be deductible.[2] The amount of the deduction is limited to $15,000 and applies to a partnership and to each partner.

Credit for Access for People with Disabilities

Eligible small businesses that pay or incur reasonable and necessary expenses to provide access to persons with disabilities may qualify for a disabled access credit. An eligible business is one that for the preceding year did not have more than 30 full-time employees or did not have more than $1 million in gross receipts. A full-time employee is one who was employed at last 30 hours per week for 20 or more calendar weeks during the preceding year. The maximum credit is $5,000 per year per individual owner or partner. For partnerships, the credit applies to the partnership and each partner. A business cannot take a double benefit for the credit. Only amounts that exceed the credit may be deducted, capitalized, or used to figure other credits. If the business is eligible for other business credits, the disabled access credit may be limited.

   Eligible expenses are those that enable a business to comply with ADA requirements, such as removing barriers; providing interpreters or other methods of delivering audio materials to individuals with hearing impairments; providing readers, taped texts, and other methods of delivering visual materials to individuals with visual impairments; acquiring or modifying equipment or devices for individuals with disabilities; and providing other similar services, modifications, materials, or equipment.

Jobs Credit

The jobs credit is an incentive designed to encourage employers to hire persons from targeted groups, including people with disabilities, that have a particularly high unemployment rate or other special employment needs. Employers can choose to take a jobs tax credit for qualified wages paid to members of targeted groups. Among the targeted groups are vocational rehabilitation referrals.

Summary

Many government-supported programs help people with disabilities become more independent, find and keep jobs, and enjoy the same travel and recreational pursuits as their nondisabled peers. These programs, many operated by the states, include rehabilitation and educational programs at all levels, library services, employment in the public and private sectors, financial assistance and disability payments, rehabilitation, medical insurance, work incentives, and individual income tax credits and deductions.

To complement the tax breaks given to individual taxpayers with disabilities, the federal government has provided special deductions and jobs and tax credits as incentives for businesses to encourage the elimination of barriers to accessibility and to promote the hiring, training, development, and utilization of people with disabilities.

For Further Reading*

Akabas, Sheila H., Lauren B. Gates, and Donald E. Galvin. *Disability Management: A Complete System to Reduce Costs, Increase Productivity, Meet Employee Needs, and Ensure Legal Compliance*. New York: AMACOM, 1992.

Assistive Technology Funding Workbook. Washington, D.C.: RESNA Press, 1987.

Bowe, F. *Rehabilitating America*. New York: Harper & Row, 1980.

Clearing House on Disability Information. U.S. Department of Education. *Pocket Guide to Federal Help for Individuals with Disabilities*. Washington, D.C.: U.S. Government Printing Office, 1989.

————. *Credit for the Elderly or the Disabled*. Publication 524. Annual. Obtainable from IRS Forms Distribution Centers.

————. *Information for Persons with Handicaps or Disabilities*. Publication 907. Obtainable from IRS Forms Distribution Centers.

Nackley, J. V. *Primer on Workers' Compensation*. 2d ed. Washington, D.C.: Bureau of National Affairs, 1989.

Planning and Implementing Augmentative Communication Service Delivery. Washington, D.C.: RESNA Press, 1988.

Rehabilitation Technology Service Delivery. Washington, D.C.: RESNA Press, 1987.

Rehabilitation Technology Service Delivery Directory. Washington, D.C.: RESNA Press, 1989.

Taylor, Humphrey, Michael R. Kagay, and Stuart Leichenko. *The ICD Survey II: Employing Disabled Americans*. New York: Louis Harris and Associates, 1987.

*Full addresses for the organizations in this listing are found in Appendixes B and C.

Notes

1. Adapted from the *Pocket Guide to Federal Help for Individuals with Disabilities* (Washington, D.C.: Clearinghouse on Disability Information, U.S. Department of Education, September 1989).
2. Department of the Treasury, Internal Revenue Service, *Information for Persons with Handicaps or Disabilities*, Publication 907. Available from IRS Forms Distribution Centers.

4

Recruiting and Hiring

Hiring is one of the primary functions of all managers and heads of staff elements. It is also one of the areas in which human resources managers can be most helpful to executives, line managers and supervisors, and staff officers. Since the passage of the Americans with Disabilities Act (ADA), many managers have become anxious about the implications of the law. Some have become paralyzed by fear of litigation, a worry that has resulted in what one author has called "ADA minimalism."[1] Those attitudes must be overcome if the promise and intent of the law—equal employment opportunity for people with disabilities and the same protections and guarantees that the Civil Rights Act of 1964 granted African Americans and other minorities—are to be achieved. The key to success is a true management approach to hiring and then to training and development. This chapter sets forth guidelines to accomplish that objective.

The Environment Surrounding Hiring Practices

Before we look at policies and procedures that will promote successful screening and selection of people with disabilities and avoid the pitfalls associated with the process, we need to examine the environment in which the process will be conducted.

The most critical aspects of that environment are the perceptions, feelings, and reactions of nondisabled people to people with disabilities; hiring misconceptions; elements of the hiring process; discriminatory hiring practices; and the hallmarks of successful hiring.

Attitudes of People toward Disabilities

To ignore how people perceive, feel about, and react to people with disabilities is fraught with hazards. And when those attitudes are negative, as they are certain to be in at least some instances, steps must be taken to change those perceptions and feelings or, at the very minimum, ensure that unfavorable feelings do not result in discriminatory behavior. One study showed that of those surveyed:

- 92 percent admire disabled people because they must overcome so much.
- 74 percent feel pity.
- 58 percent feel uneasy or awkward around people with disabilities because they don't know how to interact with them.
- 47 percent reacted with fear because they might themselves become disabled.
- 19 percent felt that people with disabilities are an inconvenience and react with anger.
- 9 percent expressed resentment for what they consider special privileges, such as handicap parking.[2]

The study also reported that the majority of those surveyed feel that they are relatively ignorant about the lives of people with disabilities. Those who know or work with someone who is disabled were somewhat more comfortable than those who did not. However, 78 percent of those surveyed were aware that people with disabilities are discriminated against in jobs, housing, transportation, and access to public facilities.

When presented with possible remedies to the foregoing situations, eight of ten respondents stated that putting persons with disabilities to work would be a boost to the nation. Most also favored increasing the number of persons with disabilities working with them, would be willing to spend money to integrate them into the mainstream, and support setting up affirmative action programs to end employment discrimination.

Hiring Misconceptions

The process of finding new employees can be complicated, time-consuming, and costly. Getting the right people for the right jobs while conforming to the law is a significant challenge, and one made more formidable by the ADA. Mistakes, misunderstandings, and misinterpretations abound in many organizations, the result of misconceptions, prejudices, stereotyping, naiveté, ignorance, incompetence, and defective or illegal policies and procedures. Too many managers and staffers underrate the capabilities of people with disabilities of any type. To hire the right people and further the goals of equal employment opportunity for all Americans, the people responsible for implementing hiring policies must change their attitudes toward people with impairments and master the skills and techniques needed to do the job compassionately, conscientiously, and legally. To do less than that is to court charges of discrimination, litigation, and substantial fines.

Elements of the Hiring Process[3]

The hiring process includes the following elements, all critically important to success in matching jobs and people:

- Formulating job descriptions and applicant specifications
- Designing application forms and interviewer evaluation forms
- Constructing or selecting tests and other forms of evaluation instruments
- Preparing advertisements for position vacancies
- Conducting employment interviews
- Making reference checks
- Evaluating candidates and making the hiring decision
- Arranging for medical examinations
- Assigning, orienting, and training the new employee
- Maintaining records and following up

Discriminatory Hiring Practices

No employer may make employment-related decisions based exclusively on the fact that an individual is disabled. In addition, employers are required to make reasonable accommodations for the specific limitations imposed by *known* disabilities of applicants who are otherwise qualified to perform the essential functions of the job if the accommodations do not create undue hardship. Here are specific examples of discriminatory hiring practices:

- Failing to hire an otherwise qualified applicant solely because the organization would have to make a reasonable accommodation.
- Failing to make a reasonable accommodation for an otherwise qualified applicant with a disability unless the accommodation would impose undue hardship.
- Selecting or administering preemployment tests in a way that reflects the impact of a sensory, motor, or speaking capability rather than measuring relevant job skills, unless the purpose of the tests is to measure those skills.
- Using qualifying standards, requirements, and tests that screen out applicants with disabilities unless they are job related and consistent with business necessity.
- Rejecting qualified job candidates with disabilities for employment

opportunities unless no reasonable accommodation can be made to enable the individual to perform the essential functions of the job.

- Denying employment opportunities to a qualified job applicant solely on the basis of association or a family situation.
- Adversely affecting the opportunities (such as training and development) or status (such as promotion or assignment) of an individual with a disability by limiting, segregating, or classifying that individual on the basis of disability.
- Participating in contractual relationships with contractors and vendors that result in discrimination against employees or applicants for employment with disabilities. (Under ADA, an employer is liable for the discriminatory practices of its contractors and vendors.)
- Denying employment to a qualified applicant simply to avoid increases in benefits costs. However, companies may continue to offer employee benefit plans that contain exclusions and limitations based on risk classifications so long as they are consistent with state laws and are not used to circumvent the objectives of ADA.

Hallmarks of Successful Hiring

Successful recruitment and employment (as well as successful training, utilization, development, and advancement) of people with disabilities hinges on these factors:

- The attitudes and comfort level of people at all levels of organization toward people with disabilities
- The desire of top executives, managers, and supervisors to hire and promote people with disabilities
- The sensitivity of employees at all levels to the needs and capabilities of people with disabilities and overcoming common myths and stereotypes about people with disabilities
- The training the organization provides for managers, supervisors, and other groups of workers
- The policies, strategies, and techniques used to train and develop people with disabilities
- The total integration and acceptance of employees with disabilities into the workplace

An effective screening and selection system is:

- *Standardized.* Every applicant for a position goes through the same screening system.

- *Efficient.* It avoids unplanned duplication or overlap of information about applicants.
- *Comprehensive.* It evaluates all factors required for success on the job.
- *Nondiscriminatory.* It guarantees equal employment opportunity to all prospective employees regardless of age, race, color, age, sex, national origin, religion, or disability.[4]

Exceptions to Reasonable Accommodation

Under Equal Employment Opportunity Commission (EEOC) regulations, employers are *not* required to:

- Make adjustments or modifications or provide assistive devices, such as wheelchairs, prosthetics, hearing aids, or eyeglasses, that help an individual perform his or her daily activities on or off the job.
- Provide amenities or conveniences, such as refrigerators or hot plates, that are not job related and are not provided to nondisabled employees.
- Provide an accommodation that imposes an undue hardship (requires significant difficulty or expense) on the operation of their businesses.
- Provide the most expensive accommodation possible, so long as the accommodation provided meets the job-related needs of the individual.
- Make accommodations for a person with disabilities who is not otherwise qualified for the job.

Recruitment

Vacant positions in an organization can be filled by either or both internal or external recruitment and selection processes. Because most organizations have limited numbers of employees with disabilities, external recruitment is likely to be the most common source of new employees in the foreseeable future. However, the internal source, including current employees with disabilities, should not be overlooked when new positions are created or higher-level, better-paying positions become vacant.

External Recruitment

External recruitment is the process of seeking applicants for openings from outside the organization: walk-ins, direct mail, telephone recruitment, schools, job announcements and advertisements, employment agencies, and agencies and organizations serving people with physical, mental, emotional, and learning disabilities (see Appendix B).

Organizations and agencies provide some or all of the following services:

- Evaluation of clients' work potential
- Skills training
- Information about hiring incentives, such as Targeted Jobs Credit, wage subsidy, and training grants
- On-the-job training and coaching
- Counseling and follow-up
- Awareness training for managers and supervisors

Internal Recruitment

Internal recruitment is the process of attracting and screening current employees for promotion or assignment to newly created or vacant positions in the organization. If the talents and potential of these employees are to be used to the fullest and if incentives and rewards are to be provided to boost motivation and morale, wherever possible internal human resources should be given priority. Internal recruitment sources include self-nominations by employees, employee referrals, nominations by managers and supervisors, and in-house advertisements or job posting.

Job Advertisements and Notices

Advertisements of position vacancies must reach the target audience, produce qualified applicants, and enhance the image of the organization as an equal employment opportunity employer. Advertisements and notices can be placed in company publications, on in-house bulletin boards, in trade and professional journals, in newspapers, and on radio. Notices can also be sent to schools, public and private health and rehabilitation agencies, and organizations that offer assistance to people with disabilities. Although not required by ADA, in all cases a telecommunications relay services (TRS) number should be included in the advertisement or notice, and staff should be trained in how to take a relay call.

Employers should state in job announcements and notices that they do not discriminate on the basis of disability and that job information is accessible to people with different disabilities (such as braille, large print, or audiotape). It is also important to include information on the essential functions of the job so that people with disabilities will not be discouraged from applying. For example, if "good oral skills" are not required, listing that qualification may discourage people with speech impairments from applying for that position.

Regardless of the medium used, advertisements should:

- Appear in media that will reach persons with disabilities, such as publications directed to consumers with disabilities and taped messages for people with vision impairments.
- Capture the reader's or listener's attention by clearly identifying the target respondents and providing an incentive to investigate further.
- Make it clear that all positions, not just entry-level jobs, are open to qualified candidates with disabilities.
- Emphasize the company's commitment to equal employment opportunity and nondiscrimination and a human-affirming environment.
- Make positive references to persons with disabilities by including photos of employees with disabilities with supporting written copy.
- Describe the organization fully.
- Identify the position by title and hierarchical placement, career ladder, salary range and benefits, and training and development opportunities.
- Describe position requirements in terms of essential functions (major duties and tasks) or business necessity.
- Describe qualifications in terms of education, training, experience, skills, and personal traits.
- Use every device to emphasize the company's desire to attract, develop, and retain persons with disabilities, not as tokenism but as recognition of the contributions they can make to the organization.
- Deal with issues of potential concern to people with disabilities (e.g., cite the absence of barriers to promotion).
- State that potential applicants will be notified of the accommodations that will be made.

ADA requires employers to post a notice describing the provisions of ADA in an accessible format to applicants as well as to employees and members of labor organizations. The EEOC stocks posters summarizing legal requirements and provides guidance for making the information available in accessible formats for people with disabilities.

Documents for Screening and Selection

Job Descriptions

Although they are not required by the ADA, current and accurate job descriptions are essential to proper planning and implementation of the hiring, training, performance review, and employee development processes. They can also be very useful for providing legal support for line managers and the human resources staff under the ADA. They have long been advocated by the EEOC, which advises that job descriptions be prepared or revised as an ongoing (rather than a one-shot) hiring activity. Nonetheless, job descriptions prepared before advertising, interviewing, and selecting job applicants are likely to be considered as significant evidence, along with other relevant practices and factors, if charges of discrimination are filed by an employee with a disability.

For example, if a job requires the employee to recall and use highly technical material, the essential function would be "to learn and apply technical processes," not the ability "to read technical manuals." The latter description would disqualify people with visual impairments. The former would eliminate a barrier and provide accommodation by permitting the hiring of people with visual impairments. They could use assistive devices, such as audiotapes, to acquire the needed knowledge and skills and therefore perform the function.

Effective job descriptions are tailored to an organization's needs. They provide the guidelines needed to hire, promote, and supervise with maximum confidence and effectiveness. They are complete, well written, and contain precise explanations of duties, tasks, and authority that leave no room for interpretation or confusion.

Software packages can eliminate much of the work of writing job descriptions, although they do not eliminate the need for job analysis. One program, *DescriptionsWrite Now* (available from KnowledgePoint) contains more than 2,400 job titles, has been adapted to meet ADA requirements, runs on IBM or compatible computers, and requires 640 kilobytes RAM and 3 megabytes hard-disk capacity. The *ADA Position Analyzer* (available from William Steinberg Consultants), a program developed with occupational and rehabilitation specialists, produces detailed reports describing the physical requirements and environmental conditions that affect a job. All the user has to do is answer a series of multiple-choice questions for a specific job.

The key to writing credible job descriptions lies in identifying the *functions, duties,* or *tasks* of the job that are essential to the success of the business. They focus on what the *results* are to be and not on *how* to attain them. To the maximum extent possible, they should include observable and measurable parameters. Examples are shown in Figure 4-1.

The ADA identifies any one or more of the following as a criterion for an essential function:

- A position exists to perform the function.
- A limited number of other employees is available to perform the function or among whom the function can be divided.
- The function is highly specialized, and the incumbent of the position is hired for his or her special expertise or ability to perform the function.

Equal employment opportunity regulations and other materials identify other distinguishing features of essential job functions:

Figure 4-1. Excerpts from functional job descriptions.

Job Title	Task	Functional Description
Data entry clerk	Keyboarding	Perform data entry, both letters and numbers, using a standard keyboard at the rate of 75 words per minute with less than 1 percent error.
		Requires reading ability; two-handed hand-eye coordination; full mobility of arms, wrists, hands, and fingers; ability to concentrate fully for periods of up to 10 minutes; ability to remain seated for periods of up to 1 hour.
		Requires viewing a computer screen from a distance of about 18 inches for a full workday of 8 hours (less rest periods of 10 minutes every hour).
Bridge painter	Climbing	Perform climbing tasks that require above-average upper-body strength, stamina, and agility, and tolerance of heights of up to 250 feet, above ground or water, using ladders, scaffolding, boatswain's chairs, and safety harnesses.
		Requires full mobility of shoulders, arms, elbows, wrists, hands, fingers, and legs.
		Requires horizontal lifting and carrying capability of 50 pounds for 50 feet and vertical lifting and carrying capability of 20 pounds for 20 feet.

- The employer's judgment of required performance standards
- The existence of a written job description prepared before the hiring process begins
- The amount of time spent performing the function
- The consequences of not requiring a job incumbent to perform the function
- The terms of a collective bargaining agreement
- The work experiences of people who have performed the job in the past and those who currently perform similar jobs
- Other relevant factors (such as the nature of work operations and organizational structure)

The essential functions of a job are best identified by job and task analysis, accomplished by following these steps:[5]

1. Develop a plan for collecting and analyzing job and task data.
2. Screen, select, and train the job analysis team.
3. Review available documentation (e.g., organization and functions manual, current job descriptions, procedures manuals, training reports).
4. Interview line managers and supervisors to identify position requirements.
5. Interview and observe current incumbents of the position being analyzed.
6. Tabulate and summarize the data into a draft job analysis report.
7. Subject the draft report to review by a sample of managers and supervisors and revise as needed.
8. Prepare a draft job description, check back with managers and supervisors, and revise as needed.
9. Update the job description as experience with it dictates.

There are alternative or supporting means of identifying essential job functions as well:

- Surveying and analyzing the actual work experiences of employees in the job
- Determining the time required to perform a duty or task
- Identifying the job-related consequences of not requiring a worker to perform a function
- Reviewing the terms of the collective bargaining agreement or union contract

The President's Committee on Employment of People with Disabilities lists the following questions to ask about each job task:[6]

- How is the task performed? What methods, techniques, and tools are used?
- How often is the task performed? Are the tasks performed less frequently as important to success as those done more frequently?
- How much time is allotted to perform the task? Is the pace consistent?
- Why is the task performed?
- Where is the task performed?
- How is success measured?
- What happens if the task is done wrong?
- What aptitudes are necessary (potential to learn a skill)?
- What knowledge is necessary (level of general or technical information)?
- What skills are necessary (applied ability through training)?
- How much physical exertion is required (lifting, standing, bending, reaching, twisting, and crawling)?
- What happens if the task is not completed on time?
- What are the environmental conditions (hot, cold, dust, wet, etc.)?
- How much mental exertion?
- How much emotional exertion?

The matrix shown in Figure 4-2 can be used for determining the physical demand level of a job. And the job analysis form shown in Figure 4-3 is very useful in identifying job requirements.

Applicant Specifications

For every job description there should be a corresponding set of applicant specifications that describe the qualifications *essential* to success on the job. Applicant specifications describe what an applicant *should know* (the technical, professional, and managerial knowledge required), what the candidate should be able to *do* (the technical, professional, and managerial skills needed), and what the applicant should *be* (the personal qualities, educational background, and kind and amount of experience sought). Here again, to ensure nondiscrimination, the documents should focus on education, training, knowledge, skills, experience, and personal traits that are directly related and essential to successful job performance or are clearly and unequivocally business necessities.

An effective set of applicant specifications contains the following items:

- Title of the position and its location within its department
- Authority and responsibility

Figure 4-2. Matrix for determining the physical demand level of a job.

	PHYSICAL DEMANDS FOR JOB DESCRIPTIONS					

The following matrix is a guide to help you determine the overall physical demand level of a job. This does not determine the actual lifting capacity of the position.

For example, if a description requires that occasionally (0–33 percent of the time) a worker will be handling 100 lbs., then the physical demand level of the job description would be heavy some of the time. Frequently (34–66 percent of the time) would indicate the physical demand level of the worker's job description most of the time, and constant (67–100 percent of the time) would indicate the physical demand level all of the time.

	Sedentary	Light	Medium	Med. Heavy	Heavy	Very Heavy
Occasional (0–33%)	10 lbs.	20 lbs.	50 lbs.	75 lbs.	100 lbs.	over 100 lbs.
Frequent (34–66%)	Negligible	10 lbs.	20 lbs.	35 lbs.	50 lbs.	over 50 lbs.
Constant (67–100%)	Negligible	Negligible	10 lbs.	15 lbs.	20 lbs.	over 20 lbs.

Source: Reprinted, by permission of publisher, from Kirsten Shingleton, "Job Audits as Interviews: Define Physical Requirements," *HRfocus,* 1992 © 1992. American Management Association, New York. All rights reserved.

- A description of principal and essential job functions (major duties and tasks)
- Personal specifications: Type and level of training/education, kind and amount of experience, skills and abilities essential to job success, and temperament and personality demanded by the job
- Identity of positions to which incumbents can aspire
- Salary range and benefits, including training and development opportunities

Excerpts from applicant specifications are shown in Figure 4-4.

Application Forms

Applications that will pass the test of close ADA scrutiny are essential. Such forms must (1) be available in accessible locations, (2) provide alternatives for people who are unable to complete standard printed forms

(Text continues on page 80.)

Figure 4-3. Job analysis form.

Agency _____ Position _____ Salary _____ Reference _____

1. Job Description

2. Physical Requirements	Weight/Reach	% of Time	Adaptations	Remarks
Carrying				
Cleaning				
Climbing				
Collating				
Dialing				
Driving				
Filing				
Hearing				
Holding				
Indexing				
Inserting				
Lifting				
Maintaining				
Opening				
Pulling				
Pushing				
Removing				
Scheduling				
Sitting				
Sorting				
Speaking				
Stamping				
Standing				
Stapling				
Threading				
Turning Pages				
Typing				
Unfolding				
Unlocking				
Using Keyboard (coding)				
Walking				
Weighing				
Writing				

(Continued)

Figure 4-3. Continued.

3. Cognitive Requirements	Level/Type	Recommendations
Education Math Problem Solving Reading Reasoning Training		

4. Site Evaluation	Dimensions	Adaptations

Job Site
  Desk
  Door
  Door Mechanism
  Elevators
  Entrance
  File Cabinets
  Floor Covering
  Obstacles
  Steps
  Threshold		

Bathroom
  Door
  Grab Bars
  Sink
  Toilet		

Cafeteria Accessibility		
Parking		

5. Comments:
   Operation of Equipment

_____

_____   _____
Job Analyst   Date

Source: Reprinted from the Job Development Bank and Enhanced Productivity for Severely Disabled Persons, K. Mallik and S. Yuspeh, 1979, G. Washington University Rehabilitation Research and Training Center, Washington, DC, Grant #G008300123, NIDRR, Department of Education.

Figure 4-4. Excerpts from applicant specifications.

Job Title: Warehouse Specialist

Essential Duties:

- Ability to operate a fork lift
- Ability to lift and carry 30- to 50-pound objects a distance of 20 feet without help and 51 to 125 pounds with the help of another person
- Ability to read and follow printed instructions and handwritten order forms in English
- Ability to inventory (count and record materials and supplies) on a prepared form

---

Job Title: Electronics Theory Instructor, Human Resources Development Department

Job and Advancement Opportunities: Incumbent receives periodic intensive in-house instructor training and upgrading to develop, enlarge, and extend instructional skills. Opportunities are provided for advanced electronics and computer training related to assigned duties. Attendance at one professional/technical conference per year at company expense is encouraged. Individuals with advancement potential are eligible for promotion to instructor team chief positions. The line of progression for additional advancement is senior instructor, master instructor, instructor supervisor, branch chief, division chief, and department director.

Job Title: Director of Logistics, Human Resources Development Department

Authority and Responsibility: Reports to the HRD manager for performance of major functions and duties and to the corporate director of purchasing for procurement activities. Provides general supervision and direction to four division chiefs (facilities, equipment, maintenance, and supply), general direction to an administrative staff, and direct supervision to an administrative assistant and a stenographer. Total logistical staff numbers 40 and consists of supervisors, technicians, clerks, equipment maintenance workers, and supply personnel. Coordinates with heads of all HRD department elements on a continuing basis.

Job Title: Coordinator, Management Development, Human Resources Development Department

Personal Specifications:

A. Education. A master's degree in general education, business administration, industrial education, human resources development, or psychology (A.M., M.S., Ed.M., or M.B.A.)

(Continued)

Figure 4-4. Continued.

B. Experience. A minimum of five years of professional educational experience that includes assignments of two or more of the following types: manager of a multiple-level training activity in business, industry, government, military, or public education; conducting advanced training for instructors; experience in management development, evaluation, and instructional technology; or teaching at the college or technical school level involving the development of supervisors or managers.

C. Skills and abilities. Candidates must possess the ability to conduct meetings and conferences, must have skill in interviewing, must be able to deliver information and decision briefings, must have the ability to prepare statements of work and negotiate contracts, and must be able to prepare and track plans and budgets.

D. Personal qualities. Must be reasonably stable emotionally, poised and self-confident, must like people and be skillful in dealing with them, must be articulate, must be open-minded and receptive to change, must be innovative, must be completely ethical, and must see his or her job as a challenge and not as a routine way of earning a living.

(for example, offering assistance in completing the application or allowing the candidate to take the form home), and (3) avoid inappropriate questions. The last item is especially critical. Application forms must not contain disability- or health-related questions. Specifically, questions relating to the following are inappropriate:

- Physical conditions or defects
- Mental conditions or defects
- Medical or health problems
- Drug or alcohol treatment
- Treatment for other conditions or diseases
- Prescription drugs
- Hospitalization
- Absences from employment due to illness
- Treatment by medical or psychological practitioner
- Receipt of workers compensation

Under certain conditions, applications may include questions that focus on the applicant's abilities. For example, job applicants who have been provided a job description or list of essential job functions may be asked whether they can perform the listed job duties and tasks with or without accommodation. If the applicant indicates that an accommodation would be required to perform the functions, he or she may be asked what would be needed and how the task would be performed. However, the information about the needed accommodation may not be used in making the hiring decision.

Résumés

Résumés submitted by job applicants can be valuable sources of information for initial screening and preparation for the employment interview. Review of résumés can prevent the great waste of time that occurs when people who are obviously not qualified for a position are interviewed. Careful review of the document will also provide leads for questions during the interview to elicit information of great value in making the hiring decision. Persons involved in the screening and selection processes must guard against rejecting applicants for reasons unrelated to the performance of essential job functions or clear business necessity.

Preemployment Tests

Tests are samples of performance taken under standardized conditions. They are used to measure knowledge, skills, abilities, aptitudes, interests, honesty, and personality. Tests used in screening and selecting personnel must meet these standards:

- *Essentiality.* They test only knowledge or skills required to perform necessary job functions or reflect a clear business need.
- *Validity.* They measure only what they are supposed to measure.
- *Reliability.* They yield consistent results.
- *Objectivity.* They eliminate the judgment or bias of administrators and scorers.
- *Nondiscrimination.* They are administered to all job candidates and do not disadvantage persons of a certain age group, sex, race, creed, color, or disability.
- *Administrability.* They can be given with relative ease under non-discriminatory conditions.
- *Standardization.* Items have been selected under prescribed conditions and scored under definite rules.

For people with disabilities, testing accommodations are often needed. Applicants should be notified in advance that alternate means of testing are available. If the effectiveness and appropriateness of a particular test are questionable for a certain type of disability, ask the applicant if he or she has taken a test of that type, whether he or she was comfortable with it, and whether there was anything that would have been helpful. The EEOC has identified the following acceptable accommodations:[7]

- *Substitution:* An oral test or instructions for a written test or instructions or vice versa, for people with vision or hearing disabilities

- *Format changes:* Use of large print or braille, computer, audio recordings, or administration by a reader, for people with visual or other reading disabilities
- *Response options:* Recording answers by means of a tape recorder, dictation, or computer, for people with visual, learning, or motor disabilities
- *Time:* Providing more time for people with physical, mental, or learning disabilities to complete a test
- *Vocabulary adjustments:* Simplifying test language for people with limited language skills caused by a disability
- *Scheduling:* Allowing rest breaks for people with mental or other disabilities who need such relief
- *Accessibility of facilities:* Making the test site accessible or taking the test in an accessible location, for people with physical disabilities
- *Setting adjustments:* Conducting the test in a separate room if a person's disability prevents optimum performance when there are distractions or altering lighting conditions
- *Alternative measures:* Evaluating the skill or ability using other means, such as interview, evaluation of education and work experiences, licensure or certification, and on-the-job trial periods, for people with physical or learning disabilities

In addition, rooms in which interviews and tests are to be conducted must be accessible to persons with all types of disabilities, and at least one person in the organization should be trained to administer tests designed for candidates with sensory, motor, or speaking deficits.

Job applicants have the responsibility under ADA to request an alternative test format, but EEOC suggests that employers inform applicants in advance that a test will be given so that the applicant can notify the employer of a need for accommodation or an alternative format. If an applicant does not request an accommodation in advance, the employer may need to reschedule the test or provide another type of accommodation if the requested one is unavailable when the test is administered.

Interviewer Evaluation Forms

Forms used by interviewers during the selection process must be constructed to facilitate fair and objective evaluation of candidates. A rating scale-type form serves that purpose well. The form should employ an odd-numbered scale, say 1 to 5, for each item to be evaluated, and provide sufficient space for the interviewer's comments. The following items typically are evaluated:

- Appearance and manner
- Experience (kind, amount, and relevance)
- Education and training (general and specialized)
- Intelligence (as revealed by responses to questions, ideas, and sense of purpose)
- Special aptitudes and skills (e.g., technical or mechanical)
- Interests and activities (in terms of breadth, depth, type, and job relevance)
- Motivation, disposition, and personality (e.g., dependability, persistence, sociability, self-confidence)

Although the foregoing represent commonly used criteria, they must be reviewed carefully for relevance to essential job functions or clear business necessity. Items that do not pass muster should be deleted from the form.

The Employment Interview

The employment interview communicates information about the organization and the job to the candidate; draws out information that applicants are not likely to put in writing; assesses characteristics that can be evaluated only in face-to-face contacts; assists in making judgments about the applicant's ability to do the job; and validates the results obtained from other means of screening.

Interviewers judge the individual's training, education, experience, poise, resourcefulness, and creativity in relation to the requirements of the position. If there is a question as to how an applicant with disabilities would function in the position, the interviewer should ask. For example, for a marketing position, the interviewer might explore the ability of a person with a visual impairment to read print by asking, "Would it be a problem for you to review daily computer printouts?" For an accounting position, a question might be, "Would you have a problem traveling to six branch offices located along the eastern seaboard once each quarter?"

Although employers may ask questions relating to an applicant's work experience before making a job offer, they may not inquire into a candidate's workers compensation history. After making a conditional offer of employment, however, an employer may so inquire.

Although ADA allows employers to prohibit the illegal use of drugs and alcohol in the workplace and comply with the Drug-Free Workplace Act of 1988, they cannot discriminate against rehabilitated drug and alcohol abusers who are not currently addicted to those substances. Thus, they may *not* ask applicants if they are drug addicts or alcoholics or whether they have ever been in a drug or alcohol rehabilitation program. They *may* ask job applicants if they drink alcohol or use drugs illegally, and they may refuse to hire, discipline or terminate an alcoholic whose job performance or conduct is impaired, provided that the individual is not a "qualified individual with a disability" under ADA.

Interviewing Sites

Accessibility standards apply to all sites, on company premises or at other locations, used for recruitment and selection activities. That means that companies must ensure that their employment offices and any other sites where candidates come to get information or in search of a job must be accessible to people with physical disabilities of any type. If facilities cannot be made accessible without incurring "undue hardship," options must be offered to candidates for positions, such as alternative sites and individual assistance.

Greeting the Candidate

The interviewer greets applicants with disabilities just as he or she would any other candidate and uses vocabulary common to the job. If in doubt as to whether to help the applicant get around the limitations caused by the disability, he or she can ask, "May I be of assistance? Is there anything I can do to make your visit more comfortable?" There are as well guidelines for interviewers that pertain to specific disabilities:

- *Vision disability:* Identify yourself, shake hands, and offer the person the option of taking your arm for direction if you need to move to another location.
- *Hearing disability:* Look directly at the individual, speak in a normal tone of voice, and be prepared to communicate in writing. If an interpreter is necessary, reschedule the appointment to a time when one can be obtained. When an interpreter is used, always speak to the applicant, not the interpreter.
- *Mental, developmental, or emotional disability:* Do not try to "talk down" to him or her. Speak as you would to any other applicant.

Conducting the Interview

The reliability of data collected in the interview and the quality of the judgments reached depend on the skill of the interviewer. Interviewer biases and prejudices, likes and dislikes, and value judgments often get in the way of the facts. This is particularly true of inexperienced interviewers facing an applicant with an obvious disability. Interviewers should know what is appropriate and inappropriate language and the code of disability conduct.

The validity of an interview is governed by how relevant the questions and responses are to the purpose of the interview. The interviewer's primary objective is to identify from among the candidates the best-qualified person for the position. That requires the interviewer to learn enough about the applicant to make an informed decision. Concerns about violating antidiscrimination laws and offending the individual with a disability may cause the interviewer to avoid questions that would yield valuable information—and thus invalidate the process. Direct questions focused on job-relevant matters should not be skirted or avoided.

Much of what has been said earlier about questions on the application form apply equally to the interview. The following questions are unlawful:

- Do you have any impairment or disability that might affect your ability to perform this job?
- Do you have any mental or physical impairments?
- Are any of the members of your family disabled?
- What illnesses or disabilities have you had in the past?
- How many days of sick leave did you use during the last year?
- Have you ever filed a workers compensation claim?

There is no discrimination involved, however, when an applicant is asked to describe his or her qualifications for the vacant position, but the order in which important questions are asked is critical. Questions relating to job requirements (essential functions) and the applicant's qualifications (education, training, and experience) must be asked before any issues pertaining to disability are raised.

The interviewer can ask the applicant questions about his or her ability to perform job-related functions, as long as the questions are not phrased in terms of a disability. For example, someone applying for a secretarial position could be asked, "Can you use a typewriter or word processor?" A warehouse operator could ask an applicant, "Are you able to lift containers weighing 50 pounds?" An applicant can also be asked to describe or demonstrate how, with or without reasonable accommodation, he or she would perform job-related functions or tasks.

When the job and qualifications have been examined, potential difficulties in performing specific job duties and tasks can be addressed. If the applicant reports a disability, his or her ability to perform essential job functions should be discussed, potential accommodations should be explored, and a tentative selection of the most appropriate accommodation, from the standpoints of both applicant and the employer, should be made. The interview should close with assurance to the candidate that the hiring decision will not be affected by the need for reasonable accommodation and that the company does not discriminate.

Interviewing People with Hearing Disabilities. To interview deaf persons, the most productive approach, but also the slowest, is to use handwritten notes. The interviewer can also use body language, facial expressions, pantomime, and finger spelling. He or she should face the light source; speak slowly and clearly directly to the person; reinforce comments with facial expressions and body language; and ask simple yes and no questions. The best alternative is to take a short workshop on the basics of American Sign Language, such as the two-day seminar offered by the Padgett-Thompson Division of the American Management Association, or learn sign language by computer.[8]

No matter what approach is taken, the main goal of the interviewer is to communicate. He or she should not be afraid to repeat. People who are deaf are accustomed to "speaking" with people who are not signers or with those who are not proficient signers. They are used to having statements and questions repeated. Any communication can be repeated in different words and with facial expressions and body language to help convey the meaning.

Interviewing People with Speech Impairments. When an interviewer is interviewing a person who has difficulty in speaking, the following guidelines will be helpful:

- Give him or her complete attention.
- Speak directly to the candidate.
- Show patience; never speak for the person.
- Try to ask questions that require only a short answer or a nod or shake of the head.
- Never pretend to understand if you are having difficulty in doing so.
- Repeat or paraphrase questions or comments and look for facial expressions or body language that connote understanding.

Interviewing People with Vision Impairments. When interviewing a person with blindness or severe vision impairments, all of the rules of disability conduct, including what are and are not appropriate questions, apply. The following guidelines are more specific:

- Speak in a normal tone of voice.
- Identify yourself (and anyone else who may be with you) and your position with the company.
- Always voice the name of the person you are addressing.
- Use common expressions.
- Clearly indicate when the interview is over.

Closing the Interview

If the candidate is not qualified, the interviewer must tell the person, being specific. The interview of a potentially successful candidate should end with a visit to the worksite. If the candidate is qualified but a job offer is not extended immediately, he or she must be told that a decision will be made in a few days and that he or she will be notified. In either case, the candidate is thanked for coming in.

Other Selection Instruments

Medical Examinations

Medical testing and evaluation are circumscribed by the ADA. Medical examinations administered before an offer of employment are strictly prohibited. However, they may be given after an offer of employment if:

1. The exam is directly related to the essential functions of the job or has a clear business necessity.
2. All candidates for the position are required to undergo the exam.
3. The results of the exam are kept confidential and are stored in a set of files separated from the general personnel files.
4. The exam is not used to reject an applicant unless it reveals a condition that prevents the person from performing essential job functions with or without a reasonable accommodation.

Voluntary postemployment medical exams are permitted if confidentiality and nondiscrimination protections and provisions are assured.

In addition, medical examinations may be required by employers under the following conditions:

- If a worker demonstrates behavior that relates to job performance or safety
- To determine whether a worker in a physically demanding job continues to be fit for duty in that job

- When the examination is conducted to comply with federal laws (such as those for transportation workers and airline pilots)

Psychological Tests and Drug Tests

Psychological tests may be used if they are designed to assess job-related criteria; however, any test that tends to screen out individuals with a disability must be demonstrably job related and consistent with business necessity.

Preemployment drug tests are not considered medical examinations. They are not prohibited, but ADA does not encourage or authorize them. ADA allows an employer to reject an applicant who tests positively for use of illegal drugs or unlawful use of prescription drugs. Treatment for drug addiction is not deemed a reasonable accommodation and is therefore not required. An individual who has successfully completed a drug rehabilitation program is considered to be a person with a disability and is protected under the ADA. Information from drug tests, whether administered before a job offer is made or following employment, must be treated as confidential; however, drug tests may be used as a basis for disciplinary action by an employer.

Reference Checks

Reference checks must be made to confirm or validate information obtained by other elements of the screening and selection system and to gather information not provided by the system. They can be used to check an applicant's character and habits and follow up leads obtained during the interview or from other elements of the selection system.

Reference checks should be made near the end of the selection process. Whether conducted by mail, telephone, or face-to-face contacts and whether they involve the candidate's past employers, educational institutions, or others, they can be very useful. The more recent the references are, the better they serve as reliable sources of information and predictors of on-the-job behavior and performance. As with other screening and selection devices, care must be taken to collect only data that are directly related to essential job functions or clear business necessity, and not to a disability.

Making the Hiring Decision

Under ADA, an employer is free to hire the most qualified applicant available and to make decisions based on reasons unrelated to disability. The decision to hire or to reject an applicant must be made on the basis of an assessment of all the objective evidence collected during the entire screening and selection process. To the maximum extent possible, subjective evaluation—biases, hunches, intuition—should be kept out of the decision. The best way to do that is to have a group discussion of the candidate's credentials and performance by two or three people who had ample opportunity to interview the candidate and review the evidence.

Employers are not required to hire an individual who does not meet minimum job qualifications, such as a college degree, state certification, driver's license, or typing speed. Nor must they hire individuals who pose a significant risk of substantial harm to the health and safety of themselves or others in the workplace. However, they cannot refuse to hire individuals because of a slightly increased risk. The determination that an individual poses a direct threat must be based on objective and factual evidence relating to his or her ability to perform essential job functions. If the employer determines that the applicant would pose a direct threat to the health or safety of anyone, consideration must be given to eliminating or reducing the risk to an acceptable level with a reasonable accommodation.

An employer may not base an employment decision on the assumption that an applicant's disability or past record may cause an increase in workers compensation costs in the future. However, an employer may deny employment or discharge an individual who is unable to perform a job without posing a significant risk of substantial harm to the health or safety of the individual or others, if the risk cannot be eliminated or reduced by reasonable accommodation. An employer may refuse to hire or terminate an employee who knowingly provides a false answer to a lawful postoffer inquiry about his or her condition or workers compensation history.

Once an applicant has been hired, employers cannot ask questions about a disability unless they can show that the questions are job related or consistent with business necessity. Any information gained from such inquiries must be kept confidential and maintained in separate files.

The true test of an organization's commitment to nondiscrimination and implementation of the ADA is the record. The hiring record should demonstrate that:

- Managers and staffers have made their employment decisions using legal and appropriate standards and processes.
- Biases, stereotypes, and false assumptions were not involved in the selection process.
- They have made their decisions on the basis of ability, not disability.

- Reasonable accommodations have been made to remove barriers to employment.
- Qualified candidates with disabilities did apply and were hired.

The final decision should be made by the manager or supervisor to whom the individual will report. Then the job offer should be made to the candidate, and all applicants for the position should be notified of the decision by telephone or letter.

Following Up

Effective follow-up can make the assimilation of newly hired personnel, particularly newly hired employees with disabilities, smooth and pleasant. The newcomer should be oriented to the organization and the job. For people with disabilities, in addition to group orientation activities, it is important that induction be personalized. That will go a long way toward engendering a feeling of acceptance and belonging, generating enthusiasm and high morale, and developing positive attitudes and loyalty toward the company, its policies, and its personnel. The progress of all new employees should be closely followed during the early months of their employment, and they should be given all the help they need.

Record Keeping

Under ADA, employers must maintain employment records, including application forms submitted by job applicants; other records related to selection; requests for reasonable accommodation, promotion, demotion, transfer, layoff, or termination; rates of pay or other terms of compensation; and selection for training or apprenticeship (for permanent, temporary, and seasonal positions) for one year after making the record or taking the action, whichever occurs later. If a charge of discrimination is filed or an action is brought by the EEOC, the employer must retain all personnel records related to the charge until its final disposition. In addition, to meet the requirements of Title VII, Executive Order 11246, and EEOC's Uniform Guidelines on Employee Selection, records must be retained on job applicants, active employees, and former employees.

Applicant records are maintained to analyze, monitor, and report recruiting, and screening, and selection activities. In addition to completed application forms and résumés, completed candidate evaluation forms, and the results of tests, these records contain the referral source of each applicant, the position applied for and the date of the application, whether a job offer was made, which job was offered and why, whether the applicant accepted or rejected the offer and why, and name and title of the individual who made the employment decision.

For tests used in screening and selection, the following records should be maintained:

- Statistical data, indexes, and graphics demonstrating the relationship between the instruments and job performance
- Mean, median, and modal scores of the instrument for all relevant company subgroups, by sex, minority, and nonminority groups
- Cutoff or minimum qualifying scores for each test or measure
- The names of test administrators, scorers, and evaluators, together with the date of each action, for each test used.

Records of all interviews must be filed. They should contain the following information:

- The name of the applicant
- The title of the position
- The date of the interview
- The identity of the recruitment source
- The tests administered and scores
- The ratings and comments of the interviewer
- The date of hiring or reasons for nonselection
- The date and means of notifying those nonselected
- The name and title of the interviewer

Statutory requirements and organizational needs must be considered in establishing records retention policies. Minimum statutory requirements for some personnel records follow:

- *Basic employee information:* Three years for the Fair Labor Standards Act, Walsh-Healy Act, Age Discrimination in Employment Act, Immigration Reform and Control Act, and Davis-Bacon Act
- *Records of promotion and transfer:* One year for the Age Discrimination in Employment Act, Vocational Rehabilitation Act, Vietnam Era Veterans Readjustment Act, ADA, and Title VII
- *Recruitment and selection:* One year (permanent jobs) and 90 days (temporary jobs) for the Age Discrimination in Employment Act, Vocational Rehabilitation Act, Vietnam Era Veterans Readjustment Act, ADA and Title VII
- *Termination, layoff, recall, demotion, and disciplinary action:* One year for Age Discrimination in Employment Act, Vocational Rehabilita-

tion Act, Vietnam Era Veterans' Readjustment Act, ADA, and Title VII

Computer software can help employers document recruitment, selection (including applicant tracking and evaluation), assignment, promotion, training and development, and other human resources practices. It can lend objectivity to the processes, make them more systematic and efficient, reduce paperwork, and make compliance with the many federal and state reporting requirements easier, faster, and less costly.

The main steps in the preoffer and postoffer employment processes are shown in Figures 4-5 and 4-6.

Summary

Hiring people with disabilities attests to a company's commitment to the concept of equal employment opportunity and demonstrates that an organization recognizes that people with disabilities can make substantive contributions to the business.

A well-designed selection system is based on organizational goals, objectives, staffing forecasts, personnel and skills inventories, projections of position vacancies, and detailed job descriptions and applicant specifications. Advertisements, application forms, tests, interviewer rating forms, medical examinations, and other recruitment, screening, selection devices, and hiring procedures must be tailored to specific jobs and be complete and nondiscriminatory, conforming with EEOC and ADA guidelines and standards.

Successful candidates must be selected solely on the basis of merit as required by sound management and applicable legal and regulatory requirements. Good hiring practice today turns what many have long considered a formidable challenge (some would say a legal minefield) into a management opportunity—one that motivates and empowers employees and enhances productivity. To achieve that goal, the focus in hiring activities must be exclusively on ability, not disability. In all phases of the hiring process, decisions must be based on a determination as to whether the candidate can perform the essential functions of the job, with or without accommodations.

For Further Reading and Viewing*

American Educational Research Association, American Psychological Association, and the National Council on Measurement and Education. *Standards*

*Full addresses for the organizations in this listing are found in Appendixes B and C.

Figure 4-5. The ADA preoffer employment process.

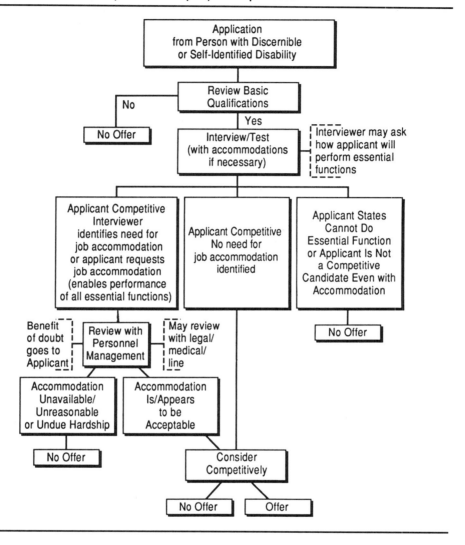

for Educational and Psychological Tests. Washington, D.C., 1985. Available from American Psychological Association.

Arthur, Diane. *Workplace Testing: An Employer's Guide to Policies and Practices*. New York: AMACOM, 1994.

Breaking the Attitude Barrier: Learning to Value People with Disabilities. 33-minute videocassette, closed and open captioned. Available from MTI Film and Video.

Bureau of National Affairs. *The Americans with Disabilities Act: A Practical and Legal*

Figure 4-6. The ADA postoffer employment process.

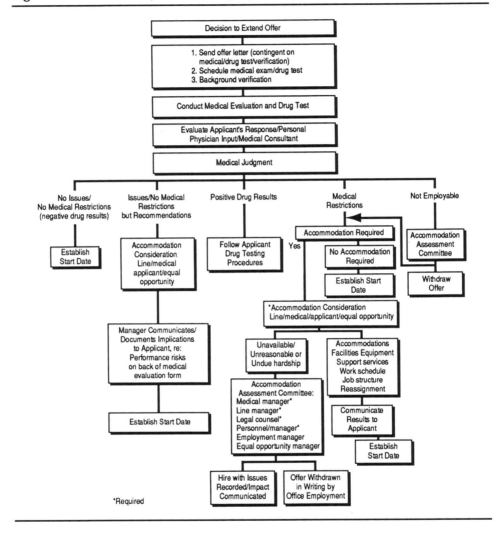

Guide to Impact, Enforcement, and Compliance. Washington, D.C.: Bureau of National Affairs, 1990.

Byham, William C. "Recruitment, Screening, and Selection." In *Human Resources Management and Development Handbook.* 2d ed. Edited by William R. Tracey. New York: AMACOM, 1994.

Cook, Mary F. (ed.). *The AMA Handbook for Employee Recruitment and Retention.* New York: AMACOM, 1992.

DescriptionsNow! HR Pro Edition. Computer job description software. Available from KnowledgePoint.

Employability: Integrating People with Developmental Disabilities into the Workplace. 1993. 27-minute videocassette. Available from Woolworth Corporation.

Equal Employment Opportunity Commission. *Americans with Disabilities Act of 1990.* Washington, D.C.: EEOC, Office of Communications and Legislative Affairs, 1990.

Friedman, Lee, Carl T. Cameron, and Jennifer Mikulka Fletcher. *User's Manual for EMPLOY: A Job Placement System for Workers with disAbilities.* San Antonio: Psychological Corporation, 1994.

Gateway to Opportunity: Interviewing Job Applicants with Disabilities. 1992. 18-minute video. Available from Advantage Media.

Goldberg, Adin C. "What You Can and Cannot Ask." *HRfocus* (Special Report), American Management Association, 1992, p. 6.

Greenberg, Susan, and Raymond Bello. "Rewrite Job Descriptions: Focus on Functions." *HRfocus* (Special Report), American Management Association, 1992, p. 10.

Horwitz, Harry A. "New Guidelines for Medical Examinations." *HRfocus* (Special Report), American Management Association, 1992, p. 7.

It's Your Choice: Selection Skills for Managers. 1993. Available from Films.

Job Analysis. Software system that integrates job requirements and environmental and social conditions into an electronic spreadsheet, creating a job standards data bank. Available from Health Management Technologies.

Jones, Timothy L. *The Americans with Disabilities Act: A Review of Best Practices,* AMA Management Briefing. New York: AMA Membership Publications Division, 1993.

Lotito, Michael J., Michael J. Soltis, and Richard Pimentel. *The Americans with Disabilities Act: A Comprehensive Guide to Title I.* Alexandria, Va.: Society for Human Resource Management, 1992.

Lotito, Michael J., Richard Pimentel, and Denise Bissonnette. *What Managers and Supervisors Need to Know about the ADA.* Alexandria, Va.: Society for Human Resource Management, 1992.

Making the ADA Work for You. 1992. 23-minute videocassette. Available from American Foundation for the Blind.

Making the ADA Work for You: A Video Training Seminar. 1992. 2-hour videocassette. Available from American Foundation for the Blind.

Martin, Scott L., John W. Jones, and John A. McDonald. *Personnel Selection under the ADA.* Rosemont, Ill.: London House/SRA, 1992.

Naeve, Robert A., and Ari Cowan. *Managing ADA: The Complete Compliance Manual.* Colorado Springs, Colo.: Wiley Law Publications, 1992.

Perkins, Nancy L. "Defining Employers' Obligations under the New Disability Act." *Management Review* (January 1992): 33–35.

Perritt, H. H. *Americans with Disabilities Act Handbook.* New York: Wiley, 1990.

Pitone, Louise. "Employee Records." In *Human Resources Management and Development Handbook.* Edited by William R. Tracey. New York: AMACOM, 1994.

Plachy, Roger J., and Sandra J. Plachy. *Results-Oriented Job Descriptions.* New York: AMACOM, 1993.

President's Committee on Employment of People with Disabilities. *Ready Willing and Available: A Business Guide for Hiring People with Disabilities.* Washington, D.C.: President's Committee on Employment of People with Disabilities, 1992.

Richardson, Gerald M. "Applicants and Employees with Mental Disabilities."
    HRfocus (Special Report), American Management Association, 1992, p. 8.
The Right Choice. 1991. 20-minute videocassette. Available from Films.
Sack, Steven Mitchell. *The Hiring and Firing Book: A Complete Legal Guide for Em-
    ployers.* Merrick, N.Y.: Legal Strategies, 1993.
Shingleton, Kristen. "Job Audits as Interviews: Define Physical Requirements."
    HRfocus (Special Report), American Management Association, 1992, p. 11.
Tompkins, Neville C., and Lynn Atkinson (eds.). *The Job Descriptions Encyclopedia:
    An ADA Compliance Manual.* Madison, Conn.: Business and Legal Reports,
    1993.
Tracey, William R. "Hiring: Matching People and Jobs." In *Critical Skills: The
    Guide to Top Performance for Human Resources Managers.* New York: AMACOM,
    1988.
Vega, Zoila Garlaza, and Gail Haney. *Employee Selection Plus . . .* 3d ed. Atlanta,
    Ga.: LOMA, 1992.
Vernon-Oehmke, Arlene. *Effective Hiring and ADA Compliance.* New York: AMA-
    COM, 1994.
Welcome to the Team: Disability Etiquette in the Workplace. 1992. 20-minute video.
    Available from Advantage Media.
When Can You Start? 1988. 27-minute video. Available from Films.

Notes

1. Timothy L. Jones, *The Americans with Disabilities Act: A Review of Best Practices,*
   AMA Management Briefing (New York: AMA Membership Publications Division, 1993), p. 7.
2. Louis Harris, *Public Attitudes toward People with Disabilities,* a study conducted
   for the National Organization on Disability (1991).
3. Adapted from William R. Tracey, "Hiring: Matching People and Jobs," in *Critical Skills: The Guide to Top Performance for Human Resources Managers* (New York:
   AMACOM, 1988).
4. Ibid.
5. See William R. Tracey, "Collecting and Analyzing Job Data," in *Designing
   Training and Development Systems* 3d ed. (New York: AMACOM, 1992), for detailed instructions on job and task analysis.
6. President's Committee on Employment of People with Disabilities, *Ready
   Willing and Available: A Business Guide for Hiring People with Disabilities* (Washington, D.C.: President's Committee on Employment of People with Disabilities, August 1992), p. 5.
7. "Uniform Guidelines on Employee Selection Procedures," *Federal Register,*
   August 25, 1978, and "Questions and Answers on the Uniform Guidelines on
   Employee Selection Procedures," *Federal Register,* March 2, 1979.
8. American Sign Language (ASL) is quite different from speaking in English.
   Like French, Italian, Russian, or Japanese, it is a totally separate language,
   with a unique vocabulary, sentence structure, word order, and style. See
   American Sign Language, 800K public domain diskette, catalog 590-5235.
   Available from Chariot Software Group.

5

Breaking Down Barriers

As more organizations begin integrating workers with disabilities, many challenges must be met to reap the benefits of an additional source of talent and a diverse workforce. First among them is the need to build increased awareness and positive, accepting attitudes about people with disabilities and upbeat attitudes among those who are disabled. Others relate to expectations, work and social experiences, inaccessible facilities, lack of accommodations, and dearth of instructor know-how.

Types of Barriers

The most obvious barriers to the complete integration of people with disabilities into the workforce are physical, but there are less obvious barriers that require attention.

Low Expectations

Studies have shown that parents and youth with disabilities often have delayed career plans and job expectations—or none at all. Young people especially may think, "It's hopeless. I can't do anything." Society's perception of many disabilities reinforces these attitudes and adds another barrier to employment.

Expectations can be raised by involvement. Organizations have a responsibility to involve workers with disabilities in job, facility, equipment, and procedure redesign projects. Such participatory activities will go a long way toward convincing persons with disabilities that they can do the jobs that are needed and make valuable contributions to the achievement of corporate goals.

Lack of Work Experience

Research has demonstrated that many adolescents with disabilities have had little or no job experience, in contrast to most nondisabled teens. This is probably a reflection of the limited employment prospects that young people with disabilities and their parents envision.

Managers and trainers must do whatever is necessary to compensate for this lack of workplace know-how. The first step is to ensure that all corporate training and development programs and services, including coaching, mentoring, and on-the-job training, are modified to accommodate workers with disabilities. To do that, human resources managers and trainers must learn about job accommodations of all types—from computer programs to raised desks for wheelchair users—and then make those accommodations. They must also learn about sources of information, equipment, and materials and use them.

Public Attitudes

Many people, including some physicians, believe that the millions of people who have disabilities that cannot be cured have lives that are not worth living. As a consequence, they devalue people with disabilities. In contrast, many people with disabilities have a much more positive outlook. They believe that they have a reasonably good life. The key is attitudinal change.

Management Attitudes

Many managers feel uncomfortable with persons with disabilities or even fear them; they worry about misunderstanding them or their needs or are apprehensive about saying or doing the wrong thing. Some managers and supervisors believe that people with disabilities can perform only nonskilled or entry-level jobs, or that they are accident prone or unreliable. Those beliefs are fictitious; people with disabilities can work successfully at any level in any type of work (and are likely to be more careful and have fewer accidents), and they are just as dependable as other employees.

Employees with disabilities can be hired and fired just like everyone else. People with disabilities, as well as nondisabled people, who fail in doing a job need to be told, not sheltered. If they can't or won't do a good job, they should be terminated. In short, managers must rid themselves of inaccurate perceptions about trainees with disabilities and replace them with correct understandings. They need to make the human resources or training department a model and standard for the organization in the way it accommodates, manages, and trains people with disabilities.

Coworker Insensitivity

Employees at all levels may display discomfort with coworkers who are disabled as do managers and supervisors and for some of the same reasons. But the primary reasons for their insensitivity is their lack of understanding of disabilities and their tendency to stereotype those who have them. Workers need to know about the obligations they and their organizations have to hire and advance people with disabilities. They need to learn more about people with disabilities—what they can do, what kinds of accommodations they need, and how they can contribute to the attainment of organizational goals and objectives.

Attitudinal and behavioral changes can be accomplished by training that addresses the concerns and questions of nondisabled employees at all levels about working with and supervising people with disabilities and training for managers, supervisors, and other employees to develop sensitivity to the potential and needs of employees with disabilities. That training should involve workers in such activities as simulations, group discussions, video and multimedia presentations, volunteerism, mentoring, and other ventures that foster contact, understanding, empathy, acceptance, and friendships among workers with and without disabilities. A videotape that will help sensitize workers to the needs and capabilities of persons with disabilities is *Part of the Team* (see the Resources at the end of the chapter).

Inadequate Social Skills

All workers need effective social skills—that is, the ability to relate to others in a positive and mutually satisfying way. They need to be able to approach others in a friendly way, engage in appropriate conversation, provide compliments, and cooperate. Many persons with disabilities lack those skills because of limited social contacts. People who are new to workplace situations where interaction with others is essential need help in adjusting so that they can fit in. Without that help, they are likely to suffer psychological distress and drop out.

Eight basic skills are required: self-awareness, social interaction, assertiveness, active listening, direct communication, empathy, conflict resolution, and problem solving. Small-group counseling programs conducted by social workers, psychologists, mental health counselors, or mental health nurses are one solution, but supervisors can also do much to help by providing encouragement and support.

Inaccessible Facilities

People with disabilities are often shut out of training rooms and laboratories because they are inaccessible. Until recently, no one has seen to it that workers with disabilities have the same opportunities for training and development as their nondisabled coworkers. The ADA now requires that training spaces—covering everything from parking spaces to drinking fountains—must be made accessible.[1]

Meager Instructor Know-How

Instructors often harbor the same misunderstandings and misconceptions found among managers, supervisors, and other workers. In addition, they typically lack the knowledge and skills needed to establish and maintain effective and efficient learning conditions for trainees with disabilities. Many rely on one or two basic instructional methods, such as the lecture and group discussion, or demonstration and performance, supplemented by large numbers of audiovisuals. With nondisabled persons, such approaches may work reasonably well, but with trainees who are vision or hearing impaired, and students with other types of disability, those methods will not suffice. To be effective, instructors must enlarge and expand their repertoire of approaches.

Communication Problems

The problems encountered by trainees with visual and hearing impairments are evident. Equally apparent are the communication restrictions that challenge persons with mental and emotional disabilities. Not so obvious are the communication problems of persons with other types of disabilities. In many cases, the isolation imposed on them by their illnesses or disabilities has made broadscale contact with others difficult or impossible, and the resulting lack of interaction with others in social or work situations has often resulted in limited speaking and listening skills. Similarly, those who have been chronically ill all or most of their lives have not had the formal education that their nondisabled coworkers have experienced. The solution lies in providing employees with disabilities secure and penalty-free opportunities to communicate with each other and with their nondisabled coworkers.

Learning Problems

Loss or diminished capacity of one of the primary senses, such as deafness or blindness, invariably results in learning difficulties. Most, however, can be ameliorated, if not totally overcome. Even dyslexia can become a much less serious impediment to learning. Those who train and develop workers with disabilities must be sensitive to their learning problems, alert to the need to compensate for them, and diligent in their efforts to overcome them.

Lack of Accommodations and Training Opportunities

Training and development are keys to employment and promotion. Workers rarely arrive at the workplace with all of the knowledge, skills, and abilities needed to produce the goods and services that organizations are established to provide. Large and small private companies and public organizations and institutions must provide training for all workers to give them the required skills. Persons with physical, mental, emotional, and learning disabilities and impairments must be provided equal access to corporate training and development systems, primarily in an integrated setting. To do that, organizations must make the necessary changes in the physical plant, facilities, and equipment and in training programs, instructional strategies, techniques, aids, and devices.

Removing Attitudinal Barriers

The real problem of disability is not the disability itself but the mistaken notions, misunderstandings, and attitudes toward disability that remain widespread in the workplace and society at large. Disability, to too many, signifies inferiority, dependence, even helplessness. Those attitudes can and must be changed.

Organization Culture and Climate

Organization culture is an organization's basic beliefs and values about itself and its employees and its clients, customers, suppliers, and the public at large. It also encompasses an organization's view of its value to society embodied in the way things are done in an organization as defined by written and unwritten policies, procedures, and practices. It is manifested in how the organization defines success and how people are rewarded and punished—the organizational norms that have become accepted and encouraged (or prescribed) by management. One of the most powerful aspects of an organization is its beliefs and values about people with disabilities.

Organization climate is the corporate atmosphere—the product of the collective impact of goals, objectives, priorities, beliefs, values, expectations, managerial techniques, and leadership styles on the motivation of people to accomplish the mission. It is revealed by employee attitudes, beliefs, feelings, opinions, and perceptions. Organization climate is co-equal in power with organization culture as reflected in the way it supports or fails to promote and nurture employees with disabilities.

Organization culture must communicate to all of its constituencies a belief in the value of a diversified workforce, one that includes people with a variety of disabilities. It must express its conviction that, regardless of impairments of one sort or another, people have a role to play, talents to deliver, and the capacity to contribute to the attainment of the goals and objectives of the organization.

A proper and principled organization climate must be demonstrated by credible policies, goals, priorities, beliefs and values, managerial style, and employee attitudes that result in the cultivation and nurturing of the skills and abilities brought to the organization by its diversified workforce.

Information Strategies

Communication up and down and laterally is an important key to the removal of barriers. Communication is the process by which facts, ideas, information, opinions, meanings, emotions, and understanding are exchanged. It employs speaking and listening, seeing, reading and writing, and posture, motions, facial expressions, and body language. All must be used to get people to understand and become accepting of workers who are in some way different.

All forms of communication and the media used to transmit information must reflect the commitment of the organization to the development and advancement of people with disabilities:

Meetings and conferences
Oral directions
Coaching and counseling
  sessions
Performance reviews
Training and development
  programs
Job and exit interviews
Labor negotiations
Audiovisuals and graphics
One-on-one dialogue
Panels and symposiums

Decision and information
  briefings
Correspondence
Memos
Messages
Reports
Minutes and summaries
Staff studies and position
  papers
Proposals
Policy statements
Contracts

Manuals	Advertisements
Brochures	Marketing
Press releases	Promotional materials

These must reflect the organization's concern for people with disabilities in terms of tone, style, and word choice.

Management and Supervisory Training

Little will be gained by providing top-notch training and development programs for employees with disabilities unless those responsible for supervising and evaluating their on-the-job performance have the required skills and attitudes. Training designed specifically for executives, managers, and first-line supervisors is essential. It requires top-level support, both financial and moral.

The keys to successful integration of workers with disabilities are sensitivity, understanding, and acceptance. All are the result of knowledge. If the myths and stereotypes that have surrounded people with disabilities are to be stamped out, managers must change their perceptions before they can change their behaviors.

ADA presents three significant training needs for managers and supervisors: detailed knowledge of the law; policies, strategies, and procedures for cost-effective compliance with the law; and strategies to reduce the attitudinal barriers to the successful employment, utilization, and advancement of people with disabilities.

Employee Training

The coworkers of people with disabilities need training and attitudinal change if they are to accept workers with disabilities with enthusiasm and a positive attitude and provide encouragement and assistance. Training designed to dispel myths and build positive attitudes toward workers with disabilities is vital for employees at all levels. Even when managers and supervisors have the proper attitudes and display positive and supportive behaviors, if their workers do not exhibit the same attitudes and behaviors, employees with disabilities will not be accepted and will be unable to make a full contribution to the organization.

Making Facilities Accessible

ADA regulations require removal of barriers to accessibility in existing places of public accommodation when removal of barriers is "readily achievable." ADA regulations have established these priorities for barrier removal:

1. Provide access to facilities from public sidewalks, parking areas, and public transportation.
2. Provide access to areas where goods and services are made available to the public.
3. Provide access to rest room facilities.
4. Take any other measures needed to provide access to the goods, services, facilities, privileges, advantages, or accommodations of places of public accommodation.

By January 1993, any major construction required for public accommodations had to comply with ADA standards. Adaptable facilities have certain structural features that make it possible to modify them to accommodate people with a wide range of physical disabilities. Appendix A contains a comprehensive checklist to make sure that training facilities meet ADA standards.

ADA holds an employer responsible for making training accessible to employees with disabilities, even if the training is conducted by others. Employers may not do anything through a contractual or other arrangement or relationship that it is prohibited from doing directly. The organization would be required to provide a training site for the employee with the disability that is accessible and usable unless to do so would create an undue hardship.

Job Accommodations

Employers have several options for accommodating workers with disabilities (Figure 5-1), all of which have the advantages of being useful, productive, and cost-effective.

Job Adaptation and Restructuring

Job adaptation is the process of developing or redesigning the dimensions of a job by identifying major functions, duties, and tasks and documenting them in a written job description. Restructuring a job by adding, deleting, or changing duties, tasks, or elements is one alternative.

Job analysis and one of its products, job descriptions, are key elements of job redesign. Job analysis is the process of collecting, tabulating, grouping, analyzing, interpreting, and reporting data pertaining to the work performed by individuals. A job description is the document that

Figure 5-1. ADA employee accommodation consideration.

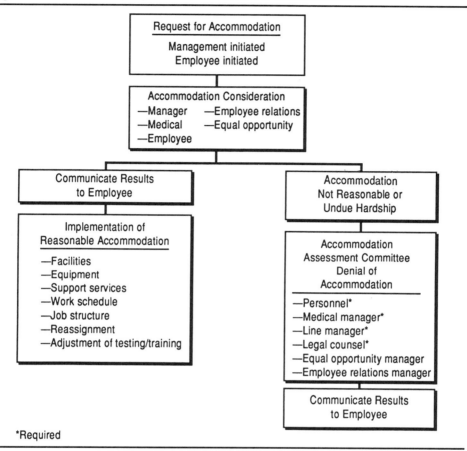

describes the major duties, functions, and authority assigned to a position and the relationships between the position and other positions in the department, and, when appropriate, the relationship of that job to positions in other departments. It is one of the main products of job analysis.

Job analysis focuses on the duties, tasks, and elements that make up a job. The results of job analyses are used to:

- Identify and organize content for writing and revising job descriptions and applicant specifications.
- Provide detailed job data that can be used to identify personnel requirements resulting from installation of new equipment, tools, work methods, or processes, and from development of new products and services.

- Project future personnel requirements resulting from restructuring or downsizing.
- Establish accurate and objective information for job evaluation.
- Provide guidance for decisions relating to compensation and benefits, assignment and transfer, on-the-job training and development, and promotion.
- Aid in the development of more effective recruitment, screening, selection, assignment, and classification instruments and procedures.
- Establish measurable job performance standards.
- Identify factors that induce job satisfaction, raise morale, and improve productivity.
- Identify and locate health and safety hazards.
- Design training and development systems.

Job Sharing and Job Splitting

Jobs can be restructured, divided and shared by two mutually dependent employees, or split into two distinct independent jobs. Detailed analysis of the jobs to be performed and the duties and tasks required by them, coupled with analysis of the capabilities of workers with disabilities and the accommodations they require, will often reveal how those jobs can be restructured to achieve gains in efficiency and effectiveness.

Two solutions are job sharing and job splitting, arrangements that allow employees to fulfill needed job functions by dividing a job and the workday or workweek between employees who are unable to work a full 8-hour shift or a 40-hour week. For example, one employee may work from 8:00 A.M. to noon and the other from 1:00 to 5:00 P.M., or one employee may work Mondays, Wednesdays, and Fridays and the other Tuesdays and Thursdays.

There is a distinction between job sharing and job splitting. In job sharing, the two employees' duties overlap; they think of each other as an extension of themselves and therefore must communicate. Their shifts may overlap to facilitate such communication, but it is not an essential feature because they may communicate by E-mail or periodic meetings, telephone calls, or notes. In job splitting, two clearly distinct jobs are created from one job. No communication between incumbents is needed.

Work Hardening and Transitional Jobs

When workers are absent from their jobs because of injury or illness, employers must replace them temporarily, increase the workload of the existing workforce, or pay overtime. Because these costs are high and growing, anything that can be done to reduce the amount of time a worker is away from the job will be of considerable help.

Work hardening programs provide one solution to the problem of getting employees back to work sooner. They are four- to six-week training programs provided to injured workers following physical or occupational therapy to give them the self-confidence and stamina need to resume an active role in the workforce. They often simulate the work that got employees injured in the first place to get them back on the job.

Creating transitional jobs is another solution. Such jobs provide alternative work for a limited time that will be useful to the organization and at the same time serve as rehabilitative assignments. Rather than paying disability benefits, the organization brings workers back to the workplace as soon as medical providers approve of the return and places them in temporary modified-duty, light-duty, or restructured jobs until they are sufficiently recovered to return to their original positions.

Facilities and Furnishings

Much that has been said about making facilities accessible applies to work areas, but there are some additional measures that can be taken to ensure that people with disabilities will be able to carry out the duties, tasks, and responsibilities of their jobs. For example, storage of goods and materials can be planned or modified to make it possible for people in wheelchairs to have ready access to them. Shelving is one obvious example.

Job Placement System

If people with severe and multiple disabilities are to be employed in large numbers, they must be successfully evaluated for job placement. A new system, EMPLOY, holds promise of overcoming the problems of improving the match between workers with severe disabilities (e.g., Down syndrome, autism) and the jobs to be filled.[2] The system features a job analysis–worker analysis instrument designed specifically to assess task, skill, and ability requirements for low-skill, entry-level jobs and evaluate and place individuals with disabilities in those jobs. The instrument was validated using a diverse set of jobs from gathering materials for recycling, to fast food counter service, to hotel and motel housekeeping.

Using the instrument, a worksite supervisor rates the extent to which each of the activities and working conditions pertain to a job, while supported employment staff rate the extent to which the worker is capable of performing those activities or under those specific conditions. The system also includes recommendations for more than 250 interventions or accommodations that have been used successfully on the job to ameliorate, if not eliminate, the problems posed by the activities and working conditions that comprise the 81 EMPLOY items—in many cases, items that relate to the essential functions of a job.

The separate worker and job analysis rating scales, each with 81 items, deal with such factors as grasping and holding, decision making and reasoning, social interaction, and work pace.

Work Hours

Appropriate adjustments in work hours, including part-time work, are often an effective means of making reasonable accommodations. This option is feasible for persons with all types of disabilities and is often the key to their successful employment. Modifying work hours is especially suitable for people whose disabilities cause difficulties in making convenient transportation arrangements or that limit the number of consecutive hours of work they can tolerate.

Performance Evaluation

Performance review and evaluation is one of the most sensitive areas in managing and supervising employees with disabilities. Although performance evaluations for people with disabilities should not be conducted differently from those of nondisabled employees, there are several areas where the system, manager, or supervisor can go wrong unintentionally and discriminate. These pitfalls can be avoided if the following criteria are met:

- Performance standards are objective, relate only to essential job functions, and are clear to both the employee and the supervisor.
- Items to be evaluated are identified in terms of the performance of job tasks, not in terms of personal traits, characteristics, or the effects of disabilities.
- Supervisors have the right attitudes toward people with disabilities and a thorough understanding of their capabilities and limitations.
- Supervisors' expectations with regard to job performance are neither too high nor too low.
- Needed accommodations are provided but are not taken into account in evaluating performance. Only *results*, and not the means of achieving them, are evaluated.

Reassignment

In a period of restructuring, downsizing, and other effects of a highly competitive business environment, transfers of employees are common.

Reassignment of workers with disabilities to different geographic locations or new jobs poses a special problem. Although theoretically a worker's disability should not be a factor in such personnel actions, there are some conditions or situations that demand recognition and accommodation.

The needs of people with mobility and motion disabilities, particularly people who use wheelchairs and require accessible transportation services, must receive attention before moving them to a site where such services may not be available. For people with health and medical problems, a different environment may seriously exacerbate the effects of the disability. And people with mental and emotional disabilities may fear separation from familiar surroundings and the support to which they have become accustomed and refuse the reassignment.

The solution is full and open discussion of the need for reassignment with the employee to reach a solution that is acceptable to both the employer and the worker. If agreement cannot be reached and the reassignment is imperative (a matter of business necessity), the employer has no obligation under ADA to create a new job for the employee.

Discipline

Managers and supervisors face no greater challenge in superior-subordinate relationships with workers with disabilities than the area of discipline. Cooperative efforts toward enterprise goals depend on discipline, so management has the primary responsibility for developing and maintaining discipline among all employees. Many managers find it difficult to discipline, and most find the task of disciplining people with disabilities a formidable challenge. They fear the emotionalism of the disciplinary scene, from both their own and the worker's standpoints.

Decisions to discipline, including termination of dismissal, must be supported by incontrovertible evidence of misconduct or substandard performance and be made independently of the employee's disability. An acceptable disciplinary system should be:

- Constructive. It is designed to correct behavior or performance, not to punish.
- Preventive. It is crafted to remediate, not to penalize.
- Job related. It is shaped to be clearly, directly, and reasonably related to job tasks.
- Predictable and certain. It is fashioned to herald the consequences of infractions.
- Appropriate. Its consequences are suited to the seriousness of the transgression or failure.

- Timely. It averts unnecessary delay in its imposition.
- Consistent. It is fair and dependable, avoiding whimsy or caprice.
- Impersonal. It involves censure of the behavior or performance, not the person.
- Subject to appeal. It provides for relief through a written grievance procedure.

Any disciplinary action that meets these specifications can and should be applied to all employees, including those with disabilities.

Psychological Accommodation

The integration of people with disabilities into the workforce can be made much easier by providing reasonable psychological accommodation: communicating to the staff the individuals' previous accomplishments prior to their arrival, asking disabled workers what they would like to have communicated to coworkers about their disabilities, and demonstrating or modeling the tasks to be performed.[3] Job coaches, to help the disabled individuals learn and do the job, and mobility instructors, to help people with various impairments get around the facility, are useful as well.

Recognition and Rewards

Employees with disabilities should receive appropriate recognition and rewards for outstanding performance on the same basis as nondisabled employees. That means that such designation as "outstanding handicapped (disabled) employee of the year" will be abandoned because it segregates people with disabilities and establishes a separate performance criterion for them. It also means that employees with impairments must be eligible and successfully compete for incentives and rewards, such as promotions, bonuses, certificates and trophies, honorary titles, and public acknowledgment of achievements.

Adaptive and Assistive Technologies

A wide variety of new technology and assistive devices is available to help disabled workers in activities of daily living and participation in the workplace. The devices range from simple appliances to sophisticated computer systems.

According to a National Rehabilitation Information Center (NARIC) report, the most important device criteria are effectiveness, ease of use and maintenance, expense, reliability, durability, safety, comfort, and attractiveness. Other factors include the amount of training, time, and energy required to use the device, portability (transport and storage), and convenience to others. User requirements for devices may vary according to the environment in which they will be used.[4]

Workplace Assistive Devices

The key to successful accommodation is to choose the technology that will make employees with disabilities as productive as their nondisabled peers. Employees with disabilities must be competitive with their peers. It is one thing to make it possible for a worker with an impairment to perform a task using one type of device, but if it takes him or her three, five, or ten times as long to perform it or exhausts the employee to the point where a prolonged rest is needed, a different device may be required.

The first step in making a choice of adaptive equipment is to ask the worker involved; he or she probably has a fairly good idea of what is needed. Professionals employed by hospitals and rehabilitation agencies, such as occupational therapists, can also be helpful. (See Appendix B.) In addition, a system is now available to help people choose the most appropriate technology based on the limits imposed by their disability. It is an expert system, AC/ES, developed by the Adaptive Computing Technology Center at the University of Missouri-Columbia. For example, if a person is blind, uses braille, and has a job involving accounting work on a computer, the system delivers a list of equipment that will fill the requirements; some are sophisticated and costly and others low tech and inexpensive.

Types of Assistive Devices

The computer is an important way to achieve the objective of opening jobs to persons with disabilities. Because not everyone can use a traditional keyboard or even a mouse, devices have been invented to make it possible for such persons to use computers.

One of the most common assistive devices for people with mobility impairments is the wheelchair. Others are leg braces, walkers, canes, scooters, and power chairs. These are critical devices because mobility is often the key to participation in the workforce.

Finally, among the many special tools and equipment that are readily available are scanners that put print into speech for persons who are deaf and hearing impaired and low-power magnifiers, stronger bifocal lenses, extra lighting, and closed circuit TV (used to photograph and magnify reading materials up to 70 times on the screen) for workers who have visual impairments.

Cost of Accommodations

The cost of most types of accommodations is much lower than most people expect. Worksite accommodations are minimal, and only the most sophisticated types of adaptive and assistive devices are expensive. But even for those, some help may be available.

According to one report, data from several studies conducted by federal government agencies indicate that only 22 percent of employees with disabilities need accommodations at the worksite.[5] A second study estimated the average costs of accommodations, as follows:

No cost to the employer	31 percent
Between $1 and $50	19 percent
Between $50 and $500	19 percent
Between $500 and $1,000	19 percent
Between $1,000 and $5,000	11 percent
More than $5,000	1 percent

Most types of adaptive and assistive technology are computer related, designed to make the computer accessible to people with disabilities. These devices range in cost from the hundreds to the thousands of dollars.

There are several funding sources for devices to enhance personal functioning and independence. For devices used as an accommodation for newly hired employees with disabilities, the primary option is employer funding. For current employees who become disabled on the job, the options include total insurance, partial insurance, state vocational rehabilitation agency, and employer funding.

Among other sources are state vocational and rehabilitation departments, physicians (who may be asked to write prescriptions for devices, which are then paid for by Medicaid), corporate and private philanthropic foundations and organizations.[6]

Training Strategies

Adults with disabilities often need training opportunities to meet the challenges of the workplace, and they may also need a longer training period to feel confident in performing job tasks. In general, the more severe the disability is, the longer an individual may take to learn new skills. Similarly, adults with disabilities may need more individualized training, even if they are mainstreamed, so they can pace themselves. As different skills are learned, pressure to compete with nondisabled employees is likely to be counterproductive. Adults with disabilities may need extra support and encouragement from instructors and supervisors during the learning period.

Basically, there are three strategies for meeting the training needs of employees with disabilities: mainstreaming, providing special assistance, and separation. Other strategies involve the provision of special accommodations for people with disabilities. Each option should be available to every trainee with disabilities according to his or her needs and abilities as determined by systematic assessment. And no trainee should be locked into one strategy but should have the option of alternative placement as his or her needs change.

Mainstreaming

The first strategy, and the one that should take precedence, is mainstreaming: keeping persons with special needs in regular training classes rather than segregating them for separate instruction. Mainstreaming, in its ultimate form called "inclusion," is a commitment to educate or train people with disabilities, to the maximum extent possible, in the school or classroom they would attend if they did not have a disability. It involves bringing support services to the person rather than moving the person to the services. Thus, trainers and supervisors must be prepared to alter support systems for trainees as their needs change so that they can achieve and experience success; individualize the instructional program for all and provide the resources every trainee needs; and include trainees with disabilities supportively in as many as possible of the same testing and evaluation experiences as their nondisabled peers.

Providing Special Assistance

The second strategy may take one of two forms: coworker training or supported employment. The first approach involves training a group of employees, representing all levels of organization from hourly workers to managers, in one-on-one techniques of training coworkers with disabilities—on-the-job training, coaching, and mentoring—and then assigning them the responsibility for guiding the training of an employee with a disability.

The second approach, a viable option for people with severe disabilities, is to take full advantage of the expertise and special assistance of social service or rehabilitation agencies. Many agencies have arrangements called supported employment, whereby a job coach is sent along with one or more of their clients with disabilities and stays as long as needed. In some cases the job coach learns the job and then teaches it to the employee on the job. The agency may "buy" the service or "deliver" the service.

Separation

The third strategy, separation, should be adopted only when mainstreaming and assistance are not practicable. In most cases, separation amounts to segregation and the denial of equal opportunity. Therefore, trainees with disabilities should be separated for training when it is the only way to help them function effectively in the average workplace environment and when they agree to it. Modified or separate participation for persons with disabilities must be a choice, not a requirement.

Other Strategies

To provide a course or training program in an accessible place and manner for persons with disabilities, it may be necessary to adopt alternative strategies. Some of the most common and feasible approaches are as follows:

- Modify the training program format or requirements (e.g., allow additional time for completion of a course module or the entire training program).
- Provide auxiliary aids and devices unless that option would result in a fundamental alteration of the training program or result in an undue burden.
- Administer the training program in a facility that is accessible or provide alternative comparable arrangements, such as offering the program on videocassette, audiocassette, CD-ROM, interactive video, or prepared notes.

Supplementary Aids and Services

Decisions about what supplementary aids and services must be provided are unique for each trainee.

Instructor Consultation and Training

The most common supplementary aids and services are consultation and training for the instructor. For example, an instructor who receives a blind trainee for the first time needs initial guidance in arranging the classroom or meeting room and continuing help in adapting lessons to help the trainee understand the concepts and skills to be taught. Such support can be provided by an in-house resource person or be obtained from local public or private special education, vocational rehabilitation, and community- and corporate-sponsored training programs on an as-needed basis.

Electronic Aids and Devices

Electronic aids—computers, speech synthesizers, FM amplification systems, and so on—are becoming increasingly common. Other less sophisticated aids are large-print materials, strategic seating, or modified desks and work benches. It is important to provide regular access to support staff to help the instructor locate equipment or devices that permit trainees with disabilities to benefit from the instruction.

Life-Support Measures

Some trainees need life-support equipment; others need frequent medication, access to an epinephrine "pen," or blood sugar monitoring. Necessary support may include both the equipment and trained personnel to perform these tasks.

General Training Techniques and Devices

Trainers who work with workers who are disabled must possess the knowledge and skills required of all corporate trainers.[7] Trainers establish the conditions of learning, set the standards, provide the motivation, guidance, and assistance, and furnish the subject matter expertise. They also play an important role in evaluating the progress and accomplishments of trainees.

With the enactment of ADA, all corporate trainers will have people with disabilities in their classrooms and shops and must have the attitudes, skills, and abilities that will enable them to achieve success in training those workers. Among the additional knowledge and skills, trainers must be able to:

- Use or develop corporate and community resources to provide needed support services.
- Provide liaison among trainees, supervisors, managers, and medical, community, and professional resources.

- Use their knowledge, understanding, ingenuity, and creativity to facilitate the complete integration of trainees with disabilities into the workforce.
- Have a keen understanding of people and be able to communicate with people with a wide range of abilities and backgrounds.
- Keep abreast of resources, technologies, and trends relating to the employment, training and development, and utilization of people with disabilities.
- Teach each individual trainee rather than trying to gear instruction to the average of a group.
- Use many different instructional strategies and techniques and shift among them as needed.

Many different techniques and devices can be used to improve the training and development of employees with disabilities. The first accommodation is to be sure that trainees with disabilities have the necessary tools, equipment, modifications, and adaptations to permit equal and competitive participation in every aspect of the training program. In general, organizations must:

- Hire and work with consultants who have expertise in designing and modifying training programs that involve employees with disabilities.
- Find, recruit, and hire training and training development specialists skilled in training and developing programs for *all* adults, including those with disabilities.
- Hire specialists to train all in the training department to adapt their instructional strategies, methods, and teaching techniques to accommodate persons with disabilities of all types.
- Hire trainers and training developers who have disabilities.

Instructional Approaches

The principles, techniques, and arrangements used in training workers with disabilities are identical to those used for years in training and educating children with special needs, with the modifications needed to support adults. Here are some of the most important:

- Base training on thorough analysis of the tasks required to perform a job.
- Translate the task analysis into the series of discrete steps required to accomplish each task.

- Prior to training (before trainees arrive) ask enrollees if they need interpreters or any special assistance for the training session(s).
- Consider the needs of participants with disabilities when choosing a training facility; arranging seating; developing program content; selecting and placing furniture, furnishings, equipment, and audiovisuals; designing learning aids; preparing documentation; and scheduling learning activities.
- Keep the front of the classroom or meeting room well lighted. Make special accommodations when darkening the room to show visuals.
- Identify needed support services, such as interpreters, note takers, and job coaches, and make arrangements to get them.
- Offer front-row seats to trainees with hearing impairments so they can see well enough to speech-read.
- Speak slowly and carefully and only while directly facing the group. Watch facial expressions to detect problems. Rephrase sentences to help increase communication.
- In addition to calling for trainee questions, invite trainees to write unsigned questions that can be answered near the end of the training session.
- Use visual aids that are clear, large, and easy to understand.
- Keep lips and face free of visual obstructions such as bushy mustaches, long hair, or frequent gestures around the face.
- Begin by carefully defining the objectives of the training in terms of what the trainees must be able to do, under what conditions, and to what standard following the training.
- Clearly describe what is expected of trainees with regard to attendance, attitude, participation, concentration, and actions and demeanor.
- Focus first on the ability of the trainees, their talents and skills. Concentrate then on the disabilities—the limitations they impose and what needs to be done to enable trainees to perform the tasks required by the job.
- Stress demonstration and performance.
- Use techniques and tactics that involve as many senses as possible: facial expressions, gestures and physical cues, oral instructions, examples and illustrations, visual prompts, and audiovisual aids.
- Speak clearly and with appropriate volume; avoid complex words and sentences; make transitions to new topics carefully; repeat key points.
- Treat trainees with disabilities the same way as nondisabled trainees are treated, but be sure that activities are adaptable to their capabilities.

- Whenever possible involve trainees with disabilities in classroom discussions and other group activities; call on them for responses, and use questions.
- Adjust the pace of learning activities to the needs of trainees: allow extra time for tests and practice, use breaks judiciously, and include frequent brief breathers.
- Provide ample opportunities for practice, and make continual use of encouragement, feedback, and reinforcement.
- Identify exactly where, how, and why elements of a task are not completed or are performed incorrectly.
- Measure results; adapt tests to accommodate those with disabilities (oral versions or modified performance tests).
- Chart progress and accomplishment.
- Withdraw assistance and prompts gradually as the training progresses and trainees acquire the needed knowledge and skills.
- Provide rewards for progress and accomplishment that focus on smiles, nods, complimentary comments, pats on the back, and direct, on-the-spot public praise.

Training Activities

When designing and conducting training activities, the following guidelines are helpful:

- Involve people with disabilities in the planning and curriculum development processes.
- Give special attention to the needs of people with disabilities when performing needs assessment and analysis.
- Incorporate examples of dealing with people with disabilities into small-group discussions, simulations, role plays, case studies, and other learning activities.
- Sensitize instructors and facilitators to the needs of people with disabilities and language and actions that they might find offensive, patronizing, or inappropriate.
- Train instructors and facilitators in means of accommodating trainees with disabilities.
- Keep records of all accommodations made for training people with disabilities. Documentation helps demonstrate compliance with ADA.
- Follow up training by checking on the resources, tools, job aids, and other accommodations that the organization and its managers and supervisors provide to facilitate the productivity, comfort, job satisfaction, and advancement of people with disabilities.

- Consider the needs of customers and clients with disabilities when developing training for marketing and sales personnel, dealers, and distributors.

Devices

Deeper understanding of the special needs of persons with disabilities, coupled with technological breakthroughs, have provided many effective options for trainers to make communication and efficient learning achievable for people with physical, mental, and emotional disabilities. Additionally, ADA rules and regulations require that appropriate auxiliary aids and services be furnished persons with disabilities to ensure that communication with them is as effective as communication with others.

Tests and Examinations

Tests and examinations related to applications, licensing, certification, or credentialing for secondary or postsecondary education, professional, or trade purposes must be given in a place and manner accessible to persons with disabilities or be made accessible through alternative means.

The following rules must be observed:

- Ensure that the examination is valid (measures what it is intended to measure) and does not reflect the individual's sensory, manual, or speaking skills.
- Modify the format when necessary (e.g., permit additional time or administer the examination orally).
- Provide aids (e.g., taped exams, interpreters, large-print answer sheets, or qualified readers) unless they would fundamentally alter the measurement of the skills or knowledge that the test or exam is intended to measure or would result in an undue burden.
- Offer the examination, whether modified or not, at equally convenient and accessible locations, as often, and in as timely a manner as are other exams or provide alternative arrangements, such as giving the exam at an individual's home with a proctor.

Performance Evaluation

Performance evaluation systems used as one basis for career planning and development activities should be handled in the same way for all workers. Evaluation should focus on the tasks the worker with disabilities is expected to perform using the same standards or criteria established for satisfactory performance by nondisabled workers.

Career and Self-Development

Another myth about people with disabilities is that they are grateful just to have a job and are happy to remain in entry-level positions. Most people with disabilities are no different from nondisabled workers in the intensity of their enjoyment of new challenges and their desire to get ahead. Employers have an obligation to provide career development and opportunities for workers with disabilities to move up to positions of greater responsibility and higher pay.

Goal Setting

Managers need to set time aside to discuss career goals and workplace aspirations with all workers, including those with disabilities. If their goals seem to be unreasonable or unreachable, the manager can ask them to describe what they believe it would take to achieve them. If the goals are unrealistic for business reasons, he or she can say so, but should ever assume that the disability will be the primary barrier. No one can define the limits of an employee's capabilities with total accuracy.

Teamwork

Today's employees want opportunities to participate in corporate goal setting, planning, and decision making, and they demand more meaningful relationships and interesting and challenging work. Membership on work teams can provide opportunities for employees to satisfy those needs. It also helps achieve organization goals and objectives more effectively and enhances job satisfaction for the employees involved. In short, team assignments serve the purposes of aligning personal and company goals, increasing organizational effectiveness, increasing commitment and job satisfaction, identifying and building employee strengths, improving communication, reducing conflicts, and improving motivation and morale. Workers with disabilities must have the same opportunities to serve as leaders and members of task forces and work groups as their nondisabled peers.

Networking

Networking—the process of informally acquiring, cultivating, and using a community of people with similar business, professional, and technical interests and concerns to get advice, information, assistance, and contacts—is a means of expanding one's learning resources at little or no cost.

Informal employee professional, social, and recreational events and activities are just as important to the full development of the individual as formal work groups. It is a mistake to assume that because a worker uses a wheelchair or has a hearing disability that he or she would not be interested in a company activity. Employees with disabilities must be given the opportunity to participate in all events, which must be held in accessible facilities.

Mentoring

Mentoring is a strategy designed to assist employees to learn, mature, and become more productive members of the workforce. Senior, experienced, and respected managers or staffers are assigned to serve as role models, coaches, counselors, advisers, and advocates for younger or less experienced persons, but they are not directly involved in their charges' personal or work lives. Employees with disabilities should be encouraged to become involved in the organization's mentoring system, as mentees or mentors. Mentors of workers with disabilities may be either nondisabled or those with disabilities.

Advocacy, Self-Help, Mutual Aid, and Support Groups

There are more than 500,000 nonprofit support groups in the United States, including those concerned with addictions and dependencies, disabilities, physical health, mental health, and others, such as stuttering. (See Appendix B.) These groups provide information, referrals, legal assistance, advocacy, support, publications, training, scholarships, or consultative and advisory services to individuals, groups, and public and private organizations. Most involve informal group meetings, one-on-one exchanges, and social gatherings. Some have hot lines for immediate aid to persons in need; others have outreach programs. Some are organized to help persons with specific types of disability to achieve equality of access and opportunity. Some assume advocacy roles, working to increase the availability of needed services, encouraging and supporting research, and sensitizing professionals and the general public to the needs of their members. Some groups are professionally run; most, however, are operated primarily by and for their members—peer groups of people who share a common experience or situation and who help each other without forms or fees for services.

Self-help groups provide valuable services by (1) offering relief from isolation and fear that physicians and other health care professionals cannot provide; (2) supplying emotional support and practical information; (3) preventing problems from escalating to the point where professional intervention or treatment is needed by reducing tensions and pressures; (4) supplementing professional treatment by providing coping and survival skills; and (5) providing follow-up services to reduce setbacks. In return, professionals play a variety of roles in support of self-help groups: referral, group adviser and consultant, and guest speaker.

Summary

Barriers to the employment, training, and development of people with disabilities are both many and formidable. Some are attributable to the people with disabilities themselves: their low expectations, lack of work experience, inadequate social skills, communication problems, and learning problems. However, most of the obstacles that people with disabilities face are due to the insensitivity of the general public and skills and attitudinal deficiencies of managers, supervisors, trainers, and coworkers. Adding to the difficulties are the problems caused by the inaccessibility of worksite and training buildings, facilities, equipment, and furnishings. If business and industry is to tap the large pool of talented and disabled Americans, people who want and need to be employed, these barriers must be removed. That will be accomplished by making accommodations, not just in removing physical and attitudinal barriers, but also in jobs, work arrangements, supervisory practices, and training, and through the use of adaptive and assistive technologies and devices.

For Further Reading and Viewing*

ABC's of ADA. Computerized database of ADA issues. Available from Wonderlic Personnel Tests.

ADA-TALK. 1992. 30-minute video. Available from BNA Communications.

A Guide to Barrier-Free Meetings. Waltham, Mass.: Harold Russell Associates, 1992.

Akabas, Sheila H., Lauren B. Gates, and Donald E. Galvin. *Disability Management: A Complete System to Reduce Costs, Increase Productivity, Meet Employee Needs, and Ensure Legal Compliance.* New York: AMACOM, 1992.

The Americans with Disabilities Act: Impact on Training. INFO-LINE 9203. Alexandria, Va.: American Society for Training and Development, 1993.

The Americans with Disabilities Act: Techniques for Accommodation. INFO-LINE 9204. Alexandria, Va.: American Society for Training and Development, April 1992.

Assistive Technology Sourcebook. Washington, D.C.: RESNA Press, 1990.

*Full addresses for the organizations in this listing appear in Appendixes B and C.

Breaking the Attitude Barrier: Learning to Value People with Disabilities. 1992. 33-minute video. Available from MTI Film and Video.

Building Bridges—Access to America's Hot New Market. 1991. 40- or 17-minute video. Available from National Easter Seal Society.

Butler, Cynthia G. "A Guide to Barrier-Free Meetings." *Meeting Manager* (March 1992): 54–58; (April 1992): 38–42; (May 1992): 40–45.

Choices, 2nd Edition. 1988. 12 interactive videos, 15-minute average run time. Available from BNA Communications.

Department of Transportation. *ADA Accessibility Guidelines for Buildings and Facilities.* Appendix A to Part 37, Standards for Accessible Transportation Facilities. *Federal Register,* September 6, 1991.

Dole Foundation. *The Workplace Workbook: An Illustrated Guide to Job Accommodations and Assistive Technology.* Available from National Easter Seal Society.

Eastern Paralyzed Veterans Association. *Removing Barriers in Places of Public Accommodation.* Jackson Heights, N.Y.: EPVA, 1992.

Employed Ability: Blind Persons on the Job. 1991. 14-minute video. Available from American Foundation for the Blind.

Fersh, Don, and Peter W. Thomas. *Complying with the Americans with Disabilities Act: A Guidebook for Management and People with Disabilities.* Westport, Conn.: Quorum Books, 1993.

Focusing on Ability. 1992. 25-minute video. Available from United Training Media.

Friedman, Lee, Carl T. Cameron, and Jennifer Mikulka Fletcher. *User's Manual for EMPLOY: A Job Placement System for Workers with disAbilities.* San Antonio: Psychological Corporation, 1994.

Given the Opportunity: A Guide to Interaction in the Workplace. 1993. 24-minute video. Available from United Training Media.

Johnson, Samuel E. "Create a Barrier-Free Work Environment." *HRfocus* (Special Report), American Management Association, 1992, p. 15.

Jones, Timothy L. *The Americans with Disabilities Act: A Review of Best Practices,* AMA Management Briefing. New York: AMA Membership Publications Division, 1993.

Making a Difference—A Wise Approach. 1992. 20-minute videocassette. Available from National Easter Seal Society.

Matthes, Karen. "Awareness Training: First-Hand Experience Working with Disabilities." *HRfocus* (Special Edition), American Management Association, 1992, p. 19.

Mello, Jeffrey A. "Perceptions in the Workplace: A Double Dilemma." *HRfocus* (Special Edition), American Management Association, 1992, p. 18.

Mendelsohn, Steven. *Financing Adaptive Technology: A Guide to Sources and Strategies for Blind and Visually Impaired Users.* New York: Smiling Interface Publishers, 1993.

Naeve, Robert A., and Ari Cowan. *Managing ADA: The Complete Compliance Manual.* Colorado Springs, Colo.: Wiley Law Publications, 1992.

No One Is Burning Wheelchairs. 1992. 20-minute video. Available from National Easter Seal Society.

Participants with Disabilities: How to Address Their Needs. INFO-LINE 8704. Alexandria, VA: American Society for Training and Development, April 1987.

Part of the Team. 1991. 17- or 40-minute video. Available from the National Easter Seal Society.

Reasonable Accommodations. 1992. 21-minute video. Available from United Training Media.

Schneid, Thomas D. *The Americans with Disabilities Act: A Practical Guide for Managers.* New York: Van Nostrand Reinhold, 1992.

Shapiro, Joseph P. *No Pity: People with Disabilities Forging a New Civil Rights Movement.* New York: Times Books, 1993.

Smith, Brenda, et al. *Managing Disability at Work: Improving Practice in Organizations.* Briston, Pa.: Taylor and Francis, 1991.

Tompkins, Neville C. "Tools That Help Performance on the Job." *HRMagazine* (April 1993): 84–91.

Training. Special Issue on Liability. June 1992.

Urbain, Cathleen. *Supported Employment: A Step-by-Step Guide.* Minneapolis: PACER Center, 1992.

Vernon-Oehmke, Arlene. "Management Needs: Understanding and Sensitivity." *HRfocus* (Special Report), American Management Association, 1992, p. 20.

Wai, Francine. *Equality in Training: A Guide to Improving Access for Persons with Disabilities.* Chatsworth, Calif.: Milt Wright & Associates, 1993.

Welcome to the Team: Diversity Etiquette in the Workplace. 1992. 20-minute video. Available from United Training Media.

White, Barbara J., and Edward J. Madara (eds.). *The Self-Help Sourcebook: Finding and Forming Mutual Aid Self-Help Groups.* 4th ed. Denville, N.J.: American Self-Help Clearinghouse, 1992.

Notes

1. For specifications, see *ADA Accessibility Guidelines for Buildings and Facilities,* Appendix A to Part 36, Standards of Accessible Design, *Federal Register,* July 26, 1991.
2. Lee Friedman, Carl T. Cameron, and Jennifer Mikulka Fletcher, *User's Manual for EMPLOY: A Job Placement System for Workers with disAbilities* (San Antonio: Psychological Corporation, 1994).
3. *Levinson Letter,* December 1, 1992.
4. Betsy Phillips, "Technology Abandonment from the Consumer Point of View," *NARIC Quarterly* 3 (2–3).
5. Eastern Paralyzed Veterans Association, *Understanding the Americans with Disabilities Act* (Jackson Heights, N.Y.: The Association, 1991), p. 5.
6. Many state agencies have administrative requirements that prevent them from purchasing equipment for state residents who are already employed.
7. For details about the knowledge and skills required of trainers, see William R. Tracey, *Designing Training and Development Systems,* 3d ed. (New York: AMACOM, 1992), chaps. 15, 18.

Part II

TRAINING STRATEGIES AND TOOLS

6

Vision Disabilities

My first contact with a person with a severe disability was with my Uncle Ed. In his early teens, Ed became totally blind as a result of glaucoma. Ed was the manager—and a worker—on my grandfather's dairy farm in northern New York State. I worked with him part of the summer of 1940. There was nothing he wouldn't or couldn't do. He fed the animals, milked a dozen cows morning and night, loaded hay onto the wagon and into the barn, drove the milk wagon to the railroad station with old Cliff's (a horse) help, chopped and stacked wood, and cooked his own meals. When my grandfather died, Ed stayed on the farm alone, with the nearest neighbor about a half-mile away. He remained through the freezing Canadian-border winters, often snowbound. His energy source for heat and cooking was a wood stove. He didn't need electricity (there was none). During the war years, Ed was employed by General Electric at its Burlington, Vermont, plant as an assembler of machine parts.

Many people with vision disabilities have sight useful for some purposes that has caused them to try to rely on their partial vision in situations where alternative techniques would be more effective and efficient. They are frequently aided by uninformed professionals who do not believe that a blind person can function competently and see alternative techniques and assistive devices as badges of inferiority.

It is easy to be misled with respect to the capacity of a blind individual by believing that deprivation of sight renders a person incapable of learning or less capable than those who do not have vision impairments. Although the brain and nervous system rely heavily on and assimilate visual information, sight is only one of the brain's sources of information, and most people with vision disabilities have lost only one of those sources. Given proper training and opportunity, the average blind person can do the standard job in the typical place of business—and do it as well as his or her sighted neighbor.

Types of Vision Impairments

Blind people and those with vision impairments have no sight at all or have sufficient loss of vision to place limitations of varying severity on personal, social, or occupational pursuits. A relatively small percentage of the 750,000 blind people in the United States are totally blind. Most, roughly 0.2 percent of the population (about 500,000), are termed legally blind. Each year about 50,000 people become blind.

As defined for governmental services and benefits, "legally blind" means people who have a central visual acuity of 20/200 or less in the better eye with correcting glasses (they can see only at 20 feet what a person with normal vision can see at 200 feet) or have a field of vision that at its widest diameter faces an imaginary angle no greater than 20 degrees. Essentially, then, a person is legally blind if he or she has 10 percent or less of normal vision in either of these ways. A more meaningful definition than the legal one says that "a person is blind if in a substantial number of situations it would be more efficient to use alternative, nonvisual techniques (traveling with a long white cane, reading and writing Braille, and so on) instead of relying on sight, regardless of the type of visual loss."[1] Another author agrees:

> Before we can talk intelligently about the problems of blindness or the potentialities of blind people, we must have a workable definition of blindness. . . .
>
> One is blind to the extent that he must devise alternative techniques to do efficiently those things which he would do with sight if he had normal vision. An individual may properly be said to be "blind" or a "blind person" when he has to devise so many alternative techniques—that is if he is to function efficiently—that his pattern of daily living is substantially altered. It will be observed that I say *alternative* not *substitute* techniques, for the word *substitute* connotes inferiority, and the alternative techniques employed by the blind person need not be inferior to visual techniques. In fact, some are superior.[2]

Some eye conditions are hereditary; others result from injury to the fetus caused by maternal disease or deficiency. The leading cause of blindness is retinal degeneration, a disease that affects about 2.5 million Americans. There are several retinal degenerative diseases, among them retinitis pigmentosa, and diabetic retinopathy. Another disease is Usher's syndrome, which causes both deafness and blindness. The third disease is macular degeneration, the leading cause of blindness in people over age 60. Other common eye conditions are albinism, amblyopia, cataracts, color blindness, congenital eye defects, corneal disease, injury and burns, myopia, optic nerve atrophy and hypoplasia, retinal breaks and detachment, strabismus (crossed eyes), trachoma, tumors, and uveitis.

Diabetic Retinopathy[3]

Diabetic retinopathy is a complication of diabetes that is caused by changes in the blood vessels of the eye. The retina is a nerve layer at the back of the eye that senses light and helps to send images to the brain. When blood vessels in the retina are damaged, they may leak fluid or blood, and grow fragile, brush-like branches and scar tissue. This can blur or distort the images that the retina sends to the brain.

Diabetic retinopathy is the leading cause of new blindness among adults in the United States. People with untreated diabetes are said to be 25 times more at risk for blindness than the general population. The longer a person has diabetes, the more the risk of developing diabetic retinopathy increases. About 80 percent of the people who have had diabetes for at least 15 years have some blood vessel damage to their retina. People with Type I, or juvenile, diabetes are more likely to develop diabetic retinopathy at a younger age.

It's important to know that today, with improved methods of diagnosis and treatment, only a small percentage of people who develop retinopathy have serious vision problems. Early detection of diabetic retinopathy is the best protection against loss of vision.

Retinitis Pigmentosa[4]

This condition is characterized by degeneration of the retina and choroid (the back portion of the uveal tract, a pigmented vascular layer behind the iris), usually involving development of excess pigment. It is hereditary and begins to develop at ages 10 to 12 (and sometimes much younger) with night blindness, followed by tunnel vision. Visual loss is progressive, by the time most individuals reach young adulthood, they are legally blind. Many adults with the disease have a very tiny field of vision in which they see well under good light. Total blindness often results. There is no known treatment for retinitis pigmentosa.

Usher's Syndrome[5]

This is an inherited disorder present at birth or early in life. It involves hearing loss and a progressive loss of vision caused by retinitis pigmentosa. Although hearing loss may be from mild to profound, it usually does not progress. However, retinitis pigmentosa does follow the usual pattern of progressive loss of vision. There is no treatment for the visual effects of the disease. Cochlear implants may provide some benefit for those with severe hearing loss.

Macular Degeneration[6]

Macular degeneration is damage or breakdown of the macula of the eye. The macula is a small area at the back of the eye that allows us to see fine details clearly. Macular degeneration makes close work—like threading a needle or reading—difficult or impossible.

Although macular degeneration reduces vision in the central part of the retina, it does not affect the eye's side, or peripheral vision. Macular degeneration alone does not result in total blindness. Most people continue to have some useful vision and are able to take care of themselves.

Various low-vision optical devices can help people to continue with many of their . . . activities. These devices include:

- Magnifying devices
- Closed-circuit television
- Large-print reading materials
- Taking or computerized devices

Glaucoma[7]

Glaucoma is another of the leading causes of blindness in the United States, accounting for about one in every seven or eight cases. The causes of glaucoma are not fully understood; however, some cases are hereditary and some are due to complications of other eye disorders. Still other cases are due to injuries, certain drugs (such as steroids), tumors, inflammation, and abnormal blood vessels.

Glaucoma is a disease of the optic nerve. The transparent fluid inside the forward part of the eye does not drain normally, excess pressure builds up within the eye, and the optic nerve is damaged. Its symptoms may include severe blurred vision, headache, nausea and vomiting, inability to adjust the eyes to darkened rooms, seeing colored halos around lights, and reduced side vision. Glaucoma may be acute, appearing as a sudden attack characterized by intense pain as the eye pressure increases. More often glaucoma is of the chronic type, in which there is no pain, and damage to vision is so gradual that it may not be noticed for a long time.

Many cases of glaucoma are controlled by eye drops, sometimes in combination with oral medication, which relaxes and unblocks the drainage channels of the eye. In most cases, medical treatment can control the disease completely; however, sometimes surgery is required. Early detection and treatment are important.

Cataract[8]

A cataract is a clouding of the normally clear lens of the eye. It can be compared to a window that is frosted or "fogged" with steam. The amount and pattern of cloudiness within the lens can vary.

The most common type of cataract is related to aging of the eye. Other causes of cataract include:

- Family history
- Medical problems, such as diabetes
- Injury to the eye
- Medications, such as steroids
- Long-term, unprotected exposure to sunlight
- Previous eye surgery

Surgery is the only way an ophthalmologist can remove a cataract. However, if symptoms from a cataract are mild, a change of glasses may be all that is needed to function more comfortably.

Retinal Detachment[9]

A retinal detachment occurs when the retina is pulled away from its normal position. The retina does not work when it is detached. Vision is blurred, like a camera picture would be blurry if the film were loose inside the camera. A retinal detachment is a very serious problem that almost always causes blindness unless it is treated. Most retinal tears need to be treated with laser surgery or cryotherapy (freezing), which seals the retina to the back wall of the eye. Almost all patients with retinal detachments require surgery to put the retina back in its proper position.

Low Vision

An individual is said to have low vision when ordinary eyeglasses, contact lenses, or intraocular implants cannot provide sharp sight. Such people still have useful vision, which can often be improved with aids. Low vision can be the result of birth defects, inherited diseases, injuries, diabetes, glaucoma, cataracts, aging, or macular degeneration (the most common cause). Forms of low vision include limited central vision, decreased peripheral vision, reduction in or loss of color vision, or the eye's inability to adjust properly to light, contrast, or glare.

Work and Blind Persons

Many people believe that the positions for which blind persons can be trained are limited. They are wrong. The Job Opportunities for the Blind (JOB) program, operated by the National Federation of the Blind in partnership with the U.S. Department of Labor, lists more than 75 different positions in which blind people who have received assistance from JOB are now working. Here is a sample from that list:[10]

Airline reservationist	Lawyer's legislative aid
Assembler, electronics	Masseur
Banker, senior vice president	Medical administrator
Chaplain	Micrographic technician
Child care assistant	Minister
Collections officer	Nutrition education
Computer analyst	coordinator
Computer programmer	Occupational health and safety
Cosmetologist	specialist
Counselor, adolescent	Personnel interviewer
Counselor, college	Pharmacist
Dispatcher	Photo finish worker
Dog groomer	Professor of psychology
Engineer, electrical	Quality control specialist
Engineer, safety	Sales executive
Estate analyst	Sales, retail
File clerk	Social worker
Fund raiser	Teacher's aid
Information specialist	Teacher, elementary music
IRS, financial assistant	Teacher, social studies
Janitor	Telephone operator
Job development specialist	Travel agent
Labor relations specialist	Typist receptionist

General Approaches to Training

Two of the leading problems that face those responsible for training and developing people with vision impairments are determining the medium that is most appropriate to compensate for an individual's visual loss and finding information and materials in that medium or an organization that can provide it.

Selecting and Training Staff

The first and most important task is to sensitize the whole staff, including those who are not directly involved in the training program (but are likely to have contact with trainee contact, such as support staff, secretaries, food and beverage workers, clerks, and maintenance personnel), to the importance of treating trainees with courtesy and avoiding any trace of condescension. It is also wise to be especially cognizant of the potential levels of frustration, anxiety, and even anger among blind persons. Sensitizing can be accomplished by training sessions, using role-playing exercises, the great variety of excellent videos currently available (see the Resources section at the end of the chapter), and discussion and handouts.

Next in importance is selecting and training those who will interact with people with visual impairments in the training environment. In addition to the normal requirements, trainers must have more than the usual amount of patience; they should be empathic but not pitying; and they must be objective. To be successful, they must have a solid knowledge of the impact of visual impairments on learning and knowledge of available adaptive materials and equipment, and they should have had experience working with people with visual impairments. That background can be acquired though seminars and workshops sponsored by such organizations as the American Foundation for the Blind or through college and university programs.

Removing Barriers

The second requirement is to make certain that people can move around the facility with as few obstructions or barriers and as much accommodation and facilitation as possible. Trainees may need a special arrangement of desks or tables or both to have ample room to use special equipment and materials. Nevertheless, seating should be arranged so that the trainees are an integral part of the group and that students with visual impairments are placed where they can use their vision, optical, and auditory aids optimally.

In addition to eliminating physical barriers, it is important to attend to chair comfort, heat, light, and ventilation, as well as fragrance.

One of the most important conditions for success in training with people with impaired vision is to remember that they are adults. They can contribute to the training by indicating how best to explain the job or task.

Building Self-Esteem

The third requirement has to do with expectations. People with disabilities are often easily discouraged; they have experienced setbacks and failures and anticipate similar disheartening happenings. At least to some extent, people who are blind or have low vision are affected emotionally, physically, communicatively, and vocationally. They may lack self-confidence, have difficulties with mobility, problems with spoken and written communication, and reduced job opportunities. Those who work with them must be upbeat—constantly emphasizing expectancy of success and unfailingly rewarding and reinforcing achievements, large and small, by words and deeds. Building self-esteem must be a continuing objective.

Identifying Needs

The fourth action is to determine which trainees need adapted materials or assistive devices, the type(s) required, and obtain them. This must be done as far in advance of the first training session as possible. The trainees themselves can provide information on visual condition, corrected acuity and its functional significance (visual field, light sensitivity, color recognition, and so on), at-work activities for which they need no assistance, activities and tasks that require accommodations (for example, time to complete work in braille), the role of an aide if one is provided, and how the trainer can best help them.

Because the original print size of tests, manuals, worksheets, and other materials varies widely, enlarging all materials by the same proportion will result in some print too small or too large for effective use. It is always helpful to obtain three measures of print size requirements for each trainee with visual impairments: the optimal and the largest and smallest the individual will tolerate. That will necessitate contacts with the head of the training element, the supervisor of the trainee, and the trainee.

Emphasizing Nonvisual Approaches

When dealing with people with severe visual impairments, trainers must base approaches on the auditory, tactile, and olfactory.[11] Music, sound effects, and radio-drama techniques are the most effective. One caution is not to appeal to too many senses at once. Sensory overload is a recurring danger for blind persons. Play up imagery, but let the people with disabilities furnish their own images. It is important for the trainer's voice to be pleasant, well modulated, clear, and intelligible.

Following Up on the Job

Following training, it is critically important to the organization, as well as to the trainee, that the trainer provide a written report of the trainee's accomplishments, in terms of specific skills acquired, to the trainee's immediate supervisor. It is also useful to take the time to meet with the supervisor to go over the report, answer questions, provide suggestions for on-the-job follow-up, and encourage the supervisor to give the trainee support and positive feedback.

Specific Techniques for Training

The following guidelines will help trainers or supervisors improve the conditions of learning for visually impaired employees in the classroom, shop, laboratory, or workplace:

- Make trainees feel safe, comfortable, and welcome.
- Give trainees preferential seating. They should not have to face bright lights or windows. A front seat is best in most situations.
- When possible work one-on-one or at the very least with trainees of identical or closely similar levels of vision.
- Speak when you enter a room where there is a blind person. He or she wants to know who is in the room.
- Talk to blind persons as you would to anyone else. They will not be offended by everyday language, such as using the word "see." Use normal expressions, such as, "It's nice to see you here."
- Speak in a normal tone of voice—clear, well modulated, intelligible, and pleasant.
- Don't assume that because you know one blind person and his or her capabilities, you know all blind people. There is as much variation in competencies among blind people as there is among sighted people.
- Ask how much sight they have and how you can best assist them. Don't be afraid to discuss just how much help they require.
- Always address your questions to the blind person, not to the person accompanying him or her.
- Before giving instructions, test and practice them in advance. Then give them carefully and repeat them.
- Show the blind person the locations of things he or she needs to know (e.g., the door, closet, the window, the light switch).
- Find ways to repeat instructions and major points without becoming trite and tedious.

- Verbalize and explain in detail training activities, visuals, and board work.
- Address the individual directly by name so that he or she can locate you.
- When writing on a chalkboard or easel, clarity is critical. Don't jumble the letters together. Print using a black felt pen on white paper to create enough contrast to allow a visually impaired person to read what is written.
- If tests or exercises must be completed using large print or braille, allow a minimum of one and a half times the usual time for large print and twice the usual time for braille.
- Responses to test items should be made on the adapted test or answer sheet. Responses are then transferred to the standard answer sheet by the trainer or an aide.
- When you leave a blind person, say that you are leaving. Don't embarrass the person by allowing him or her to continue talking thinking that you are still there.
- Don't pet a working guide dog. Always ask permission before attempting to interact in any way with the animal. Plan ahead for the animal's needs (e.g., rest area under the owner's table, water, periodic exercise).
- When guiding a blind person, offer your arm. Never grab the person's arm; instead touch his or her hand. Let the person take your elbow and walk slightly behind you. Walk at a normal pace or at a pace set by the individual with low vision. Identify obstacles, such as curbs and low-hanging branches, and pause slightly before stepping up or down.
- If you want to signal the blind person to change arms, move the elbow of your arm toward the back. For example, when traversing a narrow passage or door, place your elbow close to your side and toward your back. This will signal the individual to change hands and fall in behind you.
- If there is a handrail on stairs or on your route of travel, place the blind person's hand on it.
- When guiding a blind person into a car, place his or her hand on the door handle. If the door is open, place the hand on the top of the door so that he or she can feel where the corner is and reach in to feel the seat.
- When helping a blind person to a chair, guide his or her hand to the back of the chair and tell whether the chair has arms. Allow blind persons to seat themselves.
- When giving directions, be very specific. For example, say, "Go down the hallway, and take your first left after the third door. The

office is the first door on your right beyond a set of swinging doors.''

- If a blind person seems to need help, offer it, but don't help unless you have received permission to do so, and let him or her explain how you can help.
- Be especially sensitive to the potential for high levels of frustration, anxiety, and even anger among those who have lost their sight late in life.
- If you know that someone is losing eyesight, don't hesitate to ask, "Do you have difficulty seeing me?" Questions like this will break the ice. Loss of sight is devastating. Opening the subject to discussion will help you and the person with the loss.
- Pay close attention to the environment, especially light, heat, ventilation, seating, table size and height, and room arrangement.
- As much as possible, leave furniture in the same place every day. Changing it around could be disorienting or a safety hazard.
- Leave doors completely open or shut. Leaving them ajar is unsafe.
- Don't automatically exclude blind people from discussion, work, or social activities. Let them make the decision.
- Emphasize sound, feel, and taste. Use sound effects, music, radio-drama, and hands-on techniques and approaches as much as possible.
- Use the senses one at a time and successively. Avoid sensory overload.
- Emphasize the positive; communicate high expectancy of trainee success with the learning.
- Use participant materials that are appropriate for low vision and blind persons—oversized print for the visually impaired and braille for blind trainees.
- Plan well ahead for the production of printed and audiovisual materials in alternative formats and for descriptive narration of videotapes.
- Allow plenty of time for incubation, illumination, comprehension, insight, and understanding.
- In a mixed group of blind, low-vision, and sighted people, keep visuals to a minimum. When you do use them, be sure to describe and explain them orally. Avoid using flipcharts.

Assistive Equipment, Devices, and Materials

Equipment, devices, and materials for persons with visual impairments range from simple and inexpensive to sophisticated and costly. The former include:

Low-glare paper
Bold-lined paper
Use of sans serif print (Figure 6-1)
Prelined message pads
Braille paper
Felt-tip pens
Braille or large-print books (14 point type or larger)
Taped texts and tests
Postcard slate and stylus (used to write braille)
Reading/writing stands

Hand-held and stand magnifiers
Monoculars
Individual lamps
Dome magnifiers
Audiotape
Cassette recorders
Audio recordings
Speaker telephones
Large-key telephones
Giant-button telephone adapters

More sophisticated devices and systems designed to assist individuals with vision impairments are also available. Low-vision devices and techniques are designed to magnify or increase the size of images or objects so they can be seen by individuals with impaired vision. For individuals with little or no useful vision, other devices are available for communicating visual information by alternative means, such as voice or braille. This section presents a sample of the possibilities of assistive technology solutions.

Optical and Nonoptical Devices

There are two types of low-vision aids: optical and nonoptical. Optical aids use lenses or combinations of lenses to provide magnification, such as magnifying spectacles, telescopes, and closed-circuit television. Non-

Figure 6-1. Samples of various sizes of print.

This is 14 point sans serif print.

This is 16 point sans serif print.

This is 18 point sans serif print.

This is 20 point sans serif print.

This is 22 point sans serif print.

This is 24 point sans serif print.

optical aids include large-print books, newspapers, and magazines; check writing guides; and high-contrast watch faces. Other nonoptical aids are auditory aids, such as machines that "talk" (timers, clocks, and computers) and machines that scan print and convert it to sound.

Magnifying spectacles are stronger than ordinary eyeglasses. Designed for close work, they leave both hands free to hold reading material. Hand magnifiers allow the user to hold the material at a normal distance. Stand magnifiers, some with a self-contained light source, rest on the reading material. Telescopes are used for distance magnification and may be either hand-held or mounted in spectacles.

More expensive devices include braillers, enlarging copiers, electric typewriters and stands, modems, video magnifiers, video imaging equipment, voice synthesizers and software, and computer-aided devices. Other accommodations include qualified volunteer or paid interpreters and readers, notetakers, and drivers.

Braille Materials and Devices

Advances in technology have lowered the cost and improved the efficiency of brailled materials. Braille printers make most written materials accessible to anyone who can read braille.

Duxbury Braille Translator (available from Duxbury Systems and Apple Computer) is a program that translates text to braille, and vice versa. The system reads documents from any Macintosh or IBM word processor, offers a range of formatting options, and produces an output that is compatible with the VersaPoint Braille embosser. It comes with full instructions in print, braille, and disk.

The Duxbury Braille Front for Adobe Type Manager (available from Apple Computer) was designed to be used with the Duxbury Braille Translator. The font is compatible with any program, including Aldus PageMaker and QuarkPress, that uses Adobe Type Manager of Type fonts. It requires system software version 6.0.7 or later.

The Telesensory VersaPoint Braille Embosser (available from Apple Computer) brings desktop publishing power to creators of braille documents. The system offers plug-and-use simplicity with any Macintosh computer. VersaPoint embosses braille dots that are high, consistent, and easy to read in both 6- and 8-dot formats for a wide range of math, science, and business applications, on a variety of paper stocks. It requires braille translation, such as Duxbury Braille Translator.

Braille Blazer (available from IBM) is a small, lightweight braille embosser that prints in either 6- or 8-dot braille on 8½- by 11-inch braille paper or standard computer paper. Using the special light paper mode, the user can print on standard paper for proofreading or making notes.

A built-in speech synthesizer can be used as a speech output device for a computer.

Computer-Driven Aids

Computer-driven devices also range from simple to sophisticated. On the low end of complexity is software for people with visual impairments that expands the size of letters on the monitor screen or reverses them to black letters on a white background, the equivalent of large-print books. This software is a built-in feature of most new Macintosh computers and is available for IBM compatibles.

The next level of complexity consists of screen readers, software that interacts with a voice synthesizer that reads and voices whatever is on the computer screen. These devices make it possible for people with no vision to "read" any document that can be put on a computer screen.

With a scanner added to the screen-reader system, the top level, a blind person can "read" books, newspapers, magazines and even correspondence. It is essentially a complete reading machine.

Screen Enlargement Software. Screen enlargement systems allow users with vision impairments to increase the size of computer screen text and graphics to suit their individual needs. The following are compatible with the IBM Screen Reader: LPDOS and LPDOS Deluxe (Optelec US), MAGic (Microsystems Software), VISTA (TeleSensory), and Zoom-Text (Al Squared).

Readers. The Arkenstone Reader II (Arkenstone) consists of three components: a scanner recognition card, a full-page scanner, and associated Arkenstone Reader II software. The Reader formats scanned text so that it can be imported into more than 50 popular PC applications, all without keyboard entry.

The Kurzwell Personal Reader (Xerox Imaging Systems) allows persons who are visually impaired or blind (or have dyslexia) to read independently at their own pace. Single sheets or bound volumes can be scanned, and then the user can listen to the text immediately, store it, save it to most common word processing programs as an ASCII file for editing, or convert it to braille.

Alternative Input and Output Devices. Adaptations to input and output devices have been made to electronic technologies for people with visual impairments. These have taken the form of braille keyboards and braille printers—hardware and software systems that allow users to enter or receive information in their own language system. Trainees can take notes in class using a computer with either a braille keyboard or voice input capabilities, and these notes can be reviewed later using voice output or hard copy.

Voice recognition systems allow the computer to recognize and interpret human voice and sound. The computer is trained to recognize the user's voice or sound commands. Each word or phrase to be used in the system must be individually entered into the computer's memory, a time-consuming but necessary process if a practical vocabulary of reasonable size is to be developed.

Computer voice output allows users to hear what is written on the screen. There are two types of voice output systems: analog (the more common), a system that uses phonemes to create words, and digital, a system that stores human speech word for word, thereby yielding highly intelligible communications. The main disadvantages of analog systems are limited vocabulary and artificial sound. The greatest disadvantages of digital speech output are the large memory required to store the dictionary of words and the time required to access words and phrases needed to create sentences. Those drawbacks will soon be overcome by using interactive video disc technology, CD-ROM.

DADAEntry (ComputAbility) consists of software and a "black box" that connects the computer and a selected input device, such as a keyboard, mouse, joystick, or switches. Speech utilities allow the user to send characters, words, or phrases to a speech synthesizer. Data entry can also be made easier by assigning multiple keystrokes to a single key and changing the key repeat speed or turning off the repeat function.

DARCI TOO (WesTest Engineering Corp.) has a special entry mode that allows users who are blind or visually impaired to control an IBM Screen Reader, and it can be customized to meet special needs. The device allows the computer to be controlled by a video fame controller, joystick, switches, Morse code, or a special joystick called DARCI code. The IBM keyboard remains functional at all times.

AccessDOS software is a utility for keyboard access. It provides the IBM DOS user with visual impairments helpful features that offer specialized control (e.g., toggle keys that beep when they are active).

T-TAM (trace-transparent access module) (Prentke Romich Company) connects the computer and the keyboard, mouse, and/or a serial communication aid. It has toggle keys that beep when active. Data entry can be simplified by assigning multiple keystrokes to a single key and modifying the numeric keypad so that it simulates a mouse. The keyboard and mouse remain fully functional.

Unicorn Smart Keyboard (Unicorn Engineering) plugs directly into the keyboard port, with no additional hardware or software required. The keyboard has oversized key shapes and an 8- by 10-inch touch-sensitive surface that includes special overlays for customizing. The Setup Overlay provides features such as customized keyboard sensitivity, repeat rate, and key sound.

The IBM Personal System/2 Accessible Workstation provides display, system controls, function keys, screen/text movement keys, home row locator keys, and cursor control keys that are easy to locate by touch. Other IBM products provide alternatives to keyboard entry. AID + ME plugs into the keyboard and serial ports of the computer, allowing the computer to be controlled by membrane keyboard, joystick, scanner, switches, or Morse code or a serial communication aid. An on-board speech synthesizer enables blind persons to convert text to speech by character, word, or phrase. AID + ME also allows the user to simplify data entry by assigning multiple keystrokes to a single key or redefine key locations on the keyboard and offers support for mouse emulation.

Graphics. NOMAD (American Printing House for the Blind) is a device that makes tactile graphics talk by using as a work surface a high-resolution touch-sensitive pad with 9,600 individual points that can be programmed with speech. NOMAD connects via a serial port to any IBM or compatible desktop or laptop computer running MS-DOS.

Berkeley Systems' outSpoken (available from Apple Computer) is a talking interface for a graphics-based computer. The software makes the Macintosh completely accessible by replacing visual icons with spoken words. The user can select a folder, and the system reads its name aloud. He or she can open a document and hear it spoken aloud by letter, word, or line or pull down a menu and hear a list of commands. Full mouse emulation is provided via keypad functions, and single-stroke commands permit movement among windows; speed, pitch, and volume control; and reference to a talking text and graphics dictionary. The system works with any text-based Macintosh software, including word processing, desktop publishing, spreadsheet, database, and telecommunications programs. It comes with full documentation in print and cassette formats, plus tactile sheets representing typical Macintosh screens. A braille manual is available without charge. It requires a Macintosh Plus or newer computer.

Recent developments include devices that make graphical user interface (GUI) systems accessible to people who are blind or visually impaired. GUI software written for such operating systems as the Apple, Macintosh, MicroSoft's Windows, and IBM's OS/2 uses pictures (drawings, graphics, or window-type frames) or information that is drawn on the screen to provide information to the user. The systems allow several files to be open at the same time, on what is called the "desktop," so that the user can move and interact with any of the files.

Speech Synthesizers. One of the most significant technological advancements is the development of print-to-voice devices—machines that can read printed text and translate the information into voice using a speech synthesizer. Although the quality of the voice is rather artificial, it does permit people with visual impairments to access books, manuals, and journals that formerly would have to be converted to braille.

Speech synthesizers convert various types of text signals, such as keyboard, scanner, and switch input, into speech. Most synthesizers provide inflection, tonal quality, and variable pitch, and many can be customized for special acronyms, words, and trade terms. Examples are Accent (AICOM Corporation), Apollo Speech Synthesizer (EVAS), Audapter Speech System (Personal Data Systems), Braille 'n Speak (Blazie Engineering), CallText 5050 (Centigram Communications Corporation), DECtalk (Digital Equipment Corporation), Personal Speech System (PSS) (Vysion), Prose 2020 (Centigram Communications Corp.), and Type 'N Talk (Vysion). All of these systems support the IBM Screen Reader.

IBM's Screen Reader/2 for OS/2 software converts screen information to speech, thereby making IBM's GUI accessible to persons who are blind. Among its feature are voice output of all OS/2P screen information; autospeak, which allows visual focus and reads screen menus automatically; and the ability to recognize and verbalize objects or icons on the screen and to emulate mouse functions such as pointing and clicking. A dedicated 18-key keypad controls Screen Reader functions. This software runs on any system that can run OS/2 with 2 MB available fixed disk space, plus any supported text-to-speech synthesizer and one serial port. It is available from IBM's Independent Series Information Hotline.

Slimware Window Bridge (available from Syntha-Voice Computers) is a memory-resident screen review program for IBM and compatibles that allows a speech synthesizer or braille display to provide users who are blind access to both Microsoft Windows and DOS using integrated software strategies. The system automatically identifies important information within Windows, such as window title, menu selections, and command buttons. Within Windows applications, the user can choose to navigate the mouse, automatically identifying each item of information as he or she moves, and hear the mouse pointer move on the screen. The user can also control the mouse pointer using the keyboard and achieve the same functions as using the mouse. He or she can identify the font, style, point size, screen attributes, and screen colors of the text through synthetic speech or braille output.

outSpoken 1.7 (available from Berkeley Systems) is an upgrade of the speech access program for Apple Macintosh computers. It uses the Mac's built-in speech synthesizer and features System 7 compatibility, easy-to-access commands, flexible screen review, full mouse emulation, full access to the GUI, and compatibility with standard application programs. It requires Macintosh Plus or better.

Audicon (Visuaide 2000) is an interface system that allows direct manipulation of the objects on an electronic desktop, uses sound icons instead of graphical icons, and permits multimodal access to both audio and tactile information. It consists of a graphics tablet, a sound card, and a speech synthesizer and/or braille display. The contents of the screen are projected onto the horizontal plan of a tablet, which provides guidemarks by means of grids that can be felt with the fingers. To explore screen contents, the user moves the mouse on the tablet, thus giving him or her a good idea of the position of the cursor on the screen. Graphical data are provided in the form of sounds, which represent the objects or events on the screen. Text information on the screen can be read in voice synthesis or braille.

Other devices include the Echo II with TEXTALKER Speech Processor hardware and software (available from American Printing House for the Blind, APHB). This system allows Apple II+ or Apple //e computers with at least 64K memory for DOS 3.3, and 128K memory for ProDOS software to talk, give oral instructions, and provide reinforcement. APHB has released the next generation of TEXTALKER screen access software, Textalker-gs, designed specifically for use on the Apple IIGS computer. Textalker-gs remains in the background, permitting voice access to hundreds of Apple programs, including public domain, noncopy-protected, and many copy-protected programs. The program requires an Apple IIGS computer with at least 512 of RAM, a 3.5-inch disk drive, and an Echo speech synthesizer. APHB also offers the Echo Commander speech synthesizer, which is compatible with the Apple II+, //e, and IIGS computers.

Speaqualizer (available from APHB) is a completely hardware-based speech access system for IBM PCs and compatibles. It enables the user to hear data from any text-based off-the-shelf software. The device requires IBM PC, XT, AT, or compatible with 13-inch slots.

The Braille 'n Speak system (Blazie Engineering) is a compact talking braille note taker with many capabilities. It uses a simple command structure that is easy to learn and remember. Braille 'n Speak is offered in two packages. The Snap-Pac includes the Braille 'n Speak with calculator, carrying case, and interface kit that can be used as a print-to-braille transcriber, note organizer, talking braille notebook with 200K memory, talking computer terminal, battery-powered speech synthesizer, and portable word processor. The Braille 'n Speak 640 has all of the features of the Braille 'n Speak Snap Pac, 640K of file memory, and 256K of program memory.

Special Techniques

There are several other techniques that can be used to help persons who are blind or have vision impairments to access information. Some of the most useful are audiodescription, filing strategies, and tactile labeling.

Audiodescription

Audiodescription is the art of describing in words for visually impaired viewers the visual aspects and physical action seen in presentations such as live theater, television, films, videos, and museum exhibits.

Filing and Retrieving Information[12]

It is important for workers and trainees with low vision to have a way of filing and retrieving information. Filing systems can be set up using one or a combination of the following options:

1. Large print — Print with a dark pen on a card and file under the appropriate raised or printed letter index divider.

2. Tape recorder — Record each line of keys and their markings, reading from left to right. Refer to the bottom line, which includes the SPACE BAR, as line one. (See item 7.)

3. Closed circuit TV — To enlarge print or hand written material up to 60 times. The CCTV could double as the computer monitor.

4. Raised letter index — To create an audible file system using Talk/cards. These raised letter index dividers are available from Maxi Aids (1-800-522-6294).

5. VOXCOM (Card Recorder/Player) — To record information on Talk/cards to be filed under raised letters, Brailled, or large print index dividers. Talk/tags, Raised Letter Index Dividers, and Raised Print Labeler available from Maxi/Aids (800/522-6394).

6. Braille — Information can be Brailled on a card and filed. Braille characters can be placed upside down on the backs of index dividers.

7. Voice indexing — To file voice indexed information on a tape recorder, simultaneously depress RECORD and FAST FORWARD and record the name of the subject. Depress STOP, and then RECORD the material at regular speed. To retrieve

subject titles, simultaneously depress PLAY and FAST FORWARD. Depress STOP after you hear the title you want, then PLAY at normal speed to hear the material.

Tactile Methods of Labeling[13]

Tactile labels can be made using the 3M EA200 Raised Letter Labeler, which produces raised ½-inch capital letters on ¾-inch "peel-off" tape. Labels can be made reusable by clicking the Labeler once to leave space for a rubber band to be inserted. They can be used in the classroom, office, shop, or home to label audio- and videocassettes, computer disks, and CD-ROM discs, as well as on files and index dividers, file boxes, food, medicines, and the like. Raised letters is a tactile method of labeling and is not intended as a method of reading.

When learning the feeling of raised letters, it is vital that the trainee be made aware of the differences in the formation of each letter. Some may be able to do this immediately, but others may need help. If a trainee is having difficulty, have him or her visualize each letter as the formation is being taught: the letter A, two slanted lines, open at the bottom, pointed at the top, with a line across the middle; the letter B, a straight line on the left with two half circles attached; C, a circle with the center portion of the right side open; D, a straight line on the left and a half circle attached on the right half; and so on.

Color-coded labels can be used on clothing, fabrics, thread, paper supplies, and other materials, and objects. To make labels to denote color, use the first and last letters of the color unless to do so would be confusing. Use "BU" for blue and "BG" for beige. When one letter is enough, use only one, for example, "Y" for yellow. Although "R" could mean red, it could also mean rust or raspberry, so use the first and last letters.

Summary

Visual impairments take many forms and are due to many causes. Their severity ranges from minimal loss of vision to total blindness. The most common forms are diabetic retinopathy, retinitis pigmentosa, macula degeneration, and glaucoma. Despite the difficulties involved, persons with visual impairments can be trained for many jobs, ranging from assembly line worker, through clerical and administrative positions, to technical, managerial, and professional posts. Training for these jobs and actual job performance are made possible through accommodations and/or assistive equipment, devices, and materials.

For Further Reading and Viewing*

ADA Customer Courtesies. 1993. 20-minute video. Available from United Training Media.

ADA for Retail. 1993. 12-minute video. Available from United Training Media.

Alonso, Lou. *Student Teaching Guide for Blind and Visually Impaired University Students: Adapted Methods and Procedures.* New York: American Foundation for the Blind, 1987.

The Americans with Disabilities Act: Impact on Training. INFO-LINE 9203. Alexandria, Va.: American Society for Training and Development, March 1993.

The Americans with Disabilities Act: Techniques for Accommodation. INFO-LINE 9204. Alexandria, Va.: American Society for Training and Development, April 1992.

A Picture Is Worth a Thousand Words for Blind and Visually Impaired Persons Too! An Introduction to Audiodescription. New York: American Foundation for the Blind, 1991.

As a Blind Person. 1991. 29-minute video. Available from American Foundation for the Blind.

Assistive Technology Sourcebook. Washington, D.C.: RESNA Press, 1990.

Blind Enough to See. 1993. 25-minute video. Available from Video Publishing House.

Dickman, Irving. *Making Life More Livable.* New York: American Foundation for the Blind, 1983.

Edman, Polly K. *Tactile Graphics.* New York: American Foundation for the Blind, 1992.

Employed Ability: Blind Persons on the Job. 1991. 14-minute video. Available from American Foundation for the Blind.

Finkelstein, Daniel, with the National Federation of the Blind. *Blindness and Disorders of the Eye.* Baltimore: NFB, 1989.

Frank, Mildred. *Seeing with the Brain.* Rev. ed. Daytona Beach, Fla.: Mildred Frank, 1991.

Goldberg, Marge, Paula F. Goldberg, and Cathleen Urbain. *Opportunity Knocking: The Story of Supported Employment.* Minneapolis: PACER Center, 1988.

Griffin-Shirley, Nora, and Gerda Groff. *Prescriptions for Independence.* New York: American Federation for the Blind, 1993.

Jernigan, Kenneth (ed.). *What You Should Know about Blindness, Services for the Blind, and the Organized Blind Movement.* Baltimore: National Federation of the Blind, 1992.

Longuil, Carolyn. *Oh, I See!* 1993. 7-minute video. Available from American Foundation for the Blind.

No Two Alike. 1991. 19-minute video. Available from American Foundation for the Blind.

Orr, Alberta L. (ed.). *Vision and Aging: Crossroads for Service Delivery.* New York: American Foundation for the Blind, 1992.

*Full addresses of the organizations in this listing appear in Appendixes B and C.

Participants with Disabilities: How to Address Their Needs. INFO-LINE 8704. Alexandria, Va.: American Society for Training and Development, April 1987.

Sauerburger, Dona. *Independence without Sight or Sound: Suggestions for Practitioners Working with Deaf-Blind Adults.* Brooklyn, N.Y.: American Foundation for the Blind, 1993.

The Seven Minute Lesson. 1993. 7-minute video. Available from American Foundation for the Blind.

Urbain, Cathleen. *Supported Employment: A Step-by-Step Guide.* Minneapolis: PACER Center, 1992.

Work Sight. 1992. 28:07-minute video. Available from Braille Institute of America.

Notes

1. Daniel Finkelstein, *Blindness and Disorders of the Eye* (Baltimore: National Federation of the Blind, 1989).
2. Kenneth Jernigan, "A Definition of Blindness," in Kenneth Jernigan (ed.), *What You Should Know about Blindness, Services for the Blind, and the Organized Blind Movement* (Baltimore: National Federation of the Blind, 1992), pp. 11, 15.
3. Excerpted from *Diabetic Retinopathy.* © 1993, American Academy of Ophthalmology, P.O. Box 7424, San Francisco, CA 94120-7424. Reprinted with permission.
4. Finklestein, *Blindness*, p. 35.
5. Ibid., pp. 39–40.
6. Excerpted from *Macular Degeneration.* © 1993 American Academy of Ophthalmology, P.O. Box 7424, San Francisco, CA 94120. Reprinted with permission.
7. Finkelstein, *Blindness*, pp. 27–28.
8. Excerpted from *Cataract.* © 1993 American Academy of Ophthalmology, P.O. Box 7424, San Francisco, CA 94120. Reprinted with permission.
9. Excerpted from *Detached and Torn Retina.* © 1993 American Academy of Ophthalmology, P.O. Box 7424, San Francisco, CA 94120. Reprinted with permission.
10. "Blind Persons at Work," *Fact Sheet* (Baltimore: National Federation of the Blind/JOB Program, 1800 Johnson Street, Baltimore, MD 21230, n.d.).
11. People with usable vision should use that capability when possible. Some may even resist approaches that are nonvisual.
12. Mildred Frank, *Methods of Filing and Retrieving Information*, 2828 North Atlantic Ave., Daytona Beach, FL 32118-3001, September 1993. Available from Council of Citizens with Low Vision, Inc. (800) 733-2258. Used by permission.
13. Adapted from Mildred Frank, *Teaching Audible and Tactile Methods of Labeling*, September 1993. Available from Council of Citizens with Low Vision, Inc. (800) 733-2258. Used by permission.

7

Hearing Disabilities

Malcolm became hard of hearing while in college due to conductive hearing loss caused by frequent ear infections. For a few years he was helped by a hearing aid, but he was totally deaf when he graduated with a B.S. in education with specialization in industrial arts. Instead of entering the teaching profession, Malcolm chose to make a career in building construction. Hired as an assistant to a project manager, he rapidly became a skilled planner.

When he lost his hearing, Malcolm faced a critical adjustment. He was uncertain that he could work in his chosen profession because it demanded frequent oral communication with architects, construction managers and supervisors, and clients. He was apprehensive about his acceptance by hearing colleagues and clients. And he also wondered what adjustments and accommodations he would need to continue in the job and progress to higher-level positions.

Although the hearing loss was traumatic, having the benefit of a formal education and day-to-day exposure to spoken language, Malcolm was fluent in English and could choose from various communication strategies that enabled him to use his language skills to best advantage—"reading" gestures and visual cues, and positioning himself so that he could see a person's facial expressions and lip movements.

Within two years of his total hearing loss, Malcolm was promoted to the position of construction project manager. He succeeded because he had perseverance, skills, and intelligence. But his success was also attributable in part to his immediate boss, who had the sensitivity and understanding to make communication adjustments and workplace accommodations that met Malcolm's special needs.

Although some people have profound hearing loss and are effectively totally deaf, many people with hearing disabilities have residual hearing that enables them to engage in some activities involving the sense of hearing. They are described as hard of hearing. Most people who live long enough will have some hearing loss. Unfortunately, people of all ages who are hard of hearing try to rely on their partial hearing in situations where alternative techniques or devices, such as the use of hearing aids, would be more effective and efficient. Many apparently feel that hearing aids stigmatize them, so they penalize themselves needlessly.

Far too many people have adopted a stereotype about deafness and hearing loss and the learning and working capabilities of a deaf individual. They believe that hearing loss diminishes learning ability or makes a person less capable of workplace performance than those who do not have hearing impairments. Of course, the brain and nervous system rely heavily on and assimilate auditory information by the auditory sense, but hearing is only one of the brain's sources of information. When used to the maximum, the remaining senses can compensate for hearing disabilities. Trainers, managers, and supervisors must remember that given proper training and opportunity, the average deaf person can perform most jobs in the typical place of business—and do it as well as or better than his or her hearing peers.

Types of Hearing Impairments

"Hearing impairment" is the general term used to describe all types and degrees of hearing loss, including nerve deafness and conductive hearing loss, and from mild to profound reductions in hearing ability. Thus it describes people who have no hearing at all and those who have sufficient hearing loss to place limitations of varying severity on their participation in social or occupational activities. The National Information Center on Deafness identifies five degrees of hearing loss. These degrees and their effects on functional hearing are shown in Figure 7-1.

Hearing loss is the most prevalent physical disability. About 24 million Americans have significant hearing impairment, and nearly 10 million are in the workforce. The causes of hearing loss range from congenital conditions to noise exposure, accidents and injuries, and disease. Although the great majority of people with hearing impairment can benefit from medical, surgical, and hearing aid assistance or through rehabilitation, many have not obtained help. There are two types of hearing loss: nerve deafness (sensorineural hearing loss) and conductive hearing loss.

Figure 7-1. Degrees and functional effects of hearing loss.

Degree of Hearing Loss (in decibels, dB)	Functional Hearing
Normal hearing (10–25 dB)	No significant difficulty
Mild (26–40 dB)	Loss may or may not be noticed by the individual; difficulty hearing faint or distant speech; can usually use the phone without difficulty
Moderate (41–55 dB)	Generally understands conversational speech if less than 5 feet away from speaker; can usually use the phone with minor adjustments
Moderately severe (56–70 dB)	Sounds must be loud and near to be heard; can use the phone with some hearing people
Severe (71–90 dB)	Shouting will not be heard; speech cannot be learned through conversation; cannot hear avoices well enough to understand spoken telephone conversations
Profound (91 dB and above)	Cannot hear sounds; may perceive sounds as vibration

These descriptions relate to the individual's degree of hearing without amplification and in a quiet environment. Noise, distance, and acoustics among other things influence an individual's ability to function in any given situation.

Source: Adapted from Eugene C. Mindel and McCay Vernon, *They Grow in Silence: The Deaf Child and His Family.* Silver Spring, Md.: National Association of the Deaf, 1971. Used by permission.

Nerve Deafness[1]

Nerve deafness, an abnormality of the inner ear, the auditory nerve, or both, is the more common hearing disability. It has many causes, but the two most common are the aging process and sudden or extended exposure to loud noise, such as noise in the work environment, motorized tools (lawn mowers and power saws), loud music, and certain hobbies (guns, hot rods, outboard motors, and so on).

Conductive Hearing Loss[2]

Conductive hearing loss, the less common cause, affects the outer or middle ear and results when sound waves are not properly conducted to the inner ear. Its causes include ear infections, immobilization of one of the bones in the middle ear, a punctured eardrum, or excessive ear wax. Nerve deafness can sometimes be medically or surgically treated, but most nerve disorders, provided that there is some residual hearing, can be helped by a hearing aid. Conductive hearing problems can often be medically or surgically corrected; most can be helped by a hearing aid.

Practitioners and Specialists

Audiologists are hearing care professionals who specialize in prevention, identification, and assessment of hearing disorders and provide treatment and rehabilitative services. Practitioners test and diagnose hearing disorders, prescribe and dispense hearing aids and assistive listening devices, instruct people in their use, develop and implement hearing conservation programs, provide aural rehabilitation services such as auditory training, speechreading, and sign language instruction, and conduct research into environmental influences on hearing, new testing methods, and new rehabilitative devices such as cochlear implants.

The Deaf Community

There are two contrasting views of the deaf community.[3] Its clinical-pathological (outsiders' view) definitions focus on the behavior and values of the hearing community as the norm and then place emphasis on how deaf people deviate from that norm. One such definition refers to an audiologically defined group of persons whose hearing loss interferes with but does not preclude the normal reception of speech. Another characterizes the deaf community as a group of hearing-impaired persons who have learning and psychological problems due to their hearing loss and communication difficulties.

The cultural view (insiders' perception) of the deaf community focuses on the language, experiences, and values of a group of people who happen to be deaf. One such definition describes the community as a group of persons who share a common means of communication (signing) that provides a basis for group cohesion and identity. Not all individuals who are deaf or hard of hearing are members of the deaf community. Some choose to function within the hearing community and do not become involved in matters affecting the deaf community.

Employment of Deaf People

People with hearing disabilities work in the same types of jobs as other nondisabled people. They are employed by private and public businesses and industries, federal, state, and local government, and public and private educational agencies and institutions. Some work for their families and others are self-employed. Some deaf people are professionals; some are technical workers; others work as skilled workers and craftspersons; and still others work in manual jobs. Although improved educational opportunities, antidiscrimination laws, increased awareness of hearing loss by the general public, and a more vocal and assertive deaf community have opened more employment doors, deaf people as a group remained underemployed.

The Career Information Registry of Hearing Impaired People in Professional, Technical, and Managerial Occupations provides a base of information on hearing-impaired persons that identifies their jobs, their employers, and the education and training that prepared them for these jobs.[4] Between December 1985 and December 1986, surveys were sent to potential registrants in California, Georgia, Illinois, Massachusetts, and the District of Columbia, areas having high concentrations of persons with hearing impairments. Registration was open to retired and currently employed individuals whose last jobs were in professional, technical, or managerial occupations and to students in the last year of an associate's or bachelor's degree program or enrolled in a graduate school. Of the approximately 5,000 forms sent, 590 were completed and returned, and 475 were eligible for inclusion in the registry. Each registrant provided information about his or her educational background, current job title, age at onset and degree of hearing loss, areas of expertise and consulting interests, particular problems faced on the job because of hearing loss, and the attempts made by the registrant to resolve these problems. Figure 7-2 shows the types of employment-related problems reported by respondents and attempted solutions.

People with hearing impairments do not usually require special equipment to perform job tasks. One-on-one communication with other workers and with supervisors presents the main obstacle, and group meetings can also constitute a major challenge. These problems are overcome by such means as speech, speech reading, writing, gestures, signs, or a combination of these means. Other means include telecommunications devices for deaf persons, interpreters (sign language or speech reading), and telephone relay services. Many individuals with hearing loss use currently available equipment and their own personal strategies and devices to ensure that they are properly equipped to do a job (e.g., E-mail and other communication software).

Forms of Communication

There are many different ways for people who are deaf and hearing people to communicate successfully with each other.

Figure 7-2. Types of employment-related problems and attempted resolutions.

Types of Problems

    Communication problem using telephone
    Communication problem with colleagues/coworker
    Communication during meetings
    Communication problem with supervisor
    Communication problem in educational setting
    Written communication problems
    Communication problem speech reading
    Insufficient education/training for advancement or securing desired position
    Restricted advancement due to communication problems
    Permitted to advance to managerial level but no further
    Employer misconceptions regarding degree of handicapping condition
    Employer misconceptions regarding skills possessed
    Limited options regarding education programs accessible to hearing-impaired persons (support services, interpreters, loop systems, etc.)
    Limited options regarding career choice
    Lack of colleague acceptance
    Medical or health problem
    Possess another handicapping condition
    Possess a primary handicapping condition other than hearing impairment
    Personal acceptance of hearing loss
    Problems due to unavailability or high cost of interpreters
    Subjected to discrimination
    Lack of funds for necessary aids
    Frustration, fatigue, and stress due to straining to hear
    No problem listed/uncodable

Solutions Attempted by Registrants

    A continuing problem, no solution evident for duration of employment/schooling
    Left school or job because of problem
    Sought legal aid
    Self-education, studied on own to keep up
    Learned new or improved skills
    Tried to effect change as much as system would allow
    Accepted situation, no change attempted
    Obtained assistive device(s) or personnel
    Retired early because of hearing loss
    Depend on hearing colleagues to answer telephones, attend meetings, take notes, etc.
    No solution offered
    Dogged persistence
    Personally accepted hearing loss and learned to cope with [lack of] self-confidence
    Changed employment to find more accepting environment

Source: Adapted from National Information Center on Deafness, *1986–87 Directory of Career Information Registry of Hearing Impaired Persons in Professional, Technical, and Managerial Occupations.* Washington, D.C.: Gallaudet University, 1987, p. 78. Used by permission.

Functional Language

Functional language is communication that permits interaction between two people, one or both of whom have underdeveloped hearing and/or speech abilities. For example, a trainer may communicate with a deaf trainee by pointing with his or her finger, with or without words. The listener will indicate understanding by nodding or pointing to a particular object or graphic. Functional language also means that words that are to be used are words that the trainee will need in interactions with others at work or socially (e.g., "man," "woman," "boss," "time," "stop," "start," "water," "break," "machine").

Manding

Manding (sometimes called mand modeling) is a method of interaction between a nondisabled person and an individual with a hearing or speech impairment. Manding demands a verbal or other response from the individual with the disability. The trainer or supervisor may say to the trainee, "Tell me what you need," or "Tell me what you would like." Manding is especially useful when a trainee is being taught to complete a sequence of steps in a job task. Because people with disabilities often forget the correct sequence of steps, the trainer may demand the correct response by saying, "Show me what to do next." If name labels for various tools are being taught, the instructor may say, "Jim, point to the hammer."

Delay Procedure

With this approach, the nondisabled person or trainer stands at least 3 feet from the worker or trainee and waits at least 5 seconds following a question, direction, or request to see whether the individual will give the appropriate response. If the person does not respond within the time allowed, the supervisor or instructor then models or provides the correct response. It is important that the supervisor or trainer not rush to provide the response. Learning will take place only if the worker or trainee is given enough time to formulate the correct response.

Aural Communication

Learning to speak without hearing is a formidable task. Deaf children do not hear people talking around them as hearing children do, so they have no stimulus for speech. Most deaf children receive speech therapy and speech-reading training from the time their deafness is diagnosed until they are young adults.

Good speech should not be equated with good hearing. It could mean that the deaf person learned to speak before losing hearing or was able to benefit more than most other people by early training. So although some deaf people learn to speak clearly, most never acquire speech that sounds natural. For that reason, some deaf persons are reluctant to use their voices. They may have been ridiculed by hearing peers while growing up or have too often been misunderstood. Other deaf persons may have developed understandable speech but are poor speech readers and are unwilling to give people the impression that they can speech read.

Visual Communication

Among the means of communicating visually are several types of sign language, gestural systems, and speech reading.

Sign Language.[5] Signing is the use of hand signals to communicate. It is not unique to deaf people; it has been a part of many human cultures for hundreds, if not thousands, of years.

American Sign Language (ASL), sometimes called Ameslan, is the language of the culturally deaf. It is not English; rather, it is a language in itself, with its own grammar and structure. It combines the use of space, hand shapes, arms, movements, finger spelling, facial expressions, eyes, head, body posture, and body movements. These shapes and movements serve as the words and intonation of the language. Some users add lip movements and/or vocalization; some don't. ASL has dialects, depending on geographical location and, in some cases, ethnicity, race, sex, and age. It is not a universal language, although it is used by about 500,000 Americans and Canadians. Very few hearing people know ASL.

Contact signing—*Pidgin Sign English* (PSE) and *Signed Essential English* (SEE)—are systems that represent the English language using the hands, facial expressions, body movements, and finger spelling. They blend the features of ASL and English. They are not a language like ASL but a visual depiction of English. The number of signs is infinite, and the rules are variable, depending on the signer's skills, the situation, the topic, and so on. Users of these systems vary in how much lip movement and vocalization they add to their signed "English." Some forms express English verbatim, including verb endings. Others use signs that are more conceptual rather than word for word and borrow ASL expressions. Pidgin Sign English is used by deaf and hearing people to communicate with each other, so the vast majority of hearing people who work with deaf people use it.

Manually Coded English (MCE) encompasses several systems invented to use signs for coding English. The best known of these systems are *Seeing Essential English, Signing Exact English,* and *Linguistics of Visual English.* The developers of these three visual-gestural codes worked together to develop guidelines and principles for inventing new signs or changing existing ASL signs to represent English words. These are not separate languages; they all attempt to represent manually the vocabulary and structure of the English language. Signed codes, however, cannot express aspects of the structure and forms of spoken language, nor can many of the forms and structures be vocalized.

Manual English, sometimes called "total communication," is a technique in which the trainer orally repeats a word as its sign is modeled for the learner. The modeling is accompanied by appropriate gestures, body movements, and facial expressions. This is the type of signing that is used by people who are deaf or partially deaf but whose vocal mechanisms are intact. Manual English may be used with trainees who have poor articulation, speech intelligibility problems, minimum vocabulary, more receptive than expressive ability, or inhibiting emotional problems.

Cued speech uses eight hand shapes and four hand positions in various combinations to display voice sounds rather than words (sounds or phonemes). The system offers the closest parallel to spoken language because it shows what we actually hear (phonetics) rather than words. It can even show accents and the vocal sounds of many languages other than English, but it does not enjoy the popularity of American Sign Language or Pidgin Sign English.

Other Gestural Systems. Pointing and natural gestures can be used with considerable success in the work environment with trainees who are deaf (or have mental retardation). No equipment or materials are needed, and they are easily learned and readily interpreted by anyone. For example, a worker who needs help could request it by making a lifting motion with both hands; one who needs a break could indicate it by symbolically wiping perspiration from his or her forehead.

In recent years, an interesting attempt has been made to create a universal system of gesturing called Gesticula. This effort is similar to the one that created Esperanto as an international vocal language. Gesticula, however, has been slow to catch on; most deaf people prefer to communicate in their own country's sign language. However, Gesticula can be seen at world conferences involving deaf people, along with an array of other sign languages.

Speech Reading. Formerly called lipreading, speech reading is a means of receiving communication. Some sounds can be interpreted by watching a person's lips; others cannot. In fact, only about 30 percent of spoken English is visible on the lips, and even the best speech readers often guess. Comprehension of what a person is saying is often dependent not only on reading the lips but on interpreting facial expressions and gestures. For that reason, the term "speech reading" is used, implying that a speaker's articulation of his or her communication is read, not just the lips.

It is important for trainers and supervisors of people with hearing impairments to realize that speech reading is usually unreliable because only 30 percent of the English language is distinguishable by observing the movement of the lips. Successful speech reading depends on the speaker, the context, the environment, the number of people involved, the abilities of the speech reader, and whether that alternative is used in conjunction with other communication modes.

Interpreters. An interpreter may be needed when conducting training, orientation, meetings, and interviews. The interpreter should be a professional who subscribes to an ethical code, can clearly sign the communication, and accurately uses spoken English to convey the communication the deaf person is signing. An organization seeking to hire an interpreter must describe the interpreting situation and the communication preference of the deaf person. If the meeting or presentation will take longer than 1½ hours, two interpreters are needed to work on an alternating basis, unless 10- to 15-minute breaks are scheduled every hour. Brief the interpreter about the session and provide written materials to supplement the briefing. The following guidelines are helpful when working with interpreters:

- Arrange seating so the deaf person can see both the presenter and the interpreter.
- Avoid placing anyone in positions with back lighting.
- Always speak directly to the deaf person rather than to the interpreter.
- Avoid private conversations within earshot of the interpreter; interpreters will sign everything they hear.
- If the interpreter is voicing for a deaf person, remember that the thoughts expressed are the deaf person's, and your responses should be addressed to him or her.
- Avoid asking the interpreter to engage in private conversation. It is unethical for him or her to do so.
- In meetings, ensure that only one person speaks at a time.

General Approaches to Training

Trainers and supervisors who work with adults who are deaf or have hearing impairments must never assume that they know what their employees want or need in the way of accommodations. People who are deaf or hard of hearing are as varied as hearing people in terms of skills, aptitudes, language competency, personality, confidence, and assertiveness. Not only does deafness involve a wide range of hearing loss, but it also encompasses a great variation in intellectual abilities. Trainers, supervisors, and coworkers must never equate hearing loss with speaking ability; one is not necessarily a predictor of the other.

The most challenging problem that faces those responsible for training and developing adults with hearing impairments is communication. They must be able to identify the employee's preferred mode of communication and do what they can to accommodate that preference. When a deaf person prefers an interpreter but that choice is not possible, other agreed-upon systems, such as E-mail, written notes, computer-assisted note-taking technology, and TDDs, must be employed.

Essential Conditions

The conditions described in Chapter 6 as essential to the classroom, shop, laboratory, and worksite training of people with vision impairments apply as well to people with hearing impairments. Nonhearing-impaired workers must be prepared to work with employees who are hard of hearing. They must be sensitive to deaf persons' special communication needs and be prepared to make simple adjustments that will make it easier for them to be productive. Words and sounds are not the only way to pass on information. With persons who are deaf or hard of hearing, trainers need to focus on other means of communication. To do that requires learning the full spectrum of communication—to learn to "talk" in other ways.

The Trainer

To be successful in working with people who have hearing impairments, trainers must have a positive attitude and be patient, open-minded, and flexible. They must be willing to learn a variety of methods of communicating and have the ability to rephrase, use body and facial language effectively, demonstrate rather than explain, and communicate clearly without using jargon, slang, or obscure idioms.

Trainers must be aware of communication alternatives, familiar with the deaf community, deafness, and deaf culture, know about community resources including interpreter services, and employ effective communication, interpersonal, supervisory, and training skills. They should know about available communication technology, such as TDDs, phone relay services, computer systems, and terminology related to hearing loss. Knowledge and skills can be acquired by attending workshops and using materials available from various organizations (see Appendix B).

Trainers must also show a willingness to learn and use sign language; to communicate and initiate communication with deaf and hard-of-hearing trainees often; provide appropriate, challenging tasks and numerous opportunities to learn; and provide unfailing understanding, empathy, support, guidance, and assistance to trainees.

Specific Techniques for Training

Following are some specific suggestions for trainers and supervisors who work with trainees and workers who are deaf or hard of hearing.

Orientation

- Use an interpreter to save time.
- Orient trainees face-to-face, and supplement communication with materials in written form for future reference.
- Have trainees wear name tags at least for the first few days of training.
- Prepare and distribute a seating plan.
- Draw and distribute a map showing the location of rest rooms, offices, snack bar, and other key places trainees will need to go.
- Provide a brief tour of facilities.
- Discuss emergency procedures for fires or other potentially dangerous situations.
- Instruct the trainees on the use of special equipment, emphasizing safety precautions as appropriate.
- Thoroughly explain requirements and standards of performance, including protocol, procedures, and break periods, as well as curriculum and study criteria and specifications.
- Discuss how you will communicate with deaf or hard-of-hearing persons (in writing, through speech and speech reading, through signs and gestures, or by using a combination of methods).
- Ask the deaf person to teach you some basic signs—phrases, terms, and expressions that are used frequently.

Conducting Training

- Whenever possible, choose a quiet environment for communicating.
- To get a deaf person's attention, wave your hand or arm, use physical contact (e.g., gently touch the person's hand or shoulder), or use other means (e.g., rapping on the table or desk, flashing the room lights, stomping on the floor).
- Use facial expressions and gestures to provide major clues to meaning.
- Face the person directly in good light so that your lips can be seen. Speak clearly with normal volume without overexaggerating lip movements and maintain eye contact.
- Keep hands and objects away from your mouth, and trim mustaches and beards away from the mouth.
- Speak slowly, and avoid shouting or exaggerated lip movements.
- Use simple words unless you're certain that the individual will understand.
- Use gestures to help understanding and communication.
- Include visual cues and written reinforcement in conversations.
- Alert the individual to changes in the subject.
- Ask the individual to repeat key points made in a conversation or presentation to ensure that the full message was received.
- When communication is difficult, use written notes.
- Use pictures, drawings, diagrams, blueprints, objects, and the like to make communication clearer.
- Determine the writing abilities of deaf and hard-of-hearing trainees by asking and by reviewing written products.
- Put as much of the presentation in writing as you can ahead of time. Prepare lists, phrases, and notes to speed up communication and aid clarity.
- When writing to a deaf or hard-of-hearing person, avoid using long sentences with complicated structure. Use short, simple sentences.
- Supplement written materials with pictures, drawings, or diagrams.
- When communicating with a hard-of-hearing person by telephone, use short messages and speak slowly and distinctly.
- If interaction among trainees is an important part of the learning strategy, engage an interpreter (unless the trainee says that one is not needed).
- Check on understanding by asking questions that require descriptive answers. Avoid asking questions such as ''Do you under-

stand?" Head nodding does not necessarily mean that the individual has understood.

- Rephrase questions or comments when the trainee does not understand rather than simply repeating the communication.

Meetings and Conferences

- Arrange seating so that persons with hearing impairments can see all members.
- Reduce background noise, if possible.
- Use a well-lighted room so participants' faces will be clearly visible.
- Avoid backlighting and visual distractions or obstructions.
- When possible, provide an agenda and handouts in advance of meetings.
- Present new vocabulary in writing and in advance so that speech reading will be enhanced.
- Use visual aids as much as possible, such as handouts, flipcharts, overhead projectors, and demonstrations.
- Have someone take notes so that persons with hearing disabilities can follow the discussion, respond to questions, and know when topics change.
- Speak the individual's name when you want to get his or her attention.
- Require participants to raise their hands and be recognized before speaking.
- Insist that presenters face the group whenever they speak, even when using an overhead projection, and avoid pacing.
- Give deaf and hard-of-hearing trainees regular opportunities to speak.
- Be alert for nonparticipating trainees. They may be having difficulty keeping up with the presentation.
- Always repeat questions and trainee responses for persons with hearing impairments.
- Make full use of short, simple, clearly written acronym-, jargon-, abbreviation-free, and well-illustrated printed or duplicated materials.
- Provide note takers (so that trainees with hearing impairments can watch without losing track of the presentation). Edit the notes, and then print and distribute them to deaf trainees.
- Position note takers next to deaf trainees so that they can keep up with details.
- Train note takers to record major points, key vocabulary, assign-

ments, and the like rather than attempting to take down everything word for word.

- When printed materials are used as in-class references, allow enough time for deaf persons to read them and look up before continuing the meeting.
- Review key points and decisions individually after the meeting.
- Use captioned versions of commercially available training films and videos whenever available. If locally produced, use a character generator to caption them. If materials are produced on contract, have them captioned.
- For other types of visuals, provide scripts for participants with hearing impairments.
- Consider providing written materials, assistive listening devices and systems, computer-assisted note-taking systems, and video-text displays.
- Consider providing professional interpreters—"signers" who use sign language and oral interpreters, who interpret and repeat messages using speech for the deaf person to speech read.

Evaluation

- Provide regular feedback on performance. Never let mistakes go unexplained. Place feedback close to the action.
- Be particularly direct with deaf and hard-of-hearing trainees; innuendo, sarcasm, and tone of voice are ineffective. Use constructive criticism as well as praise.
- When mistakes are made, try to inform the deaf or hard-of-hearing trainee before others become aware of the problem to avoid embarrassing him or her.
- Be sure that your facial expression matches your oral or gestural message to avoid confusing the individual or miscommunicating.
- Evaluate progress and accomplishment by having trainees demonstrate their understanding by explaining in their own words or by actual performance.
- When checking on understanding, never rely on "yes" or "no" responses or nods of the head.
- Don't use true-false, yes-no, or multiple-choice quiz items.
- Be specific about trainee strengths and weaknesses. Always wrap up feedback sessions with concrete actions to be taken, preferably ones that are jointly determined.
- Don't lower performance standards; require high-quality performance and allow trainees to learn from their mistakes.

Work Environment Changes

Employers and supervisors can make policy, procedural, and environmental changes to make the work environment accessible to workers with hearing impairments. Of course, these adjustments must be made only after the needs of the employee have been assessed. Here are some suggestions:

- Reduce distractions and interference in the environment by minimizing noise and vibrations and using acoustical materials to reduce echoes. Background noise obstructs, masks, or otherwise interferes with communication.
- Move employees with hearing impairments away from sunny windows to eliminate shadows from the faces of coworkers.
- Change or add lighting to increase visibility.
- Install flashing lights on telephones to signal calls.
- Install flashing lights that are activated when auditory safety alarms are sounded.
- Install visual elevator arrival signals.
- Post safety floor plans with clearly marked exits and fire extinguishers.
- Use computers (with modems) and facsimile machines to send correspondence, E-mail, graphics, and financial data.
- Install amplifiers on telephones.
- Familiarize the staff with state telephone relay stations and their use.

Assistive Equipment, Devices, and Materials

People who are deaf or have hearing impairments do not need any special devices or modifications to use computers, but other office equipment poses problems. Assistive hearing devices increase the sound for an individual with hearing impairment or communicate sounds to deaf individuals through printed words, vibration, or flashing lights. Six types of devices are available to overcome these obstacles: alternative communication systems, amplification aids, signaling devices, keyboard entry devices, telephone aids, and computer-aided devices.

For people with hearing impairments, the primary means of receiving information from a computer is visual, either in the form of screen graphics or print or in the form of visual information created on the attached impact or laser printer. The principal input device is the keyboard, although joysticks, mice, keypads, and touch screens may also be used.

The many specialized software programs available for people with hearing impairments and those who work with them provide training in speech reading, sign language, and finger spelling. Other programs use biofeedback techniques to assist people with hearing impairments to improve their oral language skills, particularly pitch and tone, by comparing their voice patterns with a visual model shown on the computer screen.

Word processing systems provide one of the most important compensatory applications for people with hearing impairments. Because their inner language systems are different from those of their hearing peers, deaf and hard-of-hearing persons must constantly translate their system into an oral and written language system that is based on the language of the hearing world. In addition, the rules of grammar pose difficulties. Word processing programs allow users to practice the rules of grammar and written language. Users can express their thoughts on the computer with their own language system and have the computer place them in proper written form using grammar, spelling, style, and other checker-type programs.

Still other programs can serve as compensatory tools for people with hearing impairments in communicating with other nondisabled individuals. Using electronic bulletin boards, the user can "speak" with other individuals at his or her own pace, organizing their messages on the computer using a word processing program. Messages are transmitted only when the sender is satisfied with the content and structure of the message.

Alternative Communication Systems

Communication boards, made of cardboard or other firm material, can be used effectively with deaf and nonverbal trainees. The face of the board is divided into small squares that are neatly divided by lines running vertically and horizontally, like a checkerboard. Each square is large enough for a sketch or photograph of an object so that the worker can point to it to tell others what he or she wants or needs. The board may be organized with one row for the subject or person such as "I" or "me." An additional column could be for verbs such as "want" and another column for prepositions such as "in." There may be columns for adjectives and for nouns that represent objects that are used often. For example, one of the object names or pictures placed in the column could be a commonly used tool such as a screwdriver. The left-top and right-top corners of the board contain the words "yes" and "no," respectively, to communicate wanting or not wanting certain items. The numbers one through ten may be placed on the top center of the board so that the individual can communicate how much of any item he or she would like. The bottom of the board contains the alphabet in block letters so that the individual can spell out different words to make his or her needs known.

Amplification Aids

These aids range from relatively simple and low-cost devices that provide amplification systems for deaf individuals in interpersonal communication situations to more expensive systems and devices designed to improve hearing ability for individuals or for groups in large areas, such as classrooms and meeting rooms. One option is small, in-the-ear hearing devices. Some types of hearing aids can be used to attenuate background noise or specific tones, as well as provide general amplification or amplification of certain tones for some people, particularly those with marginal hearing loss in the higher frequencies. The devices do not eliminate background noise; they merely reduce it.

More expensive devices include receivers worn in a chest pocket connected by wire to a molded earpiece. The Pocket Talker is a personal amplification system that includes an amplifier, microphone, miniearphone, and TV listening extension cord. The microphone is placed near the origin of the sound to be heard or is held by the speaker. Others involve the installation and use of an audio loop, an FM system, or an infrared system in meeting rooms or auditoriums.

Signaling or Alerting Devices

Signaling devices alert persons with hearing impairments that a specific sound is occurring—such as doorbells, alarm clocks, fire alarms, smoke detectors, telephones, or knocks on the door—and announce the sound by using a visual or vibrating signal. Light flashers or strobes cause room lights or lamps to flash on and off. Vibrating devices are available in a variety of types. Some are large enough to vibrate chairs or beds; others are pocket-pager style or wristwatch-size portable signalers. Some pagers with alphanumeric capability can alert through vibration and also print out a message.

AccessDOS offers the IBM DOS user with hearing impairment a way to know when the computer is signaling. IBM's ShowSounds makes a possible for the user with a hearing impairment to see what others hear. The computer screen displays a musical note alone or with one of four special symbols to indicate the type of sound the computer has made and whether the signal comes from AccessDOS or an application. The entire screen can be made to flash off and on for a more obvious alert.

Keyboard Entry Alternatives

DADAEntry (TASH, Inc.) consists of software and a "black box" that connects a computer and a selected input device, such as a keyboard, mouse, joystick, switches, or a serial communication aid. For the person who has a hearing impairment, the AsciiEntry program allows any serial ASCII[6] communication aid to be connected, making it possible to control the computer and do data entry from a communication aid such as a TDD. The user can also take advantage of DADAEntry features such as work completion and macros.

T-TAM (Trace-Transparent Access Module) (Prentke Romich Company) connects a computer, keyboard, mouse, and/or an ASCII communication aid with a serial output. Persons with hearing impairments can create customized keyboard overlays to control both the computer and the T-TAM, as well as do data entry, from a communication aid.

Telephone Aids

Telephone Amplification Systems. Telephone handset amplifiers improve the ability of persons with some hearing loss to hear telephone conversations. Amplification systems can be built into the telephone instrument with the volume control in the handset or consist of an external speaker attached as a special device to the telephone. A third style is portable and snaps over the earpiece of any telephone, amplifying the sound as it comes out of the telephone. Another option is a telephone that is compatible with the use of a hearing aid.

Telephone Direct Links. IBM's PhoneCommunicator provides telephone communications for people with hearing impairments with others via touch-tone telephone and communicates with both Baudot and ASCII TDDs, displaying a full-screen view of the dialogue from both parties. The text of the conversation can be saved and printed. Other programs remain in the background while PhoneCommunicator is active, and it can be used in conjunction with host emulators and local area networks. Users can communicate with ASCII bulletin boards to browse, inquire, and send messages. Messages can be recorded from touch-tone telephones and TDD callers, noting the time and date of the call, as well as generate and save special messages for later use in touch-tone and TDD conversations.

Telephone Communication Devices for the Deaf. TDDs use a standard telephone together with a unit that has a typewriter and a visual display. People who are deaf or hard-of-hearing (or speech impaired) can communicate with other TDD users by typing a message on the TDD and sending it over telephone lines. The TDD of the party on the receiving end displays the message. There are large-print displays for users with visual impairments and pocket-sized, portable TDDs that can be used anywhere.

Telephone Communications Relay Services (TRS). TRS allows people with hearing or speech disabilities to use the telephone through facilities that are equipped with specialized equipment and staffed by communications assistants who are highly trained to relay conversations using a text telephone and a regular telephone. A text telephone is a machine, usually electronic, that has a keyboard and a readout display (a small screen that displays one or two lines of text). Coded signals are sent and received by text telephones through regular telephone lines using a coupler or modem.

The text telephone system works in this way: The communications assistant transliterates conversation from text to voice and from voice to text. Using voice carryover (VCO), a person with a hearing disability can speak directly to the other end user. The communications assistant types the response back to the person with the hearing disability without voicing any conversation. Or, using hearing carryover (HCO), the person with a speech disability can listen to the other end user, and in reply, the communication assistant, using a readout device, reads and speaks the text as typed by the person with the speech disability without typing any of the conversation. There are no extra fees or charges for using TRS.

Each TRS provides information about its services, including carryover services, collect calls, pay telephones, personal computer text telephone settings, making suggestions, and filing complaints. State TRS outreach offices can provide information.

Computer-Aided Devices

Other adaptive technology devices involve computers. One example is IBM's PhoneCommunicator. The device connects the telephone to a computer so that the screen blinks whenever the user gets a call. When the telephone is answered, the user can type a message on the computer, and a voice synthesizer will read it to the caller. The caller can also type messages using the telephone lines and the letters associated with the numbers on the keypad of a touch-tone phone. Although numbers on the keypad stand for up to three letters, the computer makes fairly accurate guesses about the words being typed and displays the message to the person with the hearing impairment.

The Omnifone TDD Modem (Apple Computer) automatically translates between conventional TDD code and ASCII. The system allows faster, more flexible typewritten communication from Macintosh to Macintosh computer (at speeds of up to 9600 bps) or Macintosh to TDD (at 45–50 bps). Omnifone allows the user to talk and type over the same telephone line so that communication with people with hearing impairments can be achieved by using voice and text on a single call (voice carryover).

Computer-assisted note taking is a means of overcoming the problems inherent in staff meetings for people with hearing impairments: failure of staffers to speak slowly and clearly, face the person with the disability, or, when an audio loop is used, to pass the microphone from speaker to speaker or equipment failure. Computer-assisted note taking is the use of a computer to produce notes of a meeting, lecture, or group discussion as a backup to speech reading or signing as a means of receiving information. A skilled note taker types on a computer keyboard a summary of what is being said, and the notes are displayed on a projector screen or monitor. A typing speed of at least 60 words per minute is essential; however, a note taker who can type at a speed of 100 words per minute can approximate a verbatim transcript of what is said. Keyboard enhancement software can expand abbreviations into complete words or phrases of sentences on screen.

Closed Captions

Producers of commercial broadcast network and cable video and training videocassettes have overcome the limitations of their medium for people with hearing impairments by providing closed captions—essentially subtitles in print showing at the bottom of the screened image. For television sets manufactured before July 1993, a decoder is needed to put audiovoice output into print. However, the Television Decoder Circuitry Act of 1990, an amendment to the Communications Act of 1934, now requires that all television sets with screens of 13 inches or more have built-in decoder circuitry capable of displaying closed captions, making it unnecessary for people who are deaf or hard of hearing to use portable decoders.

Interpreter Services

Here an interpreter proficient with both expressive and receptive American Sign Language translates or transcribes information from the speaker to the deaf individual.

Deaf-Blindness

Although only a small number of people are totally deaf, blind, and without speech, many individuals who are considered to be deaf-blind are blind with some hearing loss or deaf with some vision loss. Many people who are deaf-blind use assistive devices designed for hearing or vision impairments. Some devices and techniques are designed specifically for individuals who are deaf-blind.

Alphabet Glove

The alphabet glove is a simple white glove with each letter of the alphabet printed on it at strategic points. "A," for example, is located on the first joint of the thumb, "B" on the second joint of the thumb, "C" at the end of the thumb, and so on. To communicate, the deaf-blind person wears the glove. The "sender" spells out a message by pressing on the appropriate letters of the glove.

Braille Hand Speech

The traditional braille system employs a system of raised dots, representing the alphabet and numbers, embossed on paper. Braille hand speech reproduces braille dots in the palm of the hand of the receiver.

Morse Code

Deaf-blind people can be taught the Morse code, a simple system of dots and dashes representing the various letters of the alphabet and numbers from one to ten. Communications are sent and received using the Morse code equivalents. For example, "A" is .- (dot dash, pronounced did dah), "B" is -... (dash dot dot dot, pronounced dah did did dit), and so on. A simple reference card can be used by people who do not know the code to communicate with a deaf-blind person who knows it. The dots and dashes of Morse code can also be signaled gesturally or transmitted to any part of the body by touch.

One-Hand Alphabet

This method of communicating was dramatically portrayed in the Helen Keller story, *The Miracle Worker*. Using a combination of finger spelling and some sign language, the "sender" manually spells words or uses common signs while the deaf-blind "receiver" feels the letters or signs by gently holding his or her hands around the sender's hand. The deaf-blind person responds using the same method.

Palm Writing/Finger Spelling

The sender simple "prints" the letters on the palm of the receiver in block letters, one at a time. The return communication is done in the same way.

Teletouch

Teletouch is a device that looks like a modified, miniature typewriter. Its keys are arranged like those of a typewriter, and by depressing a key, the corresponding braille cell is activated on the other side of the device. People who are deaf-blind place a finger over the cell and are able to read messages sent by communicating partners one letter at a time. The device does not have a storage or printout capability.

Vibro-Tactile Aids

These aids pick up sounds with a microphone and transmit them to one or more small vibrators taped to the user's chest, worn like a wristwatch, or carried on a belt or in a pocket like a pager. The vibrations generate a pattern that can be translated into meaningful messages. Silent paging devices are a type of vibro-tactile aid that consist of two parts: a monitoring unit, which is worn or placed near a telephone, doorbell or any other source of sound the user wishes to monitor, and an alerting unit, which vibrates when the specified sound activates it.

Summary

Hearing impairments include many types and degrees of hearing loss, ranging from mild to profound reductions in hearing ability. The most common types are nerve deafness and conductive hearing loss. Their causes include infections, accidents, aging, and overexposure to loud noises. People with hearing disabilities can be trained to perform the great majority of the jobs held by nondisabled people, including the full gamut of assembly line, clerical and administrative, technical, managerial, and professional. A great variety of assistive equipment, devices, and materials can be used to advantage in preparing persons with hearing disabilities for these jobs and performing them following that training.

For Further Reading and Viewing*

ADA Customer Courtesies. 1993. 20-minute video. Available from United Training Media.

ADA for Retail. 12-minute video. Available from United Training Media.

Alexander Graham Bell Association for the Deaf. *Employers of Individuals with Hearing Impairments and the ADA.* Washington, D.C.: Alexander Graham Bell Association for the Deaf, n.d.

The Americans with Disabilities Act: Impact on Training. INFO-LINE 9203. Alexandria, Va.: American Society for Training and Development, March 1993.

The Americans with Disabilities Act: Techniques for Accommodation. INFO-LINE 9204. Alexandria, Va.: American Society for Training and Development, April 1992.

Assistive Technology Sourcebook. Washington, D.C.: RESNA Press, 1990.

Co-op Bloopers (Employer Version). 1994. 9-minute video. Available from Cooperative Internship Program, Center for Career Programs, Gallaudet University.

Crammatte, Alan B. *Meeting the Challenge: Hearing Impaired Professionals in the Workplace.* Washington, D.C.: Gallaudet University Press, 1987.

Employers of Individuals with Hearing Impairments and the ADA. Washington, D.C.: Alexander Graham Bell Association for the Deaf, n.d.

Experimental Programs Off Campus. *EPOC Supervisor's Manual: A Guide for Working with a Deaf or Hard of Hearing Student.* Rev. ed. Washington, D.C.: Cooperative Internship Program of the Center for Career Programs, Gallaudet University, n.d.

Gallaudet University. *A Barrier-free Environment for Deaf People.* Washington, D.C.: Gallaudet University, College for Continuing Education, 1982.

———. *Including Hearing Impaired People in Meetings.* Washington, D.C.: Gallaudet University, College for Continuing Education, 1982.

———. *Hiring Deaf People: An Introduction for Employers.* Washington, D.C.: National Academy, 1983.

Goldberg, Marge, Paula F. Goldberg, and Cathleen Urbain. *Opportunity Knocking: The Story of Supported Employment.* Minneapolis: PACER Center, 1988.

Introduction to Sign Language: An Interactive Videodisc Approach. 1990. Two double-sided Level III interactive videodiscs, a 56-page learner's guide, and two Apple Macintosh diskettes. Available from AIT: The Learning Source.

Lucas, Ceil, and Clayton Valli. *Language Contact in the American Deaf Community.* San Diego: Academic Press, 1992.

Participants with Disabilities: How to Address Their Needs. INFO-LINE 8704. Alexandria, Va.: American Society for Training and Development, April 1987.

People with Hearing Loss in the Workplace: A Guide for Employers to Comply with the ADA. Bethesda, Md.: Self-Help for Hard-of-Hearing People, 1992.

Sauerburger, Dona. *Independence without Sight or Sound: Suggestions for Practitioners Working with Deaf-Blind Adults.* Brooklyn, N.Y.: American Foundation for the Blind, 1993.

*Full addresses of the organizations in this listing appear in Appendixes B and C.

Sheie, T. P. "Adapting Training for the Hearing Impaired." *Training and Development Journal* (January 1985): 100–102.

Speechreading Challenges on Videodisc. 1993. Ten lessons on one double-sided Level III interactive videodisc, accompanied by a 68-page learner's guide, and three Apple Macintosh diskettes. Available from AIT: The Learning Source.

Urbain, Cathleen. *Supported Employment: A Step-by-Step Guide.* Minneapolis: PACER Center, 1992.

Valli, Clayton, and Ceil Lucas. *Linguistics of American Sign Language: A Resource Text.* Washington, D.C.: Gallaudet Press, 1992.

Virvan, Barbara. "You Don't Have to Hate Meetings—Try Computer-Assisted Notetaking." *SHHH Journal* (February 1991): 25–28.

Working Together: Deaf and Hearing People. 59-minute video. Available from Cooperative Internship Program, Center for Career Programs, Gallaudet University.

Notes

1. Adapted from materials provided by the Better Hearing Institute. Used by permission.
2. Ibid.
3. Charlotte Baker and Dennis Cokley, *American Sign Language: A Teacher's Resource Guide* (Silver Spring, Md.: T. J. Publishers, 1980), p. 54.
4. National Information Center on Deafness, *1986–87 Directory of the Career Information of Hearing Impaired Persons in Professional, Technical, and Managerial Occupations* (Washington, D.C.: Gallaudet University, 1987).
5. I am indebted to the staff of the Center for Career Programs, Gallaudet University, for their contributions to this section of the chapter.
6. American Standard Code for Information Interchange (ASCII) is an 8-bit code for the interchange of information that can operate at any standard transmission baud rate.

8

Mobility and Motion Disabilities

I met Bob when I was in my first year of teaching at a rural, consolidated school housing grades 1 through 12 in a wooden frame building. My teaching assignment included classes in seventh-, eighth-, and ninth-grade general science; eighth-grade English; ninth-grade algebra; and eleventh- and twelfth-grade American history, plus management of a ninth-grade homeroom (including serving hot soup at lunch time), an occasional stint as assistant baseball coach, and substitute school bus driver.

Bob was a member of my homeroom and my ninth-grade algebra and ninth-grade general science classes. He was a very bright adolescent, blond, tall for his age, and handsome. He had one arm. He had lost his left forearm in a farm accident. He also had an "attitude," perhaps due to his disability. Over the year, his demeanor and behavior improved considerably, although there was still room for improvement. In the spring of that year so long ago, Bob tried out for the baseball team as a pitcher—the progenitor of the now famous major league one-armed pitcher, Jim Abbott of the New York Yankees. Although he was never a starter, Bob did quite well in relief. He had a very good fastball, an arching curve, and an effective change-up. He kept his glove tucked under the stump of his left arm. After each pitch, Bob would quickly stick his right hand in the glove to field any balls back to or near the mound. He could cleanly grab these grounders, tuck the glove under his stump, remove the ball, and throw to first base, all in one motion.

The next time I saw Bob was about six years later when he appeared in my Methods of Secondary School Teaching class in one of the state colleges. By that time he was a charming, self-confident young man—a natural leader and a promising teacher. He fulfilled that promise by serving as a high school mathematics teacher and later as a popular and highly effective high school principal.

It was 1942. Bert was young—19—when rheumatoid arthritis came on suddenly, invading all his joints with pain so intense he could barely function. The knuckles on his fingers and toes began to swell and the members became misshapen. He took aspirin in the beginning. And later, although his physician tried to help him with several other drugs, he got little or no relief. Bert never saw a rheumatologist, nor did he know that there was such a thing as an arthritis specialist. Nonetheless, he became a teacher—and a great one. In later years, when more became known about rheumatoid arthritis, new drugs became available, and rheumatologists became more common, Bert finally found some relief from his constant pain with nonsteroidal anti-inflammatory drugs.

Rena was a member of the freshman class in a state teachers' college when I was a senior. She was a vibrant, beautiful young woman, a top student, and a stellar athlete. She was also one of the last persons in our region to contract poliomyelitis, and although she survived the disease, it left her with paraplegia. So Rena became a wheelchair user. Despite her disability, Rena returned to college and graduated with a teaching degree with honors. She immediately enrolled in a prestigious graduate school of education, and a little over a year later graduated with an M.A. in teaching, with a specialization in the teaching of English.

    She applied for and accepted a teaching position at a medium-sized high school. Imagine the difficulties she faced getting to, into, around, out of, and from a building located on the side of a steep hill and at the top of a long set of stone steps in the days before wheelchair access. Undeterred, with the help of administrators, faculty, and students, Rena found ways to overcome the problems. She became one of the most popular, inspiring, and competent teachers in the history of the school. My youngest son was fortunate enough to benefit from her instructional expertise. Rena retired recently after more than 35 years of outstanding service.

Mobility is one of the most important independence issues for workers with disabilities. Whether it is moving from home to work, from one work area to another, or traveling long distances, the ability to get there tops everyone's list of concerns. When people are able to use wheelchairs to get around, they sense freedom, and the ability to drive a vehicle is just as important for independence and self-esteem.

From an employment perspective, mobility and motion impairments, particularly those involving the arms, hands, or fingers, constitute serious, but in most cases not insurmountable, obstacles. Most jobs require some lifting or manipulation of objects, implements, tools, keys, levers and buttons, and handwriting or keyboarding. Alternative strategies and devices can accommodate a variety of impairments.

Types of Mobility and Motion Impairments

Mobility and motion impairments involve the loss or loss of use of limbs, bones, or muscles and result in inadequacy or incapability of an individual to respond to situations requiring movement of the body, hands, arms, or legs and inability to perform psychomotor skills. The problem is complicated by the fact that a person with mobility or motion impairment can be simultaneously an emotional, a neurological, a diagnostic, and a training problem, as well as a mobility or motion problem.

Mobility and motion impairments are specific. That is, people who may be unable to perform a particular skill or make a particular movement are not automatically incapable of acquiring other kills or performing other movements. It can therefore be said that mobility and motion impairments have multiple symptoms, multiple causes, and involve multiple treatments and accommodations.

Amputation

Estimates are that in the United States, more than 2 million people have lost limbs by accident, injury, or disease. New amputations are occurring at the rate of 35,000 to 40,000 annually. Originally composed largely of relatively young males who lost a limb in military combat, the amputee population has been increasing due to accidents, burn and cold injuries, diabetes, cancer and other malignancies, chronic infection, and circulatory diseases. Upper-extremity amputation is more common in highly industrialized regions of the country; lower-extremity amputation is characteristic of areas where there is a high percentage of older or retired persons.

Amputation has minimal impact on persons working in executive, managerial, supervisory, and other white-collar positions, but important adaptations may be necessary for those who earn their livelihood by heavy labor. Physical, occupational, and social therapists can assist in selecting and applying the most appropriate adaptations.

Amputation Sites. The site of the amputation has a bearing on the kind and amount of activity that can be achieved.[1] There are four main sites of amputation of the leg, ranked in ascending order of disability and descending order of potential functional activity: (1) through the ankle (known as Syme's amputation), (2) amputation about a hand's breadth below the knee or shorter (but rarely longer), (3) through the knee joint, and (4) at any position above the knee. However, even the total loss of a limb (through the hip joint disarticulation) or even hind-quarter amputation, still permits reasonable performance of daily activities.

Upper limb amputation sites include any or all fingers, transcarpal (below the wrist), wrist disarticulation, below the elbow (long, short, or very short), elbow disarticulation, above the elbow (standard and short), shoulder disarticulation, and forequarter. Although all require changes in life-style and various degrees of adaptation, people with upper limb amputation can function in the workplace with or without prostheses.

Prostheses. Advances in prosthetics, the science of developing artificial replacements for limbs lost to amputation, have made it possible for people to work and play so well that a stranger might never know that they have had the surgery. In fact, anything that a person could do prior to the amputation can be done again, with some adaptation. Prosthetic devices are made of metal alloys and plastics light enough to make artificial limbs easily manageable. Other new materials have made them pliable and flexible, and therefore wearable for long periods of time without pain or even discomfort. Further improvements are on the way. Devices are being developed that allow amputees to feel with their artificial limbs, thereby giving them unparalleled control over their movements.

An artificial limb consists of joints and levers made of a variety of materials having high strength-to-weight ratios, such as wood, leather, cloth, or plastics (nylon, acrylics, polyester resins, polypropylene, polyethylene, flexible and rigid polyurethane, flexible urethane, silicones, and fiberglass), although wood remains a useful material because it is easily cut and shaped. Simplicity of design and ease of maintenance are key factors in good artificial limbs. An artificial foot is usually made of a rubber substitute of variable density to provide support and absorb shock. A knee joint is a simple hinge that is mechanically somewhat like the natural knee in that it is free to flex and swing but is blocked against extension beyond the vertical. An artificial hand, called a "terminal device," may be shaped like a hand or composed of two curved, slender "fingers," called a "hook." A hook is superior to the hand in that it is practical and more versatile.

One of the newest developments in prostheses is an energy-storing foot, which uses springs to simulate a normal gait. Others are the Utah arm, an electronic prosthesis that swings and reacts almost like a real arm, and the Seattle foot, a flexible, lifelike prosthesis for amputees that allows considerable freedom of movement, including participating in such active sports as basketball, baseball, and golf. These devices enable knees and ankles to bend and feet to flex so people can walk normally. Still another is an artificial hand that enables the person to pick up small objects, such as a dime, off a counter without difficulty and lift objects without injuring themselves.

Another recent development is the myoelectric arm, in which thumb and finger movements are triggered by impulses delivered from muscle twitching. Myoelectric control makes use of normally unused muscles in the stump to control a prosthesis. Minute electrical potentials generated by muscular contractions are monitored at the surface of the skin, and the surface electrodes convert these electrical potentials into commands directly to the prosthesis. The device has been used with considerable success with children but with only limited success with adults.

Other prostheses include the Utah artificial arm, IPOS leg, flex-foot, SAFE foot, British SACH foot, McKendrick foot and ankle joint, and Roe-lite foot.[2]

Arthritis[3]

Arthritis is a disorder of the joints, the junctions between bones. About 50 million people in the United States have arthritis. The disorder is serious enough to interfere with the day-to-day activities of 4.4 million, partially disables 1.5 million, is completely disabling for another 1.5 million people, and is estimated to cost about $14 billion annually on lost work, productivity, and treatment. The Arthritis Foundation estimates that each year 70 million person-days of missed work are caused by arthritis and result in an additional 500 million days of restricted activity.

There are more than 100 types of arthritis, ranging from minor stiffness to severe disability and deformity. Although it cannot be cured, its course can be slowed and its symptoms relieved. The disorder affects the synovial joint, a liquid-filled capsule made of fibrous bands of connective tissue—the ligaments—that attach adjoining movable bones. The capsule is lined with a membrane that secretes the cushioning synovial fluid, which is stored in membrane-lined packets called bursae. In healthy joints between movable bones, only a thin film of fluid covers the surfaces. A decrease in the fluid is associated with the joint stiffness that people normally feel as they age. In arthritis the amount of synovial fluid increases, swelling the joint. Opposing bones facing a joint are capped by cartilage, a flexible, bloodless tissue. In a healthy synovial joint, the slipperiness of the cartilage tips and the fluid in the joint allow the bones to move freely. Figure 8-1 shows the joints most often affected by arthritis.

Joint deterioration can be hereditary or can result from injury, infection, autoimmune disease, or the action of a drug. Although the physical changes caused by some forms of arthritis are well understood, relatively little is known about how those changes begin. Three most common forms of arthritis are osteoarthritis, rheumatoid arthritis, and spondyloarthropathies. Other less common forms are gout, scleroderma, systemic lupus erythematosus, Kawasaki disease, and strep A infection. Only the most common forms will be discussed here.

Osteoarthritis. Osteoarthritis is the most prevalent form, affecting 15.8 million Americans. This is a degenerative joint disease characterized by chronic, progressive stiffness and deformity of one or more joints of the body. The most commonly affected joints are usually those of a weight-bearing type—the hips, knees, ankles, feet, or back. The smooth cartilage padding on facing bone ends wears away, and new bone forms on the exposed ends, causing pain when joints move and a grating sensation when the dry, exposed bone ends rub against each other. In its most severe form, arthritis results in limited function. (See Figure 8-2 for a comparison of a normal and an arthritic knee joint.) Many people with arthritis use wheelchairs, while others use prostheses, crutches, walkers, or canes. In any case, the disease makes many ordinary tasks and movements difficult—such as writing, turning doorknobs, climbing stairs, driving a car, or lifting or moving objects.

There are no generalized symptoms; however, arthritis usually begins with stiffness in the joint in the morning or after being inactive. Next follows enlargement of the joint with little deformity, with pain increasing after prolonged exercise or overuse. That is followed by limited motion of the joint and an abrasive sensation with its movement. In some cases, nodules or deformities may appear on the hands or feet or their joints. Arthritis is not contagious and is treated mainly by rest and the application of heat and NSAIDS (nonsteroidal anti-inflammatory drugs) medication (such as aspirin, ibuprofen, flurbiprofen, indomethacin, and naproxen) to reduce pain and inflammation. Although potent cortisone-like drugs taken by mouth or injected into the joints has been widely prescribed in the past, their use is limited today because they can lead to osteoporosis and damage to cartilage or cause cataracts, skin thinning, diabetes, fluid retention, poor wound healing, and increased susceptibility to infection.

Other therapies include injections of gold, new biologics (body chemicals), implants, and joint replacements. (See Figure 8-3.) To help with the activities of daily living, there are tools with long handles;

Figure 8-1. Joints most often affected by arthritis.

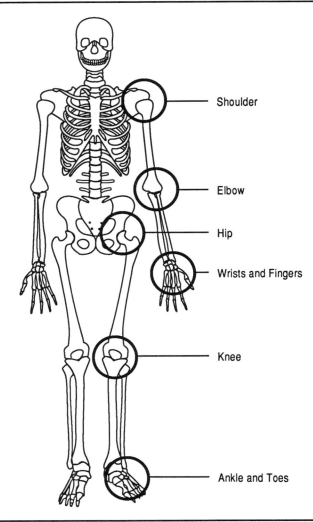

Source: Lewis Ricki, *Arthritis: Modern Treatment for That Old Pain in the Joints,* DHHS Pub. (FDA) 92-1190 (Rockville, Md.: Public Health Service, Food and Drug Administration, U.S. Department of Health and Human Services, n.d.), p. 2.

Figure 8-2. A normal knee and an osteoarthritic joint.

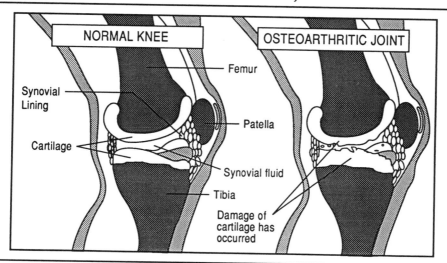

Source: Lewis Ricki, *Arthritis: Modern Treatment for That Old Pain in the Joints,* DHHS Pub. (FDA) 92-1190 (Rockville, Md.: Public Health Service, Food and Drug Administration, U.S. Department of Health and Human Services, n.d.), p. 5.

crutches and canes; and special thumb, hand, or wrist splints and gloves that can temporarily restore hand function.

Rheumatoid Arthritis. Rheumatoid arthritis is a chronic, inflammatory disease of multiple joints that usually begins in early adulthood—the 20s through 40s and more commonly in women—in the small joints of the hands and feet and progresses to larger joints. However, it can strike anyone at any age. It affects about 2.9 million people in the United States. It can be progressive, or it may burn itself out. It may be serious, mild, or somewhere in between. If progressive, the disease may result in severe disability with deformity of the joints and limited movement and function. Holding an object, such as a pencil, opening a can or bottle, or even shaking hands become overwhelming tasks, often requiring the person to use both hands to accomplish.

The causes of rheumatoid arthritis are not known, although a virus is suspected because the immune system attacks the joints as if they were the enemy. The symptoms of rheumatoid arthritis are generalized fever, loss of appetite, weight loss, and fatigue. Although it may be hereditary, rheumatoid arthritis is not contagious. Diagnosis is based on the presence of all of the following symptoms for six or more weeks:

- Joint stiffness upon awakening that lasts an hour or longer
- Swelling in specific finger joints or wrist joints

Figure 8-3. Joint replacement and implants.

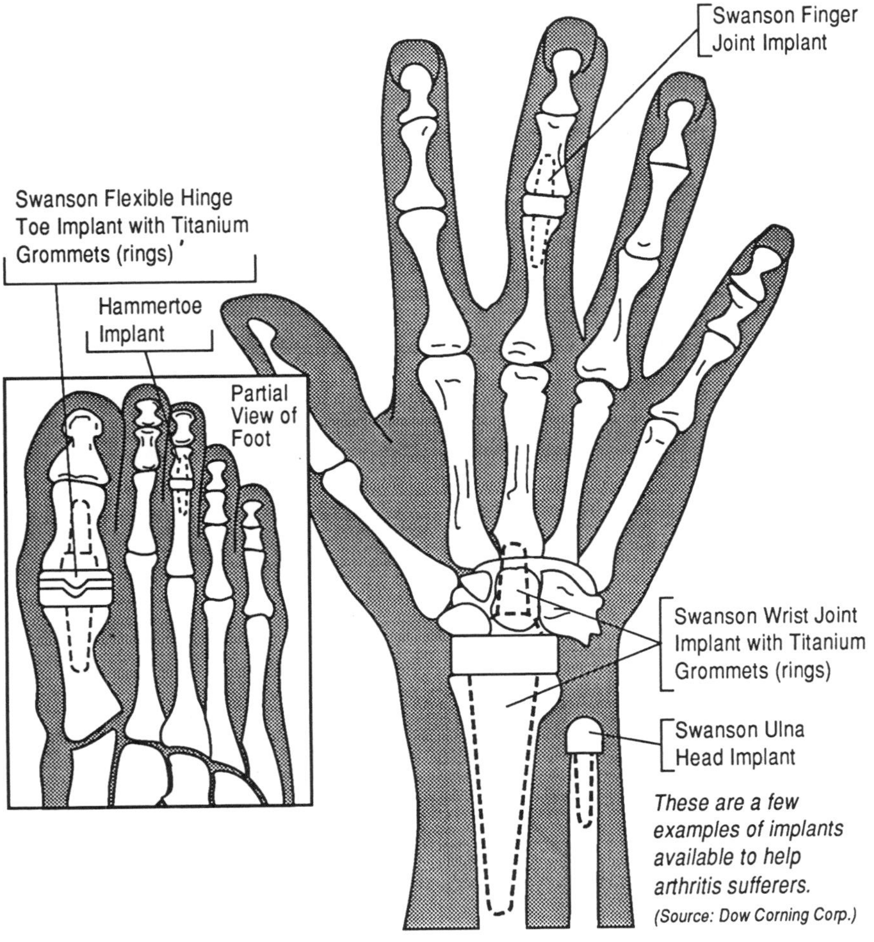

Source: Lewis Ricki, *Arthritis: Modern Treatment for That Old Pain in the Joints,* DHHS Pub. (FDA) 92-1190 (Rockville, Md.: Public Health Service, Food and Drug Administration, U.S. Department of Health and Human Services, n.d.), p. 6.

- Swelling in the soft tissue around three or more joints
- Swelling on both sides of the joint

Treatment consists of rest and control of pain, application of heat, medication to reduce inflammation of joints, and physical therapy. The most effective medications fall into three categories: (1) anti-inflammatories to reduce swelling—cortisone derivatives, such as the prescription generics (prednisone, methylprednisolone, triamcinolone, and dexamethasone) and other-the-counter drugs (aspirin and ibuprofen); (2) analgesics to reduce pain, such as prescription drugs containing codeine, and nonprescription drugs, such as Tylenol, Datril, Panadol and Anacin-3; and (3) muscle relaxants to reduce muscle spasms, such as the prescription drugs diazepam (Valium) and cyclobenzaprine (Flexeril).

The potential of dietary changes as effective treatment for both forms of arthritis is now being examined. Research into the effects of increasing intake of a class of fatty acids called omega-3s, found in oil-rich fish such as halibut, mackerel, salmon, sardines, tuna, and whiting, is promising if coupled with a reduction in the ingestion of fatty acids called omega-6s found in fried foods and vegetable oils.

Spondyloarthropathies

Spondyloarthropathies, a collection of disorders that tend to strike the spine, affect about 2.5 million Americans. Spondyloarthropathies include Reiter's syndrome, psoriatic arthritis, intestinal arthropathy, reactive arthropathy, and ankylosing spondylitis (the most common type) in which the spinal bones fuse. Symptoms include persistent diarrhea, skin and hair scaliness, and joint inflammation. Although its causes are not known, there appears to be some connection to the presence of a protein (HLA-B27) on the surfaces of people with the disease. These proteins are controlled by a group of genes that oversees immune system function. Research with animals holds promise of helping with diagnosis and treatment in humans.

Amyotrophic Lateral Sclerosis (ALS)[4]

ALS is a neuromuscular disease characterized by degeneration of a select group of nerve cells and pathways in the brain and spinal cord that leads to progressive wasting and paralysis of the muscles controlling movement. More than 5,000 people in the United States are newly diagnosed with ALS each year. Approximately 5 to 10 percent of ALS is familial, occurring more than once in a family lineage. It is estimated that the disease is responsible for one out of every hundred thousand deaths in people over age 20, and it is projected that of the U.S. population living today, more than 300,000 will die from ALS. The condition is not contagious, nor does it affect the ability to think. There is currently no cure, and it is almost always fatal within a few years.

The symptoms of ALS are as follows:

- Twitching and cramping of muscles, especially those in the hands and feet.
- Impairment of the use of arms and legs.

- "Thick speech" and difficulty in projecting the voice.
- In more advanced states, shortness of breath and difficulty in breathing and swallowing.

Treatment is aimed at symptomatic relief, prevention of complications, and maintenance of maximum function and optimum quality of life. In the later stages of the disease, nursing management is required because the patient is functionally quadriplegic with intact sensory function, bedridden, and aware that he or she is going to die.

Brain Damage

Hemiplegia, the most common type of neurologic disorder, affects all age groups, although it occurs most often in later life. It paralyzes half of the body—either the left or the right side of the trunk and its limbs. The most common cause of hemiplegia is a cerebral vascular accident, called a stroke—thrombosis of a cerebral or extracranial artery, hemorrhage in the brain or cerebrospinal space, or embolism. Other causes are brain tumor, brain abscess, head injury, and surgery. An infrequent cause is a lesion of the spinal cord. If complete recovery does not occur, the individual is left with residual hemiplegia that may be complete or incomplete.

Cerebral Palsy[5]

The term "cerebral palsy" refers to a large group of movement and balance disorders that result from brain injury just before, during, or shortly after birth. About 500,000 people of all ages in the United States have cerebral palsy—about 2 out of every 1,000 people. There are between 3,500 and 4,000 new cases annually—about 1 per 1,000 live births.

More than 90 percent of cerebral palsy cases are congenital (not genetic) that is, caused by factors related to childbearing. Cerebral palsy is often the result of lack of oxygen for a period of time, but it can also be caused by low blood sugar (hypoglycemia), general infection, or brain infection (meningitis and encephalitis). Cases of acquired cerebral palsy are due to head injuries from falls and automobile accidents, child abuse and neglect, exposure to toxic substances (such as lead, cleaning agents, medications, alcohol, and addictive drugs), and severe malnutrition.

The person with cerebral palsy usually has an awkward gait, poor balance, and impaired control and coordination of movements. Other effects include drooling, facial grimaces, involuntary movements, convulsive seizures, absent or poor speech, visual and hearing impairments, and delayed intellectual development. In early infancy the condition is characterized by slow development of motor skills. With advancing age, some muscles become rigid and controlled movements become difficult, if not impossible. The problem can range from almost imperceptible weakness that doesn't interfere significantly with function to severe and debilitating frailty. Although it is often assumed that adults with cerebral palsy have mental retardation, that is not necessarily true. For many, intellectual function may remain normal.

There is no cure for cerebral palsy, but early and intensive physical, occupational, and speech therapy is often helpful. Medication has not proved to be effective over long periods of time, except for anticonvulsant drugs given for seizures. Muscle relaxants have not been very effective either and sometimes have serious side effects. Orthopedic surgery and the use of orthotic appliances, such as braces, play a significant role in both the prevention and correction of disfigurements, particularly of the lower extremities and back.

Muscular Dystrophies[6]

The muscular dystrophies are a group of ten muscle diseases that are hereditary, progressive, and produce a pattern of weakness of muscle groups. Examples include Duchenne, Becker, Emery-Dreifus, faciosca-pulo humeral, limb-girdle, ocsular, oculopharyngeal, distal, and myo-tonic dystrophy.

Muscular dystrophy simply means muscle wasting. The primary cause of the disease is a genetic defect, which results in a gradual weakening and wasting of the muscles that may continue to advance over 20 or 30 years. The muscles become weak due to an accumulation of fat and scar tissue.

Although all of the muscular dystrophies are considered to be inherited, that does not mean that there is always a history of muscular dystrophy in an affected person's family. Often there is not, for several reasons. First, a person may have a genetic defect that has occurred for the first time—a mutation. Second, a parent may have been so slightly affected by the disease that it went unnoticed and undiagnosed, even by an experienced physician. And third, one important mode of inheritance, autosomal recessive,[7] very seldom affects more than one generation.

The most common type of muscular dystrophy is Duchenne's, which affects boys, begins in early childhood, causes weaknesses of the hips and upper legs, and progresses rapidly requiring the use of a wheelchair by about the age of ten, and usually results in death at an early age. Other forms do not become evident until early adulthood, progress slowly, and do not significantly shorten a person's life span. These disorders typically involve weakness and wasting that affects the shoulders and pelvic girdle first, then the arms, hands, and lower legs.

There is no cure for muscular dystrophy; however, much can be done to ensure maximum independence, physical capabilities, including mobility, general health, and quality of life. Treatment is focused on physical and occupational therapy to help the person adapt to the weakness and prevent the complications of pneumonia and deformities of the spine and legs.

The amount of research being conducted worldwide to combat muscular dystrophy is enormous. Each year, millions of dollars and thousands of researchers are involved in attempts to find a cure, improve methods of prevention, and apply successful research methods to achieve similar results with other forms of muscular dystrophy.

Multiple Sclerosis[8]

Multiple sclerosis (MS) is a chronic disease of the central nervous system in which simple, everyday tasks can no longer be taken for granted. Its symptoms may run the gamut from slight blurring of vision to complete paralysis. An estimated one-third of a million Americans have multiple sclerosis, with nearly 200 cases diagnosed every single week.

How is multiple sclerosis caused? Our bodies contain a fatty substance called myelin which surrounds and protects nerve fibers of the brain and spinal cord (the central nervous system) in the same way that insulation protects electrical wires. When any part of this myelin sheathing, or insulation, is destroyed, nerve impulses to and from the brain are interrupted and distorted. The result is multiple sclerosis or MS—multiple because many scattered areas of the brain and spinal cord are affected; sclerosis because "scleroses" or hardened patches of scar tissue form over the damaged myelin.

Symptoms of MS vary greatly depending upon where the scarred, or sclerosed, patches are formed in the central nervous system. They may include tingling sensations, numbness, slurred speech, blurred or double vision, muscle weakness, poor coordination, unusual fatigue, muscle cramps, spasms, problems with bladder, bowel, and sexual function, and paralysis. Occasionally there may be mental changes such as forgetfulness or confusion. These symptoms may occur in any combination and can vary from very mild to severe.

There is no way at present to predict when or even if attacks of the disease will occur. Symptoms not only vary greatly from person to person but also vary from time to time in the same person. The most typical pattern of MS is marked by periods of active disease called exacerbations or relapses and quiescent, or symptom-free, periods called remissions.

Some people have an initial attack and no recurrence afterward. Others have what is called "relapse-remitting" disease. This means that they have exacerbations, which take place unpredictably, followed by periods of remission, which may last months, or even years. Still others experience a "chronic-progressive" disease course. Thus, the disease ranges from very mild to intermittent to rapidly progressive forms.

Because MS affects individuals so differently, it is difficult to make generalizations about the extent of disability any one person may sustain. Statistics suggest that two out of three people with MS remain ambulatory over their lifetimes, but many of them will need a cane or other assistive device. MS is not contagious and it is rarely fatal.

MS strikes most people who are in their twenties or thirties—young adults who are just starting their lives. Women develop it more frequently than men; whites more frequently than blacks or Asians. The reasons are not yet understood. Studies also indicate that genetic factors may make certain individuals more receptive to the disease, but there is no evidence that MS is directly inherited.

MS is not always easy to detect or diagnose because early symptoms tend to come and go, because diseases of the central nervous system have some of the same warning signs, and because no single neurological or laboratory test definitively confirms or rules out MS.

People may be told they have "probable" or "possible" MS. However, recent advances in medical imaging, particularly MRI technology, are helping to clarify diagnosis.

Much can be done to help people with MS function at their best level on a day-to-day basis, and some treatment may help reduce the frequency and severity of relapses. There are medications that provide symptomatic relief for both acute attacks and chronic symptoms. Muscle relaxers can reduce spasms. Tension, bowel and urinary distress, pain, and other problems can be eased with medication. These and other problems should be discussed with a physician.

There are other treatments that also help. Physical therapy, exercise programs, attention to diet, adequate rest, and counseling to decrease emotional stress may all be extremely valuable in helping a person remain independent and able to lead a full life.

The cause and the cure of MS are the subject of intensive research on an international scale. The exploration extends into many fields, including virology, immunology, and the biochemistry of myelin.

Spinal Cord Injury[9]

More than 250,000 Americans are paralyzed as a result of injury to the spinal cord. Every year another 7,800 Americans, about 82 percent of them males between ages 16 and 25, sustain a spinal cord injury primarily as a result of motor vehicle accidents (about 50 percent), sports-related mishaps, or crimes of violence, such as gunshot and stab wounds. The number of new injuries per year in the United States totals 7,800—about 32 per 1 million population.

Spinal cord injury results from a trauma, lesion, infection, or disease of the spinal cord that results in paralysis of certain parts of the body and corresponding loss of sensation. Paralysis takes one of two forms: paraplegia, affecting the legs and lower parts of the body, or quadriplegia, affecting the level of the body below the neck and chest area and involving both the arms and legs.

Paralysis is often accompanied by partial or complete loss of various bodily functions and a host of other secondary medical problems such as:

- demineralization of bone
- reduction of pulmonary functions
- impairment of the circulatory system
- dysfunction of the kidney, bladder, and bowels
- sexual dysfunction
- muscle spasms
- skin sores
- chronic pain

Added to this are the psychological effects of the social, economic, and emotional adjustments that must be made to the injury.

Instructional Approaches

For most trainees with orthopedic and mobility disabilities, no special arrangements are required other than access to instructional facilities, equipment, and other aids to mobility and physical adjustments in the arrangements of classrooms and laboratories, location of facilities, use of equipment, and handling of supplies. For some trainees with severe physical disabilities, individualized instructional delivery systems may be indicated.

Following are some suggestions for trainers and supervisors who work with people with mobility and motion disabilities:

- Determine needs for special accommodations prior to the start of training; ask the individual with the disability what accommodations he or she needs to participate fully.

- Get expert help in evaluating needs.
- Check the room arrangements to be sure that they are set up in such a way that people in wheelchairs and those who use crutches have enough space to get to and from their position and park.
- Provide a handy location for clothing, accessories, tools, and materials that allow the trainee independence. He or she should be able to reach items without asking or waiting for assistance.
- Be especially wary of U-shaped conference arrangements, which do not allow space for wheelchair parking except at the ends.
- Prepare nondisabled trainees or coworkers for the individual with the disability. Focus on the goal: the development of a contributing member of the team.
- Don't assume that there are many things that they can't do; give them a chance without preconceptions. Describe what needs to be done, and then ask about abilities.
- If pretesting is needed, do it in an environment adapted for people with mobility and motion impairments, even if you have to do it off the premises.
- Make the learning climate supportive and noncompetitive.
- Check with the individual on the need for a note taker.
- Allow some flexibility; permit occasional changes in arrival and departure times.
- Be nonintrusive and considerate of the need for personal privacy; keep out of their personal lives.
- Avoid activities and situations that would place the individual at a disadvantage or where the trainee or worker might feel vulnerable or extremely self-conscious.
- When using team-building exercises, be sure to take into account the physical capabilities of people with mobility and motion disabilities. Include activities and exercises where the nonphysical strengths of people with disabilities will be evident.
- When posting notices and bulletin board illustrations, be sure that they are low enough to be read by people in wheelchairs.
- Experiment with techniques to facilitate and enhance learning.
- Keep the learning environment structured.
- Allow additional time for the completion of physical activities.
- Individualize instruction involving motor skills. Provide information about and demonstration of the best way for the trainee to position himself or herself relative to the work, how to lay out materials, what to pick up first, and exactly how to hold a tool or object.
- Provide opportunities for practice of skills in off-hours.
- Evaluate progress and accomplishment against training or job re-

quirements. Avoid normative measurement (comparison with others).

- Make full use of community-based and in-house professionals and specialists, such as vocational rehabilitation counselors and occupational therapists.
- If possible, assign a person with a similar disability to monitor and assist the individual on the job following the completion of training.

Assistive Technology

A variety of solutions is available for people with mobility impairments. Invariably, people with mobility impairments, whether caused by arthritis, spinal cord injury, multiple sclerosis, or muscular dystrophy, need customized access to and at their place of work. Some need access only to the workplace, and that can be provided by mechanical or motorized wheelchairs; battery-powered, three-wheeled scooters (with hoists installed in car trunks for loading and unloading); and accessible transportation. Others need access to keyboards and computers. Adaptive devices to meet those needs range from relatively simple and inexpensive to complex and expensive.

Ambulation Aids

The most common piece of assistive technology for individuals with mobility impairments is the manual wheelchair. Today, wheelchairs come in a variety of types and models to meet individual needs based on such factors as age, body height, weight and strength, climatic conditions, intended use, need for standard or customized supports or adaptations, and personal preference. They make use of lightweight, durable materials originally developed for space technology and aircraft manufacture.

Canes, crutches, and walkers are used by people who are able to walk with assistance. Canes provide the least support and come in many individualized styles, including single point and quad canes, each of which meets various user needs. Canadian or forearm crutches provide support on both sides of the body, reduce stress on the underarm area, and provide a more natural position for the hand to hold the crutch.

Other ambulation devices include lightweight and compact walking sticks that convert to a seat (available from Solutions) and rolling walkers (walkers with wheels and a braking system that can also be converted to a seat, fold for storage, and have optional attachable baskets, trays, or cane holders (available from NobleMotion and Able Walker). These are convenient variations for individuals who need to pause and rest or perform fatiguing tasks.

Passive Standing Aids

Standing without walking is important for workers with limited mobility. In addition to giving them additional capabilities, it may also reduce urinary problems and improve muscles, range of motion, and circulation and alleviate other physiological problems such as low blood pressure, osteoporosis, and calcium deposits.

Several products can help people stand and get the psychological, physical, and productivity benefits of passive standing. Among them are Lifestand (LDC Corporation of America), East Stand II (Alternate Medical), and Stand-Aid (Stand-Aid of Iowa).

One method, not used very much any more, is heavy braces. A new option is the Italian Boot, a lighter brace. There are also "standing stations" (some power-operated and others motorized) where a person can wheel up to the unit, strap his or her legs in, and hoist the body to a standing position. The station usually has a table top so that the person can read, write, or do other things while standing.

Orthotics

Orthotics include braces and supports that can assist individuals with mobility, activities of daily living, and workplace activities. They include such devices as cervical collars, shoe inserts that correct foot alignment, and hand splints to assist individuals with partial or spastic quadriplegia in such tasks as eating, writing, and keyboarding.

Ramps and Lifts

Portable ramps are available in a variety of styles; most are quite light in weight and can be carried in the trunk of a car. Permanent ramps are usually constructed of wood or concrete and are built to specifications for rise, length, rails, and inclusion of flat rest areas. As an alternative, stair lifts provide a platform on which a wheelchair and its user can be lifted from one floor to another; chair lifts consist of a swivel chair that is moved mechanically up or down a stairway rail.

Automatic Telephone Dialers and Flippers

Automatic telephone dialers are useful for individuals with limited upper body movement. They can dial a number simply by pressing one button instead of seven or more. Phone flippers fit over the connect button of a telephone and hold it down. They can be used by persons who cannot pick up a phone receiver and are activated by a simple flip up or down with a hand, mouthstick, or toe.

Computer Hardware

There are two primary applications of the computer to the needs of people with mobility and motion disabilities: as a prosthetic device, a tool that performs tasks that the body cannot otherwise accomplish, and as a compensatory device, which is particularly useful for alleviating specific learning problems. In both applications, the computer must be modified to permit the user to control the system. Access is achieved by single or multiple switches or voice activation, although any movement under the control of the individual can be used. The user chooses from a word or pictorial menu by using a switch. Most systems also allow the user to modify the speed with which the menus are presented. When a simple switch is used for input, the program is scanned by means of a cursor. Almost any small muscle, even an eyeblink, can be used to control the switch to enter data or retrieve information. Other types of adaptive systems include pointing devices, such as joysticks, light pens, mice, digitized tablets, touch pads, and touch screens, which permit the user to move the cursor around the screen and select the desired information.

The IBM Personal System/2 has been made accessible to people with mobility impairments. Display and system controls are of sufficient size to be usable, are easy to operate, and require a minimum of effort. The 12 function keys are organized in groups of four keys to allow more controlled access. A separate grouping of the six screen movement keys is arranged in two rows of three keys, making these frequently used keys more readily accessible than similar keys on the keypad. And a group of cursor control keys, separate from those on the keypad, is arranged in an inverted T for easier access.

Alternatives to keyboard entry input devices are also available for people with mobility impairments. AID + ME (ComputAbility) plugs into the keyboard and serial ports of the computer, allowing the computer to be controlled by a membrane keyboard, joystick, scanner, switches, Morse code, or a serial communication aid. The device allows the user to assign multiple keystrokes to a single key, redefine key locations on the keyboard, change the key repeat speed or turn off the repeat function, and set the length of time a key must be pressed for the computer to recognize a valid stroke. It also supports mouse emulation for those who cannot control a mouse.

DADAEntry (TASH Inc.) consists of software and a ''black box'' that connects a computer and a selected input device, such as a keyboard, mouse, joystick, or switches. To make data entry easier, the user can assign multiple keystrokes to a single key, change the key repeat rate or turn off the repeat function, and set the length of time a key must be pressed for the computer to recognize a valid keystroke.

DARCI TOO (WesTest Engineering Corp.), when connected between the computer keyboard and the input device, allows the user to control the computer and do data entry with a joystick, video game controller, switches, Morse code, or a special joystick input called DARCI code. The keyboard remains functional at all times, and the unit can be customized to meet special needs.

T-TAM (Trace-Transparent Access Module) (Prentke Romich Company), when connected between the computer and the keyboard, mouse, and/or a serial communication aid, allows the user to enter multiple keystrokes one key at a time, slow the keyboard response rate and avoid accidental keystrokes, adjust or deactivate the key repeat rate, and set the length of time a key must be depressed for the computer to recognize a valid keystroke. T-TAM also supports mouse emulation from the numeric keyboard. Both the keyboard and mouse remain fully functional.

Unicorn Smart Keyboard (Unicorn Engineering, Inc.) plugs directly into the computer keyboard port, requiring no additional hardware or software. The Smart Keyboard has an 8-inch by 12-inch touch-sensitive surface that requires little physical effort by the user. The oversized key shapes help persons who require more space in which to maneuver than a typical keyboard allows. Special overlays let the user customize the keyboard layout to suit personal needs. The Setup Overlay allows features such as keyboard sensitivity, repeat rate, and delay between key presses to be customized.

Other Assistive Devices

At the low end are such simple devices as mouthpicks that allow people with quadriplegia to operate computers, gooseneck telephones and telephone headsets, mechanical page turners, and lazy susan–type desktop file folder systems for people with limited physical dexterity.

Software Programs

Also at the low end are simple software programs, called keyboard solutions, that change the way the user and keyboard interact with the computer. For example, Stickykeys, a program available to both Macintosh and IBM users, allows a person with a mobility impairment to type combinations of keys using only one finger. To type a capital "E," the user hits the shift button and then the lowercase "e." The computer remembers and capitalizes the letter. Other solutions allow people with limited control of their hands to prevent the computer from typing more than one "E" before they can lift their fingers.

IBM Independence Series. Voice Type, a flexible speech recognition program that provides an affordable keyboard alternative, allows the user to control DOS and many popular text-based software programs by speaking. AccessDOS enhances keyboard access for IBM DOS users. Keyboard responses can be customized to the specific needs and abilities of people with mobility impairments.

StickyKeys allows the user to press each key separately in a multiple key operation, eliminating the need to hold down more than one key at a time. Slowkeys allows the user to set the length of time a key must be held down in order for the computer to recognize it as a valid keystroke.

BounceKeys prevents double entry of a character if the user accidentally bounces on a key when pressing or releasing it. RepeatKeys allows the user to set the key repeat rate to suit the individual's keying ability or turn it off. MouseKeys makes it possible to use the numeric keypad to move the cursor around the computer screen, simulating the use of a mouse.

Word-Predictive Software. Word-predictive software reduces the number of keys users have to type to get the words they want. For example, the computer can provide a list of words every time a key is hit. Type the letter "a," and "a," "above," "across," "after," "all," "an," "and," and "an" appear on the screen. If the desired word does not appear, the user types the next letter in the word and continues until either the correct word appears on the menu or the complete word is typed. Augmentative communication software tracks the frequency of use of words and reproduces those used most often.

Voice Output Devices. More sophisticated devices include voice output. When a word is typed, the computer voices it aloud. The computer than repeats the whole phrase or sentence. Other devices involve voice recognition systems. If the person with the disability can speak, specialized hardware and software allow him or her to speak into a microphone and put the words on a computer screen. All that is required is a pause of about 1 second between words, resulting in a speed of 40 words per minute with 90 percent accuracy. The system also learns the speech patterns of the user and adjusts itself accordingly.

Other Computer-Assisted Devices. The most sophisticated devices require no keyboards and no mobility on the part of the user. Some use eye movements that activate the computer by means of an infrared beam of light that is reflected off the cornea of the eye onto the computer screen.

Ke:nx (pronounced "connects") (Don Johnson Developmental Equipment, Inc.) is one of the most useful devices for persons who have lost a limb or have spinal cord injuries. It is a keyboard and mouse emulator that allows people with physical disabilities to operate Macintosh computers and use regular software without using the keyboard. With Ke:nx, persons with disabilities can use educational programs, graphics, design programs, databases, and word processing or do programming. It permits the use of alternative input devices to handle every aspect of computer operation: open menus, launch applications, select buttons in dialog boxes, scroll through windows, control the mouse, and find and use scroll bars. The system operates with any Macintosh computer with an ADB port, hard drive, minimum of 2 MB RAM, and System 7.0 or higher (also System 6.0.7/6.0.8).

Ke:nx On-Board provides a complete keyboard and mouse emulation. It consists of a full-featured membrane keyboard that slips over a Macintosh Powerbook (Apple's notebook-sized portable computer) that fits on a wheelchair tray. The keyboard reacts to touch instead of pressure and is adjustable for a light or heavy hand. Extra keyboard overlays and software allow the user to change the keyboard's functions. There is also a programmable speech option for all keys so that the user can listen to check for keystroke accuracy.

The Eyegaze Computer System (available from LC Technologies) enables people with severe motor disabilities, such as Lou Gehrig's disease, multiple sclerosis, spinal cord injuries, and strokes, to do many things with their eyes that they would otherwise do with their hands. By looking at control keys displayed on a computer screen, the user can perform a variety of functions, including speech synthesis, environmental control, keyboarding, operating a telephone, and running DOS-compatible software. A video camera located below the computer screen continually observes the eye, and specialized image-processing software determines the eye's orientation and projects the gazepoint on the computer display, enabling the user to control entire on-screen computer keyboards. Nothing is attached to the head or body.

TouchWindow (available from Edmark Corporation) is a device that attaches to any standard computer monitor with self-adhesive Velcro strips and plugs into a port on the computer. Users touch the screen to interact with the software. The device is available for Amiga, Apple II series, IBM and compatibles, and Macintosh SE or newer.

Madenta Communications ScreenDoors (available from Apple Computer) software puts a keyboard on a Macintosh screen and allows the user to operate it with any point-and-click device, from a mouse to a head pointer. A built-in word predictor learns the user's vocabulary as he or she types and then completes words based on the first few letters entered. The program works with any application and includes several different keyboard layouts. It requires 2 megabytes of RAM and system software version 6.0.3 or later with Multifinder.

Prentke Romich HeadMaster (available from Prentke Romich, Apple Computer) provides an alternative to a mouse for those who are unable to use their hands but have good head and mouth control. The user turns and puffs instead of pointing and clicking. It requires a keyboard emulator such as ScreenDoors.

The Madenta Communications Virtual Telephone (available from Apple Computer) allows the user to interface a telephone with a Macintosh computer. The Virtual Telephone provides 200-number speed dialing and an on-screen directory, all activated by any point-and-click device or by voice recognition. The system includes a wireless headset that allows the user to place calls by voice command from within 400 feet of the computer. It requires a Macintosh Plus or newer computer with 2 megabytes of RAM, a hard disk, system software version 6.0.3 or later, and HyperCard 2.1.

IntelliTools IntelliKeys (available from Apple Computer) plugs into the keyboard of any Macintosh computer, with no need for an additional interface, and can be adapted to suit a range of needs. It works with all existing software. The system is reconfigured by sliding in any of its six included overlays, each of which has a bar code that the keyboard recognizes. The Arrows overlay is used for mouse emulation, the Alphabet and Numbers overlay for text- and math-based input, the Basic Writing and QWERTY overlays to work with word processors, and the Setup overlay to work with special IntelliKeys functions. The system is useful for people with physical, visual, or cognitive disabilities.

Robotic Aids. Robotic Manipulator (Regenesis Development Corporation), developed by the Neil Squire Foundation, works with IBM VoiceType to make it possible for a person with mobility impairment to pick up and move objects. The manipulator is fully programmable and can be set to pick up objects and move them up and down, left and right, or rotate them. It can be used in both home and office environments.

Special Use Software. Cintex2 (Nanopac), an environmental control program, works with IBM VoiceType (Dragon Systems) to provide a full range of control functions directed by speech. The program can control up to 256 on-off devices, infrared-controlled devices, such as TVs, VCRs, and CD players, and telephone functions, including answering, dialing, conference calling, and responding to call waiting. Clintex2 includes a starter set of more than 50 voice commands that perform common functions such as "answer phone," "VCR fast forward," and "TV volume up."

Vehicle Adaptations

Many adaptations for vehicles, including even heavy construction equipment, are available to provide accessibility for operators and users with mobility impairments. Low-end adaptations include replacing bucket seats with swivel seats to allow users to enter or exit the vehicle more easily to the side or rear (particularly important when transfer to or from a wheelchair is involved).

Vans can be equipped with removable drivers' seats so that individuals who are unable to transfer from wheelchair to seat can use their wheelchairs as the driving seat. Various types of wheelchair hoists allow folded wheelchairs to be moved into a car or van after the driver has transferred to the vehicle's driver's seat.

Hand controls, which do not interfere with standard operation of the vehicle, can be permanently attached to one side or the other of the steering column of any vehicle. Van lifts can be permanently installed to allow a wheelchair user to be lifted into and out of the van, and most can be operated independently by the user from both inside and outside the vehicle or by remote control.

Because any type of disability has the potential to affect the way a person drives, each individual should go through an evaluation by a driving professional (with experience with people who have disabilities) to determine his or her capabilities and limitations, find the proper match of driver adaptive devices, and determine the need for special driver training. Rehabilitation hospitals and clinics and state departments of rehabilitation are good sources of referral for qualified driver evaluators. Other organizations that can help with evaluation and the driver training include the local or regional office of the Department of Veterans Affairs (for veterans) and national organizations for people with specific disabilities.

Evaluation should focus on two areas: visual and cognitive evaluation (a check for proper vision and reaction) and physical evaluation (a check of strength and assessment of the types of controls needed). Once the evaluation is completed, in most cases hands-on training will be required to become accustomed to the new controls and develop confidence. Because insurance does not always cover driver rehabilitation and training and private programs can run as high as $125 per hour, funding for evaluation and training is often a problem. Rotary, Lions, Elks, and other local clubs may help.

There is help available to get the vehicle the driver with disabilities needs. Chrysler Corporation, Ford and Lincoln-Mercury, and Volkswagen provide reimbursement for vehicle adaptations and other help as follows:

Manufacturer	Reimbursement for Adaptations Up To	Other Help
Chrysler Corp. (cars, trucks, and vans), (800) 255-9877	$ 500	Phone resource center
Ford and Lincoln-Mercury (cars, trucks, and vans), (800) 952-2248, (800) TDD-0312 (TDD)	750	Free cellular phone Emergency road service (1 year)
General Motors (cars, trucks, and vans), (800) 323-9935, (800) TDD-9935 (TDD)	$1,000	GMAC financing available Access America Atlas
Volkswagen (EuroVan only), (800) 444-8987	$1,000	$500 off any other VW that requires adaptive driving aids

Summary

Trainers and supervisors who work with trainees and employees who have mobility and motion impairments must give special attention to needs and accommodations. The types and severity of these types of impairments are so varied and wide that few standard prescriptions are appropriate. The range includes finger, hand, arm, and leg amputations, usually caused by accident injury, illness, or malignancy; degenerative diseases such as arthritis, cerebral palsy, multiple sclerosis, and muscular dystrophy; and spinal cord injury. The severity of these conditions extends from minimal effect on mobility or motion to complete lack of mobility and motion as exemplified by quadriplegia.

In addition to accommodations, prostheses, and the use of assistive equipment, devices, and materials, instructors and supervisors must understand the limitations imposed on employees by various types of disabilities and how they can be compensated. Of much greater importance to the development of competent workers with disabilities is the attitude of trainers, supervisors, and coworkers toward them. They must be unfailingly understanding, considerate, and supportive.

For Further Reading and Viewing*

ADA Customer Courtesies. 1993. 20-minute video. Available from United Training Media.

ADA for Retail. 1993. 12-minute video. Available from United Training Media.

The Americans with Disabilities Act: Impact on Training. INFO-LINE 9203. Alexandria, Va.: American Society for Training and Development, March 1993.

The Americans with Disabilities Act: Techniques for Accommodation. INFO-LINE 9204. Alexandria, Va.: American Society for Training and Development, April 1992.

Arthritis Foundation. *Understanding Arthritis.* New York: Scribners, 1984.

Assistive Technology Sourcebook. Washington, D.C.: RESNA Press, 1990.

Corea, James, and the Multiple Sclerosis Association of America. *MS Maintenance.* Oaklyn, N.J.: MSAA, 1991.

Department of Veterans Affairs. *Notes for Amputees: Things to Know about Amputation and Artificial Limbs.* Washington, D.C.: DVA, March 1980.

Employability: Integrating People with Developmental Disabilities into the Workplace. 1993. 27-minute video. Available from Woolworth Corporation.

Fries, James F. *Arthritis: A Comprehensive Guide.* Reading, Mass.: Addison-Wesley, 1979.

Goldberg, Marge, Paula F. Goldberg, and Cathleen Urbain. *Opportunity Knocking: The Story of Supported Employment.* Minneapolis: PACER Center, 1988.

If I Can Do This . . . I Can Do Anything! 1992. 10-minute video. Available from United Training Media.

Interactive Robotic Aids. Washington, D.C.: RESNA Press, 1986.

Lewis, Ricki. *Arthritis: Modern Treatment for That Old Pain in the Joints.* DHHS Pub. (FDA) 92-1190. Rockville, Md.: Public Health Service, Food and Drug Administration, U.S. Department of Health and Human Services, n.d.

Making a Difference—A Wise Approach. 1992. 20-minute video. Available from National Easter Seal Society.

No One Is Burning Wheelchairs. 1992. 20-minute video. Available from National Easter Seal Society.

Participants with Disabilities: How to Address Their Needs. INFO-LINE 8704. Alexandria, Va.: American Society for Training and Development, April 1987.

Part of the Team. 1991. 40- or 17-minute video. Available from the National Easter Seal Society.

Schapiro, Randall T., and the Multiple Sclerosis Association of America. *Understanding Multiple Sclerosis.* Oaklyn, N.J.: MSAA, 1991.

Seating and Mobility Needs of Severely Disabled and Elderly Persons. Washington, D.C.: RESNA Press, 1990.

Smith, Brenda, et al. *Managing Disability at Work: Improving Practice in Organizations.* Briston, Pa.: Taylor and Francis, 1991.

Sobel, Dava, and Arthur C. Klein. *Arthritis: What Works.* New York: St. Martin's Press, 1989.

*Full addresses of the organizations in this listing appear in Appendixes B and C.

Succeeding Together at Work. 1993. 7-minute video. Available from Salenger Films.

Transportation I. Washington, D.C.: RESNA Press, 1991.

Urbain, Cathleen. *Supported Employment: A Step-by-Step Guide*. Minneapolis: PACER Center, 1992.

War Amputations of Canada. *Amputation III*. Ottawa, Ontario: War Amputations of Canada, April 1986.

Welcome to the Team: Diversity Etiquette in the Workplace. 1992. 19:40-minute video. Available from United Training Media.

Wheelchair III. Washington, D.C.: RESNA Press, 1982.

Wheelchair IV. Washington, D.C.: RESNA Press, 1988.

Notes

1. Department of Veterans Affairs, *Notes for Amputees: Things to Know about Amputation and Artificial Limbs* (March 1980), p. 1.
2. See War Amputations of Canada, *Amputation III* (Otawa, Ontario: War Amputations of Canada, April 1986).
3. Ricki Lewis, *Arthritis: Modern Treatment for That Old Pain in the Joints* (Rockville, Md.: Public Health Service, Food and Drug Administration, U.S. Department of Health and Human Services, n.d.).
4. Adapted from *Facts about ALS* and *Basic Home Care for ALS Patients*, ALS Association.
5. Adapted from Leon Sternfeld, "Cerebral Palsy," *Health and Medical Horizons* (New York: Macmillan, 1991.) © 1991 Macmillan Educational Company, 866 Third Avenue, New York, NY 10022 (212) 702-2000. Used by permission.
6. Society for Muscular Dystrophy International, P.O. Box 479, Bridgewater, Nova Scotia Canada B4V 2X6 (902) 682-3086. Used by permission.
7. "Autosomal" means that the gene is not carried on the sex chromosomes, so both male and female babies can get the disease. "Recessive" means that if the gene is paired with a normal gene, the normal gene will dominate, and the person will not get the disease; however, that person will be a carrier of the gene.
8. Excerpted from *What Is Multiple Sclerosis*. © 1993 National Multiple Sclerosis Society, 733 Third Ave., New York, NY 10017-3278. Used by permission.
9. Adapted from materials provided by the National Spinal Cord Injury Association, 600 West Cummings Park, Suite 2000, Woburn, MA 01801. Used by permission.

9

Health and Medical Disabilities

At age 4, Marilyn was diagnosed as having epilepsy. Its cause could not be identified, and it remains unknown. She did not have a head injury, meningitis, or even measles, nor was there a family history of epilepsy. Although several types of medication were prescribed at that time, in the intervening years Marilyn continued to experience periodic auras, occasional generalized seizures, and simple partial seizures during which she could not control trembling or jerking of one arm or leg. These episodes continued through her high school and college years.

Marilyn did exceptionally well in high school and college. She regularly made the dean's list and was active in extracurricular activities, including the glee club, dramatic club, and field hockey and softball teams, and served as vice president of her class during her junior and senior years. Following graduation with a B.S. in accounting, she was employed as an accountant with a large accounting firm and soon began part-time study for the CPA examination. At that time, she began taking one of the new antiepileptic drugs, and the number of her auras and seizures were dramatically reduced. The chances are good that they will disappear completely as she becomes older.

Two years ago, at age 28, Marilyn passed the CPA examination on the first try and was immediately promoted to a managerial position. Her election to partnership in the accounting firm in the future appears to be a sure thing. Her intelligence, persistence, and "can do" attitude have made her a success story. But the understanding, support, and assistance of her coworkers and supervisors were equally crucial to her achievements.

People are susceptible to hundreds of health and medical conditions that can, and often do, affect not only their work lives but also their activities of daily living. Until recently, the jobs of people who contracted life-threatening or terminal illnesses, such as cancer, heart disease, acquired immune deficiency syndrome (AIDS), or even addictions, such as alcoholism, were largely unprotected. With the passage of the Americans with Disabilities Act of 1990 (ADA) that situation has changed. Workers with serious illnesses now come under the ADA definition of a "qualified individual with a disability," a person with "a disability who meets the skill, experience education, and other job-related requirements of a position held or desired, and who, with or without reasonable accommodation, can perform the essential functions of a job."

The law does not (and cannot) define the point at which a worker becomes unable to perform the essential functions of a job nor does it identify the options of an employer when that point is reached. Case law and the courts will eventually result in clearer guidelines. In the interim, employers would be prudent, as well as compassionate, to do everything possible to provide accommodations to these workers so that they can continue to work as well as avoid complaints of unlawful discharge.

Types of Medical Conditions

The following brief descriptions of some of the most common medical problems, their sources, and their control will provide a basic understanding of these conditions so that those responsible for hiring and supervising people who have them will see the need for accommodations and have some notion as to what kinds of adjustments in the work environment may be effective. Nonetheless, the best sources of help in identifying adaptations and accommodations are medical practitioners and the people with the conditions themselves.

Alcoholism

Alcoholism is a disease in which a person becomes physically addicted to alcohol and is compelled to drink alcoholic beverages. It is estimated to be the third leading cause of death in the United States, and it affects people of all ages and socioeconomic backgrounds.

The symptoms of alcoholism are regular or "binge" drinking and the fabrication of intricate strategies to obtain alcohol or conceal the fact that it was consumed. As the disease develops, other symptoms appear, such as absenteeism and tardiness, lapses in memory, frequent accidents or injuries, unusual behavior, unkempt appearance, poor nutrition, failure to function in job or family life, obvious hangovers, blackouts, and cirrhosis of the liver. As the disease progresses, it may lead to life-threatening physical complications, and it is certain to disrupt or destroy family and work relationships.

The causes of alcoholism include psychological problems and excessive tension, and there may be a hereditary element. Self-help and support groups, such as Alcoholics Anonymous, have proved to be helpful to people who have an alcohol problem. For some cases, however, intensive treatment, in either a residential facility (severe cases) or outpatient clinic (less severe problems), is required to detoxify, reeducate, motivate, and provide the needed psychological support.

Asthma

More than 15 million Americans have or have had asthma, with about 40 percent of the cases starting in early childhood. More males than females have the disease. The effects of the disease range from merely inconvenient to life threatening, although in the great majority of cases, asthma does not cause serious permanent damage to the lungs or heart.

During an asthma attack, the bronchial tubes (bronchi and the smaller bronchioles) and the lungs become swollen and inflamed, resulting in a reduction in the air supply and a feeling of tightness in the chest and breathlessness, often accompanied by a dry cough. An attack can be triggered by tobacco smoke, air pollution, cleaning solvents, hair spray, perfume, sinusitis, allergies, a viral infection, or a host of other irritants. Stress and even exercise (particularly during cold weather) can bring on an attack that can last from a few minutes to several days. (Nonetheless, regular exercise is important for people with asthma because it makes breathing easier.) The most common culprit is allergens, substances in the air caused by microscopic dust mites, insects (such as cockroaches), or dander from household pets.

Attacks of asthma can be short-circuited or controlled by a combination of medication and relaxation techniques. Medication, such as cromolyn, in the form of a bronchodilator, is self-administered using an inhaler, coating and stabilizing the airways. Used properly, inhalers provide the most relief. In addition, immunotherapy—injections of tiny amounts of the substances a person with asthma is allergic to—can trick the body's immune system into building tolerance to the allergen that can trigger attacks.

Cancer

Cancer is the number two cause of death in America today, claiming the lives of 1,375 people every 24 hours, and threatening three out of four American families.[1] Cancer is one of the most frightening diseases, perhaps because most people believe that it is beyond their control and because each of us has a one in four chance of developing it in our lifetime.

Cancer is a general name for a group of about 100 unique diseases. Among the most common are bladder, bone and bone marrow, brain, breast, cervical, esophageal, kidney, larynx, liver, lung, lymphomas (non-Hodgkins), ovarian, pancreatic, prostate, skin, stomach, testicular, thyroid, uteral and Hodgkins lymphoma, and malignant melanoma.

Cancer is an uncontrolled proliferation of abnormal cells, which often form a malignant mass or tumor. In most cases, its cause is unknown. Most forms of cancer are noncontagious. Cancer cells can multiply rapidly, invade tissues and organs, destroy healthy cells, and spread to any organ of the body, the blood, and lymph nodes through a process called metastasis. Some types of cancer progress slowly; others develop swiftly. Although some forms are almost always fatal, many are treatable.

Although the severity depends on the type and extent of the cancer, some forms—notably brain, esophageal, liver, multiple myeloma, and stomach—are likely to be fatal. In any case, people with cancer are in the workplace in large numbers. Some, over a period of time, will become debilitated and have such symptoms as fatigue and overall weakness, low-grade fever, anemia, loss of weight, nausea, choking, shortness of breath, bone and joint tenderness, swelling and pain in the affected area, and frequent infections.

Not much is not known about cancer; however, there is increasing evidence that up to 80 percent of cancers may be related to life-style— poor diet (too much fat, too little fiber, lack of vitamins, overuse of alcohol); smoking, chewing, or sniffing tobacco; overexposure to the ultraviolet rays of the sun; ingestion of air and water pollutants; exposure to radon (a radioactive gas that seeps into buildings from underground rocks); and excessive exposure to X-rays. Family history is also believed to play a role in the formation of some types of cancer.

The most commonly used cancer treatments are surgery, chemotherapy, and radiation therapy, which aim to remove or destroy the cancerous cells. Treatment for bone and mouth cancer may result in orthopedic or mobility impairments or disfigurement due to the surgery required to eliminate the malignancy. Because traditional therapies do not always work, the search for a "magic bullet" is underway—a customized treatment for a specific type of cancer that involves programming the immune system to kill the cancer. Currently under study are interferon, a substance secreted by T-cells in response to viral infections, and thymosin, a powerful hormone secreted by the thymus.

Cystic Fibrosis (CF)[2]

Cystic fibrosis, one of the most common fatal genetic diseases of Caucasians, occurs equally in males and females in about one of every 2,000 live-born white babies and about one of every 17,000 black babies. It is estimated that about 30,000 people in the United States have CF and that about one in every 20 (about 20 million people) carries one defective gene. A child must inherit one defective gene from each parent to have the disease. CF is present at birth and is usually diagnosed within the first three years, although it may not show up for a while. It is not contagious.

CF causes the exocrine (outward secreting) glands in the body to fail to function normally. These glands normally produce thin, slippery secretions, including sweat, mucus, tears, saliva, and digestive enzymes. The secretions are carried through ducts to the external surface of the body or into hollow organs such as the intestines or the airways. With CF, the mucus-producing exocrine glands often generate thick, sticky secretions that may plug up ducts and other passageways, particularly in the lungs and intestines, where they can interfere with vital body functions, such as breathing and digestion. CF affects the sweat glands in that the amount of salt and potassium in the sweat is abnormally high. When too much salt is lost due to heavy sweating during hot weather or strenuous exercise, the effects include fatigue, weakness, fever, muscle cramps, abdominal pain, vomiting, heat prostration or heat stroke, or dehydration.

The symptoms of CF include the following:

- Recurrent wheezing
- Persistent cough and excessive, thick mucus
- Recurrent pneumonia
- Failure to gain weight, often despite good appetite
- Abnormal bowel movements
- Salty-tasting skin
- Clubbing (enlargement of the fingertips and toes)

The digestive problems generated by CF, such as poor weight gain (due to failure of the body to absorb enough nutrients), abdominal pain or discomfort, and bowel function irregularities, are usually managed through dietary and nutritional changes, vitamins, and replacement of pancreatic enzymes.

While nearly every person with CF eventually develops lung disease (although the onset and the severity of the disease varies greatly from person to person), therapy can slow the damage to the lungs. The most commonly used treatments for CF-induced lung problems are chest physical therapy, exercise, aerosols, and antibiotics.

A new drug, DNase, manufactured by Genentech under the name, Pulmozyme, was approved for CF patients by the U.S. Food and Drug

Administration and Canada's Health Protection Branch in December 1993. DNase is not a cure but a way of staving off the ravages of the disease until gene therapy succeeds. It liquefies mucus that collects in the lungs, thereby reducing the number of fatal respiratory infections and improving lung function.

Treatment of CF includes prevention of salt depletion by avoiding situations that might cause excessive sweating, drinking more fluids, eating salty foods, and adding salt to other foods—or in extreme cases, salt tablets when prescribed by a physician.

With rapid improvement in diagnosis and methods of treatment, more than half of all people with CF live into their late 20s or older. Many are now living into their 40s and 50s, and a few are over 60 years of age. That means that more and more people with CF will be members of the workforce in future years and must be accommodated.

Gene therapy is now underway to replace the defective gene that causes CF. Eventually, after extensive research, this therapy may someday cure the disorder.

Diabetes Mellitus

About 13 million Americans—nearly 1 in 5 of all those over age 55—have diabetes mellitus, with its complications a leading cause of death by disease. Diabetes is a major cause of new blindness, amputations, and kidney failure. About 700,000 people will be diagnosed with diabetes this year, and about 150,000 will die from this disease.

Diabetes is a noncontagious disease in which the body is unable to metabolize glucose for energy properly. It can occur at any stage of life. It has two forms: Type I, insulin-dependent diabetes mellitus, in which the body does not produce enough insulin to help with the assimilation of glucose, and Type II, noninsulin-dependent diabetes mellitus, in which the body produces enough or nearly enough insulin but the cells of the body are not able to use it effectively. Type I, with between 500,000 and 1 million people with the condition, is less common than Type II, which numbers about 12 million people.

The symptoms of diabetes include intense thirst, increased output of urine, fatigue, and often blurred vision. There may be increased appetite accompanied by weight loss when the basic problem is little or no insulin. In any case, glucose at high concentrations in the blood can damage nerves, blood vessels, the arteries leading to the heart, and the heart itself. Although its causes are not completely understood, there is increasing evidence that insulin-dependent diabetes is genetic in origin and that nondependent diabetes is caused by obesity or heredity, or both.

Insulin-dependent diabetes is the more serious disease, in that it carries a risk of coma and grave illness if not controlled and the hazards and sometimes fatal complications of kidney disease, blindness, cataracts, nerve and blood vessel damage, severe leg pains, gangrene, and even limb amputations. For those with noninsulin-dependent diabetes, the same complications can occur but are not usually as severe. For insulin-dependent diabetes, there is the additional risk of too much insulin, which may result in coma from hypoglycemia.

Insulin-dependent diabetes is controlled by carefully balanced dosage(s) of insulin daily, administered by hypodermic needle or the use of an insulin pump, augmented by a controlled diet, daily exercise, regular (self-administered) measurement of blood sugar levels, and frequent medical evaluation. Noninsulin-dependent diabetes is controlled by weight loss for those who are overweight, oral medication to reduce blood sugar for some, and carefully regulated diet, regular exercise, a thorough education about the disease and its potential complications, and frequent medical follow-up and evaluation. For some people with adult-onset diabetes, the disease may be controlled by diet—reducing calories, consuming less fat, increasing complex carbohydrates and high-fiber foods (such as beans, grains, and potatoes), eliminating sweets, and distributing food intake throughout the day in smaller quantities.

Epilepsy[3]

Epilepsy is an ancient and baffling malady, still misunderstood. It is not a disease or a form of mental illness but a physical condition—a disorder of the central nervous system, caused by sudden brief changes in how the brain works. This results in alterations in the person's movements or actions, called seizures, for a short period of time. A seizure occurs when there is abnormal electrical activity in the brain. A person has epilepsy if he or she has recurring seizures. About 1 percent of the U.S. population—more than 2 million people—have epilepsy.

Epilepsy is not contagious and usually not hereditary. According to the Epilepsy Foundation of America, although epilepsy can develop at any time of life, about one-third of the 125,000 new cases every year begin in childhood. No cause can be found in about half of the cases. Most develop with no family history of the condition. The remaining cases may be caused by head injuries, brain tumors, genetic conditions, lead poisoning, problems in brain development before birth, illnesses such as meningitis or encephalitis, or severe cases of measles. Drug therapy is the most common way to treat epilepsy. With modern medical care, 80 to 85 percent of people with epilepsy can get complete control of seizures so long as they take their medication regularly.

The most common medications are Dilantin (phenytoin), Tegretol (carbamazepine), Depakene or Depakote (valproate), Zarontin (ethosuximide), Mysoline (primidone), and phenobarbital, but they have not been effective for everyone. In August 1993, the U.S. Food and Drug Administration approved a new drug, Felbatol (felbamate), for general use. Neurontin (gabapentin) was approved at the end of the year. Another new drug, lamotrigine, is likely to be approved. These medications are said to have fewer side effects than some of the older drugs.

The most common types of seizures are as follows:

- *Generalized tonic clonic seizures (grand mal or convulsions)* occur when the whole brain is suddenly flooded with extra electrical energy. The person falls to the ground, temporarily unconscious. The body stiffens briefly and then begins jerking movements. A frothy saliva may appear around the mouth, and breathing may become very shallow or may even stop for a few moments. Sometimes the skin turns a bluish color. The jerking movements then slow down, and the seizure ends spontaneously after a minute or two. The person regains consciousness but may feel confused and sleepy. In some cases, the recovery period is very short. Most people can go back to their normal activities after a short while.

- *Absence seizures (petit mal)* look like daydreaming or blank staring. They begin and end abruptly, last only a few seconds, and are most often seen in children. Persons having this kind of seizure are unaware of people and things around them for a few seconds but quickly return to full awareness. The seizures happen so quickly that the person, and sometimes others who are around, may not notice them.

- *Complex partial seizures (psychomotor or temporal lobe)* occur when the extra brain activity affects only part of the brain. It may begin with a feeling of fear, a sudden sick feeling in the stomach, or seeing or hearing something that is not there. The person appears to be in a trance and goes through a series of movements over which he or she has no control. He or she stares blankly, may make chewing motions, move an arm, pull at clothing or get up and walk around, all the time appearing to be in a daze. Although the seizure usually lasts only a minute or two, full awareness may not return for some time. Confusion and irritability may follow, and the person will not remember what happened. In rare cases, these seizures may cause a person to run, scream, appear afraid, or disrobe.

- *Simple partial seizures* mean that the person is conscious during the seizure but cannot control body movements—usually trembling or jerking of an arm or leg. Another type of simple partial seizure produces unusual feelings. Things may look strange, the person may "see" people or things that are not there, hear strange sounds that are not there, feel that what is happening has happened before, or feel strange sensations on one side of his or her body. Partial seizures may affect enough brain cells to spread and become a generalized tonic clonic seizure.

■ *Auras* are unusual sensations that warn of an imminent major seizure. The sensation may be a feeling of fear or sickness or an odd smell or taste. People who have this warning often have time to move away from possible hazards before the seizure starts. Sometimes the seizure doesn't spread, and all that occurs is the special sensation.

Epilepsy is in most cases a manageable condition. Most people with epilepsy lead normal lives, holding jobs and raising families. People who train those with epilepsy face two challenges that go far beyond the physical aspects of the disorder: discrimination and self-esteem. Centuries of misinformation and myths about the disorder cause serious bias problems for people with epilepsy because of the stigma attached to it. As a result, many people with epilepsy have low self-esteem. Trainers need to help their trainees become positive and upbeat and learn how to present epilepsy to employers in a way that will be reassuring to them. Trainers must also encourage people with epilepsy to do the things they can do and should constantly reinforce positive behaviors.

Heart Disease

Approximately one in four Americans has some form of cardiovascular disease. It is the number one killer in the United States, annually claiming the lives of about 1 million—about one person every half-minute.

Although a very large number of disorders can affect the heart, the most common form of heart disease is ischemic heart disease (atherosclerosis), also known as coronary artery disease or coronary heart disease. It results in a narrowing of the arteries, which causes decreased blood supply to the heart muscle, shortness of breath, mild to severe chest pain (angina pectoris), which may radiate down the left arm and to the neck, back, or jaw, and in critical cases, nausea, vomiting, sweating, and faintness—symptoms of a "heart attack." A heart attack, called a myocardial infarction, means that the supply of blood to a part of the heart muscle has been cut off, suffered irreversible injury, and died. The person who has a heart attack may become disabled or die, depending on how much of the heart muscle has been affected.

Narrowing of the coronary arteries is caused by the formation of plaque, a waxy substance containing cholesterol and cellular debris, on the walls of the artery that may block the flow of blood. As a consequence, the deprived muscle tissue creates pain and may die. Coronary heart disease can be prevented by a diet low in cholesterol and saturated fats, cessation of smoking, maintaining close to ideal weight, regular ex-

ercise, control of blood pressure and stress, and periodic medical monitoring to detect potential problems. Once it has occurred, coronary heart
disease can be treated by diet, medication, and exercise in a controlled
setting or, if effective control is not achieved, by surgery.

The severity of coronary heart disease depends on the extent to
which the arteries are blocked, the suddenness of the problem, and
whether ventricular fibrillation (a life-threatening condition where the
lower chambers of the heart do not effectively circulate the blood) occurs.
The root of the problem may be hereditary. Older men with a history of
heart disease in the family are much more likely to get coronary heart
disease than younger women with no such family history. Coronary
heart disease can be prevented or ameliorated by reducing blood cholesterol, blood pressure, and weight, eliminating tobacco, and engaging in
regular exercise.

Other forms of heart disease are congenital defects, such as a hole
in the wall between the heart's upper chambers; diseases of the heart
valves, which cause them to malfunction; and arrhythmias, when the
rhythm of the heartbeat is disrupted.

HIV/AIDS

Human immunodeficiency virus (HIV) is a microorganism that causes
AIDS (acquired immunodeficiency syndrome) and associated conditions,
such as AIDS-related complex (ARC). The disease first became a worldwide concern in 1981. On October 28, 1993, the Centers for Disease Control and Prevention reported that since 1981, 339,250 Americans have
contracted the disease and that 204,390 have died. It is conservatively
estimated that 1 million men, women, and children in the United States,
straight and gay, carry HIV. It is the number one killer of men between
the ages of 25 and 44 and the fourth leading killer of women in that age
group.

HIV is present in the earliest stages of infection when there are no
symptoms as well as in people with full-blown cases of AIDS. A positive
HIV test does not mean that the individual will develop AIDS; however,
such people can transmit the virus. Once a person is infected, the median
time before symptoms disease is just over eight years. That means that
more and more people with HIV live for years in relative good health,
able to work at the jobs for which they have been trained.

AIDS is a viral illness, assumed to be terminal, that attacks the
body's immune system, leaving it vulnerable to infection. There are at
least two viruses, HIV-1 and HIV-2, that cause AIDS. The disease is
transmitted only by the exchange of body fluids, such as through sexual
contacts, needles, cuts in the skin, and transfusions of infected blood.

Once it enters the body, the AIDS virus attacks the immune system, disabling the disease-fighting white blood cells. As the number of these cells decreases, the body's ability to combat illnesses and infections weakens. Initially the immune system fights back by developing antibodies to some of the virus, at which time the person tests HIV positive. Over time the virus wins the battle, and the person becomes defenseless and vulnerable to other illnesses and diseases, such as pneumonia, tuberculosis, Kaposi's sarcoma (a form of cancer), and other viral or bacterial infections. These diseases weaken the individual and ultimately result in death.

ARC is an early and mild form of the AIDS disease when symptoms begin to appear that may or may not develop into full-blown AIDS. Symptoms include loss of appetite, weight loss, fever, night sweats, skin rashes, easy bruising, diarrhea, fatigue, shortness of breath, lack of resistance to infection, and swollen lymph nodes. Positive results on an HIV-antibody test are also necessary for a diagnosis. Several medications are prescribed for people with ARC and AIDS, and others are being tested. To date, the effectiveness of these treatments has been questionable. Nevertheless, new drugs and improved treatments have increased the life expectancy of people with AIDS since the disease was first detected. People who used to die within a few months now can live for a number of years.

According to the Business Response to AIDS (BRTA), the resource service of the U.S. Centers for Disease Control National AIDS Clearinghouse, of Rockville, Maryland, more than two-thirds of companies with more than 2,500 workers and almost 1 in 10 employers with fewer than 500 employees have an employee with HIV or AIDS. The disease has become a subject that no employer can afford to ignore. It must be addressed in company illness policies, training for current employees and new hires focusing on work-related issues, individual and group counseling programs, educational and community relations programs, and accommodations for workers with HIV or AIDS.

Approaches to Training

The first obligation of employers to people with health and medical disabilities is to meet their psychological needs. Writing about persons with AIDS and other life-threatening illnesses, one author says, "Daily life is marked with anxiety and fear—potential loss of friends, employment, and livelihood."[4] He identifies the following needs:

- Referral for psychological and medical help
- Familiarity with benefits provisions: health insurance coverage, life insurance, leaves of absence, disability

- Other personal support (e.g., access to legal advice, child care provisions, financial planning, and other family-related matters)
- Educational support for coworkers (e.g., if it becomes known that a person has HIV)

I would add to the list these suggestions:

- Offer employees the opportunity to work as long as they can, so long as their continued employment does not endanger themselves or other employees.
- Ask employees what help or accommodations they need to continue working.
- When making job assignments, take into account the potential risk to the employee whose immune system has been damaged by disease.
- Ensure the confidentiality of health records and any medical information obtained about an employee.
- Be completely open in addressing the concerns of employees about infectious diseases.
- Provide help and services through the company's employee assistance program.
- Refer employees to community agencies and organizations that offer medical, counseling, and other support services.

Employers also have an obligation to the coworkers of people with life-threatening diseases. Following are the most important:

- Formulate and communicate company policy and specific guidelines with regard to AIDS and other catastrophic illnesses.
- Demonstrate sensitivity, fairness, compassion, empathy, and support.
- Provide training to supervisors in proper administration of emergency care, such as to a person who is bleeding.
- Ensure that the right equipment, protective clothing, gloves, and supplies are readily available, including first-aid kits.
- Provide HIV-antibody testing on request to employees who may come in contact with blood or blood products.

Accommodations

For most trainees with health or medical problems, no special accommodations other than physical adjustments in the learning environment are required. For others, any of the accommodations identified by ADA, singly or in combination, may be appropriate. These include:

Disability leave
Making facilities accessible
Restructuring jobs
Sharing or splitting jobs
Reducing workload
Reassigning to physically less-demanding work
Modifying work schedules
Adapting equipment
Making adaptive devices available
Adjusting tests and examinations
Modifying training materials
Changing policies
Providing qualified readers, interpreters, or assistants
Making assignments
Reducing workload and/or length of the training day

In any case, coordination and cooperation with medical practitioners and therapists are indicated.

Because it is inevitable that even with reasonable accommodation, at some point a person with a terminal illness will no longer be able to perform the essential functions of the job, termination becomes necessary. But before that step is taken, the employer must ensure that:

- All available alternatives to termination have been explored.
- All of the employee's sick leave and personal leave days have been expended.
- Separation does not jeopardize the employee's eligibility for disability benefits provided by the company's retirement system.
- Written documentation of the employee's inability to perform the essential elements of the job is available.
- Medical evaluation has confirmed the employee's unfitness for work.

Learning/Work Environment Changes

The following suggestions can make the learning or work environment more comfortable for people with health or medical problems:

- Modify door knobs and handles with easy-open levers.
- Install easy-touch controls for lamps and ceiling lights.
- Install soft, nonslip carpeting to reduce stress on workers' feet.
- Make sure that chairs are comfortable by adding a foam seat pad or back-support cushion.

- Use adjustable secretary-type chairs with wheels.
- Raise or lower workbenches for maximum comfort and safe use of power tools.
- Organize supply cabinets and tool cribs so as to keep items within easy reach.
- Place frequently used items, such as tools and supplies, on revolving shelves or lazy susans.
- Provide lightweight machinery and tools.
- Provide portable electrical screwdrivers.
- Provide wheeled carts for toting supplies, parts, equipment, and products.
- Make footstools available so that users can keep their knees higher than their hips and thereby avoid back pain.
- Provide step stools and long-handled tools to extend reach.
- Use height-adjustable desks and drafting tables.
- Install easily grasped drawer pulls on desks and cabinets.
- Provide oversized or curved writing instruments, such as pens, preferably with felt tips, which require a minimum of pressure.
- Supply pencils with soft lead and electric pencil sharpeners.
- Provide plastic or foam triangular or circular pencil wideners (available in stationery stores) to soften the grip.
- Provide large handled or loop-handled scissors or a clipping (razorlike) device that cuts paper without opening and closing the hand.
- Provide speaker telephones that leave the hands free or a lightweight headset that plugs into any modular telephone.
- For workers who use automobiles, provide plastic door openers, wood or plastic key turners, and back supports and cervical pillows.

Specific Techniques

Most health and medical problems will not be known or observable to trainers, supervisors, or other trainees, and under the law, employees cannot be asked to reveal their disabilities. Additionally, there are very few special techniques that trainers and supervisors can use to improve the learning environment for people with health or medical problems. Here are those few:

- If a medical or health condition is revealed by the trainee, determine his or her needs for special accommodations as soon as possible, preferably prior to the start of the training or work assignment.

- Consult with medical professionals to get help in evaluating needs.
- Never assume that there are certain things the trainee can't do. Always describe what needs to be done, and then ask the individual about his or her ability to do it.
- Make the environment positive, supportive, and conducive to learning.
- Develop clear training objectives and an effective means of measuring accomplishment.
- Encourage trainees to ask for help when they need it.
- For trainees with known medical conditions, be flexible in making assignments and defining requirements.
- Allow trainees to pace themselves; they know their own limitations.
- Break large, time-consuming operations into several smaller tasks to allow small breaks during the job.
- Never invade the trainee's privacy by questioning or probing for information about his or her illness.
- Avoid situations that would tend to place the trainee in a highly competitive or unfavorable position.
- Provide equipment and devices to avoid the need for heavy lifting.
- If possible, allow workers to perform their jobs while seated.
- Encourage workers to change positions often to loosen up and avoid stiffness.
- Allow additional time for trainees to complete physical activities.
- Be prepared to deal with emergencies, such as asthma attacks, fainting spells, epileptic seizures, and hypoglycemia. Know what to do and what not to do if they occur.
- Learn the Heimlich maneuver to deal with choking emergencies.
- Become qualified to administer cardiopulmonary resuscitation.
- Prepare, post, and distribute strip maps or written directions of the fastest and most direct route to the nearest medical facility.

Assistive Technology

Because many health and medical conditions result in loss of strength and stamina, some of the assistive devices used by people with mobility and motion disabilities (see Chapter 8) are also helpful for people with life-threatening or catastrophic illnesses. Some of the applicable devices are:

- Ambulation devices such as wheelchairs, canes, crutches, and walkers, and lightweight walking sticks that convert to a seat

- Passive standing aids
- Permanent or temporary ramps and lifts
- Reaching devices
- Automatic telephone dialers and flippers
- Computer hardware and software

Summary

The list of illnesses to which humans are susceptible is a long one. Some illnesses result in observable symptoms; many others do not. For those reasons, every trainer and supervisor will have to deal with people who have chronic and permanent or acute and temporary conditions of varying seriousness. Although most illnesses have the potential for diminished job performance, much can be done on the job in the work environment to alleviate or avoid those effects.

Among the illnesses that are most important for trainees and supervisors to understand and be able to help the individual find accommodations for are asthma, cancer, HIV/AIDS, epilepsy, and heart disease. Many accommodations are identical to those appropriate for mobility and motion disabilities.

For Further Reading and Viewing*

AIDS—An Enemy Among Us. 1993. 45-minute video. Available from Churchill Media.

AIDS: The Facts. Pamphlet available from local Red Cross chapters.

AIDS Training Tools for Employees: Slides and Guidebook. Available from Workplace Health Communications Corporation.

AIDS—What Everyone Needs to Know. 2d revision. 1993. 19:30-minute video. Available from Churchill Media.

AIDS: What Everyone Needs to Know. 1994. 9-minute video. Distributed by Churchill Media.

American Diabetes Association Staff. *Diabetes.* Denver: American Diabetes Association, 1988.

The Americans with Disabilities Act: Impact on Training. INFO-LINE 9203. Alexandria, Va.: American Society for Training and Development, March 1993.

The Americans with Disabilities Act: Techniques for Accommodation. INFO-LINE 9204. Alexandria, Va.: American Society for Training and Development, April 1992.

An Epidemic of Fear—AIDS in the Workplace. 1988. 23-minute video. Available from Impact AIDS.

*Full addresses of the organizations in this listing appear in Appendixes B and C.

Banta, William F. *AIDS in the Workplace: Legal Questions and Answers*. New York: Lexington Books, 1993.

Bernstein et al. *Asthma in the Workplace*. New York: Dekker, 1993.

Beyond Fear. 30-minute video. Available from local American Red Cross chapters. 60-minute videocassette available on free loan from Modern Talking Picture Service.

Bohl, Don L. (ed.). *AIDS: The New Workplace Issues*. AMA Management Briefing. New York: American Management Association, 1988.

Buchanan, Neil. *Epilepsy: Questions and Answers*. Philadelphia: David Company, 1989.

Bureau of National Affairs. *Alcohol and Drug Abuse in the Workplace: The Complete Resource Guide*. 2d ed. Washington, D.C.: BNA, 1989.

————. *BNA's Americans with Disabilities Act Manual*. Washington, D.C.: BNA, 1992.

Cohen, P. T., Merle A. Sands, and Paul A. Volberding (eds.). *The AIDS Knowledge Base: A Textbook on HIV Disease from the University of California, San Francisco, and the San Francisco General Hospital*. Waltham, Mass.: Medical Pub. Group, 1990.

Cooper, Geoffrey M. *Cancer Book: A Guide to Understanding the Causes, Prevention and Treatment of Cancer*. Boston: Jones & Bartlett, 1993.

Coping with AIDS. 1993. Five videos, 17–19 minutes each: *What Is AIDS?; Diagnosis of Symptoms; Treatment and Management of Opportunistic Infections; Treatment of the HIV Virus; Living with AIDS*. Available from Churchill Media.

Cunningham, James C., and Lynn M. Taussig. *An Introduction to Cystic Fibrosis for Patients and Families*. Bethesda, Md.: Cystic Fibrosis Foundation, 1991.

Davidson, Mayer B. *Diabetes Mellitus: Diagnosis and Treatment*. New York: Churchill Livingston, 1991.

Edwards, F. C., et al. *Fitness for Work: The Medical Aspects*. New York: Oxford University Press, 1988.

Employability: Integrating People with Developmental Disabilities into the Workplace. 1993. 27-minute video. Available from Woolworth Corporation.

Epilepsy Foundation of America. *Questions and Answers about Epilepsy*. Landover, Md.: EFA, n.d.

Hauser, W. Allen. *Epilepsy: Frequency, Causes, and Consequences*. New York: Demos, 1990.

Hazeldine, Peter. *Epilepsy: What It Is, What Causes It, and Advice on Its Successful Management*. San Francisco: Thorsons, 1986.

HIV Test? An Informed Decision. 1993. 10-minute video. Available from Churchill Media.

Lane, Donald J., and Anthony Storr. *Asthma: The Facts*. New York: Oxford University Press, 1987.

Learning about Cancer. 1993. Five videos: *Meeting the Challenge*, 14 minutes; *The Time of Diagnosis*, 8 minutes; *Surgery and Radiation*, 13:30 minutes; *Chemotherapy*, 11 minutes; *Coping Emotionally*, 13 minutes. Available from Churchill Media.

Managing AIDS in the Workplace: An Executive Briefing and Training Manual. Albany, N.Y.: Workplace Health Communications Corporation.

MDA on Disk. 1993. Medical Disability Advisor software. Available from LRP Publications.

National Cancer Institute. *What You Need to Know about Cancer.* Twenty-two pamphlets that discuss the symptoms, diagnosis, treatment, and other issues relating to different types of cancer. Bethesda, Md.: Office of Cancer Communications, 1987–1993.

————. *Facing Forward: A Guide for Cancer Survivors.* Pub. 93-2424. Bethesda, Md.: Office of Cancer Communications, 1992.

One of Our Own. 1992. 30-minute video. Available from United Training Media.

Participants with Disabilities: How to Address Their Needs. INFO-LINE 8704. Alexandria, Va.: American Society for Training and Development, April 1987.

Pincus, Laura B., and Shefail M. Trievidi. "A Time for Action: Responding to AIDS." *Training and Development* (January 1994): 45–54.

Powers, Paul. *A Guide to Vocational Assessment.* 2d ed. Austin, Tex.: PRO-ED, 1991.

Scanlon, Walter F. *Alcoholism and Drug Abuse in the Workplace: Managing Care and Costs through Employee Assistance Programs.* 2d ed. Westport, Conn.: Praeger, 1991.

Spread Facts Not Fear. 11-minute video. Available from local Red Cross chapters.

Stroke. 1992. 10-minute video. Available from Churchill Media.

Wallwork, John, and Rob Stepney. *Heart Disease: What It Is and How It's Treated.* Cambridge, Mass.: Blackwell, 1987.

Notes

1. National Cancer Center, undated letter.
2. Adapted from James C. Cunningham and Lynn M. Taussig, *An Introduction to Cystic Fibrosis for Patients and Families* (Bethesda, Md.: Cystic Fibrosis Foundation, 1991). Used by permission.
3. Much of this material was provided by the Epilepsy Foundation of America, *Questions and Answers about Epilepsy* (Landover, Md.: EFA, n.d.). Used by permission.
4. Don L. Bohl (ed.), *AIDS: The New Workplace Issues,* AMA Management Briefing (New York: American Management Association, 1988), p. 17.

10

Mental, Developmental, And Emotional Disabilities

Donny has Down syndrome. He was 21 years old, unemployed, and considered unemployable except in a sheltered workshop. He attended a private boarding school until age 16 and then returned home, where for the next five years he lived a life of unrelenting emptiness. Other people his age shunned or taunted him. He became fearful, depressed, sullen, and even openly hostile. Eventually he passed his days locked in his room watching television.

Placement in a sheltered workshop was recommended by a vocational rehabilitation counselor, but Donny's father rejected the suggestion because he viewed that as recreation or diversion rather than real work. Donny was finally placed in a job bagging groceries in a supermarket, but the job ended when the store closed. Donny's parents then learned of another job opportunity: cleaning cages and feeding the animals in a local veterinary hospital. Donny loved small animals and was ecstatic. The change in his attitude was nothing short of miraculous. Donny now has a full and happy life. He is working where he is needed, has friends, and has animals and people to love. He goes to movies alone, eats in restaurants, buys his own clothes, and does everything he was afraid to do before. He is now searching for an affordable small apartment.

Mental, developmental, and emotional disabilities may be categorized under two headings: mental retardation and mental illness. Persons with mental retardation have diminished intellectual capacity that is usually present at birth. Their limitations rest primarily on lowered intellectual capacity attributable to congenital or inherited defects, mental retardation, chromosomal aberrations (such as Down syndrome), disease or injury to the brain suffered before, during, or in the immediate period after birth, accidents or illnesses in childhood or adulthood, or as the conse-quence of impaired maturation due to insufficient environmental stimu-lation from family or cultural sources.

Mental illnesses consist of a group of long-term disorders that cause severe disturbances in thinking, feeling, and relating and result in dimin-ished capacity for coping with the ordinary demands of life. Mental ill-nesses can affect persons at any age and can occur in any family. People with mental illnesses usually have normal intelligence. In May 1993, the Federal Center for Mental Health Services, Public Health Service, offi-cially defined mental illness. Henceforth, adults who have or have had in the past year a diagnosable mental, behavioral, or emotional disorder that interferes with one or more major activities of life, like dressing, eating, or working, are considered to be seriously mental ill. The defini-tion provides a national uniform standard designed to be used by the states in determining eligibility for treatment in state and local clinics that receive federal funds or where patients are treated at no cost or reduced rates.

The definition is broad—some say too broad—but it covers disorders that have long been considered serious conditions, such as bipolar or unipolar illness, depressive illnesses, schizophrenia, severe anxiety and panic disorders, phobias, personality disorders, and obsessive-compul-sive behavior.

People who have some form of mental illness are likely to exhibit persistent difficulties in employment, such as developing and maintain-ing good interpersonal relationships with supervisors and peers, a self-image that interferes with job performance (such as dependency needs, lack of self-confidence, and indecisiveness), and a poor or erratic work record (has held many jobs usually for short periods of time, inability to get along with coworkers or supervisors, or extreme or disorganized reactions to normal job pressures).

The number of jobs now open to people with moderate to severe mental, developmental, and emotional disabilities continues to grow. In-itially confined to menial, low-paying, repetitive jobs, these people are now learning to perform meaningful and productive work in manufac-turing, construction, retail establishments, food service, and janitorial and clerical positions, and some work in convalescent and long-term care facilities for the terminally ill and aging.

Employment of people with mental retardation and other types of disabilities has taken two forms: sheltered workshops and supported em-ployment. Sheltered workshops, now called rehabilitation facilities, were established to provide skills that could be transferred to jobs in business and industry. However, many such workshops became dead-end set-tings where people worked at very low-level (usually menial) jobs for pennies an hour. Such workshops still exist.

Since the 1980s, supported employment has been growing nation-wide. This approach involves direct support to participants in finding employment in community businesses and industry, assisting them to learn the skills needed, and providing continuing counseling and assistance on and off the job. Service agencies and community resources provide the support to people with even severe mental and developmental disabilities.

MENTAL RETARDATION

The population of individuals who share the label of mental retardation is remarkably diverse. It includes people who are little different from so-called normal people, as well as those who are almost totally dependent on others. Those who assume that people with mental retardation are helpless and not employable lack awareness of the fact that many persons who cannot meet ordinary employment standards can be productive and useful workers, and even display unexpected levels of competence. A negative judgment is often a reflection of limited direct and indirect experience with people who have mental retardation.

Persons with mental retardation, rightly or wrongly, have been categorized by scores on intelligence tests, designated as intelligence quotients (IQs). (It should be noted that the IQ represents only the current functioning of the individual at the time the test is administered.) The classifications are slow learners (IQ range of 75–90), retarded (IQ range of 50–75), severely retarded or trainable (IQ of below 50), and perceptually disabled (brain injured). The term "borderline intelligence" has often been used to describe those who score consistently in the 70 to 90 IQ range.

It is now recognized, however, that IQ is only one variable in intelligence, and a rather questionable one. IQ is not immutable; it can be raised or lowered by the influences of a rich or barren environment. Mental age is probably more meaningful than IQ; both mental age and IQ are related to tests and testing conditions. Many factors other than verbal intelligence influence the ability to learn. Supervisors and trainers should also know that "slow" is not necessarily inadequate, that the components of intelligence can be remediated, and that learning is measured directly as achievement and only indirectly and theoretically as verbal intelligence.

A distinction must be made between generalized mental slowness and retardation in specific fields. Anyone may be a slow learner in one area and a quick read in others. There are many different areas, kinds, and ways of learning—cognitive, affective, and motor, to identify just a few. Some people are most likely to retain and use information that is transmitted orally. Others depend most on visual stimulation—body language and images. Others learn best when they touch and manipulate objects, using their tactile sense. Still others learn best when they read, reflect on what they have read, and then read again. And still others learn best when they are required to explain a concept or principle.

Mental Retardation Defined

The American Association on Mental Retardation defines and explains mental retardation in these terms:

> *Mental retardation* refers to substantial limitations in present functioning. . . . Mental retardation is defined as a fundamental difficulty in learning and performing certain daily life skills. The personal capabilities in which there must be a substantial limitation are conceptual, practical, and social intelligence. These three areas are specifically affected in mental retardation whereas other personal capabilities (e.g., health and temperament) may not be.
>
> *It is characterized by significantly subaverage intellectual functioning.* . . . This is defined as an IQ standard score of approximately 70 to 75 or below, based on assessment that includes one or more individually administered general intelligence tests developed for the purpose of assessing intellectual functioning. These data should be reviewed by a multidisciplinary team and validated with additional test scores or evaluative information.
>
> *Existing concurrently.* . . . The intellectual limitations occur at the same time as the limitations in adaptive skills.
>
> *With related limitations.* . . . The limitations in adaptive skills are more closely related to the intellectual limitation than to some other circumstances such as cultural or linguistic diversity or sensory limitation.
>
> *In two or more of the following applicable adaptive skill areas.* . . . Evidence of adaptive skill limitations is necessary because intellectual functioning alone is insufficient for a diagnosis of mental retardation. The impact on functioning of these limitations must be sufficiently comprehensive to encompass at least two adaptive skill areas, thus showing a generalized limitation and reducing the possibility of measurement error.
>
> *Communication, self-care, home living, social skills, community use, self direction, health and safety, functional academics, leisure, and*

work. . . . These skill areas are central to successful life functioning and are frequently related to the need for supports for persons with mental retardation. Because the relevant skills within each adaptive skill area may vary with chronological age, assessment of functioning must be referenced to the person's chronological age.

Mental retardation manifests before age 18. . . . The 18th birthday approximates the age when individuals in this society typically assume adult roles. In other societies, a different age criterion might be determined to be more appropriate.

The following four assumptions are essential to the application of this definition. . . . These statements are essential to the meaning of the definition and cannot be conceptually separated from the definition. Applications of the definition should include these statements. Each statement has clear implications for subsequent assessment and intervention.

1. *Valid assessment considers cultural and linguistic diversity as well as differences in communication and behavioral factors.*
2. *The existence of limitations in adaptive skills occurs within the context of community environments typical of the individual's age peers and is indexed to the person's individualized needs for support.*
3. *Specific adaptive limitations often coexist with strengths in other adaptive skills or other personal capabilities.*
4. *With appropriate supports over a sustained period, the life functioning of the person with mental capabilities will generally improve.*[1]

Factors in Learning Ability

Several factors influence the development and degree of learning ability:

- Absence of drive or motivation
- Accidents, infections, and diseases
- Cultural or language deprivation
- Emotional trauma or disturbances
- Family problems, tensions, or incohesiveness
- Inconsistencies among factors of ability, achievement, and aspiration
- Lack of acceptance
- Low parental expectations

- Meager educational resources in the home or community
- Physical factors based on sight, hearing, malnutrition, or other health problems
- Poor self-image
- School-related factors such as irregular attendance, poor study habits, repeated failure, or inadequate teaching and curriculum
- Socioeconomic limitations

Employment Potential

When considering the employment potential of people with mental retardation, we need to think in terms of their resources—that is, their personal, social, and vocational skills—which are determined by what has happened to them as well as by their inherent resources. A person's employment potential is greatly affected by the kinds of opportunities he or she has had to develop his or her resources: the immediate and extended family, the neighborhood and community, and the school. All of these are crucial to the ultimate development of individuals with mental retardation.

The contribution of the school to readiness for employment does not hinge on academic achievement since the average person with mental retardation cannot be expected to reach higher than the third- or fourth-grade level in reading and number skills. That level of academic achievement rules out all skilled or professional-level employment. Some people with mental retardation have good manual aptitude and with training can aspire to semiskilled jobs; most, however, will be employed in unskilled jobs, such as maintenance tasks and repetitive types of assembly operations, where the key to success is good work habits. To be a productive worker, an individual must be capable of understanding and following directions, attending to a task, remembering instructions, making judgments about the adequacy of his or her performance, and either calling attention to or coping with unexpected events.

People with mental retardation can and do work successfully, especially in jobs that can be well defined, highly routinized, and reasonably and consistently paced. They hold semiskilled as well as unskilled jobs in a variety of workplaces (Figure 10-1).

Types of Deficits

People with mental disabilities are likely to have problems of the following types:

Figure 10-1. A sample of jobs filled by persons with borderline and mild mental retardation.

Building Services	*Farmwork*	*Office Work*
Custodian	General farming	Clerk
Elevator operator	Helper	Copy machine
General maintenance	Poultry care	operator
Janitor		File clerk
Porter	*Fishery*	Mail handler
Watchman		Messenger
	Shellfishing	
	Hatchery	*Personal Services*
Cleaning and Room	Helper	
Preparation		Beauty shop helper
	Food Services	Hospital aide
Home		Nurse's aide
Hospital	Bus person	Orderly
Motel/hotel	Counter server	Washroom attendant
Nursing home	Dishwasher	
	Helper	*Sales*
	Waitperson	
Construction		Helper (retail sales)
	Industry	Packer/wrapper
Helper		Stock clerk
Laborer	Grounds maintenance	
	Helper	*Trades and Services*
	Janitor	
Delivery Services	Sewing machine	Car wash
	operator	Helper
Delivery person	Small parts assembly	Machine operator
Driver helper	Solderer	Painter
		Parking attendant

- Difficulty in acquiring abstract concepts.
- Deficits in their use of learning strategies, ranging from lack of study, note taking, and outlining skills to lack of awareness that knowledge acquisition strategies are needed and useful.
- Inability to plan, schedule, predict outcomes, and monitor and evaluate their efforts, accomplishments, and shortfalls.
- Deficiencies in language and communication ability, such as vocabulary, grammar usage, poor speech intelligibility, or pronunciation problems.
- Deficits in short-term memory.
- Inability to generalize acquired skills and transfer them from the learning environment to the workplace.

- Acquired (rather than innate) personality problems, such as over-dependence, excessive anxiety, low frustration threshold, aggression, and rigidity in thinking and acting.
- Although the great majority will have normal physical skills, some will have poor hand-eye coordination on tasks requiring fine dexterity and even slow execution on gross motor tasks.

People with mental retardation have the same needs as other persons, although their needs are influenced by their disability in terms of relative intensity (for example, self-esteem) and the likelihood of their being met. Success on a job helps those with mental retardation achieve self-esteem because the job offers opportunities for gaining approval from significant others, a sense of usefulness, and a feeling of achievement.

Capabilities of People with Mental Retardation

Instead of focusing on what people with mental retardation cannot do, employers and trainers need to concentrate on what they can do.

Intelligence

Intelligence is more closely related to the complexity of a job than to employability. People with IQs below 50 can perform simple maintenance tasks and the repetitive tasks common to assembly operations. Although intelligence is an important determinant of academic achievement, it is not a determinant of skill level potential. If a job does not require mastery of extensive information—facts, nomenclature, principles, and concepts—or making complex judgments and decisions, a person with mental retardation can usually be trained to do it.

Communication Skills

This is likely to be the most difficult problem to overcome or compensate. Poor speech intelligibility is common among those with mental retardation. Their understanding of spoken language typically exceeds their capacity to produce it. However, this deficiency is less likely to have a significant effect on jobs that do not involve the initiation or transmission of oral messages.

Reading, Writing, and Number Skills

Although the average academic achievement of adults with moderate retardation is about the third- or fourth-grade level, the absence of functional reading, writing, and number skills does not seriously restrict their employability in unskilled work. Most unskilled jobs require limited reading skill, largely confined to word recognition rather than comprehension of complete sentences, and a great many of these jobs require no reading skill at all.

Similarly, most low-skill jobs require no writing skills. Even when they are needed, writing tasks are confined to filling in information or making tally marks on printed forms in repetitive-type operations. With regard to number skills, some unskilled jobs require no number skills at all, and few demand no more than counting or tallying.

Physical Skills

Physical capabilities are extremely important in unskilled work because most of those jobs are manual in nature. However, the majority of people with mild retardation have relatively normal physical skills. The general state of their health, strength, endurance, agility, hand-eye coordination, and manual speed are typically within the usual range. Those who do not fall within the normal range often have poor eye-hand coordination and reduced speed of execution of motor tasks. They may also have chronic health problems, such as visual and auditory deficits.

Emotional Maturity

Unquestionably the most important factor in the employability of people with mental retardation is emotional maturity or stability. To hold a job, a person must be dependable—get to work on time and regularly and stick to the task. These characteristics are particularly critical for unskilled jobs, which are typically monotonous. Technical competence is less important to employers than dependability in low-skill jobs because those jobs skills are so easily acquired. But dependability is much more difficult to learn because it must be the product of experiences in the home, in school, in work training, and on the job.

Aptitudes and Talents

People with mental retardation are unlikely to have unusual physical, artistic, and creative talents, such as in sports, music, or art. Although a small number of people may exhibit what appears to be an unusual talent in one of these areas, they are exceptional only when viewed in the context of deficiencies in other skill areas. Some people with borderline or mild retardation may have above-average mechanical ability, but their reading, writing, and number skills limitations will prevent them from mastering a craft or trade. However, they may be able to master the skills and be employed as helpers in a craft or trade.

DEVELOPMENTAL DISABILITIES

Down Syndrome[2]

Down syndrome is estimated to occur in one of every 800 to 1,000 live births. Of all the children born annually in the United States, about 4,000 will have Down syndrome. Although women over the age of 35 are at greater risk (estimated at 1 in 365 versus 1 in 1,450 between the ages of 20 and 24), women under 35 years of age give birth to more than 80 percent of children with the disorder. In 20 to 30 percent of the cases, the extra chromosome originates in the father.

Individuals with Down syndrome vary widely in mental abilities, behavior, and physical development, and each has his or her unique personality, capabilities, and talents. The majority of individuals function in the mild to moderate range of mental retardation. Thirty to 50 percent of those with Down syndrome have heart defects, and 8 to 12 percent have gastrointestinal tract abnormalities present at birth. Most of those defects are now correctable by surgery.

Individuals with the disorder benefit from loving and enriching homes, early intervention, special education, appropriate medical care, and positive public attitudes. In adulthood, many persons with Down syndrome hold jobs and live independently.

Autism

Although autism is a developmental disability, from a training standpoint the condition manifests itself as a language disability. It is covered in Chapter 11.

Brain Injury and Perceptual Disability

People with brain injury are those who before, during, or following birth have received an injury to or experienced infection of the brain. As a result, defects of the neuromotor system may or may not be present. Such people may show disturbances in perception, thinking, and emotional behavior, either singly or in combination, that impede the learning process. People with perceptual disorders have difficulty in seeing relationships. Instead of seeing something as a whole, they perceive individual parts separate from the whole. They are likely to have this problem in the visual, tactile, and auditory domains. Individuals with brain injuries are inclined to give unusual, even bizarre, responses. They are easily distracted and inclined to want everything in an ordered, exact, repetitive arrangement. Behavioral disorders include a short attention span and lack of control and inhibitions.

MENTAL ILLNESSES

The causes of biologically based mental illnesses are not understood, although it is believed that the functioning of the brain's neurotransmitters is involved. Heredity may be a factor, and stress may contribute to its onset in vulnerable people. Recreational drugs may contribute to its onset, but they are unlikely to be the single cause. Although there are no cures for mental illness, treatment can substantially improve the functioning of persons with those disorders. The main types of mental illnesses are schizophrenia and depressive illnesses.

Schizophrenia[3]

Schizophrenia is one of the most serious, chronic, and disabling of the mental illnesses. It may be one disorder or it may be many. Affecting about one person in a hundred, both men and women equally, schizophrenia usually appears in the later teens or early 20s, and is uncommon after the age of 30. There is no known single cause of schizophrenia. Vulnerability to it appears to be rooted in genetic factors, however, and environmental factors may contribute to it. The probability of developing schizophrenia as the offspring of two parents, neither of whom has the disease, is 1 percent; the probability increases to 13 percent if one parent has the disease and about 35 percent if both parents have the disease. Several of the following symptoms identify the disorder:

- Unusual or distorted perceptions of the world around them
- Hallucinations—hearing and seeing things that exist only in the mind of the patient
- Delusions—false and irrational personal beliefs, such as imagined persecution
- Disordered thinking and inability to concentrate

- Showing emotion that is inconsistent with the person's speech or thoughts
- Disconnected and confusing language
- Poor reasoning, memory, and judgment
- High levels of anxiety
- Eating and sleeping disorders
- Deterioration of appearance and personal hygiene
- Loss of motivation and poor concentration
- Tendencies to withdraw from others

Several treatments and treatment combinations have been found to be helpful in reducing certain schizophrenic symptoms, such as hallucinations and delusions. Antipsychotic medications allow some persons to function more effectively; others are not helped very much. These drugs may also reduce the risk of future psychotic episodes. However, like most other medications, antipsychotic drugs have unwanted side effects, such as drowsiness, restlessness, muscle spasms, tremor, dry mouth, or blurring of vision.

Psychosocial treatments can help some people with schizophrenia, particularly those with less severe symptoms or those whose symptoms are under control, in establishing and maintaining relationships with others and overcoming work skills deficits as well. Similarly rehabilitation programs involving a wide range of nonmedical interventions have proved to be helpful. These programs emphasize vocational counseling, job training, problem solving, and social skills training. Regular individual or group psychotherapy with a mental health professional can help patients to understand more about themselves and their problems. Self-help groups, usually led by ex-patients, serve a useful function by providing information, assistance, and continuing support and comfort.

Some persons with schizophrenia recover completely; many others, usually with drug therapy, improve to the point where they can live independently. However, about 15 percent respond only moderately to medication, and another 15 percent do not respond to existing treatment.

Depressive Illnesses[4]

Every year, about 5 percent of the population (over 11 million people) have depressive illnesses, called affective disorders. They are the most common of psychiatric disorders and a major cause of suicide. However, they are usually less persistently disabling than schizophrenia. Depression affects twice as many women as men. The primary disturbance is that of mood. Depressive illness is a medical disorder that often interferes with normal functioning and causes pain and suffering not only to those with the disorder but to those who care about them.

According to a recent study, depression costs the United States $47.3 billion a year, most of it in treatment costs and reduced productivity, with employers paying more than half the total (about $23.8 billion or $180 per worker, whether or not he or she has depression, and about $3,000 for each depressed worker).[5] Included in the costs of the illness are such elements as lost workdays, lost productivity, and lost lifetime earnings due to suicide, in addition to the usually computed costs of hospitalization, outpatient care, and drugs.

Depressive illness involves the whole body and the person's mood and thoughts. It affects the way a person eats and sleeps, how he or she feels about himself or herself, and the way he or she thinks about things. Without proper treatment, symptoms can last weeks, months, or years. With appropriate treatment, most people with depression can be helped. Depression may be caused by family history and genetics, other general medical illnesses, certain medicines, drugs or alcohol, other psychiatric conditions, or certain life conditions, such as extreme stress or grief.[6]

Three of the most common types of depressive disorders are clinical or major depression, dysthymia, and bipolar disorder.

Clinical or Major Depression

Clinical or major depression (unipolar illness) is a disabling medical illness that costs society an estimated $27 billion on worker absenteeism, diminished productivity, and health care costs. In addition, it imposes intangible costs, such as reduced quality of work and ill will among co-workers.[7] Major depression interferes with working, sleeping, eating, and enjoying pleasurable activities. Its symptoms are as follows:

- Persistent feelings of sadness, anxiety, or irritability
- Feelings of helplessness or pessimism
- Feelings of guilt or worthlessness
- Loss of interest or pleasure in activities previously enjoyed, such as hobbies and sex
- A change in weight or appetite
- Sleep disturbances, such as trouble falling asleep, waking up too early, or oversleeping
- Difficulty concentrating, remembering, or decision making
- Fatigue or loss of energy
- Restlessness or slowed activity noticed by other people
- Persistent physical symptoms, such as headaches, digestive disorders, and chronic pain, that do not respond to treatment

- Thoughts about life's not being worthwhile or about suicide or death

Dysthymia

Dysthymia is a less severe type of depression that involves long-term, chronic symptoms that are not disabling but keep the person from functioning at top speed or from feeling good. Sometimes people with dysthymia also experience major depressive episodes.

Bipolar Disorder

Formerly called manic-depressive illness, bipolar disorder is not nearly as common as other forms of depressive illness, but it is often a recurring condition. It affects about 1 in 100 people. Although it can be caused by head injury or other neurological or general medical conditions, in most cases it is inherited. With bipolar illness, the person swings between high and low moods—cycles of depression and elation or mania that usually change gradually but are sometimes dramatic and rapid. Mania often affects thinking, judgment, and social behavior in ways that cause serious problems and embarrassment. Persons with this illness usually have several of the following characteristics during the period of mania:

- Boundless energy, enthusiasm, and need for activity
- Inappropriate elation or irritability
- Disconnected and racing thoughts
- Severe insomnia or decreased need for sleep
- Grandiose ideas and poor judgment
- Rapid, loud, disorganized speech
- Short temper and argumentativeness
- Impulsive and erratic behavior
- Possible delusional thinking
- Increased sexual desire
- Rapid switch to severe depression[8]

Causes, Stages, and Symptoms of Depressive Illnesses

There are three causes of depression: biochemical (low levels of neurotransmitters, such as serotonin), heredity, and life events. Some types of depression, particularly bipolar disorder, seem to run in families, indicating a genetic vulnerability. However, depression can also occur in people with no family history of the illness. Apparently, additional factors, such as a stressful environment or certain medications, may be involved in its onset. People who have low self-esteem or are overly sensitive to stress are also prone to depression. And a serious personal loss, chronic illness, a difficult relationship, a financial problem, or an unwelcome change in the work or family situation may also trigger an episode.

There are three stages of treatment for depressive illnesses: (1) acute care, to alleviate symptoms; (2) continuation therapy, to prevent relapse; and (3) maintenance, to prevent recurrence. Treatment options include antidepressant medication, psychotherapy, and, for severe, life-threatening depression where medication does not provide relief, electroconvulsive therapy. Prozac, an antidepressant medication, has become the drug of choice for many people with severe depression. Although there are sometimes serious side effects (such as blood disorders, fatal allergic reactions, and increased risk of seizures, as well as common side effects such as nausea, diarrhea, and insomnia), many patients feel that Prozac is a wonder drug. It has changed their lives by controlling their illness and allowing them to be happier and more productive.

Next to appropriate diagnosis and treatment, the most important thing that anyone can offer people with depression, including their trainers, supervisors, and coworkers, is emotional support. That emotional support should be manifested by continuing understanding, empathy, patience, encouragement, and affection. The following symptoms may be recognized by managers and supervisors:[9]

- Decreased productivity
- Morale problems
- Lack of cooperation
- Safety risks, accidents
- Absenteeism
- Frequent statements about being tired all the time
- Complaints of unexplained aches and pains
- Alcohol and drug abuse

Supervisors need to learn about depression and the sources of help in order to recognize when an employee shows signs of a problem affecting performance that may be depression related and refer him or her appropriately. They also need to discuss changes in work performance with the employee and suggest that he or she seek consultation.

An employee may voluntarily talk with the supervisor about health problems. In this case, the supervisor should:

- Not try to diagnose the problem.
- Recommend that the employee seek professional consultation

from an employee assistance program counselor or other health or mental health professional.

- Recognize that a depressed employee may need a flexible work schedule during treatment and provide it if possible.
- Remember that severe depression may be life threatening to the employee but rarely to others. Take comments like "life is not worth living" or "people would be better off without me" seriously and seek advice from a counselor or other specialist on how to handle the situation.

Other Mental Illnesses[10]

Other disabling mental illnesses include severe anxiety and panic disorders, phobias, personality disorders, and obsessive-compulsive behavior. Only panic disorders and phobias will be addressed here.

Panic Disorders[11]

A panic attack is an uncontrollable panic response to ordinary, non-threatening situations. It can occur in anyone and affects 1.6 percent of Americans (about 3 million people), most often, people in their early 20s. It is characterized by sweating, hot or cold flashes, choking or smothering sensations, racing or pounding heart, labored breathing, trembling, chest pains, faintness, disorientation, tingling or numbness in the hands, flushes or chills, dreamlike sensations or perceptual distortions, terror or feeling of dying, losing control, or losing one's mind. Anyone who experiences four or more panic attacks in a four-week period is said to have a panic disorder. It may also be indicated if a person experiences fewer than four panic episodes but has constant or recurring fears of having another panic attack, called "fearing the fear."

Panic attacks appear to run in families, suggesting that the disorder may have a genetic origin, such as defects in the autonomic nervous system. However, attacks can be triggered by a severe life stress, such as the death of a loved one, divorce or separation, or loss of job. They can also be caused by chemical or hormonal imbalances and by drugs or alcohol.

Panic disorders can be successfully treated by a combination of medication and cognitive or behavioral therapy. Medication includes antidepressants (imipramine and phenelzine), antianxiety agents (alprazolam) and beta blockers (propranolol). Therapy helps people behave appropriately by means of supported exposure and desensitization—being exposed to the feared object or situation with the support and encouragement of a therapist, family, friends, or coworkers—and slowly getting used to it.

Phobias

A phobia is an irrational, involuntary, and inappropriate fear of or response to ordinary situations or things. Phobias are usually chronic and can lead to other serious disorders, such as depression.

There are three types of phobia recognized by the American Psychiatric Association:

1. *Single (simple) phobia:* An unreasonable fear of specific circumstances or objects, such as snakes or traffic jams
2. *Social phobia:* Extreme fear of making a spectacle of oneself in public, thus forcing one to avoid public occasions or areas
3. *Agoraphobia:* Literally "fear of the marketplace," an intense fear about feeling trapped in any situation, particularly in public places, combined with an overwhelming fear of having a panic attack in unfamiliar surroundings

Phobias can be successfully treated by a combination of medication, therapy, and support.

EMOTIONAL DISABILITIES

Employees with emotional problems are not uncommon. A random study of 18,000 persons made by the National Institute of Mental Health revealed that upwards of one-fifth of those questioned had suffered a mental health problem of some kind during the previous six months.[12] National Institute of Alcoholism and Alcohol (NIAA)[13] reported that as much as 10 percent of the workforce in heavy industry included alcohol and drug abusers. NIAA also estimated that up to 18 percent of all industrial workers have personal problems serious enough to interfere with job performance.

The problems of alcoholic, emotionally disturbed, or otherwise troubled employees are too prevalent to ignore and too costly to overlook. Troubled employees can cost companies large sums of money through tardiness, absenteeism, lost productivity, errors and rejects, accidents, and compensation claims. And there are compelling reasons why managers and trainers should take action on troubled employees and trainees. Dismissal is not the best answer. The Federal Rehabilitation Act of 1973 and the Americans with Disabilities Act of 1990 explicitly prohibit discrimination based on former "handicaps" or "disabilities"; they recognize alcoholism, drug abuse, and emotional problems as covered disabilities and protect people who are in treatment for such problems.

Individuals whose limitations rest primarily on psychopathology (abnormal personality functioning) are recognizable by easily discernible disturbances of their behavior in terms of action, thought, and consciousness. These "abnormalities" may be the result of an individual's original endowment (heredity), the influence of the home and family (rearing), traumatic experiences that modified personality development, or, most common, stress stemming from the individual's emotional life, his or her inability to cope with those tensions, and defensive reactions, including use of alcohol and drugs to minimize anxiety. Emotional impairment should be regarded as patterns of reaction and behavior brought about by stress that goes beyond the limits of the individual's capacity for adaptation.

Emotional disorders are defensive and restorative in purpose but undesirably neurotic and substitutive rather than rational. Reality is sacrificed by the individual to achieve emotional comfort, maintain self-respect, or provide personal satisfaction.

THE CHALLENGE TO INSTRUCTORS AND SUPERVISORS

Although some individuals with mental, developmental, and emotional disabilities may be essentially like nondisabled people in their emotional, social, physical, and motor development, most display some important differences that make the task of teaching much more difficult. Following are the most important of those differences (keep in mind that no trainee will have all of the characteristics listed):

- Short attention and interest span
- Limited imagination and ability to think creatively
- Slow reaction time
- Apathy, diffidence, and dependence but frequent excitability and sensitivity
- Limited reading ability
- Absence of self-confidence
- Shyness, submissiveness, instability
- Inability to do abstract thinking, to handle symbols
- Limited reasoning power and judgment
- Inability to foresee consequences and propensity to jump to conclusions
- Inability to adapt to change in situations and people
- Failure to transfer ideas, concepts, and principles
- Limited powers of self-direction
- Sparse vocabulary

- Low standards of workmanship and achievement
- Low levels of initiative, concentration, and persistence
- Ease of confusion, anxieties, and fears
- Action based on impulse
- Impatience; insistence on quick results

APPROACHES TO TRAINING

Until recently, trainers (as well as professional special educators) have been preoccupied with trying to fit trainees with mental and emotional disabilities into paper-and-pencil curriculums developed for nondisabled trainees. The learning tasks presented to trainees with disabilities were similar to those for trainees without disabilities except that they were offered at a much slower pace. All too frequently, trainees with disabilities were presented with laborious, repetitive activities designed to teach them basic skills by means of abstract, classroom-based activities. Upon completing training, most entered the workforce at low-level jobs and encountered many barriers to a more successful and rewarding work life. Research shows that this approach has not been very effective.

Trainees with mild and moderate mental, developmental, and emotional deficits have psychological and physical needs that, if not met, can result at the very least in inappropriate or unacceptable behaviors and at the worst failure to acquire the knowledge and skills needed to function adequately in the workplace. Trainees need to have basic physiological and psychological needs met before they can learn. They need safety and security; they need to feel safe from psychological mistreatment from others, including other trainees. They also need to belong, to have self-respect, and to feel in control.

To meet the needs of trainees with mental, developmental, and emotional disabilities, supervisors and trainers need to provide emotional support through continuing understanding, empathy, patience, encouragement, and affection. In addition, trainers and supervisors should do all that they can do to encourage the same attitudes and behaviors among the nondisabled peers of trainees.

Specific Training Techniques

Preparation and Planning

- Provide instructor preparation related to study and assessment techniques for people with cognitive disabilities and adaptive instructional methods.

- Make instructional load and class size reasonable.
- When the safety of the trainee or worker or others is involved, require that medication for treatment be reported.
- Arrange space, furniture, and equipment for flexible grouping.
- Include trainees in planning learning activities.
- Provide readiness programs when needed.
- Individualize instruction to the maximum extent possible based on purpose, personality, capacity, learning style, and rate of learning.
- Make the learning environment as close as possible to the actual work environment: equipment, tools, materials, environmental conditions (heat, light, noise level, and so on).
- Schedule learning activities consistently to make the learning environment more structured. Then plan deliberate changes in the schedule over time to promote flexibility.
- Adjust the length of learning sessions to accommodate shorter attention spans.
- Encourage trainees to develop daily task lists and personal schedules to promote independence.
- Avoid downtime (a period when little or no instruction or learning occurs).
- Make the learning environment flexible.
- Provide a blend of diagnostic or prescriptive and exploratory activities.
- Keep the environment upbeat, and do everything possible to ensure success.
- Employ the basic essential approach, focusing on minimum essentials at an understandable level.
- Derive training objectives from job and task analysis, and base them on the essential functions of the job.
- State training objectives in writing and in performance terms, and give them to the trainees at the beginning of the course.
- Make plans clear, definite, and precise.
- Give priority in curriculum content to the knowledge and skills that must be achieved by trainees to reach an acceptable level of independent performance.
- Set up a curriculum framework that encourages flexibility in organizing appropriate modules of work for individuals and small groups.
- Give priority to skills that must be mastered before other skills can be learned.
- Break learning modules or other materials to be learned into small, discrete units.

Implementation

- Include trainees with disabilities in all activities to the same extent as nondisabled trainees.
- Get the trainees' undivided attention before presenting instruction.
- Present only one oral instruction at a time. If more than one instruction is essential, make a distinct pause between directions.
- Sequence oral instructions in the exact order the trainee is expected to perform them.
- Speak slowly, using short sentences, appropriate vocabulary, and simple word combinations.
- Maintain maximum eye contact with trainees as a means of reminding them to stay on task.
- Conduct learning activities in small steps.
- Individualize instruction to the maximum extent possible.
- Simplify materials and techniques.
- Review material frequently.
- Employ drill and practice but not meaningless and deadening repetition.
- Simplify activities; shorten in length and narrow in scope.
- Provide appropriate reading, reference, audiovisual, and other commercial and instructor-prepared learning materials.
- Set realistic schedules; allow trainees to pace themselves.
- Make assignments specific and detailed and follow up.
- Capitalize on individual talents and abilities.
- Make relationships and associations obvious.
- Pair terms and experiences that are familiar to trainees with unfamiliar terms and concepts to form associations.
- Use demonstrations frequently, and make them concrete and tangible rather verbal and abstract.
- Use audiovisuals, illustrations, and direct, hands-on experiences generously.
- For trainees with little or no reading ability, use graphics, still and motion, to show the sequence of tasks to be performed.
- Provide job aids that show in pictures how a task is to be performed; allow trainees to retain the aids and bring them to the job.
- Use color cues, arrows, underscoring, and highlighting to help trainees focus their attention and discriminate among stimuli.
- Provide plenty of cues and prompts, and gradually fade them as the trainees show progress and accomplishment.
- Stress the practical and immediately useful.

- Be alert for signs of frustration, and adjust the learning pace accordingly.
- Vary the settings, time of day, materials, and people involved in learning activities.
- Use extrinsic reinforcers (such as prizes, free time, and so on) in the initial phases of learning. Gradually fade these artificial reinforcers and rely increasingly on intrinsic reinforcers (nods, smiles, pats on the back, and so on).
- Allow extra time to complete assignments and tests.
- Use peer tutors to provide additional help and supervision of learning activities.
- Use procedures that encourage trainee self-expression.
- Give trainees ample opportunity to practice each skill under supervision and with immediate, constructive feedback on performance.
- Allow all trainees to practice skills until they have accomplished the objective by meeting the criterion or standard of performance.
- Require many repetitions of a skill, but vary the activities so that attention will be increased and boredom will be avoided.
- Require trainees to demonstrate competence of each skill at the required level before they leave the training program and report to the job.
- Avoid excessive pressure.
- Give praise freely but only when earned.
- Develop pride in the group and in accomplishment.
- Use corporate and community expertise to the maximum.

Evaluation

- Perform systematic needs assessment of all learners at three levels: application of measures of general classroom and shop performance, administration of diagnostic tests to identify trainee characteristics and specific strengths and weaknesses, and monitoring and evaluation of trainee progress using curriculum-based performance tests.
- Supplement formal assessment with behavioral observations, questioning, and reports of supervisors.
- Obtain input from professionals who have had contact with the trainee (physician, psychologist, physical therapist, psychometrist, rehabilitation specialist, and vocational specialist).
- Evaluate frequently, and provide encouragement and feedback on performance.
- Provide assistance and additional practice when performance on criterion tests is substandard.

- Consider developing compensatory skills for certain academic deficits (e.g., use of a calculator to solve mathematics problems instead of attempting to remediate basic computational skills).
- Perform error analysis to identify the specific mistakes that the trainee is making in carrying out a learning task, determine the cause, and devise a solution.
- Establish a cumulative record system to which all instructional, supervisory, counseling, and human resources staff contribute.
- Avoid normative measures; focus on tracking and analyzing individual progress and accomplishment.
- Evaluate both the process and the products, but focus on the latter using preestablished criteria, such as number, rate, and quality (conformance to standards).
- Help trainees to evaluate their own progress and accomplishment.
- Encourage trainees to discuss their own strengths and weaknesses regarding specific job tasks.
- Provide for instructor-counselor and instructor-supervisor conferences.
- Make weekly reports to supervisors on trainees' progress and accomplishment.

Specific Suggestions by Disability

People with Mental Retardation

People with mental retardation have the same needs and wants, likes and dislikes, and engage in the same kinds of activities of daily living as everyone else. Don't "talk down," but keep words clear and simple. Avoid obscure words and phrases, and use short sentences. If a person seems to need help in reading instructions or following directions, offer it, but don't give it until the offer is accepted. People with mental retardation are friendly and very eager to please. Never take advantage of their vulnerability by asking them to do things you wouldn't ask others to do.

People with Severe Mental Disabilities and Brain Injuries

Individualized instructional delivery systems may be used to stimulate trainees to the highest level of performance (many have potential far beyond that previously believed). A wide variety of materials, job aids, short periods on individual subjects (attention span is limited), and a great deal of stimulation are important. The pattern of instruction should follow a schedule, with as little change in the daily routine as possible. Coordination and cooperation with medical practitioners and therapists are advised.

People with Down Syndrome

The range of intellectual capacity of people with Down syndrome is as great and as diverse as in any other segment of the population at large, so the challenges are the same that face those responsible for training any individual with cognitive disabilities: retention of learned skills, distractibility, inability to remain focused, and difficulty in achieving social integration.

Trainers and supervisors of people with Down syndrome should have more than the normal endowment of patience and a sense of humor. In addition, they should have knowledge of developmental disabilities, excellent communication and organization skills, and experience in teaching or working in some capacity with people with cognitive disabilities. Family and life experiences, internships, and volunteer experiences can provide this knowledge and know-how.

To ensure the effectiveness of training and supervision, it is essential that information be gathered on the individual's capabilities, limitations, and training needs. Assessment must be highly individual and based on observation during the initial phases of training or employment. This is done by interviewing the individual as well as significant others in his or her life, by spending time with the individual, and observation.

Before becoming involved in vocational or job training activities, persons with Down syndrome should participate in prevocational training, where they learn to develop good work habits and engage in proper relationships with coworkers. Most persons with the disability can function independently in routine, repetitive jobs; others may require varying levels of support in the work environment. In either case, a person with Down syndrome can gain a feeling of self-worth and of making a contribution to the organization. Social interactions and recreational activities beyond the workplace can also enhance the quality of life for persons with Down syndrome and make them happier and more productive workers.

Here are some specific suggestions:

- Adjust training according to the individual's ability to grasp concepts.
- Give trainees who can read a simplified version of the task analysis for the job.

- For individuals without reading skills, use visual and oral prompts.
- Make learning incremental, and break tasks into small steps.
- Ensure that the learning environment is quiet and nondistracting.
- Use simple charts to map progress in specific areas. Pay special attention to downturns in learning.
- Attend to the individual's assessment of his or her own progress and whether it is reasonable and realistic.
- When evaluating, measure success fully in conjunction with the learner's expectations and goals.

Emotionally Impaired Adults

For trainees with emotional disabilities, the methods and techniques used depend on the degree of emotional impairment—trainees who are mildly disabled may require no special accommodations, but persons who are severely disabled are likely to require individual accommodation and treatment and coordination and cooperation with psychiatrists, psychologists, and psychiatric social workers.

AIDS AND ASSISTIVE DEVICES

Individuals with cognitive impairments often have good memories for past events but may be forgetful or have limited ability to remember new information or recent events. Many assistive technologies designed for other types of disabilities can also be useful for individuals with cognitive impairments. Other assistive technologies are designed specifically for persons with cognitive impairments. They range from high-tech items, such as computers, to simple aids, such as daily task lists and calendars, to keep track of activities. Some devices assist the individual to learn skills; others may be used to help the person perform a job or task.

Low-Tech Devices

The low end of assistive devices for people with cognitive impairments includes daily diaries, task lists, procedural guides, and checklists. These items improve memory, retention, or orientation to time and place or ensure that a workplace system or routine is precisely followed. Color coding is another low-tech solution. It can be used on files, cabinets, shelves, drawers, materials, parts, tools, and many other items to keep them in their proper place or as memory aids.

Computers and Software

People with mental, developmental, and emotional impairments can benefit from interaction with electronic technologies in communication and instructional systems. The types of electronic applications vary greatly and depend primarily on the degree of developmental delay manifested by the individual. Most people with mental disabilities need to use some form of adaptive or prosthetic input and output device to use computer technology because of their limited abilities. This is particularly true of very low functioning individuals who lack the cognitive or motor skills needed to use these systems in the usual manner. The types of hardware modifications include single switches, video printing devices, joysticks, and touch pads. In addition, special software programs are often employed to facilitate the use of the single switch or touch pad.

Drill and practice software have been used successfully to teach basic skills. Electronic technologies have been used to teach appropriate interpersonal employment skills and job attitudes, as well as specific job-related skills in both drill and practice and problem-solving formats. Modifications to industry-developed interactive video disc and simulator training programs have proved to be very effective.

Computers can provide a multisensory approach with visual cues, auditory cues through voice or sound prompts, and tactile cues through the keyboard, mouse, light pen, touch screen, or other input device. The computer can be especially helpful to people with cognitive disabilities because the user can proceed through a program at his or her own pace under nonthreatening and nonjudgmental conditions. In addition, the computer provides feedback so that the individual can track and measure progress and accomplishment.

Productivity software, used to assist persons with cognitive impairments to deal with time- or sequence-sensitive tasks, is commercially available. Such programs contain alarms and visual and auditory reminders tied to the computer's clock that prompt users with impaired memory. Software is also available to improve reading, mathematics, and other cognitive skills. Some programs make use of drill and practice, tutorials, educational games, problem solving, and interactivity.

Captain's Log (available from BrainTrain) consists of 28 gamelike, easy-to-use programs designed to train the basic cognitive functions: attention, concentration, memory, visual-motor, numeric concepts, problem solving, and reasoning skills. The programs can be used with adults with head injuries, learning disabilities, psychiatric disorders, stroke, mental retardation, and attention deficit disorders. It requires Apple IIgs, Apple IIe, Apple II + (64K), IBM PC/XT/At/PS2/jr, and IBM PC compatibles (512K).

Summary

People with mental, developmental, and emotional disabilities remain largely an untapped source of workers. Although mental disorders result in disturbances in thinking, feeling, relating, learning, and working, advances in treatment have enabled many people who have them to become productive employees. New medications, more effective psychotherapy and counseling, and improved community support services have made people employable—and not just in menial, low-paying, repetitive jobs but in meaningful work.

For trainers and supervisors, all of whom must provide at least some on-the-job training, the obstacles to success are formidable but surmountable. Such problems as short attention span, inability to do abstract thinking, slow reaction time, limited reading and computational ability, poor self-image, and low self-esteem present new challenges. If they approach the task with a positive outlook, disposition to learn, patience, and willingness to provide emotional support in the form of understanding, empathy, and encouragement, they can make people with these disabilities contributors to the achievement of organizational goals and objectives.

For Further Reading and Viewing*

ADA Customer Courtesies. 1993. 20-minute video. Available from United Training Media.

ADA for Retail. 1993. 12-minute video. Available from United Training Media.

American Association on Mental Retardation. *Mental Retardation: Definition, Classification, and Systems of Supports.* 9th ed. Washington, D.C.: American Association on Mental Retardation, 1992.

The Americans with Disabilities Act: Impact on Training. INFO-LINE 9203. Alexandria, Va.: American Society for Training and Development, March 1993.

The Americans with Disabilities Act: Techniques for Accommodation. INFO-LINE 9204. Alexandria, Va.: American Society for Training and Development, April 1992.

Baroff, George S. *Developmental Disabilities: Psychosocial Aspects.* Austin, Tex.: PRO-ED, 1991.

Down Time: A Worksite Guide to Understanding Clinical Depression. 1993. 17-minute video. Available from Wellness Councils of America.

Employability: Integrating People with Developmental Disabilities into the Workplace. 1993. 27-minute video. Available from Woolworth Corporation.

Goldberg, Marge, Paula F. Goldberg, and Cathleen Urbain. *Opportunity Knocking: The Story of Supported Employment.* Minneapolis: PACER Center, 1988.

*Full addresses of the organizations in this listing appear in Appendixes B and C.

National Institute of Mental Health. *Plain Talk about . . . Depression.* (NIH Pub. 93-3561. Rockville, Md.: U.S. Department of Health and Human Services, April 1993.

————. *Bipolar Disorder.* Rockville, Md.: U.S. Department of Health and Human Services, n.d.

————. *Depressive Illness: Treatment Brings New Hope.* Rockville, Md.: U.S. Department of Health and Human Services, n.d.

————. *Panic Disorder.* Rockville, Md.: U.S. Department of Health and Human Services, n.d.

Panic Disorder. Arlington, VA: National Alliance for the Mentally Ill, n.d.

Papolos, Demetri. *Mood Disorders: Depression and Manic Depression.* Arlington, Va.: National Alliance for the Mentally Ill, n.d.

Participants with Disabilities: How to Address Their Needs. INFO-LINE 8704. Alexandria, Va.: American Society for Training and Development, April 1987.

Public Health Service. *Depression Is a Treatable Illness: A Patient's Guide.* Pub. AHCPR 93-0553. Washington, D.C.: U.S. Department of Health and Human Services, April 1993.

————. *Depression in Primary Care: Detection, Diagnosis, and Treatment.* Quick Reference Guide for Clinicians, No. 5. AHCPR Pub. 93-0552. Washington, D.C.: U.S. Department of Health and Human Services, April 1993.

————. *Depression in Primary Care.* Vol. 1, *Detection and Diagnosis.* Clinical Practice Guideline No. 5. AHCPR Pub. 93-0550. Washington, D.C.: U.S. Department of Health and Human Services, April 1993.

————. *Depression in Primary Care.* Vol. 2, *Treatment of Major Depression.* Clinical Practice Guideline No. 5. AHCPR Pub. 93-0551. Washington, D.C.: U.S. Department of Health and Human Services, April 1993.

Richardson, Gerald M. "Applicants and Employees with Mental Disabilities." *HRfocus* (Special Report), American Management Association, 1992, pp. 8–9.

Serious Mental Illness: Myths and Realities. Arlington, Va.: National Alliance for the Mentally Ill, n.d.

Shore, David (ed.). *Schizophrenia: Questions and Answers.* IDHHS Pub. (ADM) 90-1457. Rockville, Md.: NIMH, U.S. Department of Health and Human Services, 1990.

Sticks and Stones. 1992. 60-minute video. Available from Advocating Change Together, 1821 University Avenue, Suite 363 South, St. Paul, MN 55104; (612) 641-0297.

Succeeding Together at Work. 1993. 7-minute video. Available from Salenger Films.

Urbain, Cathleen. *Supported Employment: A Step-by-Step Guide.* Minneapolis: PACER Center, 1992.

Notes

1. American Association on Mental Retardation, *Mental Retardation: Definition, Classification, and Systems of Supports,* 9th ed. (Washington, D.C.: AAMR, 1992), pp. 5–7. Used by permission.

2. Much of this material was provided by the National Down Syndrome Congress.

3. Adapted from *Mental Illness Is Everybody's Business* (Arlington, Va.: National Alliance for the Mentally Ill, n.d.), and David Shore (ed.), *Schizophrenia: Questions and Answers* (Rockville, Md.: National Institute of Mental Health, 1986).

4. National Institute of Mental Health, *Plain Talk About . . . Depression*, NIH Pub. 93-3561 (Rockville, Md.: U.S. Department of Health and Human Services, April 1993).

5. Conducted by researchers and economists from the Massachusetts Institute of Technology's Sloan School of Management and the Analysis Group of Boston and reported in the November 1993 issue of the *Journal of Clinical Psychiatry*.

6. Public Health Service, *Depression Is a Treatable Illness: A Patient's Guide*, Pub. No. AHCPR 93-0553 (Washington, D.C.: U.S. Department of Health and Human Services, April 1993), p. 2.

7. Wellness Councils of America, *Down Time: A Worksite Guide to Understanding Depression*, brochure (n.d.).

8. *Mental Illness Is Everybody's Business.*

9. *What to Do When an Employee Is Depressed: A Guide for Supervisors*, DHHS Pub. (ADM) 91-1792 (Washington, D.C.: Alcohol, Drug Abuse, and Mental Health Administration, National Institute of Mental Health, U.S. Department of Health and Human Services, 1991).

10. Much of this material was provided by the National Alliance for the Mentally Ill.

11. National Institute of Mental Health, *Panic Disorder* (Rockville, Md.: U.S. Department of Health and Human Services, n.d.).

12. *U.S. News and World Report*, October 15, 1984, p. 18.

13. D. Masi, *Human Services in Industry* (Lexington, Mass.: Lexington, Books, 1981), p. 14..

11

Learning Disabilities And Speech and Language Disorders

Mike is a telephone company laborer. When he was in elementary school, teachers often yelled at him, "Michael, you are just too slow! You make the same errors over and over. Can't you remember the difference between *b* and *d* and the words *god* and *dog*! And you still can't add or subtract correctly without using your fingers. Why don't you grow up?" Mike felt stupid.

Not much changed in high school. He was diagnosed variously as having anything from school phobia to brain damage. No one recognized that Mike had dyslexia. Teachers still criticized him thoughtlessly, and he had low self-esteem, often thinking, "Why can't I be smart like my sister? I still can't read very well. I really must be a moron." He developed an attitude that he expressed in minor delinquent acts, and eventually he dropped out of school in the tenth grade.

Paul, an army electronics technician, lost his larynx to cancer when he was in his late 30s. After his military discharge, he applied for a position at my school as an instructor. He had no voice box and spoke through a stoma, an opening in his throat just below the collar line that enabled him, following intensive training, to produce esophageal speech. Vocalization is achieved by forcing air into the stomach and then expelling it through the esophagus. The process produces a husky speech, unvarying in pitch, that is made audible by a hand-held, battery-operated, amplifying artificial voice generator.

Despite some misgivings, I hired Paul and enrolled him in instructor training. He did just fine. In fact, about a year after he was hired, Paul was chosen instructor of the month (by means of

a highly competitive selection system that focused on results as well as trainee feedback) and instructor of the year from among a field of 500 instructors.

The next year I had the honor of attending a ceremony in the office of the Secretary of the Army when Paul was awarded the Department of the Army's Meritorious Civilian Service Decoration for his outstanding service and selection as the Army's Handicapped Employee of the Year.

Two of the most difficult challenges facing trainers and supervisors lie in training and working with people with learning disabilities or speech and language disorders. Often both conditions, as well as physical, developmental, and emotional disabilities, are present in the same individual. Until recently, public and private elementary and secondary education programs were strikingly unsuccessful in dealing with these problems. In all too many cases, handling of the children and adolescents who have these disorders by uninformed, incompetent, or insensitive teachers exacerbated the situation and caused lifelong emotional damage to individuals by making them feel inept or stupid.

Competent trainers and supervisors now recognize that emotional factors can be either a cause or a result. That is, emotional disturbances as a cause can diminish the effectiveness with which a worker learns, takes part in classroom discussions, responds to questions, or selects the correct answer on a test or examination. And failure to achieve in a classroom or work environment, a result, is itself extremely disturbing emotionally to the employee and often produces disruptive behavior or retreat from the situation.

The ability of trainees to learn and communicate orally is almost a prerequisite for success in training and development programs. Similarly, a person who has a learning disability or has difficulty communicating with superiors and coworkers poses a very difficult obstacle to work unit collaboration and productivity. The sheer numbers and the variety of conditions of people who have these disorders is so large that it is inevitable that trainers and supervisors will have these employees in their classroom and shop training programs and in the work areas they supervise. They must learn to deal with them competently and compassionately.

LEARNING DISABILITIES

"Learning disabilities" is a generic term that includes a group of disorders manifested by substantial obstacles to the acquisition and use of listening, speaking, reading, writing, spelling, reasoning, or mathematics skills. It is estimated that about 25 million American workers have learning disabilities.

Learning disabilities fall into two main categories: language processing (problems with listening and understanding words, communicating clearly, and reading and writing) and visual-spatial processing (problems with seeing and remembering, judging distances, writing, and understanding mathematics). The most common names applied to these conditions are dyslexia (reading/spelling problems), dysgraphia (writing problems), aphasia (communication problems), and dyscalculia (math problems). It is not unusual for one person to experience more than one of these disabilities. People with learning disabilities are not lacking in intelligence; in fact, they are usually quite bright. However, the learning disabilities interfere with learning and work efficiency and productivity.

Learning disorders are believed to be due to dysfunction of the central nervous system. Although they may coexist with other disabling conditions, such as sensory impairments, mental retardation, or social or emotional disorders, they are not the direct result of those conditions. The term "learning disability," then, does not include learning problems that are due primarily to visual, hearing, or motor disabilities, mental deficits, emotional disturbances, or environmental deprivation. Figure 11-1 identifies the most common indicators of learning disabilities in the workplace.

Although much progress has been made in developing strategies and techniques for dealing with the needs of children with learning disabilities, there are large gaps in our knowledge of adult learning disabilities and how to overcome or compensate for them. However, some useful accommodations for adults with learning disabilities have been identified:

- Individualized instruction
- One-on-one or small-group tutoring
- Peer tutoring
- Texts and manuals on audiotape
- Demonstrations on videocassettes
- Note takers
- Extra time on assignments and tests
- Performance-based evaluation
- Job shadowing and mentoring
- Job coaching
- Reduced workload
- Job sharing
- Task substitution

Figure 11-1. Signs and symptoms of learning disabilities.

Language Processing Disabilities

Understanding

- Difficulty recalling new or complicated information
- Confuses similar-sounding words
- Can't follow directions

Speaking

- Difficulty recalling names or labels quickly
- Can't find right word
- Expresses ideas in short or broken sentences

Reading

- Mispronounces words when reading orally
- Loses place easily
- Reverses or rearranges words, parts of words, or phrases
- May read slowly and/or word-by-word
- May not comprehend what is read

Writing

- May reverse or omit letters, words, or phrases
- Can explain orally, but not in writing
- Spells poorly

Visual-Spatial Disabilities

Perception

- Forgets shapes or direction of numbers, letters, symbols
- Difficulty judging distances and sizes
- Poor comprehension of body language
- May not recognize own errors

Planning

- Disorganized drawing or writing
- Problems planning space use, layouts
- Left-right confusion
- Poor time sense, judgment of time
- Chronically early or late for appointments

(Continued)

Figure 11-1. Continued.

> *Organization*
>
> - Loses or misplaces things
> - Needs consistent routine and preorganized steps or strategies
> - Problems with the sequence of steps in a job
> - Easily distracted by irrelevant details
> - Problems following diagrams or maps

Source: © Diane L. Sauter, 2567 Erie Avenue, Cincinnati, OH 45208 and Donna McPeek, 2700 Marshall Court, Madison, WI 53705. Used by permission.

- Modified equipment, tools, and procedures
- Periodic review and retraining of critical skills

The Disabilities

Attention Deficit Disorder (ADD)

An estimated 15 million Americans have ADD, sometimes called attention deficit hyperactivity disorder, a group of symptoms that appears before the age of 7 and is a lifelong condition. About three times as many men as women are affected by ADD. The disorder has 14 symptoms, any 8 of which constitute a positive diagnosis:

Disorganization	Problems with relationships
Distractibility	Frequent job changes
Impulsiveness	Underachievement
Overactivity	High intelligence quotient
Argumentativeness	Increased creativity
Low frustration tolerance	Compensation for any of the
Mood swings	symptoms
Forgetting	

The syndrome is believed to be genetic in origin, most likely a neurochemical failure in the system of the brain that controls attention.

Medication, most commonly the stimulant Ritalin, works in about 80 percent of adult ADD cases. Ritalin normalizes brain functioning by increasing the production of neurotransmitters. For the remaining 20 percent, behavioral therapy or a combination of medication and behavioral therapy is effective. Behavioral management therapy helps people to become more aware of their actions and their consequences.

Dyslexia

Dyslexia is difficulty with language, not lack of intelligence, laziness, or a vision problem. It includes several disorders that severely interfere with the ability to learn. It is unrelated to race or age, nor is it a disease. No two people with dyslexia are alike. Some may have difficulty with reading, spelling, or expressing themselves clearly in speech or writing. Others may have trouble remembering, distinguishing right from left or before from after, or remaining organized. However, people with dyslexia may also have talents in art, drama, mathematics, or sports.

Dyslexia affects about 12 million Americans, males much more frequently than females. It is estimated that of all people with reading difficulties, between 5 and 15 percent have dyslexia. Severity varies among individuals, yet it always seems to cause problems perceiving the shapes of words and letters. To people with dyslexia, letters in words seem to weave, shift, and undulate on the page, sometimes almost jumping off its edge.

People are born with dyslexia. The National Institutes of Health estimates that up to 15 percent of the men, women, and children in the United States—one in seven—have dyslexia. Often other members of the family have had difficulty learning to read and spell. Dyslexia cannot be outgrown, although people with the disorder can learn how to learn with appropriate training.

Although several theories have been advanced for the source of dyslexia, no definite cause has been proved. Studies suggest, however, that it begins prior to birth by abnormal development of the brain, sometime between the fourth and sixth month of pregnancy, when the part of the brain that controls language develops. Some researchers believe that the disability is the result of slight injuries to the fetal brain, such as a minor stroke, maternal stress, a virus, or a hormonal (testosterone) imbalance. Other possible causes are disease, accidental brain injury, and cultural deprivation.

Dyslexia has nothing to do with intelligence. Many famous people, including Winston Churchill, Thomas Edison, Albert Einstein, and Woodrow Wilson, had dyslexia. The disability manifests itself in a variety of ways: sometimes confusion of one consonant with another, such as "b" for "d," "p" for "q," or "t" for "f" or as a reversal of syllables, words, or entire sentences. For example, the person may on one occasion see a combination of letters as "d-o-g" and another time as "g-o-d."

In training situations, people with dyslexia may exhibit these characteristics:

- Difficulty listening and following directions
- Reading, spelling, and mathematics difficulties

- Poor handwriting
- Deficient speech development and problems with oral language
- Poor study habits
- Narrow memory span
- Difficulty remembering facts and procedures
- Difficulty in associating verbal labels and directional concepts
- Time dysfunctions, inadequate sense of time or space
- Difficulty pronouncing words
- Poor auditory discrimination of vowels
- Inadequate phoneme memory for matching[1]
- Disorder of phonemic discrimination
- Comprehension disorders
- Inability to complete work on time
- Lack of concentration
- Lack of organization of tools and materials
- Distractibility
- Poor sound blending
- Maturational delay in the development of most language functions
- Unilateral stare when reading
- Mirror-imaging and writing of letters and words (e.g., "b" and "d," "was" and "saw")
- Hyperactivity, overactivity, and impulsiveness
- Poor self-image

The usual treatment for dyslexia involves intensive counseling and the use of visual and tactile aids to substitute for the traditional phonetic approaches to the teaching of reading. However, some physicians believe that medication can be helpful for dyslexia rooted in malfunctions of the vertical and horizontal fine-tuners of the inner ear, if taken under the direction of a medical doctor. These include antihistamines, stimulants, antidepressants, and vitamins.

Perceptual and Integrative Disorders

People with perceptual and integrative disorders have difficulty in understanding, comprehending, processing, and interpreting information, concepts, and principles, or they may be unable to make fine discriminations among objects or ideas. These abilities are requirements for problem solving as well as for response, storage, and retention of knowledge and previous experience and for effectiveness in categorizing objects and ideas and discerning differences. Perception and learning are essential concomitants of the thought process. Perception is not sensation; it implies the recognition of an object, an image, or an idea. Perception, therefore, is the act of knowing objects, images, and thoughts by sensory experiences or by recollective thought. It takes place only through a lengthy process of repetitive experiencing of the object, image, or thought.

Perceptual disabilities often leave a trainee confused, anxious, and frustrated. The individual whose perceptions are inaccurate, inconsistent, and misleading occupies an unpredictable world and needs to make a great amount of conscious and persistent effort to override distorted visual and auditory information.

Integrative disabilities manifest themselves as difficulties organizing new information and relating it to previously learned information. People with this condition can absorb a series of facts but are unable to answer questions using those facts. They are unable to sequence and organize newly learned information and previously learned information into an integrated whole.

Trainers of industrial processes want trainees to understand what tools can do and how different operations serve different ends. Sales trainers want trainees to understand the principles of selling and how approaches must be tailored to meet customer needs and expectations. Because concepts give power to deal with situations, understanding of new concepts is central to any learning experience. Ideas are taught because they help people interpret new situations and events.

Interpretation is the key to appropriate behavior. When a worker makes a mistake, the chances are that he or she acted out of a faulty perception of the situation. The person who is stumped by a problem either does not possess the concepts and principles needed to analyze it or does not recall them. Training improves employees' power to interpret by teaching them concepts and principles that are useful in getting at the heart of the problems. Therefore, people with perceptual and integrative disorders are at a distinct disadvantage in training situations and in the workplace. But it is important to remember that a concept or principle has no value to a trainee or worker unless he or she can recall it, know where to apply it, and know how to apply it.

Simple Memory Deficiencies

Memory may be defined as the means by which information that has been acquired and presented to consciousness through one or more of the senses is stored for later retrieval and re-presentation to consciousness. It consists of three processes: (1) reception and registration of a mental impression, (2) retention or preservation of the previously acquired perception, and (3) reproduction or recall of the impression. Memories may be categorized as recent or short term and remote or long term. Although memory is believed to involve complex electrochemical events within the brain, its physiological origins are unimportant here. What is important is that memory is purposive and tends to promote responses and reactions with minimum effort of the individual in his or her attempts to profit by earlier experience.

When memory fails or is interfered with by emotions, the result is forgetting. Forgetting, too, is purposive inasmuch as it may be regarded as the result of organizing or reorganizing the process and holdings of memory. Sensory impressions that have been generalized or subordinated, conceptualized as a means of retaining larger banks of information, or condensed to maintain an efficient working memory, tend to be forgotten. However, it is believed that everything registered as memory remains in memory unless brain structure and function are impaired by illness or injury. Yet many sensory impressions may not be recorded in permanent memory. Some memories are psychologically repressed and remain available when the conditions that induced repression are modified or eliminated.

Mental health professionals identify three types of memory disorders: (1) abnormally pronounced or vivid memory, called hypermnesia, (2) loss of memory, or amnesia, and (3) falsification or distortions of memory, or paramnesia. These are all in the category of abnormal personality functioning, or psychopathology. Here we are not concerned with such gross disturbances. Rather, we shall limit the discussion to simple memory deficiencies; disorders that result in such problems as inability to join ideas one to another in imagining, conceiving, inferring, and other processes, and the formation of new ideas from these processes; disorders in the progression of thought or "stream of thought"—a coherent sequence of related ideas passing from an initial idea to a goal idea; or frequent lapses in ability to reproduce or recall facts and ideas.

General Training Approaches

Attention Deficit Disorder (ADD)

There are three basic strategies for helping adults with ADD: education, compensatory strategies, and behavioral management strategies.

Education. Unquestionably the most important strategy for people who work with adults who have ADD is to educate themselves about the condition. Knowledge of the disorder—how it can be controlled and compensated and how workers with the disorder can be helped—will go a long way toward making those workers productive. Good resources are books, professionals, and community resources, such as self-help groups, vocational assessment and training agencies, and professional organizations.

Compensatory Strategies. Because workers with ADD are frequently unorganized, forgetful, and underproductive, helping them to implement selected behavioral strategies can overcome these deficits and help them feel more in control. Supervisors and instructors must determine which strategies work best for the individual by trial and error. The ones that work then can become a part of the workplace routine for that worker. The following suggestions for trainees or workers are useful:

- Join self-help support groups to improve interpersonal and social skills, acquire coping skills, and learn stress management and relaxation techniques.
- Learn time management skills.
- Make a daily "to do" list and keep it handy at all times.
- Maintain an appointment or planning calendar.
- Keep note pads in strategic places at home, in the car, and at work.
- Use a tape recorder to help remember if the "to do" lists don't work.
- Post appointments, schedules, and so on on strategically placed bulletin boards at home and at work.
- Use a desk, workstation, file cabinets, drawers, closets, storage boxes, or anything else that will help organize the job, tasks, tools, job aids, and materials.
- Color code objects, tools, files, and so on to make them more prominent, arresting, and memorable.
- Use a highlighter when reading to maintain attention.
- Make notes when reading.
- Divide large projects, jobs, and tasks into smaller, more manageable ones.
- Schedule daily vigorous physical exercise to burn off energy and reduce stress.
- Reserve time every day for change-of-pace activities, including rest and recreation.
- Reduce or eliminate alcohol.
- Listen to feedback from trusted coworkers, friends, and relatives.
- Set up a self-reward system for the completion of tasks.

Behavioral Management Strategies. Workers with ADD need large amounts of reinforcement, as well as stimulation and challenge. The following strategies are helpful:

- Provide career and vocational counseling to achieve a better match of skills and jobs.
- Provide regular and frequent feedback, encouragement, and positive reinforcement of progress and accomplishment to build confidence and self-esteem.
- Use praise and pats on the back freely.
- Never carp, badger, or hassle the worker about not paying attention.
- Schedule occasional breaks for changes in routine and activities involving physical exercise, such as walking to other areas or climbing stairs.
- Provide occasional highly stimulating and challenging activities to overcome boredom and encourage motivation.
- Be sure that outside distractions are not competing for attention.
- Maintain eye contact when communicating, making requests, or giving directions, and require a response to ensure that the message was received.
- Find out under what conditions the employee works best (noisy room, quiet room, with music, etc.), and provide those conditions.
- Consider writing down what is needed from the worker, and give it to him or her in the form of a list every day.
- Color code learning aids, equipment, tools, and materials.
- Break down jobs and large tasks into small ones.
- Prioritize jobs and tasks.
- Make deadlines for the completion of small tasks.
- Change activities frequently, and make them interactive as much as possible.
- Schedule regular "time-out" periods to prevent overstimulation.

Dyslexia

Because of the heterogeneity of the population of people with dyslexia, instruction must be highly individualized—person oriented rather than method focused. Adults with the disorder are typically highly motivated. Whether referred by their supervisors or self-referred, they are anxious to understand why they have difficulty reading or learning and are seeking help. They also want to know the level of their performance so that they can match their vocational goals and aspirations with their potential.

Trainers can begin by encouraging spontaneous, clear vocalization through frequent questioning and the use of positive reinforcement. They can promote accurate listening by asking the individual to repeat instructions and paraphrase answers. In addition, the following suggestions will prove useful:

- Although the ultimate objective of training may be to maximize the individual's vocational potential, begin with instruction designed to improve communication in the work environment.
- Try to identify the reading strategy used most efficiently and that used least efficiently, such as word form, sight recognition, phonetic analysis, structural analysis, and context.
- Be unfailingly understanding, patient, and sympathetic.
- Establish and maintain a learning environment that is consistent and predictable.
- Emphasize the use of multiple strategies for reading, writing, and spelling.
- Present new words in context and both as wholes and in syllables with spacing between each syllable—for example, "computer," "com pu ter."
- Emphasize multisensory methods and techniques of instruction (listening, viewing, feeling, and doing).
- Break learning elements and processes into small steps.
- Require mastery of each step before progressing to the next step.
- As the trainee learns new words, emphasize structural analysis by adding various verb endings, prefixes, and suffixes, and provide practice in lists, phrases, and context.
- Provide direct instruction in language skills and concepts.
- Provide training in language conventions (forms and usage).
- Provide practice in linguistic sequencing in conventional sentences.
- Provide ample amounts of conversation.
- Use clear, verbal directions with every prompt and cue used.
- When using cues embedded in activities and materials, make sure the cue is distinctive in color, shape, or size to direct the individual's attention to the key aspects of the stimulus.
- Don't overuse any prompt or cue that will encourage the individual to become overly dependent on it.
- Fade (gradually remove) prompts or cues as soon as possible.
- Teach all steps in a task or procedure in proper sequence.
- Focus reading or instructional materials or subjects closely related to the actual or potential job of the individual trainee.
- Check frequently on the person's ability to self-correct and monitor for meaning when reading aloud.
- Tape-record the individual reading aloud, and then play the tape back without the reading material in front of him or her and note if the trainee can identify mistakes.
- Require the trainee to perform all the steps and learned up to that point in the instructional sequence before moving on to the next.
- Provide frequent distributed practice.

Perceptual Disorders. Here are some suggestions for alleviating or compensating perceptual disorders.

- Seat trainees with perceptual disabilities in the front row near the center of the chalkboard, projector screen, or easel.
- Use different colors of felt pens or chalk when writing on the chalkboard or easel to help the trainee keep his or her place.
- Organize materials to be learned into appropriate segments and patterns to make it easier to grasp.
- Use a "whole-then-part" method in presenting material.
- Define terms as precisely as possible; use words with a definite meaning.
- Demonstrate rather than just talk.
- Make instruction more auditory than visual, or at least supplement all visual materials with auditory repetition.
- Give directions orally.
- Give clear explanations; use familiar words and short sentences; avoid complex sentence structure.
- Present difficult ideas or concepts repeatedly in different words.
- Encourage the trainee to verbalize quietly what he or she is writing.
- Allow the trainee to use a file card, ruler, or fingers under lines of print while reading.
- Encourage the trainee to highlight important terms and other information.
- Avoid lessons that involve copying from books, manuals, chalkboard, or easel; provide photocopies and handouts.
- Allow the trainee to tape-record lectures.
- Use large-print books or enlarge by means of a photocopier.
- Use reading materials that are clear, legible, and uncrowded.
- Place special emphasis on important terms or principles.
- Insist that the trainee use terms accurately.
- State principles explicitly to improve transfer.
- Make sure the trainee understands a principle thoroughly—what it means and why it is true.
- Provide practice to develop and improve discrimination.
- Use cues that help the trainee focus attention properly.
- Require the trainee to give examples of principles.
- Have the trainee explain why a principle is true by relating it to other principles.
- Provide realistic experiences—real objects and ideas that have some connection with the trainee's past experiences.

- Provide plenty of opportunities for the trainee to use principles in solving unfamiliar problems.
- Give the trainee extra time to complete assignments, tests, and other classroom activities.

Integrative Disorders. Here are some suggestions for helping trainees with integrative deficiencies:

- Help the trainee organize his or her classroom or work area, including equipment, tools, and materials.
- Provide the trainee with an assignment booklet and a calendar to keep track of assignments and projects.
- Have a nondisabled trainee see that all assignments are properly recorded.
- Issue a binder with pockets and dividers to help the trainee organize his or her work.
- Assign tasks in sequence.
- Give instructions in small segments; gradually increase their length and complexity.
- Sequence presentations carefully.
- Actively involve the trainee to keep him or her focused on the task at hand.
- Teach the trainee to talk through the steps when solving a problem.

Memory Deficiencies. Here are some suggestions for ameliorating simple memory deficiencies:

- Keep distractions to a minimum.
- Do not give directions while the trainee is doing something else.
- Repeat instructions step by step, have the trainee repeat them, and then ask him or her to demonstrate understanding of what to do.
- Never assume that the trainee will remember tomorrow what he or she knows today or that because he or she has trouble learning something today the same problem will recur tomorrow.
- Organize materials to be learned into patterns to make it easier to remember.
- Make material comprehensible and meaningful.
- Teach memory improvement strategies, such as using mnemonics, acronyms, visualization, and imaging.
- Teach the trainee how to make notes and lists to help remember information.

- Avoid exercises that emphasize memorization without comprehension (rote learning).
- Provide ample opportunities for the practice of skills to promote retention.
- Review materials previously taught until the material is overlearned.
- Require more thorough learning than is needed to perform well on an immediate test.
- Provide periodic review and practice to promote retention.
- Directly teach techniques of remembering and memorizing: studying for meaning, learning by wholes, frequent self-testing, use of rhythm and grouping, and formation and use of secondary association.
- Build trainee confidence in the payoff of learning how to remember.
- Reward improvement.

Fine Motor and Writing Difficulties. Here are some strategies that will help trainees to overcome fine motor and writing difficulties:

- Avoid long writing assignments; allow the trainee to tape-record or dictate longer reports.
- Provide writing tools, such as pencil grips.
- Provide paper and work sheets that are well spaced and clearly lined.
- Allow the trainee to use a typewriter or word processor.
- Encourage the trainee to proofread written work by reading it aloud to himself or herself.
- When possible, give oral rather than written tests and quizzes.
- Accept answers to test items in any written form, even if misspelled (unless correct spelling is critical).
- Provide immediate feedback and reinforcement for progress and accomplishment.

SPEECH AND LANGUAGE DISORDERS

Because so much dependence is placed on oral communication in the workplace as well as in daily living, even the slightest speech impairment is noticeable. The social pressure on every individual to speak "normally" is tremendous, and individuals with even slight speech difficulties often develop poor self-image as a result of the pressures and negative attitudes of those around them. Individual variations are barely tolerated. Even certain regional accents are subject to criticism because they are "different." As a consequence, much time, attention, research, and training have been expended over the years to correct speech impairments of all types.

Speech-language pathologists help people develop their communication abilities, as well as treat speech, language, and voice disorders. Their services include prevention, identification, evaluation, treatment, and rehabilitation of communication disorders including those who have had strokes and those who have language delays, stutter, or other voice and articulation problems. They also work with people who are non-speaking and use augmentative communication aids ranging from sign language to computers.[2] These professionals work in hospitals, clinics, rehabilitation centers, skilled nursing facilities, health departments, research laboratories, colleges and universities, schools, and in private practice.

Individuals with communication impairments have difficulty in making themselves understood, due primarily to neurological or mechanical disabilities involving the voice but sometimes due to difficulties in organizing their thoughts or understanding what is said by others. An individual is considered to have a speech impairment or disability when (1) speech is so deviant that listeners pay more attention to how the person speaks than to what is said, (2) speech is difficult or impossible to understand, or (3) the speaker reacts to his or her own utterance in such a way as to affect the communication adversely.

There are two basic causes of speech impairments, functional and organic. Functional (or psychogenic) speech defects are cuased by psychological factors; they have no physical origins. Organic speech defects are caused primarily by physical factors, such as accidents, disease, or heredity. Speech problems take many forms. Among the most common are the following:

- Aphasia (expressive and receptive)
- Articulation problems (lisping and lallation)
- Autism (a developmental disability)
- Cleft palate
- Laryngectomy
- Stuttering
- Voice problems (pitch and volume)

The only speech disabilities that will be discussed here are aphasia, articulation disorders, autism, loss of speech, and stuttering.

The Disabilities

Aphasia

Aphasia, a language disorder that is considered to be a defect of the integrative process, is the most disruptive of all communication disabilities. People with aphasia see, hear, and feel but cannot integrate this sensory information into logical experience patterns. Aphasia results in inability to use or comprehend words. There are two types of aphasia: expressive and receptive. An individual who can understand what is said but cannot express thought is said to have expressive aphasia. Expressive aphasia is manifested in motor inadequacies, primarily an inability to activate the muscles of the speech mechanism or loss of or reduction in gestural ability. An individual who cannot receive or understand speech has receptive aphasia. Receptive aphasia has its roots in sensory deficiencies, including either or both vision and hearing impairments. Aphasia may be partial, called dysphasia, or total.

Symptoms of aphasia vary widely. Some people with aphasia cannot read a sentence aloud, but that does not mean that they have lost the ability to understand the printed word. Some cannot understand auditory instructions. Others cannot discriminate one visual or auditory symbol from another. Some are unable to retain messages while keeping them separated from other messages. Some cannot collect and organize words into an idea to be spoken.

Aphasia is probably caused by a neurological dysfunction that does not come under the heading of mental deficiency, deafness, dyslexia, peripheral speech defects, emotional disturbances, or social, cultural, or educational deprivation. The main causes of aphasia are traumatic head injuries that cause brain damage and cerebral vascular accidents involving reduced blood supply to the brain (e.g., a stroke). Some experts believe that aphasia is often caused by lesions in the brain (brain tumors, cerebral hemorrhage, or cerebral thrombosis) or, less often, by a lag in language development.

Articulation Disorders

Articulation disorders are manifested in unclear, imprecise voicing of sounds. For example, words involving the "s" sound and its voiced correlative "z" (the most common error); "r" with a "w" substitute; "l" with an "s" substitute; and the "sh" and "zh" sounds. Lallation is a common problem of articulation. In lallation, the "r," "l," "t," "d," and/or "s" sounds are defective.

Autism

Autism is a developmental disability whose manifestations include absence of language or language delays, resistance to affection, and other problem social behaviors. Because of their inability to communicate, children with autism may resort to tantrums, or self-injuring or aggressive behavior, or they may engage in repetitive, obsessive, and ritualistic activities. About 70 percent of individuals with autism also have mental retardation. Although the causes of autism are unknown, there is some evidence that it is linked to brain abnormalities.

Following intensive education and training focusing on communication, usually in an institutional setting, autistic behavior can be changed. When training is successful, people with autism can return to their homes, move into group homes or other residential schools, and hold jobs. In certain repetitive jobs, their tendency to engage in obsessive behavior can be a plus.

Loss of Speech

Loss of speech is due to problems of the larynx, the cartilaginous structure at the upper end of the trachea or windpipe that contains and supports the vocal cords and associated structures. It is the human voice box. Laryngitis, a common ailment involving the voice box, is manifested by a change in tone or quality of the voice to a coarse, harsher sound; a need to clear the throat; difficulty in swallowing; and throat pain. Laryngitis is inflammation of the larynx due to inhaling smoke, chemical fumes, gases, vapors, or dust; excessive use of alcohol; or diseases such as the common cold, flu, bronchitis, sinusitis, tonsillitis, or pneumonia; overuse or abuse of the voice; polyps in the throat; or cancer.

If a temporary, nonserious condition, treatment for laryngitis consists of resting the larynx by not speaking, not drinking alcohol or smoking, increasing fluid intake, and medication. If symptoms persist, other treatment may be indicated. In worst-case situations, the cause may be cancer of the larynx. That condition sometimes results in a laryngectomy—removal of the voice box—and total loss of speech.

Restoration of the ability to speak is achieved by intensive therapy and training in esophageal speech, whereby vocalization is achieved by forcing air into the stomach and expelling it through the esophagus. The resulting low-volume, hoarse speech, unvarying in pitch, is made audible by a hand-held, battery-operated, amplifying artificial voice generator.

Stuttering

More than 3 million Americans stutter. Stuttering usually develops in early childhood, between the ages of 2 and 4, and it affects four times as many males as females. About 25 percent of all children go through a state of development during which they stutter—some 4 percent as long as six months or more. Although usually described as excessive repetition or a break in speech rhythm, stuttering today is described as a deviation in the fluency of speech. There are three possible causes of stuttering: (1) physical or constitutional, (2) emotional problems, or (3) learned behavior or response. It is most likely to be the result of environmental or hereditary factors or their interaction. However, no theory about the origin of stuttering has been proved.

People who stutter are just as intelligent and well adjusted as nonstutterers. Although much has been learned about factors that contribute to its development, the root causes of stuttering are not known, and there are no quick cures. Qualified speech therapists, however, can help people at any age make significant progress in overcoming the disorder.

General Training Approaches

Cueing

Trainees with speech and learning disabilities need help in learning to complete various types of job tasks that involve motor skills. One technique instructors can use is oral cues, brief instructions given to the trainee who is learning to perform a specific task. For example, if the trainee is ready to start a photocopier and is about to press the wrong button, he or she can be orally cued by the trainer, "No, try this one."

Another technique is the use of physical guidance cues. When using this type of cue, the trainer guides the trainee's hands or fingers by placing his or her hands over those of the trainee. This approach is particularly useful when it is important to prevent the trainee from making an error to avoid damage to equipment or injury to the trainee.

Modeling and Demonstration

In modeling and demonstration, the trainer shows the trainee how to do one or more steps in the job or task. For example, a supermarket grocery-bagger trainee may not understand how to place certain food items in the bag and the cart to avoid damage or a stock clerk trainee might not know how to arrange food items on shelves. The trainer would say, "Watch me," placing the items properly so the trainee can see the right way of doing it.

When using modeling and demonstration, it is important that the trainee watch the trainer carefully and that the trainer observe the trainee to be sure that his or her attention has not been diverted. Gesturing and pointing can help the trainee avoid becoming confused during a demonstration.

Observing and Correcting

The position of the trainer for observing performance of a newly learned task is critically important. The trainer should stand behind the trainee so that he or she can correct the trainee with pointing, gesturing, or oral cues without obstructing the work. Standing to the side is incorrect because the trainee will look at the trainer and become distracted. Even if the trainee does not turn to look at the trainer, he or she is almost certain to use peripheral vision to glance at the trainer and thus become diverted from the task.

The trainer should be as unobstrusive as possible and stand farther and farther away from the trainee until he or she is able to disappear completely while the trainee performs the task. Unless that is done, the trainee will learn little and is not likely to develop confidence in his or her ability to perform the task without help.

Color Coding

Color coding is a very useful training technique that can help emphasize or highlight a particular part of an operation or task. For example, if the trainee has to sort machine parts or separate rejected items from an assembly line, the trainer may color code the box where the various parts go or where the rejects go for rework.

Evaluation and Error Correction

Work performed by trainees with learning and speech and language disabilities must always be carefully evaluated to prevent the practice of errors. When errors are observed or exhibited, they must be corrected immediately. Error correction involves making the trainee aware of the steps in the task that he or she has missed or performed incorrectly, followed immediately by questioning, physical guidance, modeling, or demonstration and then practice of the correct procedure. For example, the trainer might say, "No. Do it like this." Or, when a mistake is about to be made, "Please stop. Now, what is the next step?"

The trainee's progress and performance can be followed by using a task record sheet, recording the result each time the trainee performs a task. If necessary, the individual can be retrained in performing the most difficult steps or tasks and the amount of reinforcement changed or increased. These records can be passed on to the worker's supervisor following training so that he or she will be able to determine what tasks have been learned and how well.

Work Endurance

Workers with disabilities must develop endurance if they are to be able to perform a job. That is, they must be able to work several hours per day without too many breaks. Developing endurance takes time. Some trainees require that on-the-job training time be increased gradually until they can work productively and independently a reasonable number of hours.

Reinforcement

Positive reinforcement strategies are critical to success in training people with learning and speech disabilities. They are needed to help trainees remain focused. Using various reinforcing techniques will make it possible for trainees to work steadily for relatively long periods of time. Coffee and rest breaks are one form. Pats on the back and praise are another.

Practice

Trainees with learning and speech disabilities require many more opportunities for practice with guidance and supervision than nondisabled trainees. Their ability to acquire and retain new skills is greatly enhanced by practice. Productivity is another important concern. Trainees with disabilities must be able to complete tasks at speeds much like those of nondisabled workers, and the quality of the work product must be up to standard. If maintenance practice is not provided periodically, the trainee is likely to forget how to perform the task. It is also important that the trainee's nondisabled coworkers become involved in the training so that when the trainee returns to the worksite (or the supervisor or trainer leaves the work area), coworkers will know how to help.

Follow-Up

Follow-up to determine how trainees perform when they have been placed in a job is an important component of good training. The progress and accomplishments of workers must be checked to see that they are properly adjusting to the work environment. That can be done by visiting the work area and observing and talking with the worker, meeting the immediate supervisors of workers and discussing their progress, and requesting periodic brief reports from supervisors.

Specific Training Techniques

Aphasia

Workers with aphasia need understanding and encouragement if they are to become productive. Here are some suggestions:

- Encourage frequent use of language, correct articulation of words, use of gestures to supplement speech, and association of words with concepts and objects.
- Take a positive approach. Demonstrate interest in the individual, and adopt a friendly and supporting, but not patronizing, manner.
- Remember that the basic intelligence and personality of the individual are not affected, only his or her ability to communicate.
- Simplify your speech, and supplement it with gestures.
- Never raise the pitch or volume of your voice.
- Make frequent use of questions, requests, and instructions.
- Get the individual's attention before giving directions.
- Be aware of distracting factors, and try to reduce or eliminate them.
- Present only one instruction at a time. Use the same wording each time.
- Pause between directions. Avoid making the person feel rushed.
- Sequence instructions in the order of their desired performance; make a definite transition between tasks.
- Speak slowly, using sentences with appropriate vocabulary and simple word combinations.
- Be sure that the desired response is in the individual's repertoire to reduce the potential for failure.
- Give the individual plenty of time to respond in order to sort out the incoming messages and select and formulate an appropriate response.
- When demonstrating a task, combine clear, concise verbal directions with the modeling procedure.
- Keep the demonstration process simple.
- Use positive reinforcement to establish correct procedures.

- Minimize correction and criticism.
- Review material previously covered.
- Be consistent. Get the person to know you and what you expect.

Articulation Disorders

Workers with articulation disorders are likely to be sensitive about their disability. Trainers can help by following these suggestions:

- Point out errors privately.
- Demonstrate.
- Provide opportunities for practice.
- Provide plenty of positive reinforcement.

Autism

Workers with autism often pose the greatest challenge to trainers, supervisors, and coworkers. Here are some suggestions that should help:

- Alert coworkers to the potential for bizarre, aggressive, and inappropriate behaviors.
- Provide continuing support to other employees in dealing with autistic trainees.
- Provide a consistently structured work environment.
- Be persistent; insist that trainees with autism complete their tasks.
- Be consistent and firm in giving directions, and keeping the trainee on task.
- Reinforce appropriate behavior immediately.
- Reward only appropriate and productive behavior.
- Allow more time on task to help trainees learn their particular jobs.
- Provide periodic short breaks—not longer than 5 or 6 minutes.

Stuttering

Malcolm Fraser, director of the Stuttering Foundation of America, suggests that people who stutter can learn to control the difficulty by modifying their feelings and attitudes and by eliminating or correcting the irregular behavior associated with their blocks when they stutter.[3]

The Stuttering Foundation of America includes the following "Guidelines for Greater Fluency" in one of its informational pamphlets.[4] It seems likely that almost anyone could help people who stutter follow these guidelines.

Always try to . . .

1. Speak more slowly and in a deliberate manner. Draw out the vowels, and do not skip over syllables. It won't sound as slow as you think!
2. Slide into words with light and loose movements of the lips and jaw. Feel the words as you say them.
3. Eliminate all avoidance or word substitution, habits which you may use to postpone or eliminate stuttering. Feared words only become a larger problem when you attempt to run away from them.
4. Keep moving forward in your speech. Repeating words you have already said only postpones the attempt to say the next word that you fear.
5. Maintain natural eye contact with your listener.
6. Occasionally stutter on purpose! By blocking or repeating intentionally you may feel how to control your speech mechanism during those tense moments.
7. Monitor and identify what you are doing unnecessarily when you stutter. The more you can self-analyze your stuttering, the more aware you become of how to modify the muscle coordination needed to produce more fluent speech. Stuttering does not "just happen."
8. Remember that your goal is to be more fluent—not perfect! Even normal speakers have disfluencies in their conversational speech. Perhaps you cannot control what you do after the block. Try to focus on how to resume fluency.
9. Tell your listeners that you stutter. By not pretending you are a normal speaker—and by actually confronting and discussing what you are trying to hide—the fear will lessen and fluency will come more easily.
10. Prevent anxiety or tension from overwhelming your fluent speech. Stuttering is nothing to be ashamed about, and you certainly don't do it on purpose. Instead of being embarrassed by a block, analyze what you did, try to say the word again fluently, and then move on. Don't dwell upon your failures; celebrate those moments when you succeed in speaking more fluently.

There is little question that the way a person, such as a training instructor or supervisor, reacts to a person who stutters is much more important than attempting to help them overcome the difficulty. The Stuttering Foundation of America makes these suggestions:

- Refrain from making remarks like: "Slow down," "Take a breath," or "Relax." Such simplistic advice can be felt as demeaning and is not helpful.
- You will be very tempted to finish sentences or fill in words. Try not to do this.
- Maintain natural eye contact, and try not to look embarrassed. Just wait patiently and naturally until the person is finished.
- Use a relatively slow, relaxed rate in your own conversational speech—but not so slow as to sound unnatural.
- Let the person know by your manner and actions that you are listening to *what* he or she says—not *how* they say it.
- Be aware that those who stutter usually have more trouble controlling their speech on the telephone. Please be extra patient in this situation. If you pick up the phone and hear nothing, be sure it is not a person who stutters trying to initiate the conversation before you hang up.[5]

Answering questions in class or requiring oral presentations are tension-producing situations for most people. They can be a terrifying for people who stutter. Trainers should wait for people who stutter to volunteer rather than call on them for oral responses or presentations. Other than that, people who stutter are just as "normal" or regular learners as nonstutterers. Therefore, the learning climate that is effective for nonstutterers, other than the way people react to their difficulty, is just as effective for people who stutter.

AIDS AND ASSISTIVE DEVICES

From the standpoint of assistive devices, major cognitive impairments, such as brain injury, are very difficult to deal with. Less severe disabilities, such as dyslexia and ADD, pose less severe problems. People with learning disabilities make up the largest segment of the population with disabilities. Some of the built-in features of the Macintosh computer, such as its graphical user interface and mouse, and IBM-compatible computers equipped with Microsoft Windows and a mouse, make them particularly useful for people with cognitive disabilities.

Augmentative communication devices are designed to aid or augment communication for individuals with speech impairments—not to take the place of speech but to improve a person's ability to make himself or herself clearly understood. There are three categories of augmentative devices: direct and indirect selection language systems, voice output communication aids, and other speech aids.

Facilitated communication (FC) involves the use of special devices through which people with autism, other speech disabilities, cerebral palsy, or deficient motor skills can communicate. The devices include a keyboard input device and a computer screen; the user often requires help from an aide or instructor who supports the user's arm or hand while the message is being typed by the hunt-and-peck method.

Direct and Indirect Selection Language Systems

Communication Displays

Communication displays, low-tech solutions to voice and speech disabilities, consist of a series of symbols, drawings, or pictures that are arranged on a variety of mechanisms, such as boards, books, folders, cards, wallets, and lap trays. The symbols include a mix of photographs, line drawings, picture symbols, letters, numbers, and words. The symbols selected for display are those that are most often needed by the user and his or her communication partners. Communicators simply point to the symbols on the display using a finger, hand, toe, foot, elbow, or eye gaze, or with a pointing stick attached to a hand, foot, mouth, or head. This is direct selection.

An example of communication displays is Talking Pictures (Crestwood Company), which provide a means of communication for people who have difficulty expressing their needs orally and cannot be understood by others. These kits are available in cards, portable books, and folding portable boards, some with up to 1,035 stickers depicting various needs and activities used to fabricate boards to meet individual needs.

The Mayer-Johnson Speaking Dynamically "talkative" software (available from Apple Computer) allows users to link spoken words, phrases, and sentences to a "communications board" of graphic or textual symbols. Speech is heard when the symbols are clicked. "Talking picture" boards are designed for or by the user, and up to 200 boards can be created and linked in hierarchies.

Switch and Scanning Systems

A more sophisticated form of communication display, indirect selection, is achieved through a switch and scanning system. Here the appropriate symbol is selected from an array of automatically displayed options. The system requires an electronic augmentative communication device programmed to perform a scanning function and equipped with a switch. The cursor on the screen of the device automatically moves at an adjustable speed among selected symbols, boxes, or other specified areas of the screen, stopping at each symbol long enough for the user to indicate whether it should be selected. The user makes the selection by activating a switch by finger, hand, arm, head, mouth, eyelid, eye gaze, knee, or foot or with pointers attached to the hand, head, mouth, or foot.

Voice Output Communication Aids

Laryngectomy Speech Amplifiers

These battery-driven amplifiers supplement lost or insufficient vocal tone. The most common style is a cylindrical vibrating unit that is held against the throat so that vibrations passed up through the mouth and nasal cavities allow the user to speak. These devices are equipped with tone and volume controls.

Text Telephone

The text telephone system uses a communications assistant who transliterates conversation from text to voice and from voice to text. Using voice carryover (VCO), a person with a hearing disability can speak directly to the other end user. The communications assistant types the response back to the person with the hearing disability without voicing any conversation. Or, using hearing carryover (HCO), the person with a speech disability can listen to the other end user; in reply, the communications assistant, using a readout device, reads and speaks the text as typed by the person with the speech disability without typing any of the conversation.

Telecommunication Devices for the Deaf (TDDs)

TDDs (described in Chapter 6) can be used by individuals with speech impairments for telephone communication to the extent that they are able to use the direct selection method.

Telephone Direct Links

IBM's PhoneCommunicator provides telephone communications for people with speech impairments with others via touch-tone telephone and communicates with both Baudot and ASCII TDDs, displaying a full-screen view of the dialogue from both parties. The text of the conversation can be saved and printed. Other programs remain in the background while PhoneCommunicator is active, and it can be used in conjunction with host emulators and local area networks. Users can communicate with ASCII bulletin boards to browse, inquire, and send messages. Messages can be recorded from touch-tone telephones and TDD callers, noting the time and date of the call, as well as generate and save special messages for later use in touch-tone and TDD conversations.

Other Speech Communication Aids

Technologies developed for people with vision impairments, such as screen readers, are helpful for people with learning and speech disabilities as well. For example, with a screen reader, people with dyslexia can comprehend written material voiced by the computer in half the time it would take to read it. Similarly, expanding the size of the type on the screen of a computer reduces the total amount of information presented at one time and makes it easier for the user to understand. Word-predictive software designed for people with motor or mobility impairments is useful as well for people with learning disabilities because they can choose the word they want from the menu instead of extracting it from memory.

The Don Johnson Development Equipment's Co:Writer (available from Apple Computer) is an intelligent word prediction program designed to help people with learning disabilities, language deficiencies, or physical limitations. It predicts words based on its knowledge of subject-verb agreement, grammar rules, word relationships, proper names, recency, redundancy, frequency, and user preference. The program works with any Macintosh word processor with hard drive, minimum of 4 MB RAM (with 1–2 MB RAM available for Co:Writer), and System 7.0 and higher recommended (also System 6.07/6.08 under Multifinder). It employs artificial intelligence to predict and complete the words a writer wants to use, thereby reducing the number of keystrokes used and the amount of energy expended. It also adapts to the user's style. The program helps with grammar, spelling, and subject-verb agreement and automates capitalization and spacing. It requires a Macintosh computer, 4 megabytes of RAM, and system software version 6.0.7 or later.

Several other available augmentative communication devices are ideal for patients with speech and language disorders. One such device, the Handy-Speech Communication Aide (available from Consultants for Communication Technology), offers near-human-voice quality and complete control of intonation, speed, pitch, and volume. The system consists of a speech synthesizer, software written for an IBM PC or compatible, and a laptop computer. It is accessed by keyboard, any single switch, a joystick, voice or sound, eye blink, scanning, or direct selection. The system is relatively inexpensive (under $2,000) and requires only basic reading skills.

Keyboard Entry Alternatives

DADAEntry (TASH, Inc.) consists of software and a "black box" that connects a computer and a selected input device, such as a keyboard, mouse, joystick, switches, or a serial communication aid. For the person who has a speech impairment, the AsciiEntry program allows any serial ASCII communication aid to be connected, making it possible to control the computer and do data entry from a communication aid. The user can also take advantage of DADAEntry features such as work completion and macros.

T-TAM (Trace-Transparent Access Module) (Prentke Romich Company) connects a computer, keyboard, mouse, and/or an ASCII communication aid with a serial output. Persons with speech impairments can create customized keyboard overlays to control both the computer and the T-TAM, as well as do data entry, from a communication aid.

Crestalk (available from Crestwood Company) is a lightweight, portable, and easy-to-use electronic aid for adults who have difficulty expressing their needs orally. The user presses alphanumeric keys lightly to type out messages. Each message prints 16 characters per line on a 2-line display panel, which continues scrolling for longer messages. The device has 20K memory, which enables users to preprogram hundreds of sentences and then retrieve them quickly.

Summary

Learning disabilities and speech and language disorders pose some of the most difficult challenges for trainers and supervisors because they have such an adverse effect on communication, learning, and, ultimately, job performance. The most common learning disabilities are attention deficit disorder, dyslexia, perceptual disorders, integrative disorders, simple memory deficiencies, and fine motor and writing difficulties.

Although trainers and supervisors cannot be expected to substitute for professionals whose specialties are remediation of learning disabilities and speech and language disorders, nevertheless, they can help trainees. Probably the most important strategy for them to adopt is to learn as much as they can about these disorders, how they can be controlled, and how they can be compensated. A second strategy is to take full advantage of opportunities to involve professionals in the task of determining the optimum compensatory tactic for each individual with these types of disabilities. The third strategy is to provide continuing understanding, compassion, and support for these trainees and workers.

For Further Reading and Viewing*

ADA Customer Courtesies. 1993. 20-minute videocassette. Available from United Training Media.

ADA for Retail. 1993. 12-minute videocassette. Available from United Training Media.

The Americans with Disabilities Act: Impact on Training. INFO-LINE 9203. Alexandria, Va.: American Society for Training and Development, March 1993.

The Americans with Disabilities Act: Techniques for Accommodation. INFO-LINE 9204. Alexandria, Va.: American Society for Training and Development, April 1992.

Augmentative Communication: Intervention. 1986. Available from Don Johnson Development Equipment.

Blackstone, Sarah. *Augmentative Communication: An Introduction.* Rockville, Md.: American Speech-Language-Hearing Association, 1986.

——— et al. *Augumentative Communication: Implementation Strategies.* Rockville, Md.: American Speech-Language-Hearing Association, 1988.

Burkhart, Linda. *Using Computers and Speech Synthesis to Facilitate Communication.* Baltimore: Brooks Publishing Company, 1991.

Copeland, Edna D. *Copeland Symptom Checklist for Adult Attention Deficit Disorders.* Atlanta, Ga.: Southeastern Psychological Institute, 1989.

Duran, Elva. *Teaching the Moderately and Severely Handicapped Student and Autistic Adolescent.* Springfield, Ill.: Charles C. Thomas, 1988.

Edwards, Alistaire. *Speech Synthesis: Technology for Disabled People.* Baltimore: Brooks Publishing Company, 1991.

Employability: Integrating People with Development Disabilities into the Workplace. 1993. 27-minute video. Available from the Woolworth Corporation.

Fraser, Malcolm. *Self-Therapy for the Stutterer.* 8th ed. Pub. 12. Memphis, Tenn.: Stuttering Foundation of America, 1993.

Goossens, C., and S. Crane. *Augmentative Communication Assessment Resource.* Don Johnson Developmental Equipment.

Hallowell, Edward M., and John J. Ratey. *Driven to Distraction: The Human Story of ADD in Adults and Children.* New York: Pantheon, 1994.

Kelly, Kate, and Peggy Ramundo. *You Mean I'm Not Lazy, Stupid, or Crazy?! A*

*Full addresses of the organizations in this listing appear in Appendixes A and B.

Self-Help Book for Adults with ADD. Cincinnati, Ohio: Tyrell & Jerem Press, 1993.

Langone, John. *Teaching Students with Mild and Moderate Learning Problems.* Boston: Allyn and Bacon, 1990.

Levinson, Harold N. *Smart But Feeling Dumb.* New York: Warner Books, 1984.

Participants with Disabilities: How to Address Their Needs. INFO-LINE 8704. Alexandria, Va.: American Society for Training and Development, April 1987.

Pavlidis, George T., and Dennis F. Fisher. *Dyslexia: Its Neuropsychology and Treatment.* New York: Wiley, 1986.

Rawson, Margaret Byrd. *The Many Faces of Dyslexia.* 2d ed. Baltimore: Orton Dyslexia Society, 1992.

Robin, Arthur. *ADHD in Adulthood: A Clinical Perspective.* 1992. 60-minute video. Available from Professional Advancement Seminars.

Schopler, E., and G. Mesibov. *Autism in Adolescents and Adults.* New York: Plenum, 1983.

Weiss, Lynn. *Attention Deficit Disorder in Adults: Practical Help for Sufferers and Their Spouses.* Dallas, Tex.: Taylor Publishing Company, 1992.

Wilkins, Angela, Alice Garside, and Mary Lee Enfield. *Basic Facts about Dyslexia: What Everyone Ought to Know.* Baltimore: Orton Dyslexia Society, 1993

Notes

1. Phonemes are the basic sound units of human speech—recognizable, discrete collections of sounds that, when strung together sequentially, form spoken words. They provide the small variations in sound that differentiate word meanings, such as in the word "tap" and "top" and "bet" and "bat."

2. This section is adapted from *Helping People Communicate.* (Rockville, Md.: American Speech-Language-Hearing Association, n.d.). Used by permission.

3. Malcolm Fraser, *Self-Therapy for the Stutterer,* 8th ed. (Memphis, Tenn.: Stuttering Foundation of America, 1993).

4. *Self-Therapy for the Stutterer* (Memphis, Tenn.: Stuttering Foundation of America, n.d.), pp. 2–3. Used by permission.

5. *How to React When Speaking with Someone Who Stutters* (Memphis, Tenn.: Stuttering Foundation of America, n.d.), p. 1. Used by permission.

12

Training Managers And Supervisors

Gaining the support and commitment of managers and supervisors and competent performance of tasks associated with the management of disability require careful planning, training, development, support, and feedback. Managers and supervisors provide the key to the success of workers with disabilities. They must serve as role models if they are to fulfill their responsibilities effectively and make people with disabilities an integral part of the workforce.

Managers must examine their own perceptions and biases as well. If they fail to be sensitive to the needs of people with disabilities who are assigned to their areas of responsibility and do not allow these workers to apply what they have learned in training classes because they lack either or both understanding of or confidence in the knowledge and skills acquired in corporate training programs, the best training programs will be negated. No organization can afford to leave it to chance that managers and supervisors will adopt the attitudes and acquire the knowledge and skills required to conduct on-the-job training, supervise, and develop workers with disabilities perceptively, responsively, and competently.

An essential first step in preparing to manage people with disabilities is to know what constitutes a disability and to understand the specific nature of mental, developmental, physical, and learning disabilities and the limitations they impose and do not impose on people:

> The first critical step managers must take is to become knowledgeable about the specific nature of all physical or mental disabilities their employees and job applicants may have. . . . Employing a person with one type of disability is not necessarily comparable to employing a person with another type of disabil-

ity because each disability has its own symptoms and affects the ability and capacity for work in different ways. . . . Managers who do not educate themselves about certain limiting conditions will not be able to respond to employees in a manner consistent with ADA requirements.[1]

Managers and supervisors can be prepared to meet the specific needs of individual workers with disabilities by providing written information, contacts with community resources, and coaching by those who have disabilities; however, training programs provide the most effective means of gaining their support and commitment.

Essential Conditions for Training

Any training program that deals with behavioral and attitudinal change is likely to be met with resistance by at least some of the participants. An important first step in overcoming this resistance is to demonstrate and communicate corporate-wide long-term commitment to the training. That can be manifested in several ways.

■ *Make training inclusionary.* The tendency of some organizations to restrict training in hiring, training, and developing people with disabilities to front-line supervisors—those who must deal directly with workers with disabilities on a daily basis—is shortsighted and misses the point. Everyone in the organization has an impact on the effectiveness of policies and practices related to nondiscrimination, and they will exercise this influence only if they have been trained to do so and are constantly reminded of it.

■ *Make training continuous.* Too often, managers, including human resources managers, expect to see miraculous changes in attitudes and behavior as a result of a single training workshop. But one-shot training approaches are typically short-lived or marginal in terms of results. Formal training has its limitations. It can encourage participants to adopt necessary attitudes and values, help them recognize and understand guiding principles that must be applied in working with people with disabilities, and improve specific interpersonal, communication, and supervisory skills. But to be truly effective, training must be constantly reinforced on the job by the reward system and by follow-up training.

■ *Ensure top management support and participation.* Unless the training program has the unqualified backing of top management, it is doomed to failure. Top executives must be clear about their commitment and provide consistent goals for supervisors and workers. They must support the program by allocating sufficient funds to the venture and demonstrate their commitment to its objectives by actively participating in it as both trainees and, later, as presenters. They must provide feedback to managers and supervisors, commend and reward successes, and encourage efforts to make supervisors good role models.

■ *Develop clear and detailed objectives.* Participants in the training program must know at the outset what they will learn in the program, what they will be able to do following the training, and why the program is important to them and the organization. They should also be informed in advance of the types of activities they will be expected to participate in and that they may experience some anxiety, irritation, frustration, or discomfort during simulation exercises.

■ *Provide adequate time.* Enough time must be allocated to the program to achieve the objectives. A 1-hour lecture or a 30-minute videotape without discussion is likely to produce more negative than positive results. It is also important to allow enough time between the announcement of the program and its presentation so that participants will be able to attend.

■ *Select or prepare top-notch materials.* Only the very best materials should be used in the training program. Select carefully from among the many videotapes, multimedia programs, and printed materials that are currently available. Preview them before using them and plan exactly how to introduce and follow them up.

■ *Assign competent instructor-facilitators.* Assignment of a substandard instructor or facilitator to conduct the training is certain to produce disappointing results. Not every instructor has the knowledge, skills, personality, and temperament needed to carry out this instructional program. It invariably requires special competencies, training, and experience.

■ *Use experiential exercises.* One of the best means of having trainees explore their own attitudes and the attitudes and behaviors of others toward people with disabilities and to learn how to interact properly is to conduct exercises that simulate a few of the most common types of disabilities. Trainees can be paired and rotated through a series of exercises that will enable them to experience some of the problems faced by people with disabilities and practice some of the courtesies taught earlier. Here are a few samples:

■ Coat a pair of eyeglasses with petroleum jelly and have the pairs experience the difficulty of reading a short set of directions printed in 14-point type.

- Have each pair spend about 15 minutes each taking a trip around the building while blindfolded, with one partner acting as the sighted person. (Be especially careful about safety.)
- Have each pair perform a simple task without using speech.
- Provide inexpensive ear plugs for each participant, and have each perform a simple task without using speech.
- Have each participant spend as much time as possible (a minimum of 30 minutes) in a wheelchair or on crutches, say, going on lunch break (this exercise can be spread out over the length of the training program).

Always conduct debriefings following the exercises to discuss the experience, concentrating on such questions as these:

- How did participants feel about each situation and their roles as blind, deaf, mobility-impaired, or speech-impaired people? As helpers for people in those circumstances?
- What problems did they encounter? What mistakes did they make? How could the problems have been avoided or ameliorated?
- What else did they learn? How can they use what they have learned?

It is also important for the instructor to emphasize that people with disabilities have learned to cope with many of the problems through training and rehabilitation. If that is not done, participants are likely to come away from the experiences with negative perceptions of people with disabilities reinforced.

- *Follow up and reinforce the training.* The training must be followed up and reinforced by such means as periodic group meetings, systematic evaluation, and recognition and rewards for managers who are effective in applying the principles discussed in the training.

Planning and Promoting the Training Program

A successful training program for managers and supervisors must be carefully planned, advertised, and promoted. That includes allocating sufficient time to schedule and conduct the training and preparing workshop or seminar announcements, defining objectives, selecting instructor-facilitators, and choosing the delivery system and instructional strategy.

Determining Length and Scheduling

Anything less than the equivalent of one full day is probably too little time to devote to training managers and supervisors to participate in the selection, training, development, and management of people with disabilities. The equivalent of two to three workdays is probably about right. If it is conducted by outside contractors, it is likely that full days will be scheduled—about six hours of class time per day plus breaks. If conducted by in-house trainers, it is advantageous to schedule half-days of four hours, including breaks, thereby spreading the training period over about a week. That allows managers and supervisors at least half of each day to perform their jobs and prevent them from getting behind in their work, and it also gives participants time to digest what they are learning.

Advertising and Promoting the Training Program

Training for managers and supervisors in the techniques of hiring, training, and developing people with disabilities is quite new. And like anything else that involves newness and change, training is likely to be viewed with defensiveness, misgivings, and even anxiety. Careful attention to the design of workshop announcements and promotional materials can go a long way toward overcoming potentially negative feelings. The materials must be clear and emphasize that the organization is committed to hiring, training, and developing people with disabilities and that the training is designed to help managers and supervisors deal with the problems and challenges implicit in that commitment.

Defining the Training Objectives

The importance of clear objectives is critical. Here is a sample:

Following the training, participants will be able to:

- Define disability in its legal context.
- Identify and overcome stereotypical thinking about people with disabilities.
- Use acceptable disability-related terminology.
- Practice proper etiquette when dealing with people with disabilities.
- Describe the major types and job-related effects of the most common physical (sensory and mobility and motion), mental, and learning disabilities.
- Avoid discrimination in interviewing, hiring, training, de-

veloping, promoting, and supervising people with disabilities.
- Identify and describe realistic accommodations for people
with various types of disabilities in the jobs they supervise.

Selecting Instructor-Facilitators

Some organizations have developed in-house programs to train managers and supervisors to manage people with disabilities. Others have contracted the training with external consultants and training organizations.
There are certain advantages and disadvantages to each option. In-house
trainers are likely to have a better understanding of the culture and needs
of the organization and the personalities of those who will be attending.
On the other hand, they may not have the in-depth knowledge and
breadth of experience needed to handle such a delicate and complex subject. External consultants and trainers have the advantages of expert
status and the ability it confers to address senior officers with comfort,
as well as broader knowledge and experience. When making the decision, the size of the target group of managers and supervisors, their re-
ceptivity to the training, the budget, and the availability of qualified in-
house training staff need to be considered.

If someone within the organization is chosen, he or she should show
the qualities found in any competent trainer: knowledge of the subject,
speaking ability and related platform skills, sensitivity, a sense of humor,
and the ability to encourage and handle group discussion.

If an outsider is contracted for, the qualifications and experience of
the company and the individual hired to do the training need to be veri-
fied:

- How long the company has been conducting training on the subject of disability and how many sessions it has completed
- The amount and source of formal training and experience the
trainer has in the area of disability
- The objectives of the training to be provided
- The training strategy, methods, activities, and techniques of evaluation to be applied

Choosing the Delivery System and Strategy

A live instructor-facilitator, making use of presentation, guest experts,
media, experiential activities, case studies and critical incidents, role
playing, simulations, and group discussion, is the most effective delivery

system and strategy. Formal presentations (lecturettes) should be kept short and to the point. A one-hour lecture can be and often is deadening. Guest speakers should include experts on disability from in-house or the local community: physicians, nurses, rehabilitation specialists, and people with disabilities. The speakers need to recognize that they are dealing with nonprofessionals who want not highly technical content or unfamiliar medical terminology but practical information.

Experiential exercises, case studies, role playing, and simulations should always have clear and practical objectives (e.g., to illustrate an important fact or concept, produce an awareness, or practice a skill). They should focus on exercises that develop self-awareness and understanding of the workplace effects and challenges posed by disabilities. Carefully handled, exercises that enable participants to experience the perspective of a person with a disability can be very effective. They should be tried out with a small group of managers or supervisors before using them with regular training groups to iron out the kinks and uncover potential problems.

Videocassettes in rapidly increasing numbers and quality are available to build sensitivity to people with disabilities, choose and install accommodations, and avoid discriminatory practices. The Resources sections at the end of all chapters of this book identify some of these videos.

The most effective technique is group discussion. It should always follow lecturettes, guest speaker presentations, experiential activities and exercises, role playing, and videos. During such discussions in large and small groups, participants achieve insights and begin to change attitudes.

Content of the Training Program

Different levels of management and supervision require variations in the content of training. Depending on the size of the organization, executives, line managers, staff officers, and first-line supervisors should receive somewhat different training in terms of the delivery system used, strategy and methods, focus and emphasis, and length of training. A written pretest, administered before the training begins or during the first training session, will reveal areas that need emphasis during the training and enable the instructor-facilitator to eliminate content that is already known to participants. The test may also stimulate interest and generate enthusiasm for the training.

History of Disability

To sensitize managers and supervisors to the attitudinal and behavioral problems posed for workers with disabilities by their fellow workers and others, they must be aware of the long-standing myths and biases and discriminatory laws and workplace barriers that have encumbered the work and social lives of those who have disabilities. They need to understand the rationale underlying the recent changes that have led to recognition of the potential of people with disabilities to make significant contributions to the workplace and the attainment of organizational goals and objectives.

Disability and the Law

Managers and supervisors must have more than a casual knowledge of federal and state laws and regulations that safeguard the rights of job applicants and current and past employees. They must know how to avoid discrimination in hiring, training, developing, promoting, and supervising employees with disabilities of all types—permanent and temporary—and precisely how to comply with the letter and spirit of the law.

Types and Effects of Disability

To provide managers with a clear and accurate understanding of the nature of workplace limitations caused by disabilities, presentations and discussion of the most common types of disabilities should be conducted. Material should be presented in lay terms, avoiding to the maximum extent possible medical parlance, but sufficiently detailed to describe clearly the effect of the disability on the workers. The focus should be on the potential effects of various types of disabilities on the performance of common job-related tasks. Areas for discussion include various physical, mental, emotional, and learning conditions; the impact of various conditions on the worker; and the use of special equipment and assistive devices.

Job Descriptions

Managers and supervisors must be familiar with the documents that regulate the recruitment, selection, training, performance evaluation, promotion, and termination processes. The most important of these are job descriptions. Detailed review of the job descriptions of subordinates that focus on essential jobs, duties, tasks, and functions will uncover important issues regarding employment of people with disabilities. Foremost among the issues that will emerge are those relating to job accommodations. The review process will also cause managers to probe their hiring practices, particularly those that relate to job requirements and the means used to establish qualification, such as tests.

Etiquette

The suggestions contained in Chapter 1 relating to the etiquette of disability should be presented and discussed. Particularly relevant are items dealing with conduct that is potentially offensive to people with disabilities. Another list of do's and don'ts is shown in Figure 12-1.

Cost of Accommodations for Disabilities

Managers and supervisors need to know that most accommodations, including those associated with the modification of buildings, facilities, and work areas and the purchase of specialized equipment and devices, typically cost very little and can be made or installed with little or no disruption or problems to the worksite or workers.

Responsibilities of Managers and Supervisors

The success of any disability management program hinges on recognition by managers and supervisors of their responsibilities and a commitment to carry them out.

Figure 12-1. Do's and don'ts for managers and supervisors.

DO	*DON'T*
• Respect the employee as a person. • Ask the person who has a disability which is the best way to accommodate his or her physical limitations. • Expect the same good work habits, the same quality of work and the same production levels from workers with disabilities as you would from others. • Give honest feedback to the employee who has a disability. Everyone makes mistakes, and everyone wants feedback to improve his or her performance. • Include employees in all activities, such as staff meetings or picnics. • Expect the employee to have the same ambitions as others.	• Be afraid of employees with disabilities. They won't break, and you can't catch their disabilities. • Feel sorry for the person's disabilities. Get to know him or her by discovering abilities. • Feel like the person is more fragile emotionally than others. Constructive criticism produces growth. • Assume the person can't perform a certain task. Ask how he or she will do the task. Help the person figure it out. • Talk down to employees with disabilities or treat them like children.

Source: Reprinted, by permission of publisher, from Arlene Vernon-Oehmke, "Management Needs Understanding and Sensitivity," *HRfocus* (Special Edition), 1992 © 1992. American Management Association, New York. All rights reserved.

Eliminating Discriminatory Attitudes and Actions. Doing away with discriminatory attitudes and practices must be a top priority. An important part of that responsibility is to set the example by consistently demonstrating sensitivity to disability, making programs and facilities accessible, and doing everything possible to break down barriers to employee learning, development, and performance. Those in positions of authority must show their commitment to doing all that can be done to ensure equal opportunity to persons with disabilities and not simply fulfilling their obligations under the law.

A correlative responsibility of managers and supervisors is to promote positive attitudes and behaviors toward employees with disabilities by their fellow workers. That can be done by reinforcing and rewarding behaviors that demonstrate sensitivity and concern for employees with disabilities, such as assisting them to adapt to the job and providing any needed help with task performance. It can also be encouraged by inviting nondisabled employees to serve as coaches and trainers in the context of on-the-job training programs.

Making Accommodations. Managers and supervisors must understand the need for and the means of making accommodations to allow people with various types of disabilities to perform their jobs. They should explore in some depth the several types of accommodations that can be made and examine some of the more common types of adaptive equipment. To accept the need for accommodations, managers and supervisors must understand that disabilities often affect only the way a job is performed, but do not prevent job performance. In other words, they provide alternative ways of doing a job or task.

It is also helpful to have workers with disabilities describe their experiences and feelings and what they expect and need to be reasonably accommodated. Joint discussion of potential accommodations should follow. In addition, first-hand experience for managers, such as those described earlier in this chapter (e.g., wearing a blindfold), can build sensitivity and communicate the message faster and better than any other strategy.

Other exercises involve taping participants' thumbs and forefingers together and then having them perform writing tasks. Or, to show the effects of cognitive impairment, write a question or problem backwards on a chalkboard or flip chart, and ask participants to write the answer in 20 seconds. The training should be scheduled at a site where examples of adaptive equipment and materials are located.

A word of caution is in order here. There are many controversial approaches to the tasks of working and training people with disabilities. One is the use of the blindfold in training supervisors and instructors to work with people who are blind. Used correctly and with appropriate safeguards, the blindfold can be a valuable adjunct to the training program. However, the blindfold should never be used with the idea that it will teach anyone what it is like to be blind. No matter how much time a sighted person spends blindfolded, the exercise cannot teach what blindness is. The most it can do is bring home very quickly some of the problems of blindness and some of the difficulties involved in such areas as mobility and communication.

Providing Orientation and Induction. The way new employees are introduced to the organization, their job, their work area, and their coworkers is important. If new employees, and particularly those with disabilities, are treated with indifference or lack of sensitivity to their needs and concerns or if they are left with their questions unanswered, they are unlikely to feel that they are a part of the organization. If, on the other hand, they are welcomed with respect and consideration and their initial contacts with the organization are pleasant, confidence building, and helpful, they are more likely to develop into loyal and productive members of the organization.

Orientation and induction programs introduce new employees to the organization, provide them with complete and uniform information about the firm—its organization, mission, functions and policies, compensation, benefits, and services—and introduce them to the work environment, the work group, and the job. Every orientation program should include clear definition of the company's obligation to people with disabilities and the policies that implement that obligation.

In addition to formal live presentations by staff and the use of multimedia programs, orientation and induction typically include introductions to key personnel and coworkers, tours of the office or plant and facilities, demonstration of selected work tasks, work standards, and requirements, and the like. The objective is to develop confident, loyal, effective, and productive workers and to reduce the likelihood of rule violations, accidents and injuries, discharges, resignations, and grievances.

Delivering On-the-Job Training. One of the primary responsibilities of people in managerial and supervisory positions is to provide one-on-one on-the-job training (OJT) for their immediate subordinates. As the title implies, OJT is conducted where the employee works, whether in the office or the field. The job of the supervisor is to motivate, encourage, demonstrate, guide, assist, and reward the subordinate and provide guided practice and feedback on performance. OJT requires a continuous flow of directions, comments, explanations, and suggestions from the supervisor to the employee, with the tutor observing, listening, questioning, and relating learning to the worker's experience.

Counseling. Performance, career, personal, family, and social problems inevitably surface in the lives of workers at all levels of organization, those with disabilities as well as nondisabled employees. Despondency, reclusiveness, marital difficulties, substance abuse, separation and divorce, emotional stress, insecurity, lack of self-acceptance, and various types of neuroses affect most people at one time or another. Counseling by managers and supervisors, in the form of "employee first aid," can help some of these workers, the "working wounded," to cope.

The kind of help required is most accurately described as helping people to help themselves. It is a process in which two people come together to attack a problem so that the one who has it can be helped to understand, clarify, and find a self-determined solution to it. At the very least, managers and supervisors must show sensitivity, be approachable, and be willing to refer the individual to someone who can provide the assistance required, such as the employee assistance program.

Providing Career Planning. Career planning is vital to the long-term job satisfaction of all workers. Managers and supervisors must accept responsibility for helping their subordinates figure out where they have been, where they want to be, and how to get there—the essence of career planning. They need to help them assess and analyze themselves and their career status, personality, abilities, interests, and needs. Then they need to help their subordinates set personal goals and identify precisely what they need to do to achieve them.

Making Developmental Assignments. Formal education and training cannot provide the complete solution to the problem of providing opportunities for employees to qualify for positions of greater authority, responsibility, prestige, and remuneration. To help them broaden their experience and develop new skills, they must be given assignments expressly chosen to achieve those goals. This is particularly true of people with disabilities, many of whom have had few opportunities to develop new insights and skills. But they too have hopes and dreams for their own futures that cannot be realized unless a commitment is made to personal and professional development. For many, that is not likely to happen unless their bosses provide both encouragement and incentives.

Assigning employees to committees and task forces and involving them in policy making and decision making is one option. Another is job rotation, involving assignment to nonsupervisory or managerial jobs, training positions, or assistant-to positions for specific periods of time, where the employee, under the close supervision of a seasoned manager, can receive diversified training and experience. A third option is to develop employees and build their expertise by assigning them to special projects, investigations, studies, audits, quality circles, and travel.

Encouraging Self-Development. Career growth and development are just as vital to well-being, job satisfaction, and survival in the workday world for people with disabilities as they are for nondisabled employees. Technological change, restructuring, downsizing, and takeovers are beyond the control of workers. When such changes occur, people with disabilities must be ready to change jobs, if not careers, without missing a step or taking a wrong turn.

Resources for personal and professional development are many and varied. Personal development includes attendance at formal and informal courses, seminars, and workshops; reading and study; and a comprehensive physical health program, including regular physical checkups, nutrition and weight control, exercise, and recreational activities. Professional development activities include formal training and education, use of advisers and mentors, use of learning centers and databases, networking, speaking and writing for publication, membership in professional and technical associations, and attendance at professional and technical conferences and expositions.

Providing Posthire or Posttransfer Assistance. Posthire and posttransfer assistance, always an important service for new employees, is particularly critical for those with disabilities. For some new hires, it will be their first job. How they adjust to that dramatic change in their lives will determine their future as independent and self-sufficient workers. Managers and supervisors must accept a major share of the responsibility for easing the adjustment to a new environment by organizing special information and assistance and referring employees to sources of special assistance within and outside the organization.

Managers and supervisors must know the names of the in-house staff and outside organizations and agencies that can assist them in taking the steps needed to accommodate workers with disabilities, as well as helping them, to get settled in their new jobs.

Using Company Resources. Most organizations have staff offices, individual functionaries, and professionals under contracts who provide advice and assistance on matters relating to hiring, supervising, training, and developing people with disabilities. Employee assistance offices, common in most large organizations, can provide great amounts of expertise and help. The human resources department, individual executives and managers, legal counsel, and consultants can also provide assistance in solving many problems.

Using Community Resources. Every community of any size has several organizations and agencies that can provide help to organizations and individuals who employ people with disabilities. Many of these organizations, although national in coverage, provide advice and assistance on a great variety of issues and problems. These organizations are listed in Appendix B. Other organizations are part of state or local movement. Still others are private organizations and agencies.

The First Training Session

The first challenge to trainers is to overcome any resistance to training. Although promotional materials were designed to make participants more receptive to the training program, some residual resistance is likely to remain. Trainees who understand that they are going to receive practical knowledge and techniques, that will make their jobs easier will be more receptive to training. To accomplish that goal, trainers can encourage participants to identify the problems they face, both real and anticipated. Managers and supervisors may be reluctant to do this at first, so it is usually useful for the instructor-facilitator to bring up a few of the most common problems and then invite participants to join in discussion. Another helpful technique is to demonstrate by example that many of the solutions to the problems of supervising and making accommodations for people with disabilities are quite simple. Another way to eliminate resistance is to keep the training light, interesting, informal, and nonthreatening.

The IBM Program

IBM hired its first employee with a disability in 1914 and has been committed to hiring and accommodating employees with disabilities ever since. In 1942, it began training people with disabilities for employment. The company has also worked with community-based groups to develop training centers, contributed funding and equipment, loaned employees to programs that benefit people with disabilities, and developed and promoted technology to help people with disabilities lead full and productive lives.

In 1991, IBM organized a cross-functional task force that developed a comprehensive training program for all IBM managers. Training for facilitators was conducted at three sites during February and March 1992, and manager training was conducted throughout the United States from

March to July 1992. An outline of that two-day training program is shown in Figure 12-2.

Managing Employee Disability

Management, particularly human resources management, has always been deeply concerned about employee disabilities caused by accidents, injuries, and illnesses, whether job related or not. One estimate suggests that, on average, the costs to an employer for each employee not successfully rehabilitated and remaining on disability benefits is $154,440.[2] That concern has been exacerbated in recent years by three factors: (1) the downturn in the economy, which demands that all costs be closely scrutinized and reduced; (2) downsizing, restructuring, and hiring freezes, which make it critical and imperative that all employees be on the job and that absences due to accidents and illnesses be kept to a minimum; and (3) employee dissatisfaction with personnel actions and benefits in recent years, which results in increases in costly litigation. To reduce those costs and improve the disability management, managers and supervisors need training and development.

Meeting the challenge of managing disability in any type of organization requires a multifaceted approach, including job and task analysis, using databases and computer software, assessing employee capabilities, selecting or tailoring therapies, modifying job tasks, making workplace accommodations, devising and analyzing return-to-work strategies.

Performing Job and Task Analyses

The solution to the problem of determining what a recovering employee is capable of doing lies in having detailed, accurate, and validated information about job requirements—data that can be acquired only by performing job and task analysis (systematically collecting, analyzing, and recording information about the physical and mental requirements of jobs and their essential and integral tasks).

The level of detail required to make reliable determinations of worker capability will not be found in conventional job analysis reports and their derivative job descriptions and applicant specifications. Additional data, determinable only by specialists, such as rehabilitation counselors, rehabilitation nurses, and occupational and physical therapists, must be collected. Although it undoubtedly will add to the costs of performing job and task analyses to have these specialties represented on job analysis teams, it is a prudent expenditure of funds. The information will be helpful in determining the capabilities of recovering workers and useful when

Figure 12-2. IBM's ADA training program for managers.

```
Day 1   Welcome/Opening Remarks
            IBM Overview and Video
                IBM's Long-Standing Commitment, 1914–1992
                IBM Policy
                    Nondiscrimination
                    Accommodation
                    Affirmative Action
                    Harassment-Free Working Environment
                IBM Management Philosophy
            The ADA
                Basic Principles
                    Equal Opportunity
                    Reasonable Accommodation
                    Equal Access
                    Integration
                    Focus on the Individual
                ADA Titles
                    Title I—Employment
                    Title II—Public Services/Transportation
                    Title III—Public Accommodation/Commercial Facilities
                    Title IV—Communications
            Current Law
                Rehabilitation Act of 1973
                Many State Laws
            ADA Overview—Highlights of Changes
                Essential Functions
                Additional Reasonable Accommodation Considerations
                Expanded Definition of Discrimination
                Limits on Medical Examinations and Inquiries
                Current Use of Illegal Drugs—Never Protected
                Private Right of Action
            Definitions/Discussion
                Disability
                Qualified Individuals with Disabilities
                Reasonable Accommodation
                Undue Hardship
                Direct Threat
            Case Studies (8)
Day 2   Follow-On Functional Training
                Employment
                Equal Opportunity
                Legal
```

matching the capabilities of people with disabilities with the requirements of vacant or newly created position, as well as for making the reasonable accommodations mandated by the Americans with Disabilities Act of 1990 (ADA).

When job and task data are available, the capabilities of a recovering worker can be matched against the job and task requirements. Where a fit is reached in terms of specific job tasks, even if it is not the whole job, the employee can be returned to work to perform tasks within his or her capabilities. Until the jobs in an organization can be systematically reanalyzed, as an interim measure job analyses for specific positions can be performed by having a rehabilitation specialist or therapist analyze the physical and other demands of the job as listed in the *Dictionary of Occupational Titles, Classification of Jobs Manual,* or other databases, interview the disabled worker, interview a knowledgeable supervisor or experienced worker, observe the job as it is being performed, and produce a job analysis report, including a set of guidelines for that job or task and recommended modifications of the job to accommodate workers with specific limitations. Copies of the report are provided to examining or treating physicians, rehabilitation specialists, and therapists for consideration in making disability determinations and providing treatment.

Job and task analysis data will also prove to be useful in preemployment screening for all prospective employees and in providing critical information to preferred providers, managed care providers, and in-house rehabilitation coordinators, risk managers, administrators, and outplacement specialists.

Using Databases and Computer Software

The amount and kind of information that must be collected to satisfy corporate human resources programs and activities, as well as reporting requirements of federal laws, grows almost weekly. Automated systems provide the only feasible means of handling that volume of data.

Databases and computer software to support the selection, hiring, training, and development of people with disabilities continue to grow in number and quality. For example, CrossWalk, the Employment Regulations Advisor, is a powerful, user-friendly software package created to run on IBM personal computers, compatibles, and Macintosh platforms. It is designed to support informed decision making and minimize legal exposure by managers and human resources professionals who must understand and conform to the provisions of law regarding employee disability. It includes the full texts of pertinent federal legislation, a dictionary of terms, state-by-state review of employers' incentives for hiring people with disabilities, a list of important government agencies and other ADA resources, a list of professional associations and disability groups, and information and suggestions on job accommodations and modifications, including useful products. In addition, the software provides support for creating, upgrading, and managing job descriptions and a means of analyzing up to 85 job criteria for all 12,700 job titles in its database.

Assessing Employee Capabilities

The key to making workplace accommodations, selecting or tailoring therapies, modifying jobs and tasks, and other strategies is assessment of the capabilities of employees with disabilities. The following questions can be used to determine capabilities:[3]

- What are the various job tasks performed?
- Are there extreme temperature factors in the work environment?
- Is the work surface even or uneven?
- What is the level of customer contact? Supervisory contact?
- How much has to be lifted? How often?
- Must the employee sit? Stand? Walk?
- How much stooping or bending is required? Pushing or pulling?
- Does the job require the use of ladders?

Selecting or Tailoring Therapies

Videotapes of job tasks and photographs of workstations can be used by therapists to select or tailor therapies and expedite the return of disabled workers to the job.

Modifying Jobs and Tasks

Job and task data can be used as the basis for making changes to the job, such as reducing work hours, providing rest breaks, allowing time off for therapy or exercise, and assigning tasks to another worker. They can also be used to determine the need for assistive or adaptive devices and strategies, such as reaching and grasping aids, special chairs or work surfaces, or modified tools. All of these modifications can accommodate an early return to work.

Devising and Applying Return-to-Work Strategies

Companies have four ways to go about getting injured or sick employees back to work:

1. Provide medical treatment and wait for recovery.
2. Provide therapy to restore or improve function.
3. Reassign the worker to another job.
4. Redesign the job.

The root problem is to determine what a recovering employee is capable of doing in terms of job duties and tasks. Unfortunately, physicians, therapists, and other health care providers do not always understand the job duties required of the injured or ill employee and are unable to identify possible changes in the job, or another job, that might allow the worker to return to productive work sooner. The focus remains on diagnosis and treatment, with little or no attention given to such alternatives as job changes. The result is that the disabled status of the employee is needlessly prolonged, and the costs to the employer multiply.

Making Travel and Transportation Arrangements

The individual responsible for making corporate travel arrangements must be fully aware of potential difficulties and sensitive to the needs of travelers with physical disabilities. The first step in avoiding problems is to identify those with disabilities and understand the extent of their limitations. Reservation and registration forms should ask employees and attendees to indicate that they have a physical disability. Positive responses can then be followed up with a short questionnaire and/or telephone call to get specifics.

One author suggests that the following data be obtained so that appropriate arrangements can be made with airlines and hotels:[4]

- Weight and height of traveler
- Names of medications taken
- Extent to which mobility is affected, if any
- Use of a walker, cane, crutches, or wheelchair
- Weight and dimensions of wheelchair, if used
- Type of battery (wet or dry cell) used by the wheelchair
- Ability of the traveler to transfer to and from the wheelchair without help

Summary

Training programs designed specifically for managers and supervisors are one important key to the task of achieving effective hiring, training, and development practices and to the ultimate success of organizations in integrating people with disabilities into the workforce.

If managers and supervisors are to serve as role models for other employees and fulfill the organization's commitment to nondiscrimination implicit in the employment of people with disabilities, training must be provided. Training programs related to the employment and management of people with disabilities must be inclusive, continuous, and have the unqualified support of top management, clearly defined objectives, adequate time, first-class materials, highly competent instructor-facilitators, and effective follow-up and reinforcement.

The success of training can be measured only by its results: increased numbers of successful workers with disabilities and their advancement to positions of greater responsibility, authority, and remuneration in the workplace along with their nondisabled coworkers. Such results are dependent on the actions and attitudes of managers and supervisors at all levels of organization.

Other important keys to the success of an employee disability management program are the identification and execution of appropriate management strategies; the conduct of comprehensive audits of disability policies, procedures, and programs; and the development and implementation of well-conceived ADA action plans.

For Further Reading and Viewing*

ADA 101—Final Exam. 1992. 40-minute video. Available from Society of Human Resource Management.

ADA Customer Courtesies. 1993. 20-minute video. Available from United Training Media.

ADA—Day to Day. 1992. 17-minute video. Available from United Training Media.

ADA Facts and Fears. 1992. 42-minute video. Available from Society of Human Resources Management.

ADA Maze: What You Can Do. 1992. 16-minute video. Available from United Training Media.

ADA on Video. 1992. Two videos: *Focusing on Ability*, 25 minutes, and *Reasonable Accommodations*, 21 minutes. Available from United Training Media.

ADA TALK. 1992. 30-minute video. Available from BNA Communications.

Akabas, Sheila H., "Transitional Employment Encourages Earlier Return to Work." *HRfocus* (Special Report), American Management Association, 1992, p. 21.

All You Have to Do Is Ask. 1993. 16-minute video. Available from United Training Media.

The Americans with Disabilities Act: Techniques for Accommodation. INFO-LINE 9204. Alexandria, Va.: American Society for Training and Development, April 1992.

*Full addresses of the organizations in this listing appear in Appendixes B and C.

A Tool to Work With: The Americans with Disabilities Act. 1993. 11-minute video. Available from United Training Media.

Blind Enough to See. 1993. 25-minute video. Available from United Training Media.

Bohl, Don L. (ed.). *AIDS: The New Workplace Issues.* AMA Management Briefing. New York: AMA, 1988.

Brady, Robert L. "Drinking, Drugs and Disability: What Employers Need to Know." *HRfocus* (Special Report), American Management Association, 1992, p. 9.

Choices, 2nd Edition. 1988. 30-minute video. Available from BNA Communications.

Co-op Bloopers (Employer Version). 1994. 9-minute video. Available from Cooperative Internship Program, Center for Career Programs, Gallaudet University.

Employability: Integrating People with Development Disabilities into the Workplace. 1993. 27-minute video. Available from Woolworth Corporation.

Epilepsy Foundation of America. *Questions and Answers about Epilepsy.* Landover, Md.: EFA, n.d.

Esposito, Michael D. "ADA's Impact on Employee Benefits." *HRfocus* (Special Report), American Management Association, 1992, p. 17.

Face Facts Video Tapes. 1991. Five videos: *Cleft Lip and Palate,* 25:55 minutes; *Craniosynostosis,* 26:16 minutes; *Hemifacial Microsomia,* 25:12 minutes; *Treacher Collins Syndrome,* 26:09 minutes; *Orbital Hypertelorism,* 25:36 minutes.

Froiland, Paul. "Managing the Walking Wounded." *Training* (August 1993): 36–40.

Gateway to Opportunity: Interviewing Job Applicants with Disabilities. 1992. 18:25-minute video. Available from United Training Media.

Given the Opportunity: A Guide to Interaction in the Workforce. 1992. 24-minute video with implementation guide, presentation slide set with script, leader's guide, employee handbook, and audiocassette. Available from Meridian Education Corporation.

If I Can Do This. . . . I Can Do Anything. 1992. 10-minute video. Available from United Training Media.

I Work with a Guy Who's Deaf and Blind. 1992. 11-minute video. Available from Salenger Films.

Job Analysis software system. Available from Health Management Technologies.

Jones, Timothy L. *The Americans with Disabilities Act: A Review of Best Practices.* AMA Management Briefing. New York: AMA Membership Publications Division, 1993.

Kearney, Deborah S. *The New ADA: Compliance and Costs.* Kingston, Mass.: R. S. Means Company, 1992.

Lawson, Joseph W. R., II. *The Manager's Guide to the Americans with Disabilities Act.* Chicago: Dartnell, 1992.

Lotito, Michael J., Richard Pimentel, and Denise Bissonnette. *What Managers and Supervisors Need to Know about the ADA.* Alexandria, Va.: Society for Human Resource Management, 1992.

Making the ADA Work for You. 1992. 23-minute video. Available from American Foundation for the Blind.

Making the ADA Work for You: A Video Training Seminar. 1992. 2-hour video. Available from American Foundation for the Blind.

Mello, Jeffrey A. "Perceptions in the Workplace: A Double Dilemma," *HRfocus* (Special Edition), American Management Association, 1992, p. 18.

Mirror, Mirror. 1990. 27-minute video on facial disfigurement. Available on loan for educational programs from AboutFace.

Naeve, Robert A., and Ari Cowan. *Managing ADA: The Complete Compliance Manual.* Colorado Springs, Colo.: Wiley Law Publications, 1992.

No One Is Burning Wheelchairs. 1992. 15-minute video. Available from National Easter Seal Society.

Participants with Disabilities: How to Address Their Needs. INFO-LINE 8704. Alexandria, Va.: American Society for Training and Development, April 1987.

Part of the Team. 1991. 17-minute video. Available from the National Easter Seal Society.

Reed, Presley. *The Medical Disability Advisor: Workplace Guidelines for Disability Duration.* Horsham, Pa.: LRP Publications, 1991.

Rothwell, William J. "HRD and the Americans with Disabilities Act." *Training and Development* (August 1991): 45–47.

Schneid, Thomas D. *The Americans with Disabilities Act: A Practical Guide for Managers.* New York: Van Nostrand Reinhold, 1992.

———. *The Americans with Disabilities Act: A Compliance Manual.* New York: Van Nostrand Reinhold, 1993.

Serious Mental Illness: Myths and Realities. Arlington, Va.: National Alliance for the Mentally Ill, n.d.

Serving Customers with Disabilities. 1993. 15-minute video. Available from Salenger Films.

Shore, David (ed.). *Schizophrenia: Questions and Answers.* Rockville, Md.: U.S. Department of Health and Human Services, 1986.

Succeeding Together at Work. 1993. 7-minute video. Available from Salenger Films.

Tingey, Carol. *Down Syndrome: A Resource Handbook.* Waltham, Mass.: College-Hill Press/Little, Brown, 1988.

Tompkins, Neville, and Lynn Atkinson (eds.). *The Job Descriptions Encyclopedia: An ADA Compliance Manual.* Madison, Conn.: Business and Legal Reports, 1993.

Tracey, William R. "Training and Development." In Mary F. Cook (ed.), *The AMA Handbook for Employee Recruitment and Retention.* New York: AMACOM, 1992.

———. "Counseling: Helping People Help Themselves." In William R. Tracey, *Critical Skills: The Guide to Top Performance for Human Resources Managers.* New York: AMACOM, 1988.

———. "Developing Yourself: Commanding Your Own Destiny." In *Leadership Skills: Standout Performance for Human Resources Managers.* New York: AMACOM, 1990.

———. "Assessing Training and Development Needs." In *Designing Training and Development Systems.* New York: AMACOM, 1992.

———. "Auditing the HR Function." In William R. Tracey (ed.), *Human Re-*

sources Management and Development Handbook. 2d ed. New York: AMACOM, 1994.

Unseen Courage. 1991. 23-minute video. Available from Advantage Media.

U.S. Equal Employment Opportunity Commission and U.S. Department of Justice. Civil Rights Division. *The Americans with Disabilities Act: Questions and Answers.* Washington, D.C.: EEOC, September 1992.

Welcome to the Team: Disability Etiquette in the Workplace. 1992. 19:40-minute video. Available from American Management Association. Nine Galen St., P.O. Box 9119, Watertown, MA 02272 (800) 225-3215 or (617) 926-9939.

Wood, Christopher K. "Job Analysis: A Powerful Tool for Managing Employee Disability." *Employee Benefit News* (February 1992): 43:48–49.

Notes

1. Jeffrey A. Mello, "Perceptions in the Workplace: A Double Dilemma," *HRfocus* (Special Edition), American Management Association, 1992, p. 18.
2. Christopher K. Wood, "Job Analysis: A Powerful Tool for Managing Employee Disability," *Employee Benefit News* (February 1992): 43.
3. Ibid., p. 48.
4. Julie Barker, "First Steps in Serving Disabled Travelers," *Successful Meetings* (June 1992): 37.

RESOURCES

Appendix A

Accessibility Standards

Parking Lots

- Designated parking spaces are located within 200 feet of the building.
- There is at least one accessible route from public transportation stops, accessible parking spaces, passenger loading zones, and public streets or sidewalks to an accessible building entrance.
- There is at least one accessible route connecting accessible buildings, facilities, and spaces on the same site.
- Parking spaces are clearly identified by the international access symbol.
- Parking spaces are a minimum of 96 inches wide.
- Ground surfaces that provide access from the parking lot to the building are stable, firm, slip resistant, and clear of gravel, loose impediments, and other obstacles.
- Passenger drop-off zones have curb cuts and accessible aisles parallel to vehicle pull-up spaces.
- Passenger loading zones provide access aisles at least 60 inches wide and 20 feet long (adjacent and parallel to vehicle pull-up spaces) and curb ramps.
- Vehicle standing spaces and access aisles are level with surface slopes that do not exceed 1:50 in all directions.
- There is enough space for a wheelchair lift to be lowered flat to the ground rather than to the curb.

Walks, Curbs, and Ramps

- At least one clearly marked and accessible route is available from the parking area to the building entrance.

Note: Diagrams of the material discussed in this appendix are found in *ADA Accessibility Guidelines for Buildings and Facilities*, Appendix A to Part 36, Standards of Accessibility Design, *Federal Register*, Vol. 56, No. 144, Rules and Regulations, July 26, 1991.

- For new construction, an accessible route connects accessible public transportation stops, parking spaces, passenger loading zones, and public streets or sidewalks to all accessible features and spaces within a building.
- Walks and other travel surfaces along accessible routes are firm, stable, and relatively nonslip under most weather conditions.
- Sidewalks from reserved parking areas to the building entrance are free of abrupt changes in level.
- Curbs are installed adjacent to designated parking spaces.
- Ramp approaches are identified by accessibility symbols.
- Sidewalks and ramps are a minimum of 36 inches wide, with some wider areas for turning and passing.
- Curb ramps have tactile detectable warning surfaces (raised truncated domes) extending their full width and depth.
- The maximum slope of all ramps is 1 inch of rise to every 12 inches of run.
- Ramps have a 5-foot landing at the top, bottom, and at ramp direction changes and resting levels.
- Gratings are designed so that openings are not wider than ½ inch. If elongated, the grating is perpendicular to the direction of travel.
- Ramps are visible through color change.
- Sidewalks and ramps have handrails on both sides.
- Ramps and landings with drop-offs have curbs at least 2 inches high or walls, railings, or projecting surfaces that prevent slipping.

Entrances, Corridors, Stairs, Floors, and Doors

- For new construction, at least 50 percent of all public entrances are accessible, and there are accessible entrances to enclosed parking, pedestrian tunnels, and elevated walkways.
- The approach to the building entrance is a hard surface at least 5 feet wide.
- The international symbol of access is displayed at entrances.
- Access to the building is covered to protect people during bad weather.
- An accessible single door entrance is at least 36 inches wide.
- If double doors, accessible door entrances are at least 48 inches wide.
- Door handles, pulls, latches, locks, and other operating devices have a shape that is easy to grasp with one hand and do not require tight grasping, pinching, or twisting of the wrist to operate.
- Door handles are lever operated, push type, or U shaped.

- Inner doors are a minimum of 32 inches wide and open 90 degrees measured from their fully closed to open positions.
- Door sills are flush to the floor or low enough (¾ inch beveled or ½ inch or less) to enable easy passage by a wheelchair.
- Doors have smooth kick plates on their bottoms up to a minimum of 16 inches from the floor.
- Doors have time-delay or light-pressure closers.
- Doormats are stationary, flat, or recessed and less than ½ inch thick.
- Automatic or power-assisted doors operate in a manner and direction that does not present a hazard.
- An accessible and unlocked door is adjacent to all revolving doors.
- Hallways and corridors between rooms have a clearance of at least 36 inches and occasional clear spaces of 60 inches for turning and passing.
- Stairs have uniform riser heights and uniform widths (no less than 11 inches measured from riser to riser).
- Easy-to-grasp continuous handrails, uninterrupted by newel posts or obstructions, are installed on both sides of all stairs.
- Floors are hard, stable, and regular to permit ease of negotiation by people who use wheelchairs, walkers, crutches, and canes.
- Registration desks are accessible to wheelchair users.
- Service counters have one portion that is at least 36 inches long and 54 inches from the floor.
- For new construction, each floor in a building without a supervised sprinkler system contains an area of rescue assistance (an area with direct access to an exit stairway where people unable to use stairs may await assistance during an emergency evacuation).

Signage and Warning Signals

- Signage is large enough, well lighted, and installed at an appropriate height.
- Emergency alarms give both visible and audible warnings.
- Permanent signs have raised letters or repeat their messages in braille.
- Suspended stairs are provided with sufficient warning devices to alert people with visual impairments of reduced headroom.

Elevators

- All levels of the building used by trainees are accessible by elevator.
- Inside car dimensions are a minimum of 48 inches by 48 inches.

- Elevator operation is automatic and self-leveling so that the car will be brought to floor landings with a tolerance of ½ inch under rated loading to zero loading conditions.
- Elevator call buttons and control panels are readily accessible to wheelchair users (centered at 42 inches above the floor).
- Call buttons have visual signals to indicate when each call is registered and when each call is answered.
- Raised and braille character floor designations are provided on both jams of elevator entrances 60 inches above the finish floor.
- Elevator doors are equipped with an automatic safety reopening device.
- Audible signals indicate when the elevator is going up or down.
- Floor buttons are maximum of 54 inches above the finish floor for side approach and 48 inches for front approach.
- Elevator lighting provides a minimum of 5 foot-candles of illumination at car controls, platform, and car threshold and landing.
- Elevators are large enough to allow wheelchair users to turn and face the door—a minimum of 48 inches deep and 22 feet square.
- Elevator doors are a minimum of 32 inches wide.
- The space between the floor and the elevator is a maximum of 1¼ inches.

Public Telephones

- At least one telephone in each bank of telephones is installed so that both the handset and the coin box are between 48 and 54 inches from the floor.
- Telephone booths and kiosks have a clear access path at least 30 inches wide.
- Telephone directories are at wheelchair level.
- Telephone operating instructions have raised lettering.
- At least one telephone in each bank of telephones is equipped with an amplified handset for people with hearing impairments.
- At least one telephone on each floor is a text telephone or one equipped with TDD (telecommunications device for the deaf).

Drinking Fountains and Water Coolers

- Drinking fountains and water coolers are accessible to people in wheelchairs.
- Spouts of water coolers and drinking fountains are no higher than 36 inches from the floor.
- Spouts of water coolers and drinking fountains are at the front of

the unit and direct the water flow in a trajectory parallel to the front of the unit.

- Drinking fountains are controlled by easily operated hand levers or buttons mounted at the front or side near the front edge.
- If wall or post mounted, units have a clear knee space between the bottom of the apron and the floor or ground at least 27 inches high, 30 inches wide, and 17 to 19 inches deep and with a minimum clear floor space at least 30 by 48 inches to allow a person in a wheelchair to approach the unit facing forward.

Public Rest Rooms

- Accessible rest rooms are available for men and women, clearly marked with the international access symbol.
- For new construction, public and common-use rest rooms are accessible, but only one stall must be wheelchair accessible unless there are six or more stalls, in which case two stalls must be accessible.
- Rest room doors have a clear opening of 36 inches.
- Mirrors are mounted within 40 inches of the floor.
- Sinks are mounted at least 29 inches from the floor for wheelchair knee clearance, and drains provide at least 9 inches for toe clearance.
- There is enough clear floor space in front of sinks to allow for the approach of a wheelchair.
- Hot water pipes under sinks are wrapped with a protective covering to prevent burns to wheelchair users.
- Faucet controls are of the lever or push type.
- Accessories are installed no higher than 54 inches from the floor to enable use by a person seated in a wheelchair.
- There is at least one toilet stall available with a clear opening of at least 36 inches.
- Toilet stall doors open outward and can be closed behind a wheelchair.
- There is at least one toilet stall arranged in such a way as to permit either side or front approach by someone in a wheelchair.
- Grab bars are installed behind and on the wall side of toilets, 36 inches wide at a minimum and no more than 44 inches above the floor, to facilitate transfers out of and into a wheelchair.
- Toilet seats are a maximum of 19 inches off the floor.
- Rest room toilet paper dispensers are no higher than 36 inches from the floor.

- Flush controls are fist operated and mounted no more than 44 inches above the floor.
- At least one stall-type or wall-hung urinal is installed in the men's rest room with a hand-operated or automatic flush control and an elongated rim set at a maximum height of 17 inches above the finish floor to permit use by a person in a wheelchair.

Dormitories and Guest Rooms

- For new construction, 4 percent of the first 100 rooms and approximately 2 percent of rooms in excess of 100 are accessible to people with hearing impairments (contain visual alarms, visual notification devices, volume-control telephones, and an accessible electrical outlet for a TDD) and to persons with mobility impairments.
- Barrier-free rooms are located near elevators.
- Door handles on all doors (inside and outside) are lever type.
- Doors and hallways are a minimum of 32 inches wide.
- Mirrors are a maximum of 40 inches from the floor.
- In rooms with two beds, minimum space between the beds or along one side is 32 inches.
- Carpeting is low pile with thin padding.
- Telephones, remote controls, and light switches are located next to the accessible side of beds.
- Furniture arrangement permits maneuverability for wheelchairs.
- Room thermostats are no higher than 40 inches from the floor.
- If temperature controls are on the heating and air-conditioning unit itself, the unit is accessible for a wheelchair user.
- Closets have sliding or bi-fold doors.
- Shelves and the closet clothes bar are a maximum of 48 inches from the floor.
- Shelves and hanging rods are adjustable.
- Shelves are no more than 18 inches deep.
- Peepholes on outside doors are low enough for a person in a wheelchair to see through them.
- Fire alarms are a maximum of 40 inches from the floor.
- Flashing-light alarms are installed to alert deaf and hearing-impaired guests.
- Voice alarms are installed for guests who are blind or hearing impaired.
- Bathroom floors are nonslip.
- Doors to bathrooms open out.
- Bathroom doors have a clear opening of 36 inches.
- There is a 5 by 5-foot clear space within each bathroom.

- Mirrors are mounted within 40 inches of the floor.
- Sinks are mounted at least 29 inches from the floor for wheelchair knee clearance, and drains provide at least 9 inches for toe clearance.
- There is enough clear floor space in front of sinks to allow for the approach of a wheelchair.
- Hot water pipes under sinks are wrapped with a protective covering to prevent burns to wheelchair users.
- Faucet controls are lever or push type.
- Dispenser and accessories are no higher than 54 inches from the floor to enable use by wheelchair users.
- The position of toilets permits either side or front approach by someone in a wheelchair.
- Toilet seats are a maximum of 19 inches off the floor.
- Flush controls are fist operated and mounted no more than 44 inches above the floor.
- Secure grab bars of sufficient length are mounted along the sides and backs of toilets to facilitate transfers out of and into a wheelchair.
- Secure grab bars of sufficient length, both vertical and horizontal, are mounted low along the sides, fronts, and backs of bathtubs to facilitate transfers out of and into a wheelchair.
- Tubs have securely mounted seats at the head end.
- Bathtubs have nonskid strips or surface.
- Tubs are equipped with shower spray units with hoses at least 60 inches long that can be used both as a fixed shower head and as a hand-held shower.
- There is a roll-in shower with no curb.

Cafeterias, Dining Rooms, and Lounges

- For new construction, dining areas and 5 percent of fixed tables (but not less than one) are accessible.
- Flat, nonslip surfaces provide access to facilities.
- Stairs or ramps are installed.
- Entrances have doors with a minimum clear opening of 32 inches, accessible levers, and negotiable thresholds.
- Food service lines have a minimum clear width of 36 inches.
- Tray slides are mounted no higher than 34 inches above the floor.
- Self-service shelves and dispensing devices for tableware, condiments, food, and beverages are installed at a maximum height of 54 inches above the floor.
- Counters and tables are accessible to people in wheelchairs.

- There is adequate space between tables for a wheelchair (minimum of 36 inches).
- There is a minimum of 27 inches of clearance under tables.
- Tables are a minimum of 30 inches wide.
- Cafeteria and buffet lines are a minimum of 36 inches wide and provide adequate turning space at corners.
- Menus in braille and large print are available.

Classrooms, Meeting Rooms, and Auditoriums

- Classrooms and meeting rooms are centrally located to make access easier for persons with mobility limitations.
- Upper-floor rooms are located near elevators.
- Rooms are barrier free.
- Risers have ramps with slopes of not more than 1 inch vertical to every 12 inches horizontal.
- Aisles are a minimum of 32 inches wide.
- Accessible cross-aisle seating is provided.
- Doors to rooms have a clearance of at least 32 inches.
- Doors have inside and outside lever-type handles.
- Peepholes on doors are low enough for a person in a wheelchair.
- Doors have smooth kick plates on their bottoms a minimum of 16 inches from the floor.
- Doors are a minimum of 32 inches wide and open to 90 degrees.
- Doors are flush or have ¾-inch beveled thresholds and time-delay or light-pressure closers.
- Classroom and meeting room floors are nonslip, level, and negotiable by unassisted people in wheelchairs.
- Floors have a common level throughout or are ramped at abrupt changes in level.
- Furniture placement allows sufficient turning space for wheelchairs.
- Rooms have movable tables and chairs that are adjustable in surface height.
- Storage areas are mobile or placed at the side of work surfaces instead of overhead.
- Wheelchair seating areas in auditoriums have level floors and optimum viewing areas and adjoin an accessible route.
- A minimum of 30 by 48 inches of clear ground space is available for each single, stationary wheelchair and occupant.
- Temporary ramps are available for use with raised podiums.
- Heating and cooling systems are noise controlled (dampened) to facilitate hearing by the hearing impaired.

- Microphones are available, readily accessible, and easily adjusted.
- Amplified communications equipment (assistive listening systems) is available for deaf and hearing-impaired trainees seated within 50 feet of the stage or podium.
- Tops of accessible tables are between 32 and 54 inches above the finish floor.
- Table knee space is at least 28 inches high, 30 inches wide, and 19 inches deep.
- Floor surfaces are hard, stable, and regular.
- If carpeted, floor surfaces have a firm texture and weave (industrial grade, short pile, maximum pile thickness of ½ inch) to eliminate slipping and tripping hazards for people who use crutches, canes, walkers, or wheelchairs.
- Exposed edges of carpeting are fastened to floor surfaces and have trim along the entire length of the exposed edge.
- Lighting is nonglare, nonreflecting, and nonblinking.
- Lighting is adjustable in terms of variable task-light intensities.
- Lighting provides a minimum of 50 foot-candles.
- For new construction, fixed seating assembly areas accommodate 50 or more people and have audio-amplification systems or a permanently installed assistive listening system.
- For new construction, wheelchair seating is dispersed in auditoriums accommodating more than 300 seats.
- At least 1 percent of all fixed seats are aisle seats without armrests (or removable arm rests), and mixed seating for companions is located adjacent to each wheelchair location.

Libraries and Learning Centers

- For new construction, all public areas and 5 percent of fixed tables or study carrels (or at least one) are accessible.
- At least one lane at the check-out area and aisles between card catalogs, magazine displays, and stacks are accessible.
- Doors provide a minimum of 32 inches of clear space on the pull side.
- Doors operate by a single effort (lever handles rather than knobs).
- At least one section of the circulation desk or service counter is a maximum of 26 inches from the floor.
- If registration desks and service counters are too high for people in wheelchairs, clipboards are provided.
- Tape recordings of services, directions, instructions, and so on are available.
- Card catalog drawers are no less than 18 and no more than 48

inches from the floor. If they are higher, assistance is readily available.

- There is a minimum clear aisle space of 42 inches between stacks.
- Some carrels are equipped with audiovisual equipment that can be operated by people with limited hand function.
- Carrels have adjustable lighting up to a minimum of 50 foot-candles.
- Carrel walls are designed to absorb noise without transmitting it.
- Carrels are equipped with assistive listening devices.
- Chairs are adjustable in height from the floor to the seat and the height and flexibility of the back support.
- Work areas (table tops) of carrels are between 32 and 34 inches from the floor with knee space of at least 28 inches high, 30 inches wide, and 19 inches deep to accommodate people in wheelchairs.
- Personalized help and services are offered to people with disabilities.

Appendix B

Sources of Information And Assistance

Blindness and Low Vision

ADA Consulting Group, 15 West 16th Street, New York, NY 10011, (212) 620-4232. An individualized service created by the American Foundation for the Blind to assist business and industry to meet the needs that have arisen since the passage of the Americans with Disabilities Act of 1990.

American Academy of Ophthalmology, 655 Beach Street, San Francisco, CA 94109-1336, (415) 561-8532. An organization of 20,000 ophthalmologists dedicated to preserving eye health and sight by providing total eye care (medical, surgical, and optical).

American Action Fund for Blind Children and Adults, American Brotherhood for the Blind, 1800 Johnson Street, Suite 100, Baltimore, MD 21230-4998, (410) 659-9315. Provides direct assistance to blind and deaf-blind persons, scholarships and study grants to enable blind students to continue their education, a hot line to the deaf blind (a biweekly news service in braille), and books with print and braille text and pictures so that blind parents can read with their sighted children and blind children can read along with their sighted parents.

American Association of the Deaf-Blind. 814 Thayer Avenue, Room 300, Silver Spring, MD 20910, (301) 588-6545. Established to ensure that a comprehensive, coordinated system of services is available and accessible to all deaf-blind people to enable them to achieve their maximum potential and integration into the community.

American Council of the Blind, 1155 15 Street, NW, Suite 720, Washington, DC 20005, (800) 424-8666 or (202) 467-5081. A consumer organization that acts as a national clearinghouse for information. Provides referrals, legal assistance, advocacy support, scholarships, and consultative and advisory services to individuals, organizations, and agencies.

American Foundation for the Blind, 15 West 16th Street, New York, NY 10011, (800) 232-5463; New York State, (800) 272-5463 or (212) 620-2147. An organization established to help persons who are blind or visually impaired achieve equality of access and opportunity. American Foundation for the Blind Regional Centers provide technical assistance, staff training, information and referral services to community agencies and organizations:

Eastern: AFB, 1615 M Street, NW, Suite 250, Washington, DC 20036, (202) 457-1492.

Midwest: AFB, 401 North Michigan Avenue, Suite 308, Chicago, IL 60611, (312) 245-9965.

Southeast: AFB, 100 Peachtree Street, Suite 620, Atlanta, GA 30303, (404) 525-2303.

Southwest: AFB, 260 Treadway Plaza, Exchange Park, Dallas, TX 75235, (214) 352-7222.

Western: AFB, 111 Pine Street, Suite 725, San Francisco, CA 94111, (415) 392-4845.

American Optometric Association, 243 North Lindberg Boulevard, St. Louis, MO 63141, (314) 991-4100. Provides information and pamphlets about vision and visual impairments.

American Printing House for the Blind, 1839 Frankfort Avenue, PO Box 6085, Louisville, KY 40206-0085, (502) 895-2405. Offers braille, computer disk, large-type, recorded, and regular-print computer-related books for purchase. Also manufactures the Speaqualizer, a completely hardware-controlled speech access system for IBM personal computers and compatibles.

Braille Institute of America, 741 North Vermont Avenue, Los Angeles, CA 90029-3594, (800) BRAILLE. A private, nonprofit organization established to provide free programs and services to people who are legally blind or visually impaired. Services include education and training programs, career planning, counseling, consultation, job placement, and library and reading materials in braille and recorded formats.

Council of Citizens with Low Vision International, 5705 Brockton Drive, No. 302, Indianapolis, IN 46220, (800) 733-2258 or (317) 254-1185. An international membership organization and network of persons with low vision, family members, and professionals established to provide outreach programs for the low-vision community.

Helen Keller National Center, 111 Middle Neck Road, Sands Point,

NY 11050, (516) 944-8900 (voice or TDD). Provides information and re-habilitation programs for deaf-blind persons.

Information Access Project for Blind Individuals, 1800 Johnston Street, Baltimore, MD 21230, (410) 659-9314. A joint project of the U.S. Department of Justice and the National Federation of the Blind. Offers free consultation in meeting the Americans with Disabilities Act's information access requirements. *See also* Job Opportunities for the Blind.

Job Opportunities for the Blind, c/o National Federation of the Blind, 1800 Johnson Street, Baltimore, MD 21230, (800) 638-7518 or (410) 659-9314. A joint program of the U.S. Department of Labor and the National Federation of the Blind that provides workshops, publications, and information about reasonable accommodations for the blind. Also provides a free, nationwide service to employers in locating and hiring qualified blind applicants and assists employees who are blind or become legally blind while on the job.

National Association for Visually Handicapped, 22 West 21st Street, New York, NY 10010, (212) 889-3141. Serves only the partially seeing with information and referral services, counsel, and guidance; offers large-print loan library (free by mail) and newsletters for adults and children. Works with professionals and paraprofessionals who deal with the partially seeing.

National Federation of the Blind, 1800 Johnson Street, Baltimore, MD 21230, (410) 659-9314. A consumer group of 50,000 blind Americans whose purpose is to achieve the complete integration of the blind into society by removing legal, economic, and social discrimination, educating the public to new concepts concerning blindness, and ensuring the right of all blind people to exercise to the fullest their individual talents and capacities and work along with their sighted neighbors in the professions, common callings, skilled trades, and regular occupations. With the U.S. Department of Labor, sponsors Job Opportunities for the Blind, a nationwide employment service for employers and blind applicants.

Retinitis Pigmentosa International, PO Box 900, Woodland Hills, CA 91365, (800) FIGHT-RP or (818) 992-0500. An international nonprofit organization dedicated to the fight against retinitis pigmentosa, incurable hereditary blindness. The organization raises funds for research and helps individuals and their families to accept and deal with the diagnosis of impending blindness.

Deafness and Hard of Hearing

Alexander Graham Bell Association for the Deaf, 3417 Volta Place, NW, Washington, DC, (202) 337-5220 (voice or TDD). A publication and information organization that emphasizes oral-deaf education, including speech reading and the use of residual hearing for oral communication.

American Association of the Deaf-Blind, 814 Thayer Avenue, Room 300, Silver Spring, MD 20910, (301) 588-6545. Established to ensure that a comprehensive, coordinated system of services is available and accessible to all deaf-blind people to enable them to achieve their maximum potential and integration into the community.

American Deafness and Rehabilitation Association, PO Box 251554, Little Rock, AR 72225, (501) 868-8850. Established to promote quality human services, including social services and rehabilitation, to deaf people through national organizations, local affiliates, professional sections, and individual members.

Better Hearing Institute, PO Box 1840, Washington, DC, 20013, (800) EAR WELL or (703) 642-0580. A nonprofit, tax-exempt educational organization supported by philanthropic funds that informs persons with impaired hearing, their friends and relatives, and the general public in the United States and Canada about hearing loss and available help through medicine, surgery, amplification, and other rehabilitation.

Deafness and Communicative Disorders Branch, Rehabilitative Services Administration, Switzer Building, M/S 2736, Washington, DC 20202, (202) 732-1401 (voice), (202) 732-1298 (TDD). Provides information on rehabilitative services for deaf persons.

Division of Educational Services, Office of Special Education Programs, U.S. Department of Education, Washington, DC 20202, (202) 708-5366. Provides information about Department of Education–supported postsecondary education programs for individuals who are deaf.

Ear Foundation, 2000 Church Street, Box 111, Nashville, TN 37236, (800) 545-HEAR or (615) 329-7809. A nonprofit organization established to lead the effort for better hearing and balance through public and professional education programs, support services, and applied research.

Gallaudet University, 800 Florida Avenue, NE, Washington, DC 20002, (202) 651-5000. Funded by the federal government to provide a liberal higher education for deaf persons. Offers more than 80 undergraduate and graduate programs leading to A.A., A.A.S., B.A., B.S., M.A., M.S., Ed.D., and Ph.D. degrees and a program of research relating to deafness. Provides information and publishes books and other materials on deafness.

Hear Now, 4001 South Magnolia Way, Suite 100, Denver, CO 80237, (800) 648-HEAR or (303) 758-4919. Established to make technology accessible to deaf and hard-of-hearing individuals. Raises funds to provide hearing aids, cochlear implants, and related services to children and adults who have hearing losses but do not have the financial resources to purchase their own devices.

Helen Keller National Center, 111 Middle Neck Road, Sands Point, NY 11050, (516) 944-8900 (voice or TDD). Provides information and rehabilitation programs for deaf-blind persons.

International Federation of Hard of Hearing People, Radegunder Strasse 10, A-8045 Graz, Austria, + +43 316 671327 (voice), + +43 316 681093 (TDD). An international volunteer organization consisting of national organizations of and for hard-of-hearing and deaf people, consumers, and professional organizations.

National Association of the Deaf, 814 Thayer Avenue, Silver Spring, MD 20910, (301) 587-1788 (voice), (301) 587-1789 (TDD). Established to improve the quality of products and services for deaf and hearing-impaired people. Serves as a legislative advocate for equal access to communication and employment opportunities. Provides materials, deaf awareness programs, legal defense fund, public information center, and professional leadership.

National Black Deaf Advocates, One Lomb Memorial Drive, Rochester, NY 14623, (716) 475-6367. Established to promote leadership, deaf awareness, and participation in the political, educational, and economic processes that affect the lives of black deaf citizens.

National Center for Law and Deafness, Gallaudet University, 800 Florida Avenue, NE, Washington, DC 20002-3695, (202) 651-5373 (voice), (202) 651-5373 (TDD). Provides a variety of legal services and programs to the deaf community, including representation, counseling, information, and education. Helps young adults to grow, develop, work, and participate in community life to their fullest capacity. Provides bibliographic and program services, training materials, publications, and technical assistance.

National Information Center on Deafness, Gallaudet University, 800 Florida Avenue, NE, Washington, DC 20002-3695, (202) 651-5051 (voice), (202) 651-5052 (TDD). A national centralized source of inexpensive publications and technical information on hearing loss and deafness. Collects, develops, and disseminates up-to-date information on deafness, hearing loss, organizations and services for deaf and hard-of-hearing people, education, research, demographics, law, technology, and barrier-free design.

National Institute on Deafness and Other Communication Disorders Clearinghouse, P.O. Box 37777, Washington, DC 20013-7777, (800) 241-1044 (voice), (800) 241-1055 (TDD/TT). An office of the National Institutes of Health, U.S. Department of Health and Human Services, whose mission is to support biomedical and behavioral research training in the seven areas of human communication. Established the NIDCD Clearinghouse in March 1991, a national resource center for information and resources on mechanisms of hearing, balance, smell, taste, voice, speech, and language for health professionals, patients, industry, and the public.

National Technical Institute for the Deaf, Rochester Institute of Technology, One Lomb Memorial Drive, P.O. Box 9887, Rochester, NY 14623-0877, (716) 475-6400 (voice), (716) 475-2181 (TDD). Provides technical postsecondary education to people who are deaf or hearing impaired. Disseminates information, materials, and instructional videocassettes on deafness and related areas nationwide.

Office of Career Opportunities, National Technical Institute for the Deaf, One Lomb Memorial Drive, Rochester, NY 14623, (716) 475-6400. Created by public law to provide special technical education for deaf students from all states.

Self Help for Hard of Hearing People, 7800 Wisconsin Avenue, Bethesda, MD 20814, (301) 657-2248 (voice), (301) 657-2249 (TDD). Promotes awareness and information about hearing loss, communication, assistive devices, and alternative communication skills by means of publications, exhibits, and presentations.

World Federation of the Deaf, Ilkantie 4, PO Box 65, SF-00401, Helsinki, Finland, 011 358-0-58031. Promotes the exchange of research findings, ideas, and reports about deafness. Encourages national federations of deaf people to establish aid programs for deaf people in developing countries.

Disfigurement

AboutFace, 1002 Liberty Lane, Warrington, PA 18976, (800) 225-FACE. An international information and support organization for people with facial difference and their families. Resources include training, books, videos, lending library, and bimonthly newsletter.

American Cleft Palate-Craniofacial Association, 1218 Grandview Avenue, Pittsburgh, PA 15211-9906, (800) 24-CLEFT (voice/TDD) or (412) 481-0847. Established in 1943 to encourage the improvement of scientific clinical services to persons with cleft palate and associated conditions. Membership is open to qualified professionals who are involved in the treatment and/or research of cleft lip, cleft palate, and other craniofacial anomalies. Approximately 2,600 members from 40 countries include 30 health care disciplines such as surgeons, dentists, and speech pathologists.

Burns United Support Group, 441 Colonial Court, Brose Ponte Farms, MI 48236, (313) 881-5577. A national organization established to provide information, assistance, and support to those who have survived being burned and their family and friends. Services include outreach visitation, phone support, and newsletter.

Cleft Palate Foundation, 1218 Grandview Avenue, Pittsburgh, PA 15211-9906, (412) 481-1376. A nonprofit organization dedicated to assisting patients with birth defects of the head and neck and their families. Helps patients and their families understand these birth defects through its publications, which include informational brochures and fact sheets. Through CLEFTLINE, a toll-free informational service, refers interested parties to groups of professionals in their area who are skilled in the management of cleft lip, cleft palate, and other craniofacial deformities. Also is involved in educating professionals and the public about the problems and treatment of people born with these defects.

Let's Face It, Box 711, Concord, MA 01742-0711, (508) 371-3186. The U.S. branch of an international mutual help organization dedicated to helping people with facial difference, their loved ones, and the communities in which they live to understand and to solve the problems of living with this disability. Its goals are to (1) link and educate family, friends, and professionals; (2) educate the public to value the person behind every face; (3) assist facially different people to share their experiences, strengths, and hopes; and (4) provide continuing education to medical, nursing, and allied health professionals.

Phoenix Society for Burn Survivors, 11 Rust Hill Road, Levittown, PA 19056, (800) 888-2876 or (215) 946-2876. An international organization of burn survivors established to assist people who have been burned and their families during and after the hospitalization. Holds national and international conferences and provides books, audiovisual materials, and a quarterly newsletter.

Health and Medical

Alcoholics Anonymous World Services, General Service Office, AA World Services, 475 Riverside Drive, 11th Floor, New York, NY 10115, (212) 870-3400. A fellowship of men and women who share their experiences with each other to solve their common problems and help others recover from alcoholism through interaction and support and by following AA's Twelve Steps. There are no dues; the only requirement for membership is a desire to stop drinking and stay sober. Chapters are organized in all cities and most towns nationwide.

American Cancer Society; check the Yellow Pages for the nearest ACS office or call (800) ACS-2345. A nationwide, community-based voluntary health organization dedicated to eliminating cancer as a major health problem by preventing cancer, saving lives from cancer, and diminishing suffering from cancer through research, education, and service. Provides resources, information, and guidance, programs for women with breast cancer, the Look Good . . . Feel Better program, cancer support groups, transportation, and limited financial assistance.

American Diabetes Association, PO Box 6911, Washington, DC 20090-6911, (800) 232-3472 or (202) 331-8303. A nonprofit organization dedicated to preventing and curing diabetes and improving the lives of all people affected by diabetes through research and education.

Calix Society, c/o Rolf Olson, 7601 Wayzata Boulevard, Minneapolis, MN 55426, (612) 546-0544 (mornings only). Established to help Catholic alcoholics achieve and maintain sobriety through Alcoholics Anonymous. Focuses on total abstinence and spiritual development. Publishes a bimonthly newsletter.

Cystic Fibrosis Foundation, 631 Arlington Road, Bethesda, MD 20814, (800) FIGHT CF for (301) 951-4422. A nonprofit organization established to fund research to find a cure for cystic fibrosis and to improve the quality of life for the 30,000 children and young adults with the disease. Funds its own network of 14 research centers in America, finances more than 112 care centers nationwide, offers general information publications, and supports public policy and education programs.

Epilepsy Foundation of America, 4351 Garden City Drive, Landover, MD 20785, (800) EFA-1000, (301) 459-3700. A national, voluntary health organization dedicated to the prevention and cure of seizure disorders, the alleviation of their effects, the promotion of independence, increased job preparation and employment opportunities, and an optimal quality of life for people who have these disorders. Operates the Training and Placement Service program, an employment initiative funded by the Department of Labor, that provides job search assistance, training in job seeking skills, and employer education.

National Association of People with AIDS, 1413 K Street, NW, #10, Washington, DC 20005-3405, (202) 898-0414. A national network of people with AIDS composed of 102 affiliated groups. Established to share information and serve as a collective voice for health, social, and political concerns. Publishes a monthly newsletter.

National Cancer Institute, Building 31, Room 10A16, Bethesda, MD 20892, (800) 4-CANCER. One of the 13 institutes comprising the National Institutes of Health, U.S. Department of Health and Human Services. Maintains its own research laboratories and clinics, supports cancer research, and provides information on the prevention, detection, and treatment of cancer.

National Neurofibromatosis Foundation, 141 Fifth Avenue, Suite 7-S, New York, NY 10010, (800) 323-7938; in New York State, (212) 460-8980. A nonprofit organization with approximately 31,000 associates in all 50 states (23 chapters) and 51 other countries. Its purposes are to (1) sponsor research aimed at finding the cause and cure for both types of neurofibromatosis, NF1 and NF2; (2) promote the development of clinical activities that ensure individuals with the disease ready access to the best medical care; (3) develop programs to increase public awareness of neurofibromatosis; and (4) provide support services for patients and their families.

Women for Sobriety, PO Box 618, Quakertown, PA 18951-0618, (800) 333-1606 or (215) 536-8026. Established to help women alcoholics achieve sobriety. Addresses the need to overcome depression and guilt. Provides group meetings, conferences, information and referrals, and telephone support.

Learning

Adult Attention Deficit Foundation, 132 North Woodward Avenue, Birmingham, MI 48009, (313) 540-6335. A nonprofit corporation whose mission is to identify and inform adults with attention deficit disorder (ADD) about the disorder and how it can be managed and to support research profits for further inquiry into the field of ADD in adults.

National Network of Learning Disabled Adults, P.O. Box 32611, Phoenix, AZ 85064-2611, (602) 941-5112. A national consumer-directed self-advocacy association of adults with learning disabilities established to improve their image, develop their communication skills, and encourage the formation of support groups. Publishes a quarterly newsletter.

Orton Dyslexia Society, Chester Building, Suite 382, 8600 LaSalle Road, Baltimore, MD 21286-2044, (800) 222-3123 or (410) 296-0232. An international nonprofit organization of 9,000 members in 44 branches in the United States, 1 in Canada, and 1 in Israel. Dedicated to the study and treatment of dyslexia and sharing information with its members through publications, conferences, and a network of volunteers throughout the country.

Mental, Developmental, and Emotional

Administration on Developmental Disabilities, Department of Health and Human Services, Room 329D, Humphrey Building, Washington, DC 20201, (202) 690-5910. A source of help at the national level for employers and people with developmental disabilities.

American Association on Mental Retardation, 1719 Kalorama Road NW, Washington, DC 20009, (800) 424-3688 or (202) 387-1968. A 117-year-old international multidisciplinary association of professionals, academicians, researchers, service providers, managers, parents, and consumers. Formerly known as the American Association on Mental Deficiency.

Anxiety Disorders Association of America, 6000 Executive Boulevard, #513, Rockville, MD 20852-3801, (301) 231-9350 or (900) 737-3400. A national organization of consumers, health care professionals, and others to promote the welfare of people with phobias and anxiety disorders. Publishes a newsletter.

ARC, 500 East Border Street, #300, Arlington, TX 76010, (817) 261-6003. An advocacy and direct services organization established to provide support for people with mental retardation and their families. Publishes a bimonthly newsletter.

Arc of New Jersey, Project HIRE, 985 Livingston Avenue, North Brunswick, NJ 08902, (908) 246-2525. An organization that has exemplary programs in place for recruiting, hiring, training, and developing people with Down syndrome.

Depression Awareness, Recognition, and Treatment, 5600 Fisher's Lane, Room 14C-02, Rockville, MD 20857, (301) 443-4140. A national science-based program to educate the public, primary care providers, and mental health specialists about depressive illnesses—their symptoms, diagnosis, and treatments. An agency of the federal government sponsored by the National Institute of Mental Health.

Emotional Health Anonymous, P.O. Box 429, Glendale, CA 91202-0429, (818) 240-3215. Established to help people solve common problems of mental health by sharing experiences, strengths, and hopes. Patterned after Alcoholics Anonymous's Twelve Steps. Publishes a newsletter.

Emotions Anonymous, P.O. Box 4245, St. Paul, MN 55104, (612) 647-9712. Established to achieve better emotional health and foster fellowship and sharing experiences, hopes, and strengths using Alcoholics Anonymous's Twelve-Step program.

Helping Hands, c/o Rita Martone, 86 Poor Street, Andover, MA 01810, (508) 475-3388. Established to help people with manic-depressive disorders, schizophrenia, or clinical depression to become more aware of themselves and develop a positive attitude.

Mental Illness Anonymous, c/o St. Mary's Episcopal Church, 1895 Laurel Avenue, St. Paul, MN 55106, (612) 646-6175. A self-help group of men and women with mental illness established to promote fellowship, share pain and hope, and achieve recovery. Patterned after Alcoholics Anonymous's Twelve Steps.

National Alliance for the Mentally Ill (NAMI), 2101 Wilson Boulevard, Suite B 302, Arlington, VA 22201, (800) 950-NAMI or (703) 524-9094. An organization dedicated to the eradication of mental illness and improvement in the quality of life of those whose lives are affected by those diseases. Provides information and resources to make it easier for families to deal with mental illness and supports research into causes, treatments, and cures.

National Down Syndrome Congress, 1605 Chantilly Drive, Suite 250, Atlanta, GA 30324, (800) 232-NDSC or (404) 633-1555. A membership organization of parents and professionals established to promote the availability and accessibility of persons with Down syndrome to a full range of opportunities and resources and to educate professionals, parents, and the community about Down syndrome.

National Down Syndrome Society, 666 Broadway, New York, NY 10012, (800) 221-4602 or (212) 460-9930. Promotes public education and awareness about Down syndrome, supports research about this genetic disorder, and provides vital services, including clinical information for health professionals and an information hot line for families and individuals. Its purpose is to create and carry out programs that enable people with Down syndrome to live richer, healthier, and happier lives.

Mobility and Motion

Amyotrophic Lateral Sclerosis Association, 21021 Ventura Boulevard, Suite 321, Woodland Hills, CA 91364, (800) 782-4747 or (818) 340-7500. A not-for-profit voluntary health organization dedicated to the fight against amyotrophic lateral sclerosis (Lou Gehrig's disease) through research, patient support, information dissemination, and public awareness.

Arthritis Foundation, P.O. Box 19000, Atlanta, GA 30326, (800) 283-7800 or (404) 872-7100. A not-for-profit organization whose mission is to support research to find the cure for and prevention of arthritis and to improve the quality of life for those affected by arthritis. Also conducts education programs for health professionals, provides community education and support services for people with arthritis and their families, informs the public about arthritis, and advocates the interests of people affected by arthritis.

Arthritis Research Institute of America, 300 South Duncan Avenue, Suite 240, Clearwater, FL 34615, (813) 461-4054. A research organization devoted to eliminating the pain and suffering of osteoarthritis through research. Sponsors research on related topics.

Eastern Paralyzed Veterans Association, 75-20 Astoria Boulevard, Jackson Heights, NY 11370-1177, (718) 803-3782. Provides information and assistance to organizations and individuals who work with veterans with spinal cord injuries resulting in paraplegia or quadriplegia and with individual veterans.

Multiple Sclerosis Association of America, 601-603 White Horse Pike, Oaklyn, NJ 08107, (800) 833-4MSA. A national self-help organization that offers support group meetings, information and referrals, telephone support, conferences, counseling, and a newsletter.

National Amputation Foundation, 73 Church Street, Malverne, NY 11565, (516) 887-3600. A nonprofit organization with 2,500 members, it is the largest amputee organization in the United States. Originally established to help veterans who lost a limb in World War I, it now serves both veterans and civilians of all ages and both sexes by providing legal counsel, vocational guidance, liaison with outside groups, psychological aid, training in the use of prosthetic devices, and publications.

National Multiple Sclerosis Society, 733 Third Avenue, New York, NY 10017-3288, (800) 532-7667 or (800) 227-3166. Funds research in multiple sclerosis and provides information (brochures, newsletters, and telephone contacts); individual, group, and family counseling; and self-help support groups for patients and their families. Provides help in obtaining adaptive equipment and short- and long-term equipment loans.

National Neurofibromatosis Foundation, 141 Fifth Avenue, Suite 7-S, New York, NY 10010, (800) 323-7938; in New York State, (212) 460-8980. A nonprofit organization with approximately 31,000 associates in all 50 states (23 chapters) and 51 other countries. Its purposes are to (1) sponsor research aimed at finding the cause and cure for both types of neurofibromatosis, NF1 and NF2; (2) promote the development of clinical activities that ensure individuals with the disease ready access to the best medical care; (3) develop programs to increase public awareness of neurofibromatosis; and (4) provide support services for patients and their families.

National Spinal Cord Injury Association, 600 West Cummings Park, Suite 2000, Woburn, MA 01801, (800) 962-9629 or (617) 935-2722. A membership-based, private nonprofit organization with more than 60 chapters established by the Paralyzed Veterans of America to serve as a national clearinghouse and primary resource to its members, the general public, and the media regarding spinal cord injury. Provides information and referral on job analysis, job modifications, job accommodations, job restructuring, new technology, adaptive equipment for individuals with spinal cord injuries, and information and referral on architectural modifications and building codes.

Paralyzed Veterans of America, 801 Eighteenth Street, NW, P.O. Box 96010, Washington, DC, (202) 872-1300. A nonprofit veterans' service organization chartered by the U.S. Congress to improve the care, treatment, and rehabilitation of veterans who have a spinal cord injury or disease. Funds 58 full-time service offices across the United States. Programs include veterans' benefits, counseling, spinal cord research, advocacy and legislation, barrier-free design, wheelchair sports and recreation, and public education.

Society for Muscular Dystrophy Information, International, P.O. Box 479, Bridgewater, Nova Scotia, Canada B4V 2X6, (902) 682-3086. Established to share and encourage the exchange of nontechnical, neuromuscular disorder and disability-related information. Produces a directory of worldwide sources, provides referrals to support groups, publishes a networking newsletter, and operates a publications exchange.

United Cerebral Palsy Associations, 1522 K Street, NW, Suite 1112, Washington, DC 20005, (800) 872-5827 or (202) 842-3519. A nationwide network of 180 state and local affiliated agencies that provide direct services to people with cerebral palsy, act as advocates for people with disabilities, are involved in public and professional information and education, and support research on cerebral palsy and the neurosciences.

Speech and Language

American Speech-Language-Hearing Association, 10801 Rockville Pike, Rockville, MD 20852, (800) 638-8255 (voice or TDD) or (301) 897-5700 (voice or TDD). A national professional, scientific, and credentialing organization of 65,293 speech-language pathologists and audiologists. Its mission is to ensure that all people with speech, language, and hearing disorders have access to quality services to help them communicate more effectively.

International Foundation for Stutterers, P.O. Box 462, Belle Mead, NJ 08502, (609) 275-3806. An organization established to eliminate stuttering through speech therapy in conjunction with self-help groups. Provides education for the public and professionals about stuttering.

National Cued Speech Association, 1615-B Oberlin Road, P.O. Box 31345, Raleigh, NC 27622, (919) 828-1218. Provides advocacy and support regarding use of cued speech and provides information and services for deaf and hard-of-hearing people of all ages, their families, and professionals.

National Institute on Deafness and Other Communication Disorders Clearinghouse, P.O. Box 37777, Washington, DC 20013-7777, (800) 241-1044 (voice), (800) 241-1055 (TDD/TT). An office of the National Institutes of Health, U.S. Department of Health and Human Services, whose mission is to support biomedical and behavioral research and research training in the seven areas of human communication. Established the NIDCD Clearinghouse in March 1991, a national resource center for information and resources on the normal and disordered mechanisms of hearing, balance, smell, taste, voice, speech, and language for health professionals, patients, industry, and the public.

Stuttering Foundation of America, P.O. Box 11749, Memphis, TN 38111-0749, (800) 992-9392. A nonprofit organization established to help prevent stuttering and treat those who stutter. Provides information packets for adults who stutter, publishes books and brochures on stuttering, and organizes conferences and symposia on stuttering for professionals, such as speech-language pathologists, on various topics related to stuttering. Formerly the Speech Foundation of America.

General

AbleData, 8455 Colesville Road, Suite 935, Silver Spring, MD 20910-3319, (800) 346-2742 (voice/TDD). Operated by Macro International, the company that operates the National Institute on Disability and Rehabilitation Research. Provides free information from a database listing of more than 17,000 assistive devices for all types of disabilities.

Accent on Information, P.O. Box 700, Bloomington, IL 61702, (309) 378-2961. A private nonprofit organization that offers product information through a quarterly publication and a biennial buyers' guide. Accepts telephone requests for information.

ADA Regional and Business Technical Assistance Centers, NEB-TAC, 145 Newbury Street, Portland, ME 04101, (800) 949-4232. Provides addresses and telephone sources for training on ADA provisions, disability awareness, and technical assistance.

Alliance for Technology Access, 1307 Solano Avenue, Albany, CA 94706-1888, (415) 528-0747 or ATA, 217 Massachusetts Avenue, Lexington, MA 02173, (617) 863-9966. A nationwide network of 46 computer resource centers and more than 40 technology vendors committed to the transformation of the tools of technology to open doors to education, employment, and personal fulfillment and empowerment to people with disabilities.

American Self-Help Clearinghouse, St. Charles–Riverside Medical Center, Denville, NJ 07834, (201) 625-7101. Established to reduce human suffering and isolation and increase the availability of the unique community support and expertise of "those who have been there" by offering emotional support and education in dealing with a variety of medical problems. Provides group information services and contacts for any national self-help group, a directory of national and demonstrational model self-help groups, and group/network development assistance. Publishes *The Self-Help Sourcebook*.

Apple Computer, 20515 Marinani Avenue, M.S. 43 F, Cupertino, CA

95014, (408) 996-1010. Provides information about specific Apple devices (Apple and Macintosh computers) and applications for people with disabilities.

Architectural and Transportation Barriers Compliance Board (Access Board), 1111 18th Street, Suite 501, Washington, DC 20036, (800) USA-ABLE, (202) 272-5434, (202) 653-7834 (TDD). Provides information and technical assistance regarding accessibility and standards for facilities for people with disabilities. Enforces standards and investigates complaints about the inaccessibility of buildings. Developed the ADA Accessibility Guidelines.

Association for Persons with Severe Handicaps, 7010 Roosevelt Way, NE, Seattle, WA 98115, (206) 523-8446. Advocates for educational services for persons with disabilities. Disseminates information, publishes a newsletter and a journal, and acts as an advocate for the rights of people with disabilities.

Barrier Free Environment, P.O. Box 30634, Raleigh, NC 27622, (919) 782-7823. Provides information about ADA accommodations.

Center for Assistive Technology, University of Buffalo, 515 Kimball Tower, 3435 Main Street, Buffalo, NY 14214-3079, (716) 829-3217. Provides information and materials on all types of assistive technology. Operates Project Link: Link to Assistive Products.

Center on Addiction and Substance Abuse, Columbia University, 152 West 57th Street, New York, NY 10024, (212) 841-5200. Works with experts in medicine, law enforcement, business, economics, communications, teaching, social work, and the clergy to determine and combat the impact of substance abuse on courts, housing, prisons, children, health care, crime, business productivity, and education and to inform people of the costs of substance abuse throughout society.

Clearinghouse on Disability Information, 330 C Street, SW, Room 3132, Switzer Building, Washington, DC 20202-2524, (202) 732-1245. Identifies government agencies that provide specific information about ADA.

Closing the Gap, P.O. Box 68, Henderson, MN 56044, (612) 248-3294. Publishes an annual resource directory on adaptive equipment and the companies that manufacture and distribute it.

CompuServe, P.O. Box 20212, 5000 Arlington Center Boulevard, Columbus, OH 43220, (800) 848-8199. Permits companies and individuals with modem-equipped personal or desktop computers to access news, notes, and information on referral organizations and adaptive hardware and software.

Direct Link for the Disabled, P.O. Box 1036, Solvang, CA 93464, (805) 688-1603. Maintains listings of more than 10,000 organizations and community resource centers for all types of disabilities. Responds to telephone and mail inquiries without charge.

Disabilities Awareness Network, ASTD, 1640 King Street, Box 1443, Alexandria, VA 22313-2043, (703) 683-8100. A membership group established to encourage the American Society for Training and Development as an organization to examine and explore disability issues, from language in its publications to conference accessibility and programming, and to stimulate trainers and other professionals who work with people with disabilities to network with each other.

DRAGnet: Disability Resources Activities and Groups Network, (612) 753-1943. The local outlet for many national electronic bulletin boards and independent living programs for persons in Minnesota with disabilities. It is available 24 hours a day to people with a personal computer and a modem and can also be used by people using voice synthesizers. The service is free to users in the 612 area, and plans have been made for satellite expansions statewide.

Equal Employment Opportunity Commission, Office of Communications and Legislative Affairs, 1801 L Street, NW, Washington, DC 20507, (800) 800-3202 (TDD) or (202) 663-4900 (voice), (202) 296-6312 (voice for 202 area code), (202) 663-4494 (TDD for 202 area code). Provides information about requirements of the Americans with Disabilities Act that affect employment. Also investigates and resolves complaints or charges of discrimination on the basis of disability unless there is a state or local law that provides relief.

Federal Communications Commission, Consumer Assistance, 1919 M Street, NW, Washington, DC 20554, (202) 632-7000, (202) 632-6999 (TDD). Provides information on Telecommunications, Title IV of ADA.

Health Care Financing Administration, Inquiries Staff, Room GF-3, East Lowrise Building, Baltimore, MD 21207, (410) 966-5505. Provides information and assistance relating to Medicare and Medicaid.

Helping Hands, 1505 Commonwealth Avenue, Boston, MA 02135, (800) 851-4666 or (617) 787-4419. A nonprofit organization specializing in filling nonprofessional-level jobs or entry-level professional positions. Locates, screens, and refers job candidates with disabilities in specific areas and coordinates candidate searches of disability organizations in the area. An affiliate of the Boston University School of Medicine.

IBM's Disabilities Assistance Network, 2000 Purchase Street, Purchase, NY 10577-2597, (914) 697-6595. Offers computers and software on loan at no charge to federally funded disabilities support centers (agencies and noprofit organizations designated by states to administer programs funded through the Technology Related Assistance for Individuals with Disabilities Act of 1988) across the United States.

IBM's Program to Train Disabled Persons, 2000 Purchase Street,

Purchase, NY 10577-2597, (914) 697-6595. Helped establish 53 centers nationwide that train people with disabilities for careers in information processing industries. Most centers provide programmer training for individuals with physical disabilities to learn entry-level computer programming skills and to obtain jobs. A second program provides personal computer skills-based training to people with disabilities.

IBM's Special Needs Information and Referral Center, P.O. Box 2150, Atlanta, GA 30055, (800) 426-2133. Formerly IBM's National Support Center for Persons with Disabilities, the center provides information about IBM and compatible devices and programs and reference guides and instructional request. Created to help health care leaders, employers, educators, public officials, and individuals learn how technology can improve the quality of life in the school, home, and workplace for persons with disabilities.

IBM's Workforce Solutions, 20 Old Post Road, Armonk, NY 10504, (914) 765-2000. A source of information about all IBM programs and services relating to workforce diversity, including programs for the training and development of people with disabilities.

Industry-Labor Council on Employment and Disability, Human Resource Center, 201 I.U. Willets Road, Albertson, NY 11507, (516) 747-6323. A nonprofit organization of more than 140 corporations that provides information and technical assistance to employers seeking to integrate people with disabilities into the workforce.

Internal Revenue Service (IRS), Department of the Treasury, 1111 Constitution Avenue, NW Washington, DC 20224, (202) 566-2000. Provides information about federal disability-related tax credits and deductions for individuals and businesses.

Job Accommodation Network, West Virginia University, 809 Allen Hall, P.O. Box 6123, Morgantown, WV 26506-6123, (800) 526-7234; WV (800) 526-4698; Canada, (800) 526-2262, (304) 293-7186, (800) 232-9675 (TDD), (800) 342-5526 (computer modem). An international information network and consulting resource established to help qualified workers with disabilities to be hired or retained. It enables employers, rehabilitation professionals, and people with disabilities to share information about practical ways, including methods and equipment, of making accommodations for employees and applicants with disabilities.

Local vocational rehabilitation agencies. Provide a variety of support services to individuals with disabilities and employers. Check the Yellow Pages under "Rehabilitation" or call the National Association of Rehabilitation Facilities, (703) 648-9300.

MD Technology Assistance Program, 300 West Lexington Street, Box 10, Baltimore, MD 21298-3096, (800) 832-4827, (410) 554-3202, or (410) 333-4975 (voice and TDD). Operated by the Office for Individuals with Disabilities of the State of Maryland, provides information and materials relating to the selection, acquisition, or use of assistive technology devices.

National Catholic Office for Persons with Disabilities, 401 Michigan Avenue, NE, P.O. Box 29113, Washington DC 20017, (202) 529-2933 (voice and TDD). Established to foster the inclusion of people with disabilities in all the celebrations and obligations of the Roman Catholic church. Works through a network of diocesan leaders.

National Center for Youth with Disabilities, University of Minnesota, Box 721, UMHC, Harvard Street at East River Road, Minneapolis MN 55455, (800) 333-6293; (612) 333-6293, or (612) 626-3939 (TDD). An information and resource center focusing on adolescents with chronic illness and disabilities. Its mission is to raise awareness of the needs of adolescents with chronic illness disabilities, expand the knowledge and involvement of those who provide services to youth, and promote programs and strategies that enhance the ability of adolescents and young adults to grow, develop, work, and participate in community life to their fullest capacity. Provides bibliographic and program services, training materials, publications, and technical assistance.

National Easter Seal Society, Computer Assistive Technology Service, 5120 South Hyde Park Boulevard, Suite 100, Chicago, IL 60615, (800) 221-6827; IL, (312) 726-6200. A nonprofit, community-based health agency dedicated to increasing the independence of people with disabilities. Developed CATS (Computer Assistive Technology Services) to enhance the productivity and independence of people with disabilities through the use of computer assistive technology.

National Information Center for Children and Youth with Handicaps, P.O. Box 1492, Washington, DC 20013, (800) 999-5599. Provides sources of information and assistance relating to the rights of children with disabilities and their parents, appeal procedures, and general advocacy information in the area of education.

National Organization on Disability, 910 16th Street, NW, Suite 600, Washington, DC 20006, (800) 248-ABLE or (202) 293-5960. A private nonprofit organization established to increase the acceptance and participation in all aspects of life of all men, women, and children with physical or mental disabilities.

National Rehabilitation Association, 1910 Association Drive, Suite 205, Reston, VA 22091, (703) 715-9090 (voice), (703) 715-9209 (TDD). Provides referral to more than 400 accessibility surveyors nationwide who can assist employers to meet ADA accessibility guidelines, remove physical and attitudinal barriers, conduct accessibility surveys, and train employers to conduct such surveys. Offers training programs relating to the employment of people with disabilities and publishes guidelines on accessibility.

National Rehabilitation Information Center, 8455 Colesville Road, Suite 935, Silver Spring, MD 20910-3319, (800) 346-2742, (301) 588-9284. A library and information center on disability and rehabilitation serving educators, allied health professionals, administrators, physicians, rehabilitation counselors, information professionals, students, and consumers. Publishes *NARIC Quarterly,* a newsletter of disability and rehabilitation research and resources.

National Resource Library on Youth with Disabilities, National Center for Youth with Disabilities, Adolescent Health Program, University of Minnesota, Box 721-UMHC, Harvard Street at East River Road, Minneapolis, MN 55455, (800) 333-6293, (612) 626-2825, (612) 624-3939 (TDD). A comprehensive source of information related to adolescents, disability, and transition. Contains four files: bibliographic, programs, training/education, and technical assistance.

Office of Federal Contract Compliance, Department of Labor, Washington, DC 20210, (202) 401-8818. Provides information to employers doing business with the federal government under contract and assistance to employees who wish to file complaints relative to discrimination on the basis of disability.

Office of Student Financial Assistance, P.O. Box 84, Washington, DC 20044, (202) 708-8391. Provides information and assistance relating to federal student aid programs.

Pacer Center, 4826 Chicago Avenue, South, Minneapolis, MN 55417-1098, (612) 827-2966 (voice and TDD). A coalition of 19 Minnesota disability organizations established to improve and expand opportunities that enhance the quality of life for children and adults with disabilities (physical, mental, learning, and emotional) and their families. Through the Transition and National Supports in the Workplace project, funded under a five-year grant from the Departments of Labor and Health and Human Services, Pacer helps businesses hire people with disabilities, develops the support services businesses need to incorporate them into the workforce, and identifies the school training needed to become successful employees.

President's Committee on Employment of People with Disabilities, 1331 F Street, NW, Washington, DC 2004-1107, (800) ADA-WORK or (202) 376-6200. Offers a toll-free information service about accommodation methods, devices, and strategies.

Project LINK: Link to Assistive Products, 515 Kimball Tower, 3435 Main Street, Buffalo, NY 14214-3079, (800) 628-2281 or (716) 829-3141. A free information service connecting people with disabilities and others with manufacturers of assistive devices.

Projects with Industry, U.S. Department of Education, Rehabilitation Services Administration, 400 Maryland Avenue, SW, Washington, DC 20202, (202) 732-1882 for information about nationwide projects or (202) 245-2352 to locate the nearest PWI. Federally funded programs aimed at establishing partnerships between business and rehabilitation organizations to facilitate the employment of people with disabilities.

RESNA Press, 1101 Connecticut Avenue, Suite 700, Washington, DC 20036, (202) 857-1199. Sponsors programs that provide a variety of technological approaches to overcome disability and apply science, engineering, and technology to the needs of people with disabilities.

State departments of rehabilitation services, state vocational rehabilitation agencies, and state commissions/offices on deafness. Provide employment assistance to people with disabilities and information for employers. Check the Yellow Pages under state government and "Rehabilitation" headings.

Trace Research and Development Center, University of Wisconsin, Madison, Room S-151, Waisman Center, 1500 Highland Avenue, Madison, WI 53705, (608) 262-6966. Offers literature on adaptive technology and a public information program on computer access for people with disabilities, including a database of organizations and products. No fee for mail or telephone inquiries.

U.S. Department of Justice, Coordination and Review Section, P.O. Box 66118, Washington, DC 20035-6118, (202) 514-0301, (202) 514-0381 (TDD). Provides information on Title II, Public Services, and Title III, Public Accommodations, of the ADA.

U.S. Department of Transportation, Office of Assistant General Counsel for Regulation and Enforcement, 400 Seventh Street, SW, Washington, DC 20590, (202) 366-1656, (202) 366-2979 (TDD). Provides information on Title II (Public Transportation) and Title III (Private Transportation) of the Americans with Disabilities Act of 1990.

Wellness Councils of America, Community Health Plaza, Suite 311, 7101 Newport Avenue, Omaha, NB 68152, (402) 572-3590. A national nonprofit organization of 2,000 corporate members in 27 councils established to promote healthier life-styles for all Americans, especially through health promotion activities at the workplace. Developed Well Workplace and WELL CITY USA to give companies the incentive to re-think the quality of health promotion programs, set high standards of excellence, and encourage and reward achievement. Develops products and services for companies.

World Institute on Disability, 510 16th Street, Oakland, CA 94612, (510) 763-4100. A public policy center that uses research, public education, training, and model program development to create a more accessible and supportive society.

Appendix C

Sources of Equipment And Materials

Blindness and Low Vision

AICOM Corporation, 1590 Oakland Road, Suite B112, San Jose, CA 95131, (408) 453-8251. Manufacturer of the Accent speech synthesizer.

AI Squared, 1463 Hearst Avenue, NE, Atlanta, GA 30319, (404) 233-7065. Producer of ZoomText, screen enlargement software.

American Printing House for the Blind, 1839 Frankfort Avenue, P.O. Box 6085, Louisville, KY 40206-0085, (502) 895-2405. Distributes computer-related books, manuals, and software in accessible media; portable, rechargeable, voice-output computers; speech synthesis devices; and talking utilities for Apple computers.

Arkenstone, 1185 Bordeaux Drive, Suite D, Sunnyvale, CA 94089, (800) 444-4443. Manufacturer and distributor of Arkenstone Reader II.

Berkeley Systems, 2095 Rose Street, Berkeley, CA 94709, (510) 540-5535. Distributors of outSpoken 1.7, a speech access program for Apple Macintosh computers.

Blazie Engineering, 109 East Jarretsville Road, Forest Hill, MD 21050, (410) 893-9333. Manufactures and distributes the Braille 'n Speak speech synthesizer for people who are blind or vision impaired.

Centigram Communications Corp., 4415 Fortran Court, San Jose, CA 95134, (408) 745-1818. Manufacturer of the CallText 5050 and the Prose 2020 speech synthesizers.

Digital Equipment Corp., Terminals Business Unit, 146 Main Street, Maynard, MA 01754-2571, (800) 832-6277. Manufacturer of the DECtalk speech synthesizer.

Duxbury Systems, 435 King Street, P.O. Box 1504, Littleton, MA 01460, (508) 486-9766. Produces and distributes the Duxbury Braille Translator.

EVAS, P.O. Box 371, Westerly, RI 02891, (800) 872-3827. Manufacturer of the Apollo Speech Synthesizer.

IBM Corporation, Special Needs System, P.O. Box 1328, Boca Raton, FL 33429-1328, (800) IBM-3333; in Canada, (800) 465-1234. Produces and distributes computer hardware and software solutions for people with vision impairments.

Independent Living Aids, 27 East Mall, Plainview, NY 11803, (516) 752-8080. Produces and distributes Can-Do Products for people with low vision and other physical disabilities, from household items to talking watches, calculators, and clocks and large-print games.

Lighthouse Low Vision Products, 36-20 Northern Boulevard, Long Island, NY 11101, (800) 453-4923. Distributor of talking and low-vision watches, clocks, calculators, telephones, cassette players, lighting, writing supplies, games, and many household items.

Lorin Software, 365 Brassie Drive, Orlando, FL 32805, (407) 872-3245. Develops and markets educational software for special needs students. Focuses on products for people who are blind and visually impaired, such as tactile graphics (produced on braille embossers).

MAXIAids, P.O. Box 3209, Farmingdale, NY 11735, (800) 522-6294 or (516) 752-0521. Distributor of aids and appliances for people with vision, hearing, motion and mobility, and health-related disabilities. Publishes a catalog of aids and appliances.

Microsystems Software, 600 Worcester Road, Framingham, MA 01701, (508) 879-9000. Producer of MAGic screen enlargement software.

Optelec US, P.O. Box 796, Westford, MA 01886, (800) 828-1056. Producer of Large Print DOS (LPDOS) screen enlargement software.

Personal Data Systems, 100 West Rincon Avenue, Suite 217, Campbell, CA 95009, (408) 866-1126. Manufacturer of the Audapter Speech System.

Seeing Technologies, 7074 Brooklyn Boulevard, Minneapolis, MN 55429, (612) 560-8080. Manufactures and distributes a variety of video magnifiers.

Syntha-Voice Computers, 125 Gailmont Drive, Hamilton, Ontario L8K 4B8, (416) 578-0565 or (800) 263-4540. Distributes Slimware Window Bridge for use with Microsoft Windows and DOS.

TeleSensory, P.O. Box 7455, Mountain View, CA 94039-7455, (800) 227-8418. Producer of VISTA screen enlargement software.

Visuaide 2000 955 D'Assigny, Suite 143, Longueuil, Quebec, Canada, J4K 5C3, (514) 463-1717. Distributes graphical interface equipment for DOS.

Vysion, 30777 Schoolcraft Road, Livonia, MI 48150, (800) 521-1350. Manufacturer of the Personal Speech System and Type 'N Talk speech synthesizers.

Xerox Imaging Systems, Kurzweil Reading Machine Division, 185 Albany Street, Cambridge, MA 02139, (800) 343-0311. Manufacturer and distributor of the Kurzweil Personal Reader.

Deafness and Hard of Hearing

Caption Center, 125 Western Avenue, Boston, Mass. 02188 (617) 492-9225. A nonprofit service of WGBH Educational Foundation. Produces captions for all segments of the entertainment and advertising industries and offers off-line captions, real-time captions, and open captions. Sells open-captioning software and QuickCaption to enable agencies to caption their own programs.

Caption Films/Videos for the Deaf, Modern Talking Picture Service, 5000 Park Street, N, St. Petersburg, FL 33709, (800) 237-6213. Makes free loans of educational and entertainment captioned films and videos for deaf and hard-of-hearing people. Publishes *Captioned Films/Video Newsletter.*

Crestwood Co., 6225 North Sidney, Milwaukee, WI 53209, (414) 352-5678. Specializes in communication aids for people who have difficulty hearing or speaking clearly and those who cannot read.

Hal-Hen Co., 35-53 24th Street, Long Island, NY, (718) 392-6020. Provides devices for people who are deaf or hearing impaired.

Heidico, 3320-East 4th Plain, Vancouver, WA 98661, (206) 694-0446. Provides devices for people who are deaf or hearing impaired.

Nationwide Flashing Signal Systems (NFSS), 8120 Fenton Street, Silver Spring, MD 20910, (301) 589-6671 (voice), (301) 589-6670 (TDD). Provides devices for people who are deaf or hearing impaired.

National Technical Institute for the Deaf, Rochester Institute of Technology, One Lomb Memorial Drive, P.O. Box 9887, Rochester, NY 14623-0877, (716) 475-6400 (voice), (716) 475-2181 (TDD). A clearinghouse of educational materials relating to deafness. Disseminates information, materials, and instructional videocassettes on deafness and related areas nationwide.

Phone-TTY, 202 Lexington Avenue, Hackensack, NJ 07601, (201) 489-7889 (voice), (201) 489-7890 (TDD). Provides devices for people who are deaf or hearing impaired.

Phonic Ear, Petaluma, CA 94952, (707) 769-1110. Manufactures and distributes Phonic Ear, an assistive listening device, both permanently installed and portable, for people with hearing impairments, used primarily at group meetings and conventions.

Pioneer New Media Technology, 600 East Crescent Avenue, Upper Saddle River, NJ, (201) 327-6400. Producer and distributor of the Pioneer/

ADA Interactive Training System, which includes a LaserDisc player with bar code reader and the *Americans with Disabilities Act: New Access to the Workplace* laser disc produced by Coronet/MTI Film and Video.

Silent Call Corporation, P.O. Box 868, Clarkson, MI 48347-0868 (313) 391-1710 (voice), (313) 391-1799 (TDD). Provides devices for people who are deaf or hearing impaired.

Sonic Alert, 1750 West Hamlin, Rochester, MI 48309, (313) 656-8347 (voice/TDD), Provides devices for people who are deaf or hearing impaired.

Telecommunications for the Deaf, 8719 Colesville Road, Suite 300, Silver Spring, MD 20910-3939, (301) 589-3786 (voice), (301) 589-3006 (TDD). A consumer-oriented organization that sells caption decoders and a directory of deaf people. Advocates and supports legislation relating to the use of TDDs, ASCII code, 911 emergency access, telecaptioning, and visual alerting systems in the public, private, and government sectors.

Tele-Consumer Hotline, 1910K Street, NW, Suite 610, Washington, DC 20006, (800) 332-1124 (voice or TDD), (202) 223-4371 (voice or TDD). A nonprofit and independent telephone consumer information service. Provides free telephone assistance and publications on special telephone equipment, TDD directories, troubleshooting, selecting a telephone, telephone fraud, money-saving tips, and relay services.

Learning

BrainTrain, 1915 Huguenot Road, Richmond, VA 23235, (800) 633-1221 or (804) 794-4841. Produces and distributes software to teach a variety of skills, such as basic living, language arts, mathematics, and reading.

R. J. Cooper & Associates, Adaptive Technology Specialists, 24843 Del Prado #283, Dana Point, CA 92629, (714) 240-1912. Researches and develops special software for persons with moderate to profound developmental and acquired disabilities, both mental and physical, including touch-pad-oriented programs that help persons with severe communications disorders learn about and use language.

Mental and Developmental

BrainTrain, 1915 Huguenot Road, Richmond, VA 23235, (800) 633-1221 or (804) 794-4841. Produces and distributes software to teach a variety of skills, such as basic living, language arts, mathematics, and reading.

Conover Company, P.O. Box 155, Omro, WI 54963, (800) 933-1933. Provides multimedia employability skills and workplace literacy programs for special needs, at-risk, and disadvantaged youths and adults in computer software, computer network, video, and print formats.

R. J. Cooper & Associates, Adaptive Technology Specialists, 24843 Del Prado #283, Dana Point, CA 92629, (714) 240-1912. Researches and develops special software for persons with moderate to profound developmental and acquired disabilities, both mental and physical, including touch-pad-oriented programs that help persons with severe communications disorders learn about and use language.

Laureate Learning Systems, 110 East Spring Street, Winooski, VT 05404, (800) 562-6800. Distributes materials for low-cognitive-functioning people, including persons with severe developmental disabilities, requiring no reading.

Mobility and Motion

Able Walker, 1122 First Avenue, Building C-2, Blaine, WA 98230, (800) 663-1305. Manufacturer and distributor of rolling walkers.

Alternate Medical, 913 South Washington, Redwood Falls, MN 56283, (800) 782-6324. Manufacturer and distributor of East Stand II.

Apple Computer, Apple Catalog, One Apple Plaza, P.O. Box 9001, Clearwater, FL 34618-9001, (800) 795-1000 (voice), (800) 755-0601 (TDD). Provides hardware and software to enable access to computers for people with disabilities.

Bureau of National Affairs, 1231 25th Street, NW Washington, DC 20037, (800) 372-1033 or (202) 452-4200. Publishes more than 70 print and electronic services in the legal, economic, business, human resources, environmental, safety, and tax fields, including CD-ROM resources, easy-access online reports, and software.

Cleo Inc., Rehab Shoppe, 3957 Mayfield Road, Cleveland, OH 44121, (800) 321-0595 or (216) 382-9700. Distributors of a catalog of products for people with motion or gripping and holding disabilities.

ComputAbility, 40000 Grand River, Suite 109, Novi, MI 48375, (313) 477-6720. Manufacturer and distributor of the AID + ME alternative computer input device.

Consultants for Communication Technology, 508 Bellevue Terrace, Pittsburgh, PA 15202, (412) 761-6062. Manufactures and distributes the Handi-Speech Communication Aide. Also integrates complete systems that address the issues of environmental control, word processing, and telephone communications.

R. J. Cooper & Associates, Adaptive Technology Specialists, 24843

Del Prado #283, Dana Point, CA 92629, (714) 240-1912. Researches and develops special software for persons with moderate to profound developmental and acquired disabilities, both mental and physical, including touch-pad-oriented programs that help persons with severe communications disorders learn about and use language.

Chrysler Corporation, 1200 Lynn Townsend Drive, Detroit MI 48231, (800) 255-9877. Manufacturer of adapted cars, trucks, and vans.

Edmark Corporation, P.O. Box 3903, Bellevue, Washington 98009-3903, (800) 426-0856. Offers a special line of computer software designed specifically for touch input. Covers basic math skills, spelling and writing, social and behavioral skills, vocational preparation, and language development.

Ford Motor Company, American Road, Dearborn, MI 48121, (800) 952-2248 (voice), (800) TDD-0312 (TDD). Manufacturer of adapted cars, trucks, and vans.

General Motors Corporation, General Motors Building, Detroit, MI 48202, (800) 323-9935 (voice), (800) TDD-9935 (TDD). Manufacturer of adapted cars, trucks, and vans.

IBM Special Needs System, P.O. Box 1328, Boca Raton, FL 33429-1328, (800) 426-7282; in Canada, (800) 465-1234. Develops, markets, and oversees the manufacturing of IBM products under the Independence Series trademark. Developed the disk operating system AccessDOS, free to anyone, that enables people with motor and mobility impairments to interact with a computer.

Don Johnson Developmental Equipment, P.O. Box 639, 1000 North Rand Road, Building 115, Wauconda, IL 60084-0639, (800) 999-4660 or (708) 526-2682. Producers and distributors of computer access, communication, and literacy materials and assistive devices.

Laurel Designs, 5 Laurel Avenue, Belvedere, CA 94920, (415) 435-1891. Markets carrying bags that fit on wheelchairs, walkers, and crutches.

L. C. Technologies, 9455 Silver King Court, Fairfax, VA 22031, (800) 733-5284 or (703) 385-7133. Manufacturer of the Eyegaze Computer System, an advanced adaptive system that makes computers accessible to people so severely paralyzed that they can move only their eyes.

LDC Corporation of America, 20 Independence Court, Folcroft, PA 19032, (800) 782-6324. Distributor of Lifestand, a passive standing aid.

LRP Publications, Department 440, 7747 Dresher Road, Suite 500, P.O. Box 980, Horsham, PA 19044-0980, (215) 784-0860. Publisher and distributor of the Medical Disability Advisor, MDA on Disk software.

Nanopac, 4833 South Sheridan Road, Suite 402, Tulsa, OK 74154-5718, (918) 665-0329. Manufacturer and distributor of Clintex2, an environmental control program.

NobleMotion, P.O. Box 5366, Pittsburgh, PA 15206, (800) 234-WALK. Manufacturer and distributor of rolling walkers.

Prentke Romich Company, 1022 Heyl Road, Wooster, OH 44691, (216) 262-1984. Manufacturer and distributor of Headmaster and the T-TAM alternative computer input device.

Regenesis Development Corporation, 4381 Gallant Avenue, North Vancouver, B.C., Canada V7G-1L1, (604) 929-6663. Manufacturer and distributor of the Robotic Manipulator.

Solutions, 13700 Northwest Science Park, P.O. Box 6878, Portland, OR 97229, (800) 342-9988. Manufacturer and distributor of Seastick, an ambulation device.

Stand-Aid of Iowa, P.O. Box 386, Sheldon, IA 51201, (800) 831-8580. Manufacturer and distributor of Stand-Aid.

TASH, 70 Gibson Drive, Unit 12, Markham, Ontario, Canada, L3R4C2, (416) 475-2212. Manufacturer and distributor of DADAEntry alternative computer input device.

Therapy Skill Builders, 3830 East Bellevue, P.O. Box 42050-TS4, Tucson, AZ 85733, (602) 323-7500. Publisher and distributor of adult rehabilitation and cognitive rehabilitation materials.

Unicorn Engineering, 5221 Central Avenue, Suite 205, Richmond, CA 94804, (800) 899-6687. Manufacturer and distributor of Smart Keyboard alternative computer input device.

Volkswagen of America, 3800 Hamlin Road, Auburn Hills, MI 48326, (800) 444-8987. Manufacturer of adapted cars and EuroVans under its Mobility Access Program.

WesTest Engineering Corp., 1470 North Main, Bountiful, UT 84010, (801) 298-7100. Manufacturer and distributor of DARCI TOO alternative computer input device.

Speech and Language

Communication Skills Builders, 3830 East Bellevue, P.O. Box 42050-E91, Tucson, AZ 85733, (602) 323-7500. Distributor of assessments, computer software, and games for articulation and phonology, cognitive rehabilitation, communication, and remediation of language and motor-speech disorders.

Consultants for Communication Technology, 508 Bellevue Terrace, Pittsburgh, PA 15202, (412) 761-6062. Manufactures and distributes the HandiSpeech Communication Aide. Also integrates complete systems that addresses the issues of environmental control, word processing, and telephone communications.

R. J. Cooper and Associates, Adaptive Technology Specialists, 24843

Del Prado #283, Dana Point, CA 92629, (714) 240-1912. Researches and develops special software for persons with moderate to profound developmental and acquired disabilities, both mental and physical, including touch-pad-oriented programs that help persons with severe communications disorders learn about and use language.

Crestwood Co., 6225 North Sidney, Milwaukee, WI 53209, (414) 352-5678. Specializes in communication aids for people who have difficulty hearing or speaking clearly and those who cannot read.

Don Johnson Developmental Equipment, P.O. Box 639, 1000 North Rand Road, Building 115, Wauconda, IL 60084-0639, (800) 999-4660 or (708) 526-2682. Producers and distributors of computer access, communication, and literacy materials and assistive devices.

Laureate Learning Systems, 110 East Spring Street, Winooski, VT 05404-1898, (800) 562-6801. Publisher and distributor of programs for children and adults with special needs, including talking software for language-learning disabilities, aphasia, and traumatic brain injury.

National Captioning Institute, 5203 Leesburg Pike, Falls Church, VA 22041, (800) 533-9673 (voice), (800) 321-8837 (TDD), (703) 998-2400 (voice and TDD). Provides closed-captioning services for television networks, program producers, cable-casters, advertisers, and other organization in the federal and private sectors. Distributes Telecaption decoders and Audiolink Personal Listening Systems to retailers.

General

Access to Recreation, 2509 East Thousand Oaks Boulevard, Suite 430, Thousand Oaks, CA 91362, (800) 634-4351. Publishes and distributes a catalog for adaptive fitness and recreational products and books and videos on practical subjects for adults with disabilities.

Apple Computer, Apple Catalog, One Apple Plaza, P.O. Box 9001, Clearwater FL 34618-9001, (800) 795-1000 (voice), (800) 755-0601 (TDD). Provides hardware and software to enable access to computers for people with disabilities.

Avenue, 1199 Avenida Acaso, Suite K, Camarillo, CA 93012, (800) 848-2837. Markets clothing, both career and casual, for wheelchair users, other accessory items, and fitness equipment for people with disabilities.

Dragon Systems, an IBM authorized industry remarketer, (800) 825-5897 or call IBM at (800) IBM-3333 for the number of the nearest branch office.

IBM Corporation, Special Needs Systems, P.O. Box 1328, Boca Raton, FL 33429-1328, (800) IBM-3333; in Canada, (800) 465-1234. Producer and distributor of computer hardware and software for people with vision, hearing, mobility, and speech disabilities.

Don Johnson Developmental Equipment, P.O. Box 639, 1000 North Rand Road, Building 115, Wauconda, IL 60084-0639, (800) 999-4660 or (708) 526-2682. Producers and distributors of computer access, communication, and literacy materials and assistive devices.

Laureate Learning Systems, 110 East Spring Street, Winooski, VT 05404-1898, (800) 562-6801. Publisher and distributor of programs for children and adults with special needs, including talking software for language-learning disabilities, aphasia, and traumatic brain injury.

Laurel Designs, 5 Laurel Avenue, Belvedere, CA 94920, (415) 435-1891. Publishes and distributes a catalog of clothing products for wheelchair users.

Nanopac, 4833 South Sheridan Road, Suite 402, Tulsa, OK 74154-5718, (918) 665-0329. Manufacturer and distributor of Clintex2, an environmental control program.

Project LINK, Center for Therapeutic Applications of Technology (CTAT), University of Buffalo, 3435 Main Street, 515 Kimball Tower, Buffalo, NY 14214, (800) 628-2281 or (716) 829-3141. Offers a free information service to help people learn about assistive products and where to get them.

Revdyne Medical, 691 East 20th Street, Suite 111, Tucson, AZ 85719, (602) 623-4275. Markets a guide, *Adaptive Equipment for Persons with Disabilities* ($15.95 plus $4.00 shipping and handling) that lists more than 200 products, including vendor and funding information.

J. E. Stewart, Teaching Tools for Special Educators, 18518 Kenlake Place, NE, Seattle, WA 98155, (206) 486-4510. Markets software for the classroom or worksheet computer, such as the Washington State Cooperative Curriculum for children and adults with severe and profound handicaps.

Trio Publications, 3600 West Timber Court, Lawrence, KS 66049, (913) 749-1453. Publisher and distributor of *Illustrated Directory of Handicap Products* catalog. Contains product photographs and descriptions with manufacturers' telephone numbers for about 1,000 products in 21 categories. $12.95 postpaid.

Media Distributors

About Face, 1002 Liberty Lane, Warrington, PA 18976, (800) 225-FACE; in Canada, (800) 665-FACE.

ACT, 1821 University Avenue, Suite 363 South, St. Paul, MN 55014, (612) 641-0297.

Advantage Media, Inc., 21356 Nordhoff Street, Suite 102, Chatsworth, CA 91311, (800) 545-0166.

AIMS Media, 9710 DeSoto Avenue, Chatsworth, CA 91311-4409, (800) 367-2467.

AIT: The Learning Source, AIT Dept; #SL/SCVI Box A, 1111 West 17th Street, Bloomington, IN 47402-0120, (800) 457-4509 or (812) 333-4278.

Alpha Media, 4501 Glencoe Avenue, ground floor, Marina Del Rey, CA 90292-6372, (800) 832-1000.

American Management Association Video, Nine Galen Street, Watertown, MA 02272, (800) 225-3215 or (617) 923-1875.

Barr Films, 12801 Schabarum Avenue, P.O. Box 7878, Irwindale, CA 91706-7878, (800) 234-7878 or (818) 338-7878.

BNA Communications Inc., 9439 West Avenue, Rockville, MD 20850-3396, (800) 233-6067.

Chariot Software Group, 3659 India Street, Suite 100C, San Diego, CA 92103.

Churchill Media, 12210 Nebraska Avenue, Los Angeles, CA 90025-3600, (800) 334-7830 or (310) 207-6600.

Cooperative Internship Program, Center for Career Programs, Gallaudet University, 800 Florida Avenue, NE, Washington, DC 20002-3695, (202) 651-5240.

Films, Inc., 5547 North Ravenswood, Chicago, IL 60640, (800) 323-4222, Ext. 44 or (312) 878-2600, Ext. 44.

Forward Face, Institute of Reconstructive Plastic Surgery, NYU Medical Center, 560 First Avenue, New York, NY 10016, (800) 422-FACE or (212) 263-6656.

Health Management Technologies, Country Club Road, Suite C, Morage, CA 94556, (510) 631-6750.

Impact AIDS, 3692 18th Street, San Francisco, CA 94110, (415) 861-3397.

Knowledge Point, 1311 Clegg Street, Petaluma, CA 94954-1191, (800) 727-1133 or (707) 762-0333.

LRP Publications, Dept. 440, 747 Dresher Road, P.O. Box 980, Horsham, PA 19044-0980, (215) 784-0860.

Meridian Education Corporation, Department 123, 236 East Front Street, Bloomington, IL 61701-9961, (800) 727-6607.

Modern Talking Picture Service, 5000 Park Street, North, St. Petersburg, FL 33709, (813) 541-7571.

MTI Film & Video, 820 Academy Drive, Northbrook, IL 60062, (800) 621-2131.

Pioneer New Media Technology, Inc., 600 East Crescent Avenue, Upper Saddle River, NJ 07458-1827, (800) LASER-ON or (201) 327-6400.

Professional Advancement Seminars, P.O. Box 746, Worcester, MA 01602, (508) 792-2408.

The Psychological Corporation, 555 Academic Court, San Antonio, TX 78204-2498, (800) 228-0752 or (210) 299-3628.

Salenger Films & Videos, Inc., 1635 12th Street, Santa Monica, CA 90404, (800) 775-5025 or (310) 450-1010.

Society for Human Resource Management, 606 North Washington Street, Alexandria, VA 22314-1997, (703) 548-3440.

United Training Media, 6633 West Howard Street, Niles IL 60714-0718, (800) 424-0364.

Video Publishing House, Inc., 4 Woodfield Lake, Schaumberg, IL 60173, (800) 824-8889.

Wellness Councils of America, Community Health Plaza, 7101 Newport Avenue, Suite 311, Omaha, NE 68152, (402) 572-3590.

Wonderlic Personnel Test, Inc., 1509 North Milwaukee Avenue, Libertyville, IL 60048-1380, (800) 323-3742.

Woolworth Corporation, 233 Broadway, New York, NY 10279, (212) 553-2042.

Workplace Health Communications Corporation, 4 Madison Place, Albany, NY 12202, (800) 334-4911; in New York, (800) 942-1002.

Index